I0203025

Printed in the United States of America

First Printing, 2017

ISBN 978-0-692-70389-2
ISBN-10: 0692703896

Wild Bernie Press,
Salem, MA 01970

Dedicated to Thomas "Professor Truth" Coleman

TABLE OF CONTENTS

Book No.________ 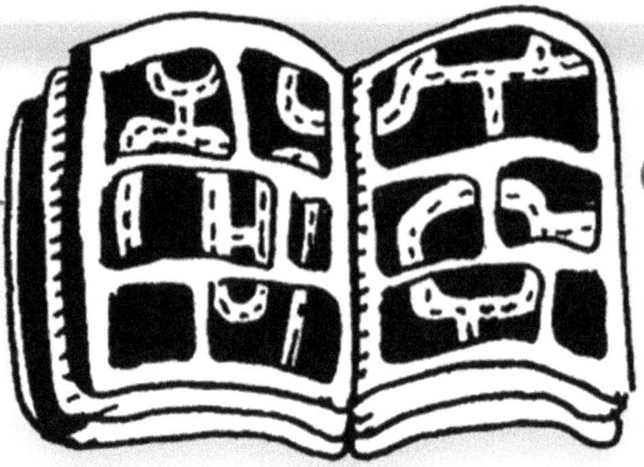 Cost____________

WARNING: The following Bookloaf features strong graphic content, adult situations, potty language, and the gratuitous use of caffeinated beverages. Reader discretion is advised.

Signature of Pupil	Date Loaned	Date Returned	Condition

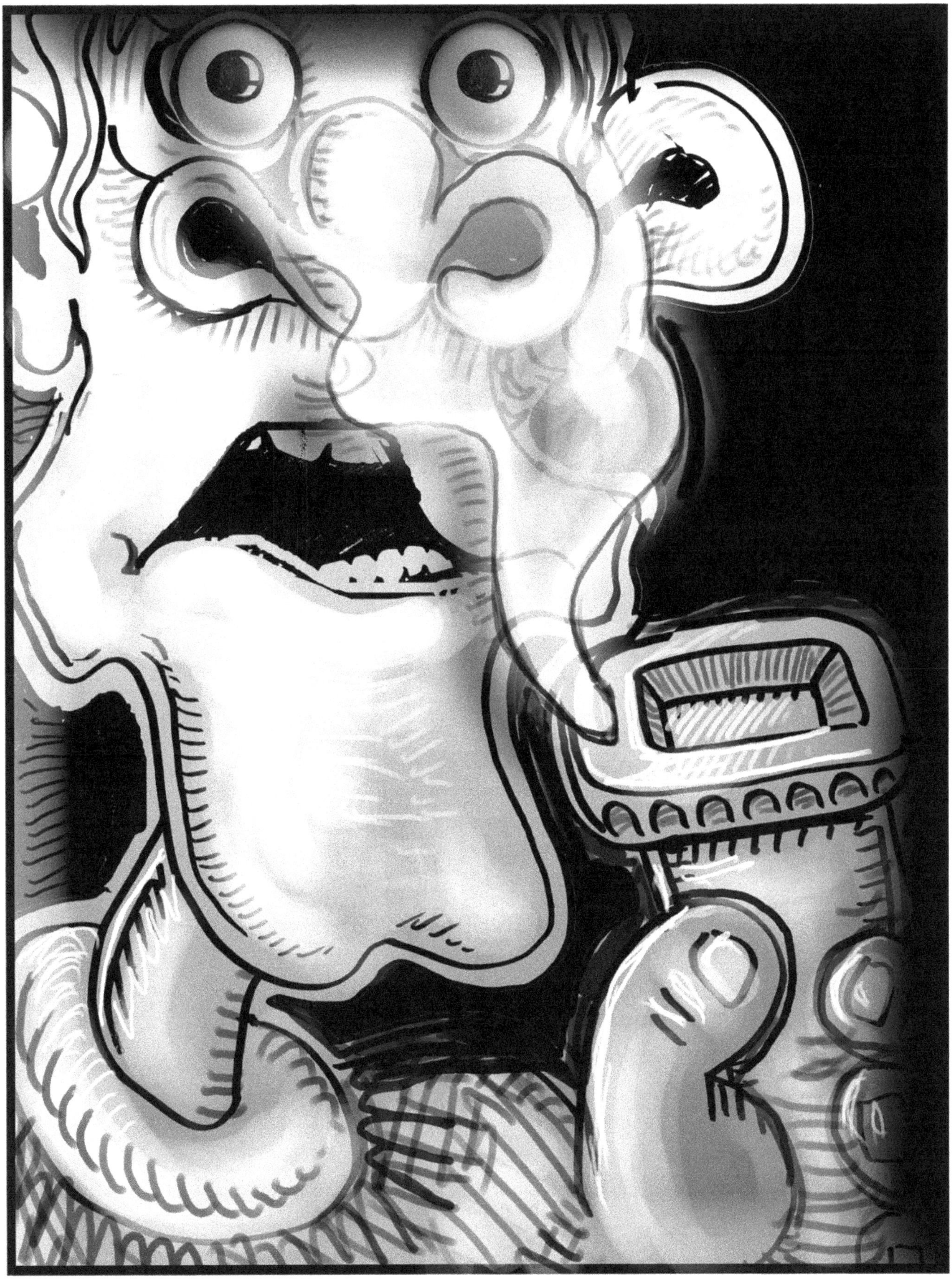

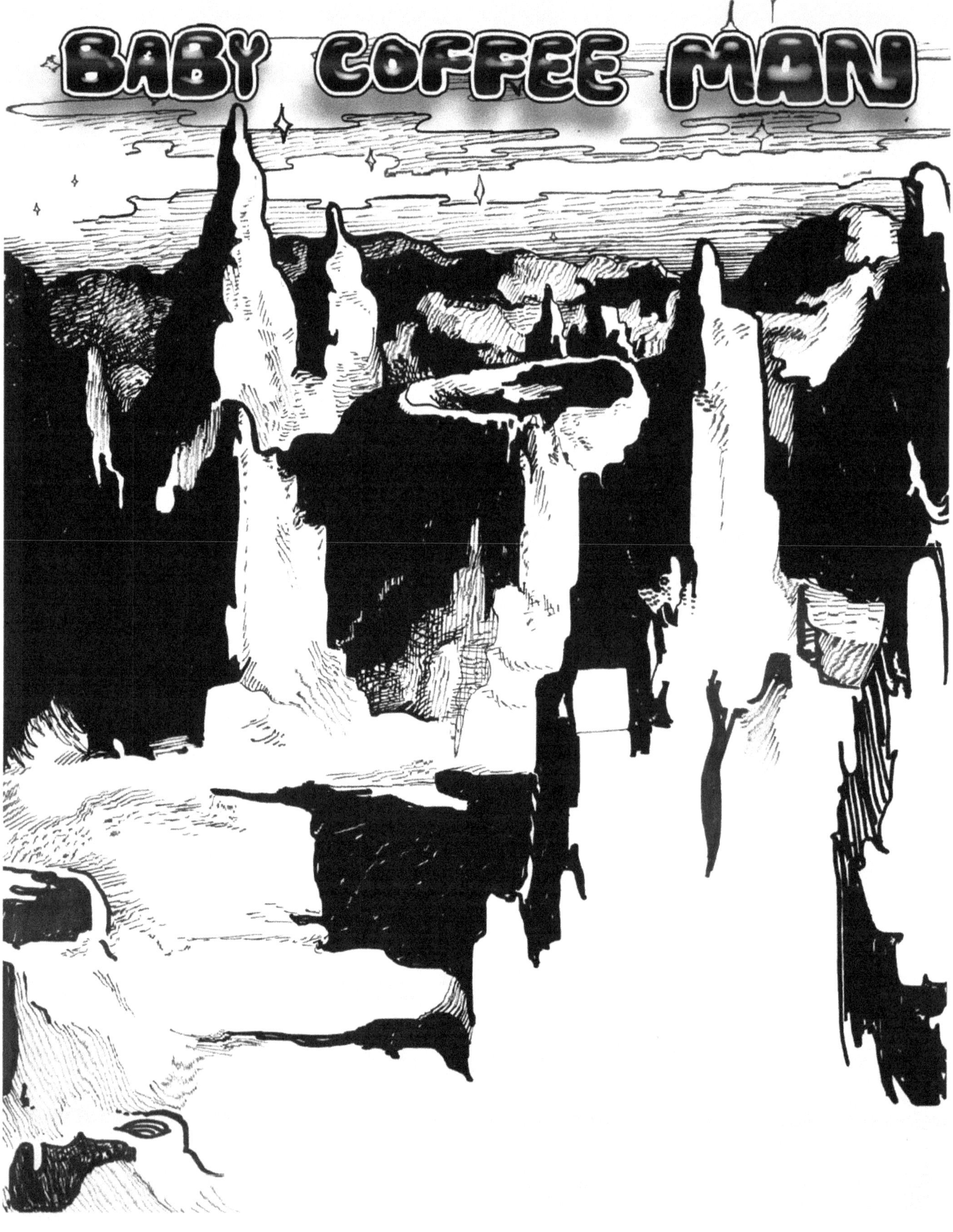
BABY COFFEE MAN

WE MUST FIND AND DESTROY THE BLUBLUBULA ONCE AND FOR ALL.
YEAH BUT HOW WILL WE FIND HIS BASE?
TRUST ME, WE'LL FIND IT.
I GOT AN INSIDE GUY, BUT I CAN'T SAY MUCH ELSE.
WELL WHY THE FUCK NOT?
I JUST CAN'T.
AW, NICE HELMETS CAN I GET ONE ?!

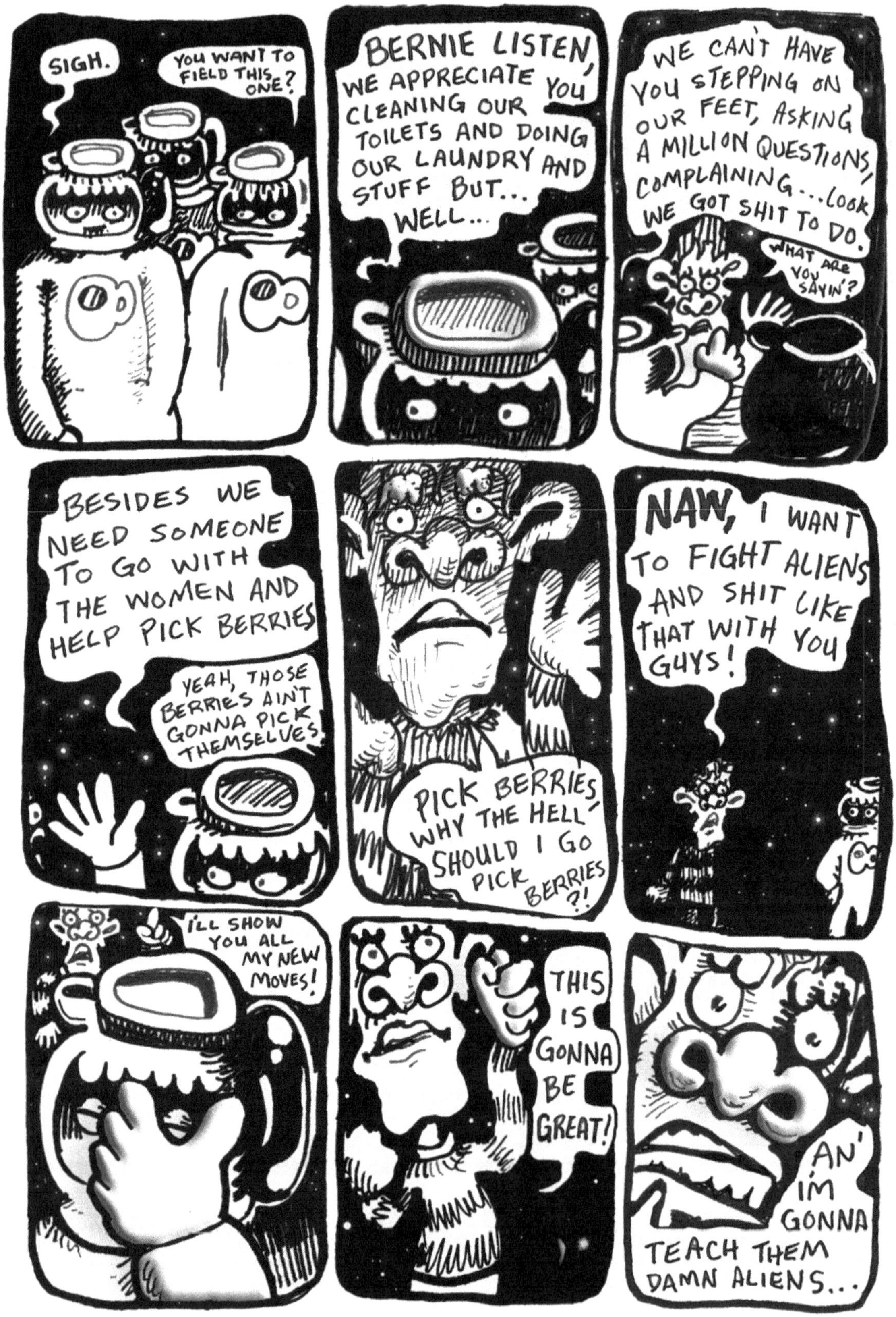

SIGH.
YOU WANT TO FIELD THIS ONE?
BERNIE LISTEN, WE APPRECIATE YOU CLEANING OUR TOILETS AND DOING OUR LAUNDRY AND STUFF BUT... WELL...
WE CAN'T HAVE YOU STEPPING ON OUR FEET, ASKING A MILLION QUESTIONS, COMPLAINING... LOOK WE GOT SHIT TO DO.
WHAT ARE YOU SAYIN'?
BESIDES WE NEED SOMEONE TO GO WITH THE WOMEN AND HELP PICK BERRIES
YEAH, THOSE BERRIES AIN'T GONNA PICK THEMSELVES
PICK BERRIES, WHY THE HELL SHOULD I GO PICK BERRIES?!
NAW, I WANT TO FIGHT ALIENS AND SHIT LIKE THAT WITH YOU GUYS!
I'LL SHOW YOU ALL MY NEW MOVES!
THIS IS GONNA BE GREAT!
AN' I'M GONNA
TEACH THEM DAMN ALIENS...

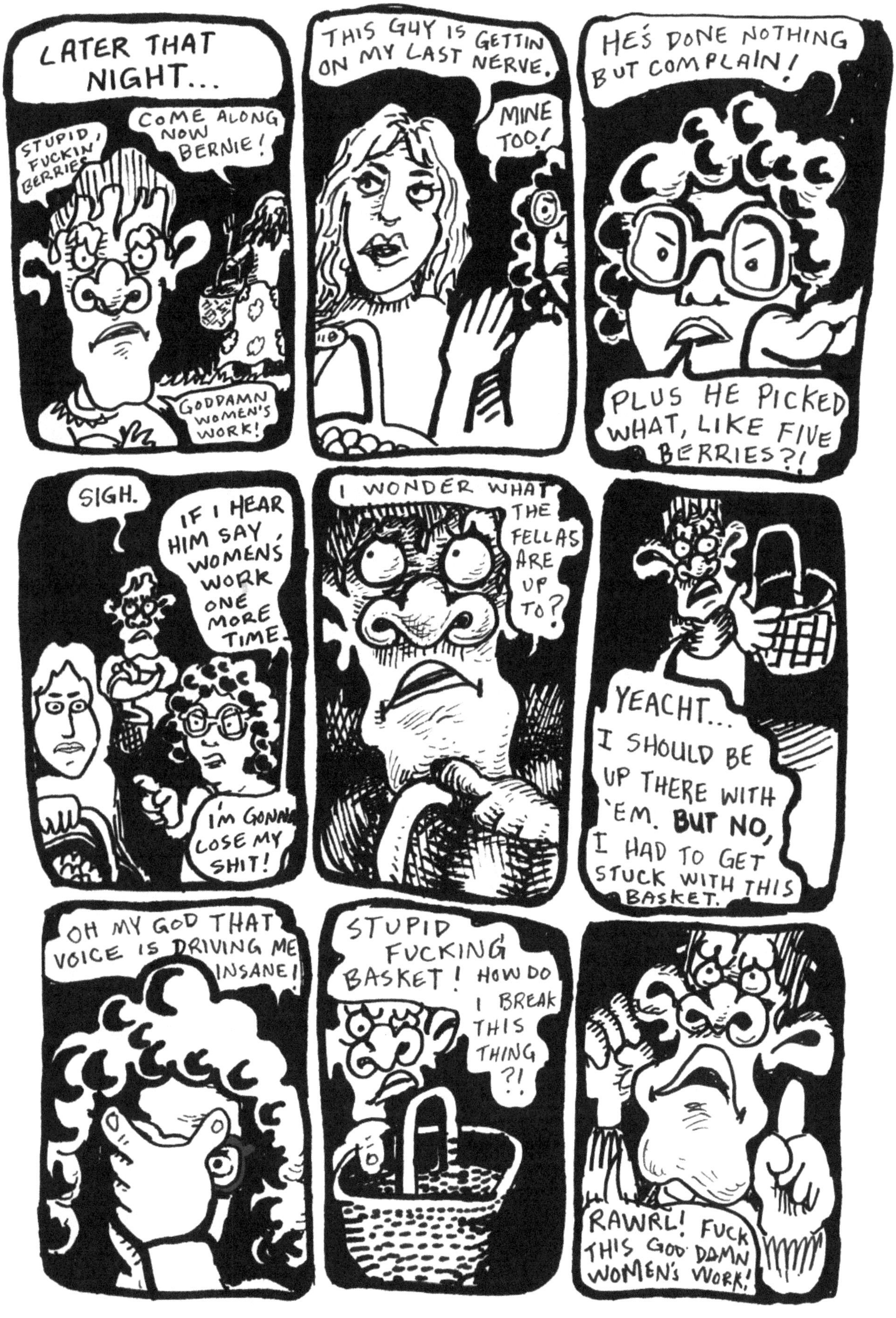
LATER THAT NIGHT...
STUPID FUCKIN' BERRIES
COME ALONG NOW BERNIE!
GODDAMN WOMEN'S WORK!
THIS GUY IS GETTIN ON MY LAST NERVE.
MINE TOO!
HE'S DONE NOTHING BUT COMPLAIN!
PLUS HE PICKED WHAT, LIKE FIVE BERRIES?!
SIGH.
IF I HEAR HIM SAY WOMENS WORK ONE MORE TIME.
I'M GONNA LOSE MY SHIT!
I WONDER WHAT THE FELLAS ARE UP TO?
YEACHT... I SHOULD BE UP THERE WITH 'EM. BUT NO, I HAD TO GET STUCK WITH THIS BASKET.
OH MY GOD THAT VOICE IS DRIVING ME INSANE!
STUPID FUCKING BASKET! HOW DO I BREAK THIS THING?!
RAWRL! FUCK THIS GOD DAMN WOMEN'S WORK!

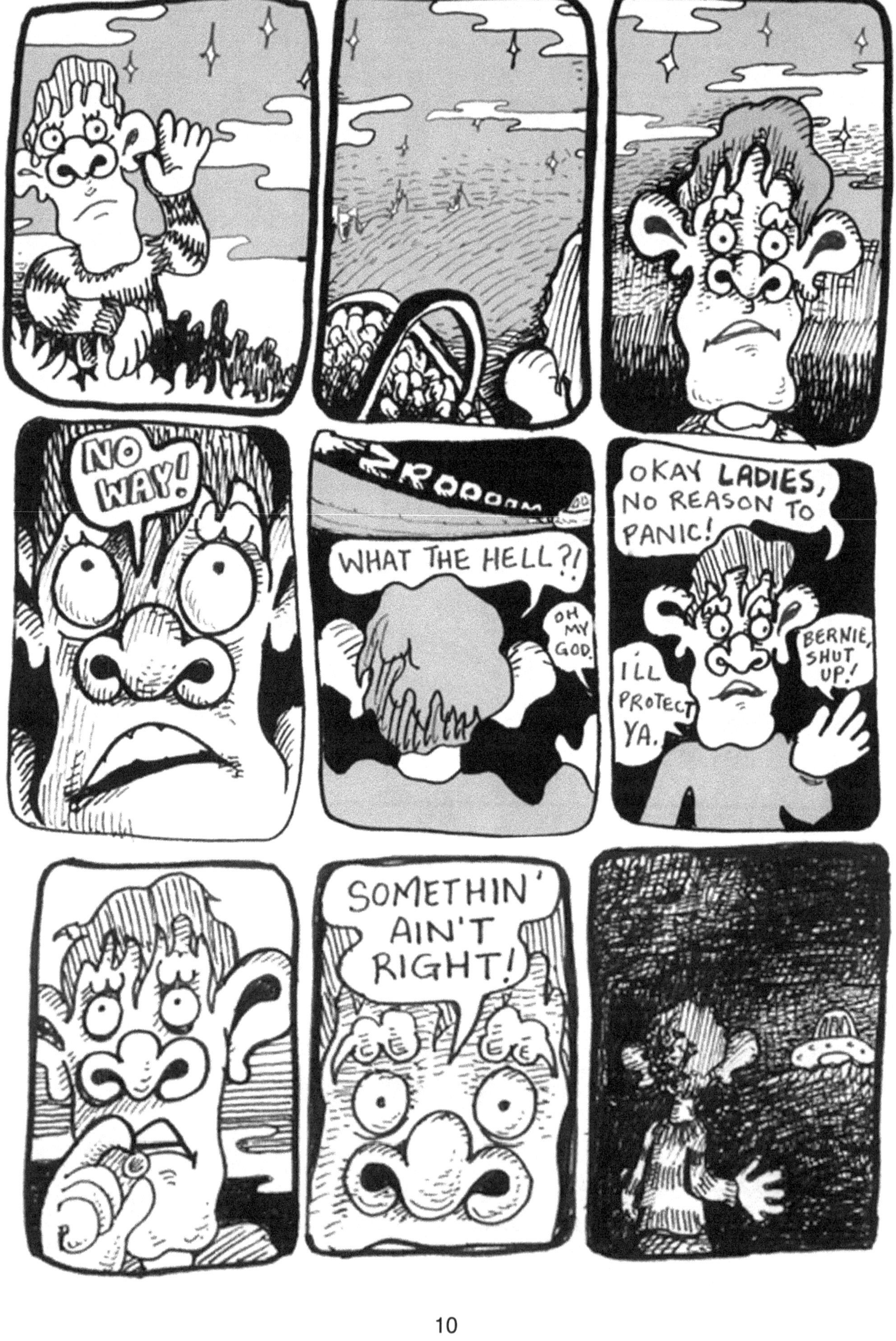
NO WAY!
ZROOOOM
WHAT THE HELL?!
OH MY GOD.
OKAY LADIES, NO REASON TO PANIC!
I'LL PROTECT YA.
BERNIE, SHUT UP!
SOMETHIN' AIN'T RIGHT!

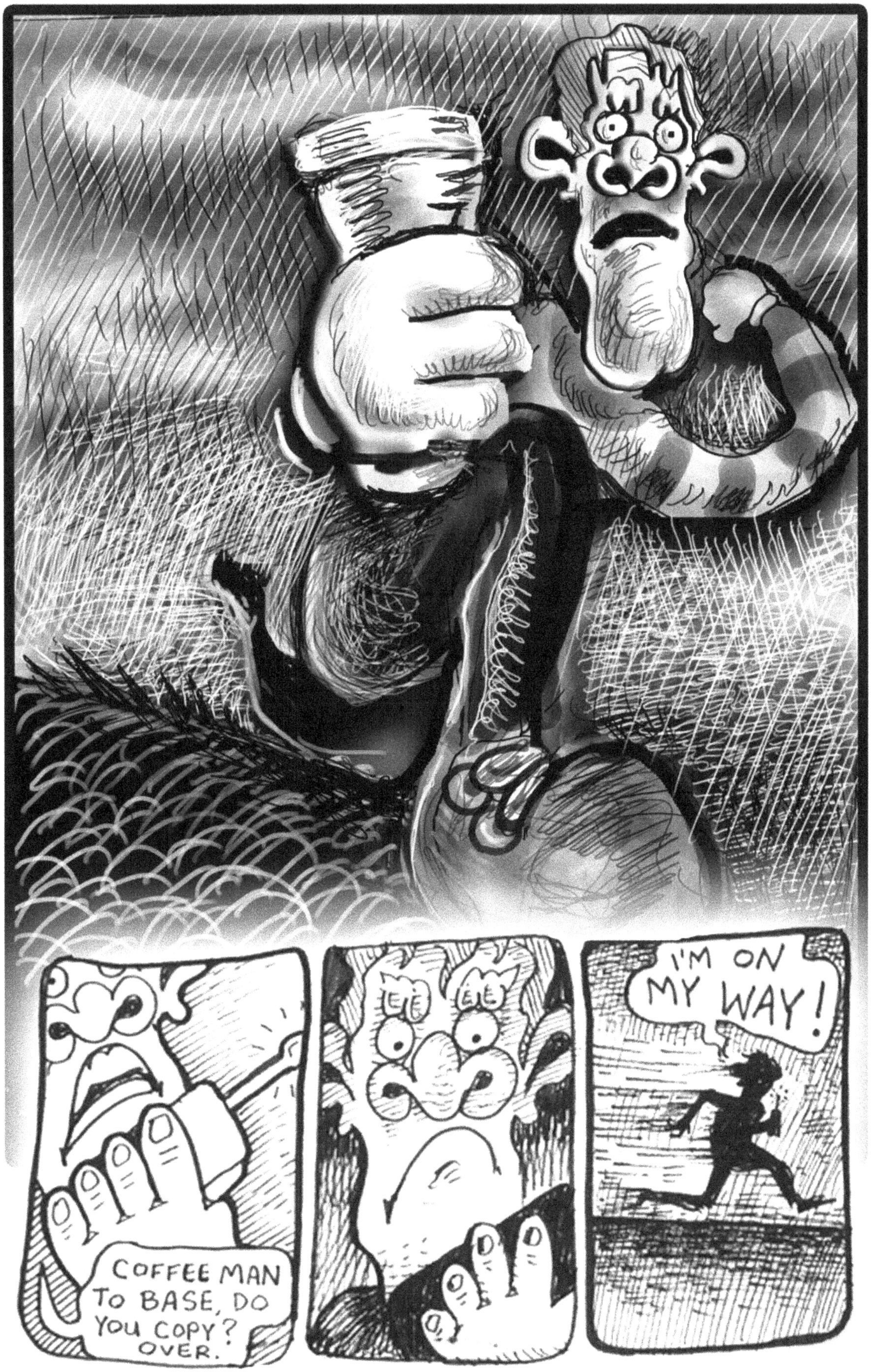
COFFEE MAN TO BASE, DO YOU COPY? OVER.
I'M ON MY WAY!

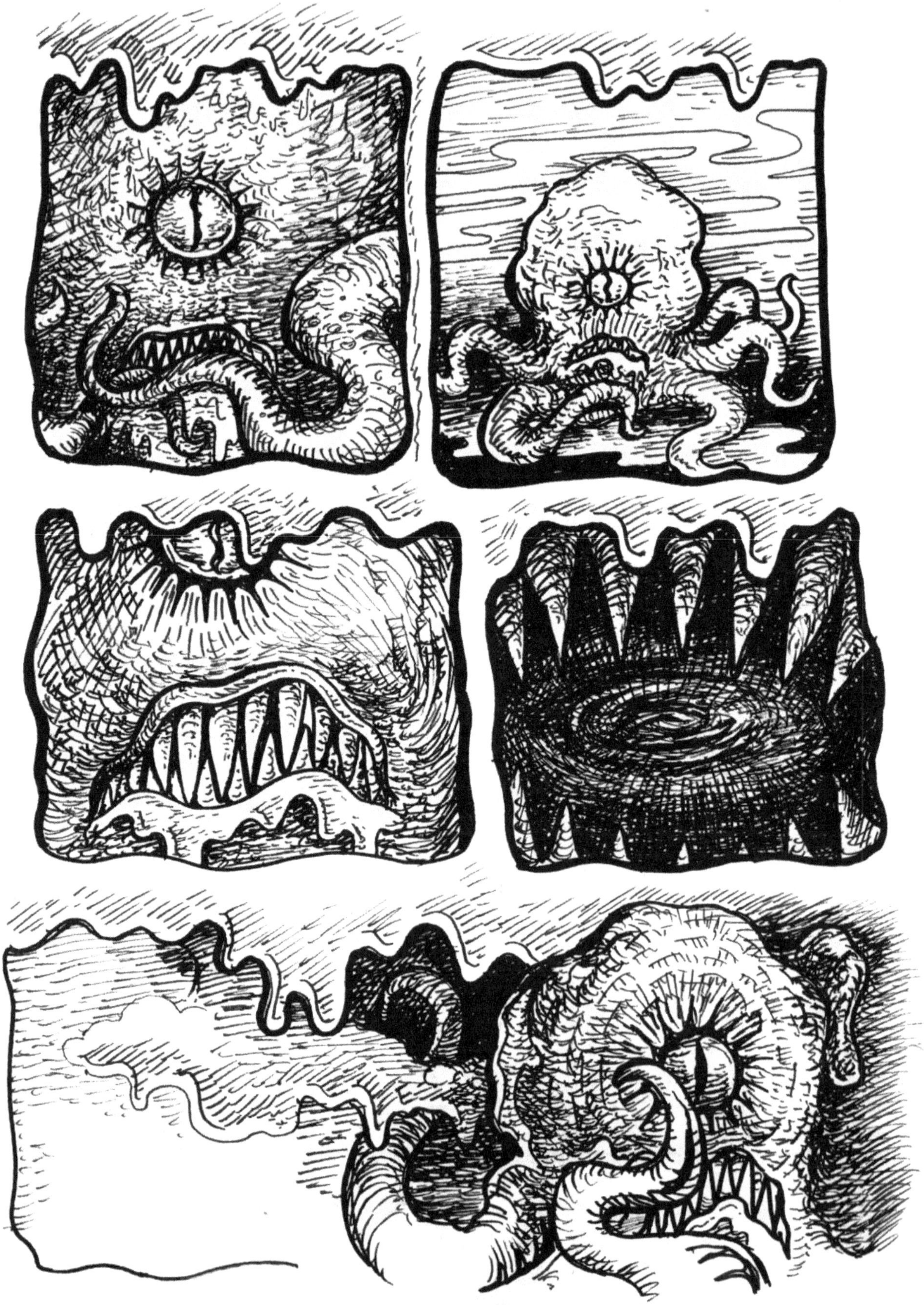

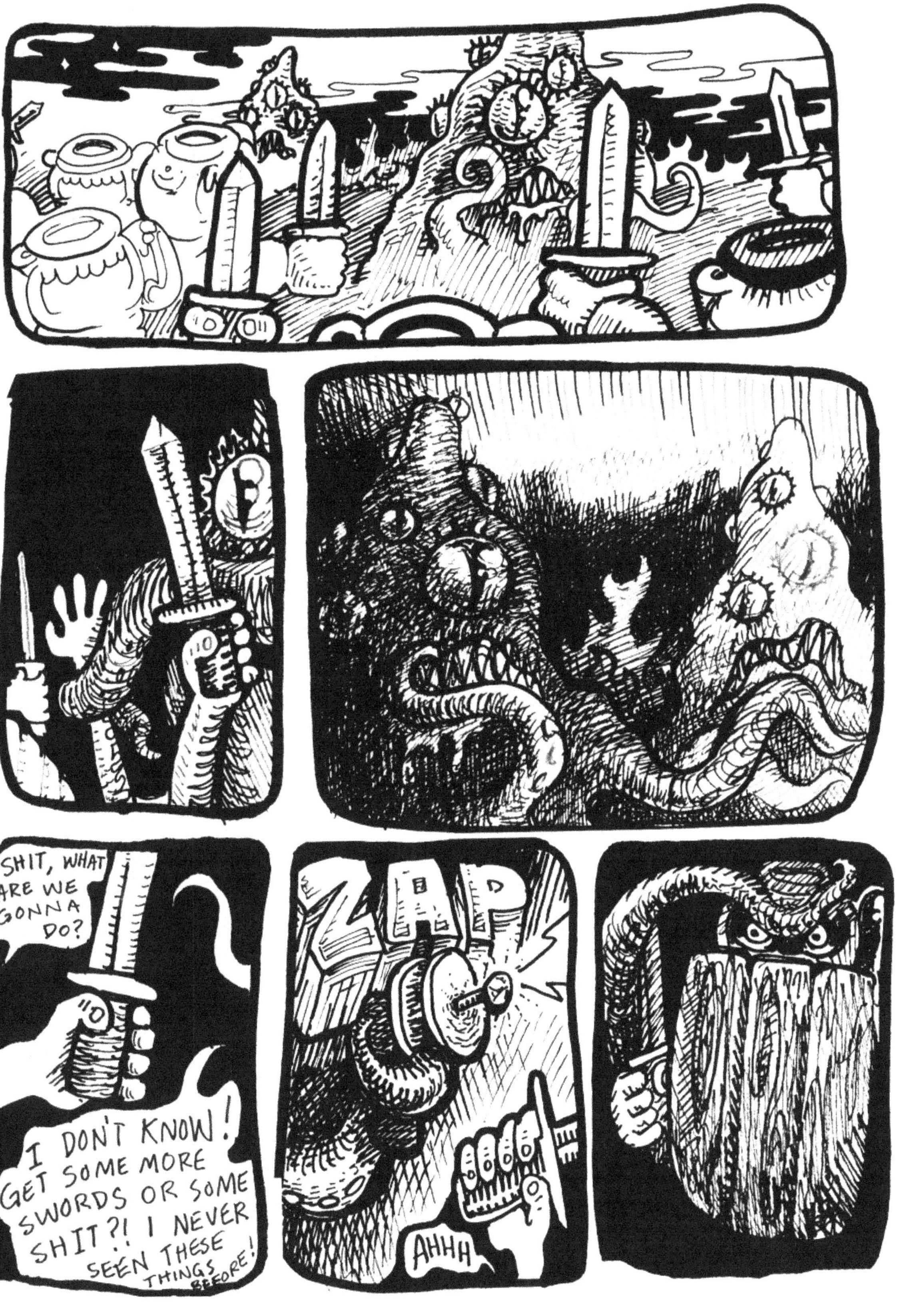
SHIT, WHAT ARE WE GONNA DO?
I DON'T KNOW! GET SOME MORE SWORDS OR SOME SHIT?! I NEVER SEEN THESE THINGS BEFORE!
ZAP
AHHH

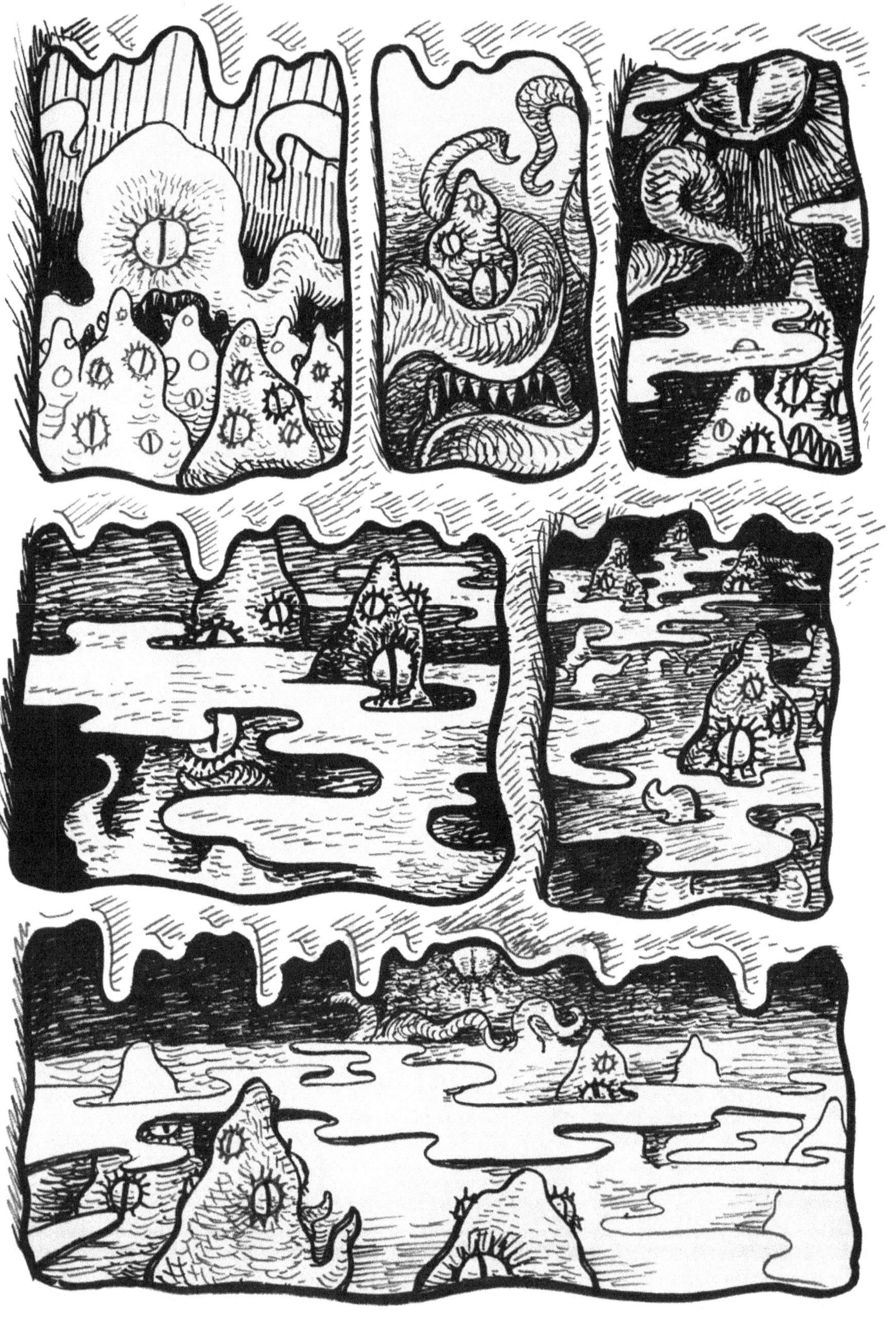

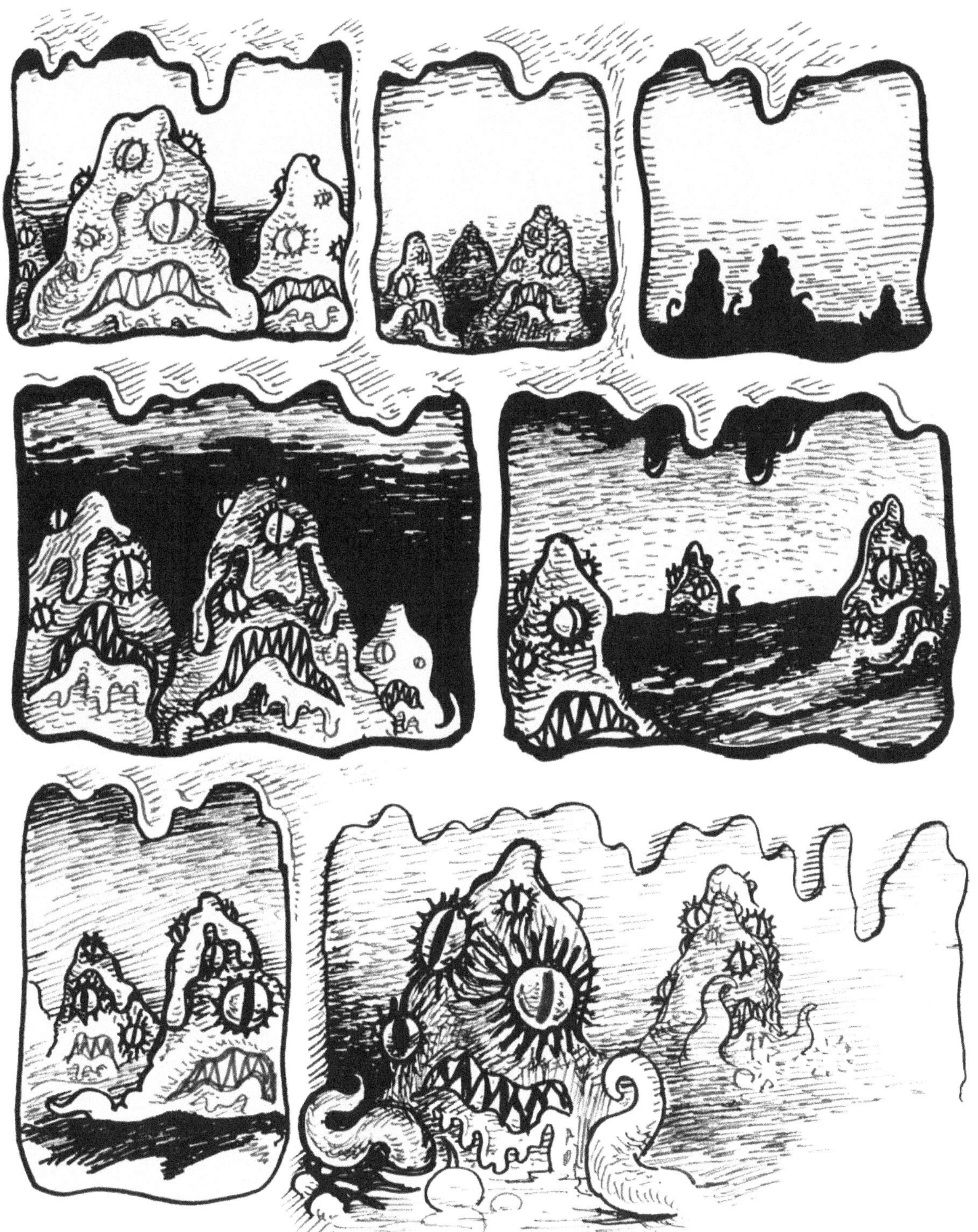

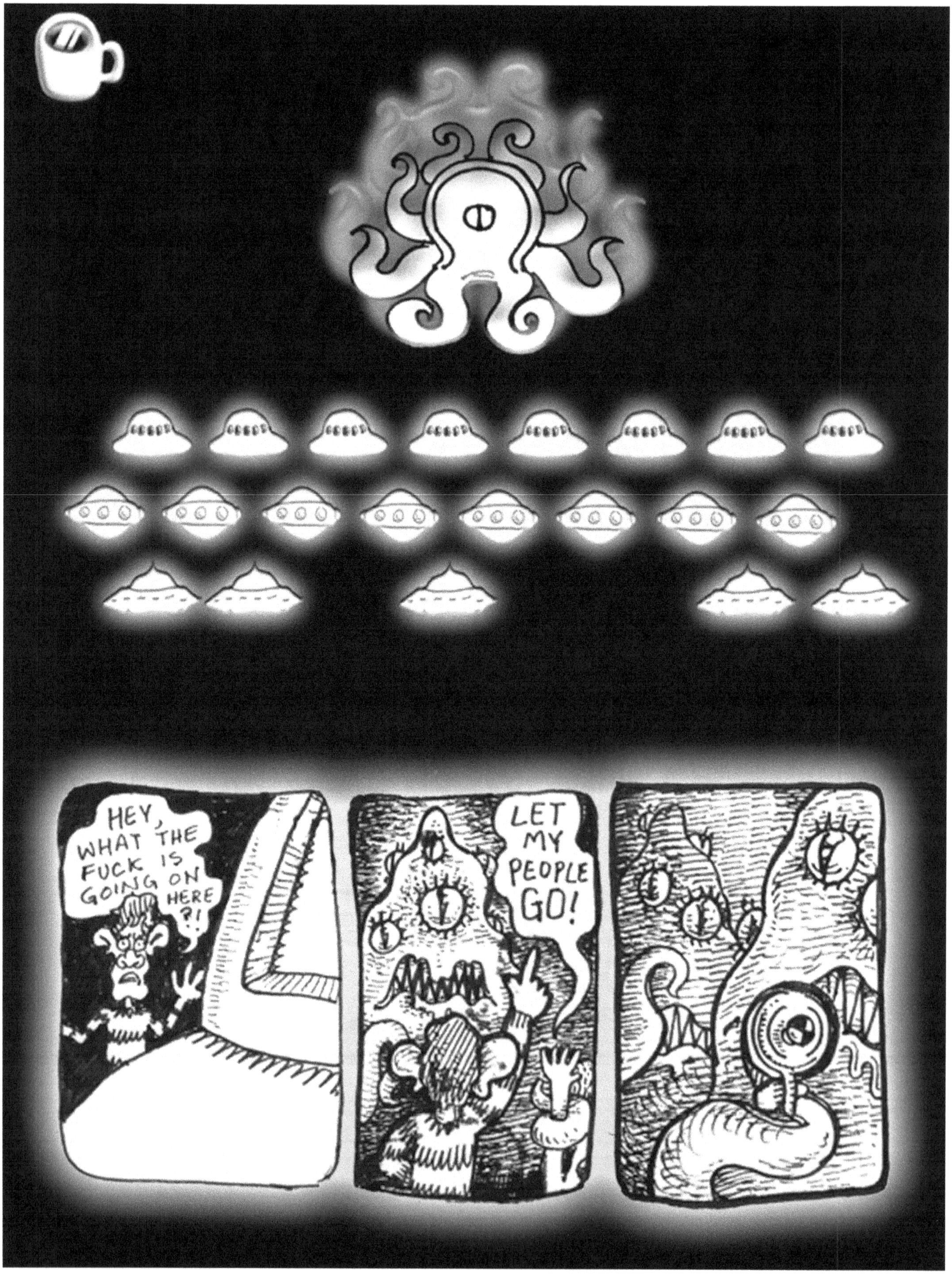
HEY, WHAT THE FUCK IS GOING ON HERE ?!
LET MY PEOPLE GO!

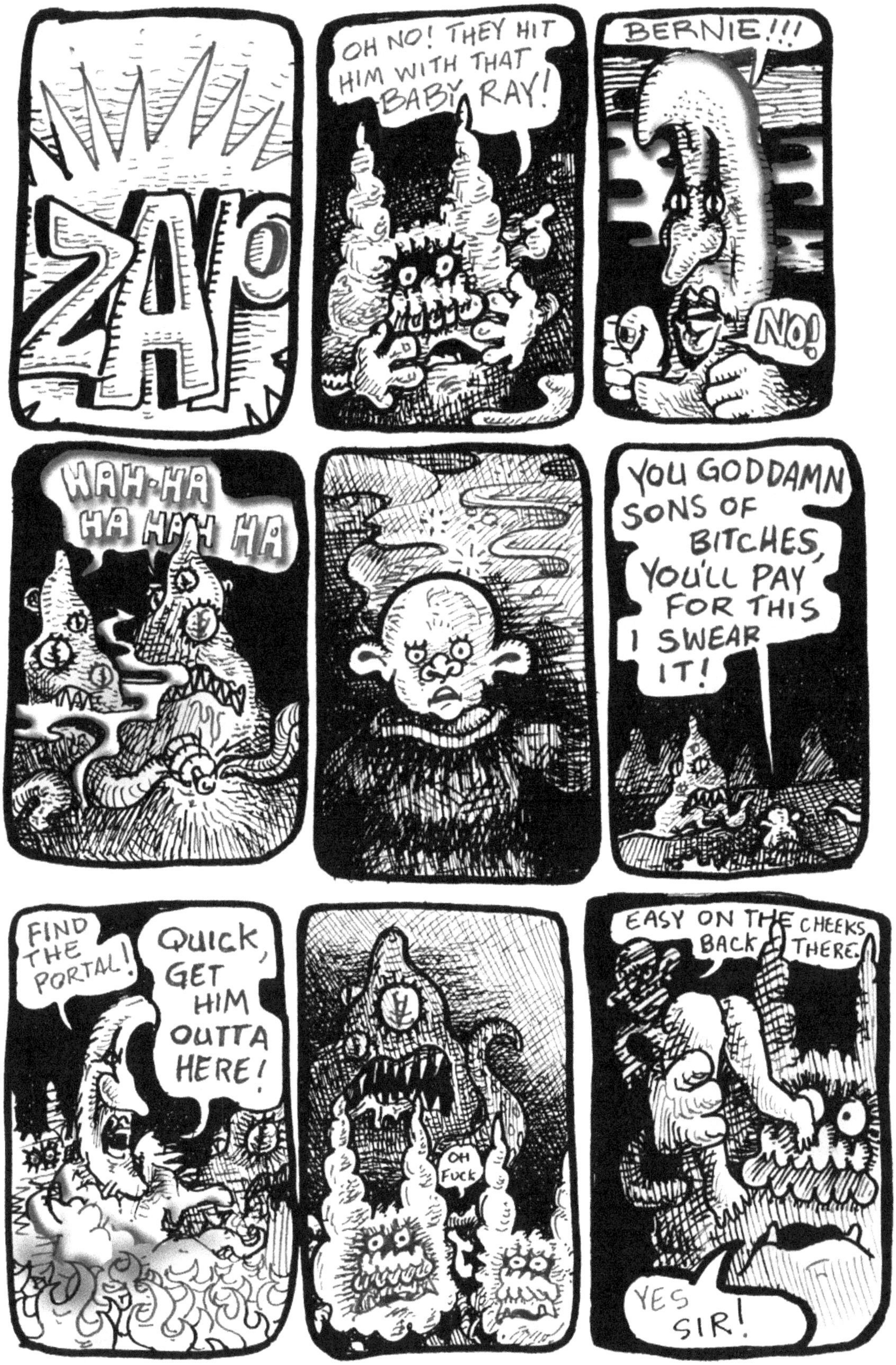
ZAP
OH NO! THEY HIT HIM WITH THAT BABY RAY!
BERNIE!!!
NO!
HAH-HA HA HAH HA
YOU GODDAMN SONS OF BITCHES, YOU'LL PAY FOR THIS I SWEAR IT!
FIND THE PORTAL!
QUICK, GET HIM OUTTA HERE!
OH FUCK
EASY ON THE CHEEKS BACK THERE.
YES SIR!

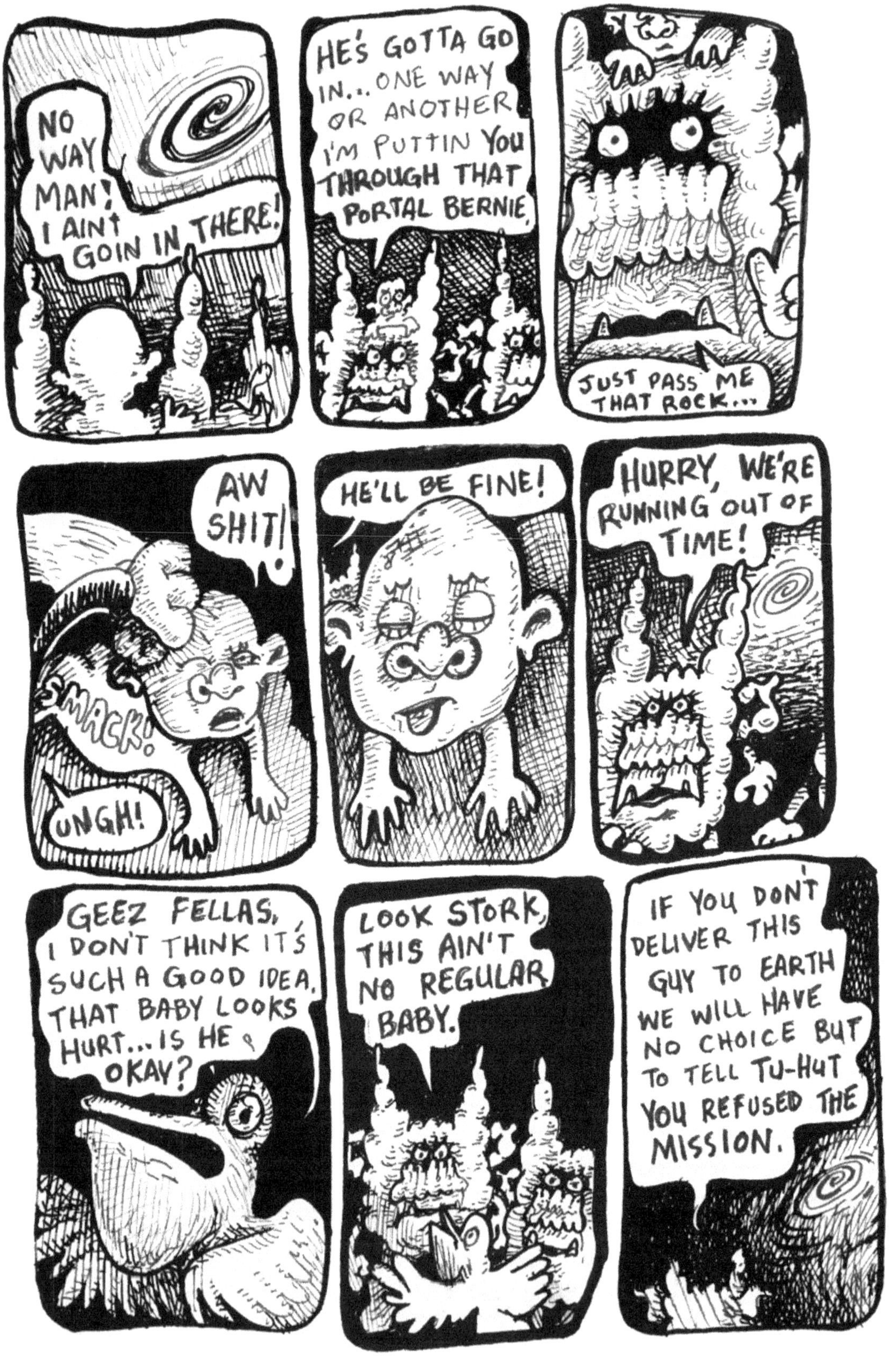
NO WAY MAN! I AIN'T GOIN IN THERE!
HE'S GOTTA GO IN... ONE WAY OR ANOTHER I'M PUTTIN YOU THROUGH THAT PORTAL BERNIE.
JUST PASS ME THAT ROCK...
AW SHIT!
SMACK!
UNGH!
HE'LL BE FINE!
HURRY, WE'RE RUNNING OUT OF TIME!
GEEZ FELLAS, I DON'T THINK IT'S SUCH A GOOD IDEA. THAT BABY LOOKS HURT... IS HE OKAY?
LOOK STORK, THIS AIN'T NO REGULAR BABY.
IF YOU DON'T DELIVER THIS GUY TO EARTH WE WILL HAVE NO CHOICE BUT TO TELL TU-HUT YOU REFUSED THE MISSION.

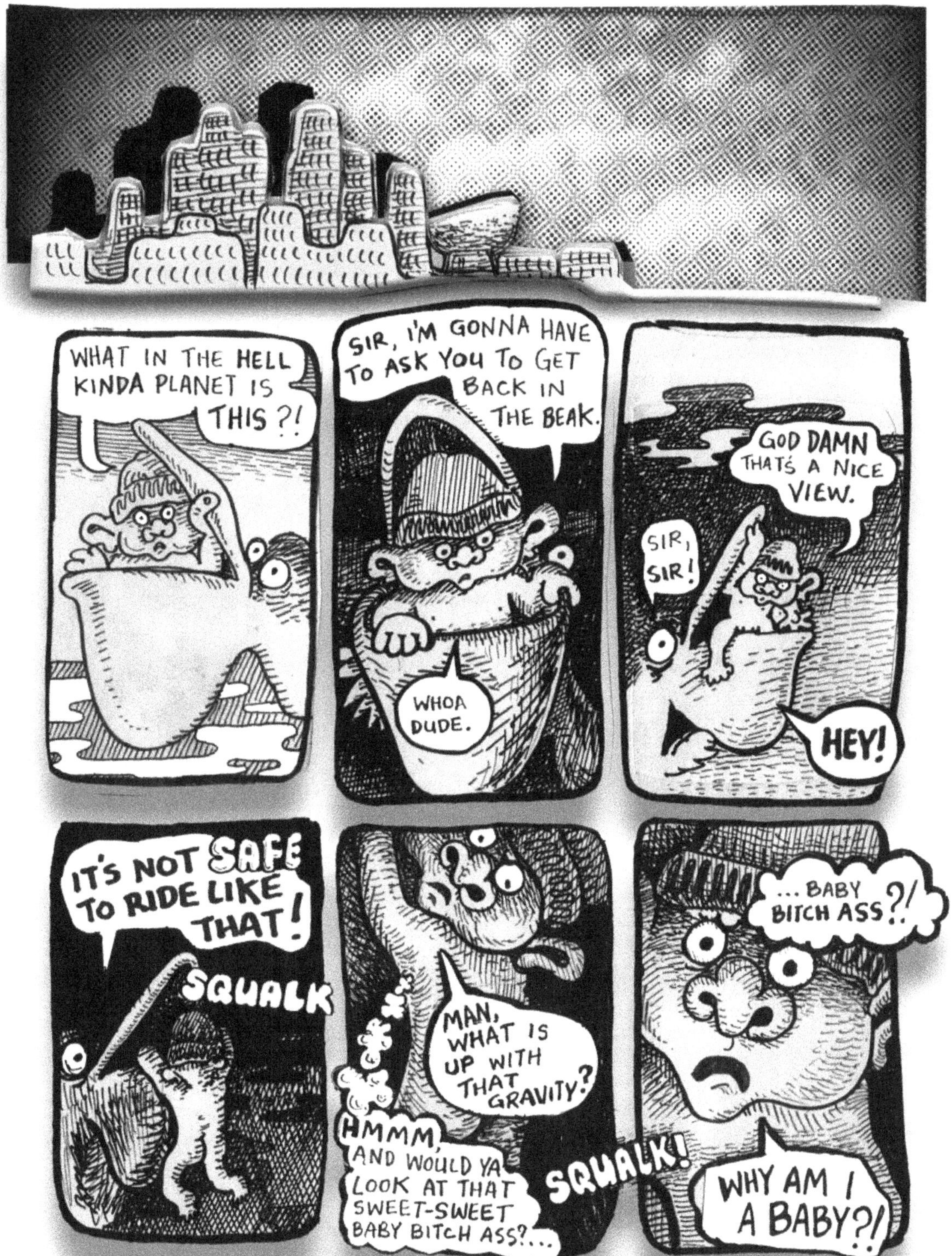
WHAT IN THE HELL KINDA PLANET IS THIS ?!
SIR, I'M GONNA HAVE TO ASK YOU TO GET BACK IN THE BEAK.
WHOA DUDE.
GOD DAMN THAT'S A NICE VIEW.
SIR, SIR!
HEY!
IT'S NOT SAFE TO RIDE LIKE THAT!
SQUALK
MAN, WHAT IS UP WITH THAT GRAVITY?
HMMM, AND WOULD YA LOOK AT THAT SWEET-SWEET BABY BITCH ASS?...
SQUALK!
... BABY BITCH ASS?!
WHY AM I A BABY?!

I BETTER FIND OUT WHAT THIS BIRD KNOWS.
SQUALK SQUALK
SQUALK!
AY! SHUT THE FUCK UP FOR A MINUTE I'M TRYIN' TA THINK!
I CAN'T FLY LIKE THIS, PLEASE, SIR!
SQUALK WE'RE LOSING ALTITUDE... I CAN'T KEEP MY NECK STRAIGHT!
OH FOR PETE'S SAKE!
YOU NEED TO CLIMB BACK IN, AHH! I CAN'T SEE WHERE I'M GOING!
NOW LOOK BIRD, I'M GONNA NEED SOME ANSWERS! WHO SENT YOU?!
GET OFF ME!
NO ONE SENT ME DON'T BE RIDICULOUS!
RIDICULOUS?!
I DON'T NEED THIS SHIT, OH MY GOD!..THAT DOES IT!
THIS IS MY LAST DELIVERY!
WHO YOU CALLIN' RIDICULOUS ?!
POP
HOW'S THAT?
POP
STOP
OW! OW!
SNARL
UNGH
YEA!
YOU LIKE THAT ?!
WTF ?!
YOU THINK I'M MESSIN AROUND?!
COUGH GLAK
NOW EITHER YOU TELL ME WHO SENT YA OR SO HELP ME GOD I'LL PULL THESE DAMN FEATHERS OUT ONE BY FRICKIN ONE!

OW!
OW!
SPIT IT OUT BIRD!
OW!
YOU'RE GONNA KILL US BOTH, STOP!
GIVE ME A NAME!
NOW!
GLARK
GLUH
HXXT
COUGH
CHOKE
COUGH
COUGH
SQUALK! OKAY, OKAY, I'LL TALK. HE GOES BY THE NAME TU HUT!
GLARK COUGH WHEEEEZE
I'M JUST THE DRIVER! (GLARK COUGH) STOP!
GASP
I KNEW IT! JUST AS I SUSPECTED...
IF TU HUT'S BEHIND THIS IT MUST BE SOME KIND OF TOP SECRET MISSION.
EITHER THAT OR THIS IS ALL SOME KIND OF JOKE.
EITHER WAY, I'D BETTER PROCEED ACCORDINGLY... THE BIRD'S GOTTA GO. I CAN'T AFFORD TO RISK HIM SQUALKIN'... SHIT I WASN'T BORN YESTERDAY.

IT WAS ALL COMING BACK TO ME. I KNEW THAT TU HUT MUST HAVE PUT ME HERE FOR A PURPOSE. SURE I WAS IN BABY FORM, BUT MY MIND WAS STILL IN DECENT SHAPE.

SORRY DUDE, I GOTTA LET YOU GO. NOTHING PERSONAL, OF COURSE.

WHAT?! LET ME GO? Y-YOU MEAN... YOU'RE GONNA KILL ME?!

-FRAID SO. Y'SEE, I'M A SPACE REFUGE. I CAN'T AFFORD TO BE COMPROMISED... I'M A WANTED MAN.

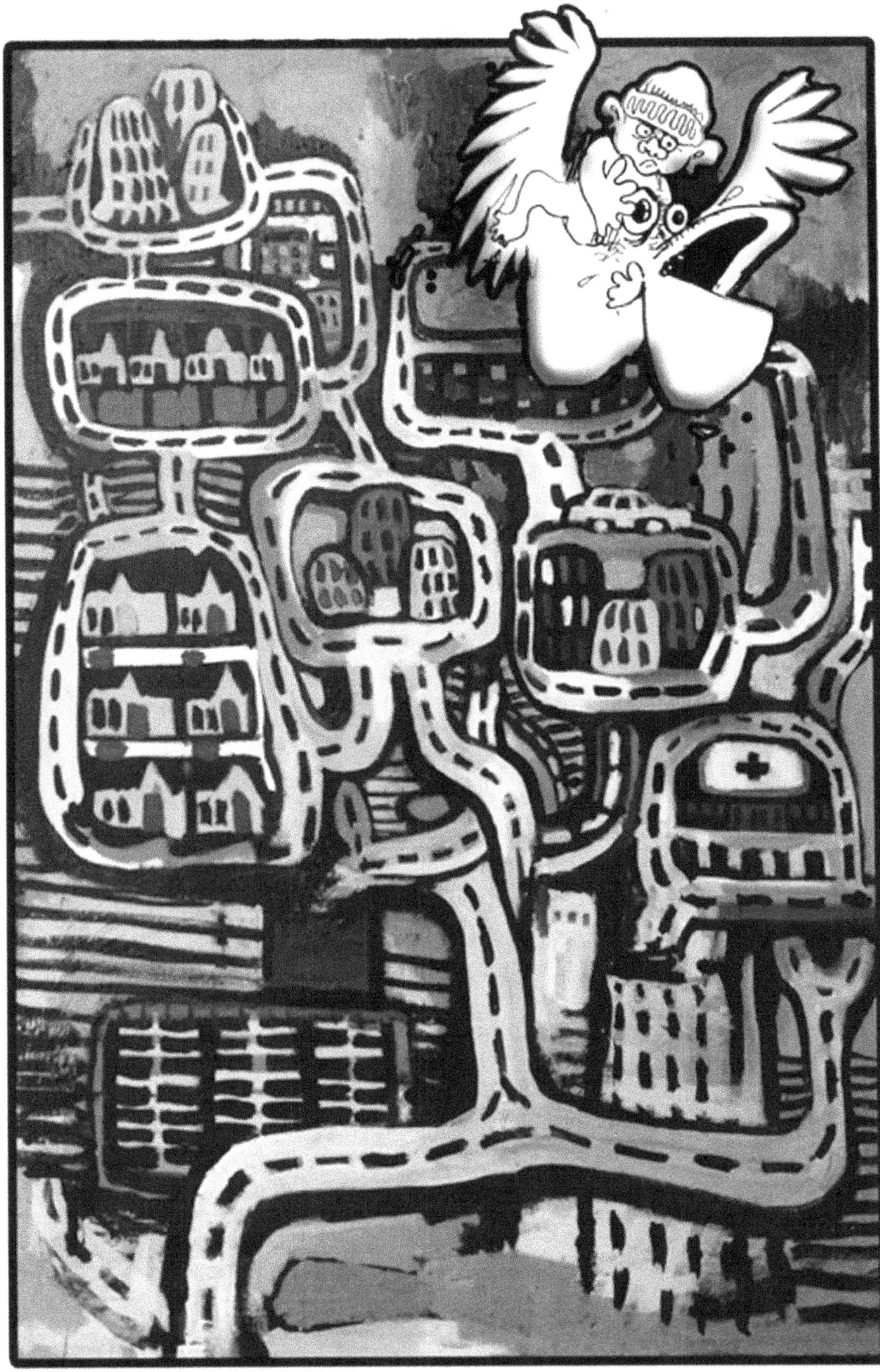

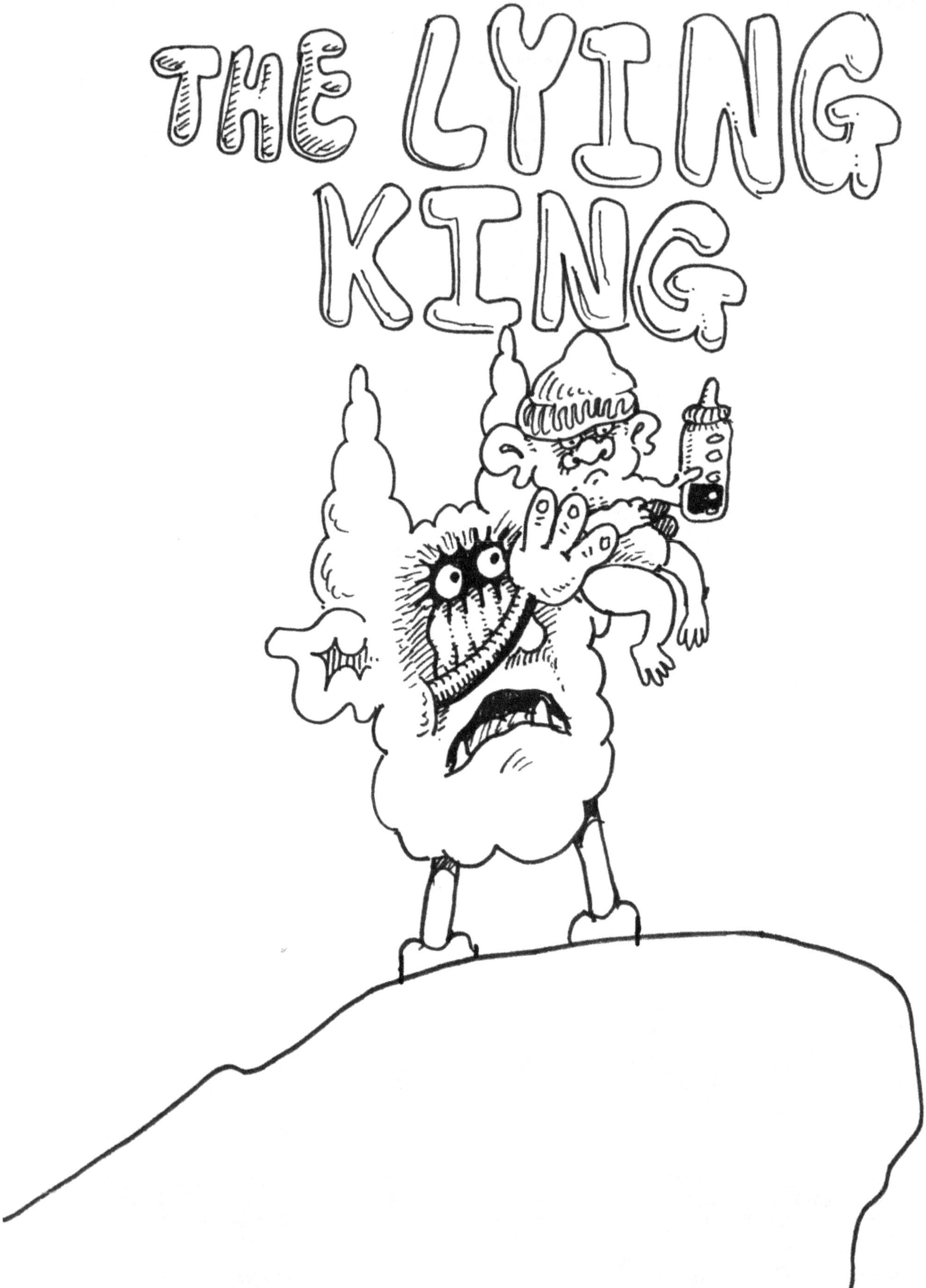
THE LYING KING

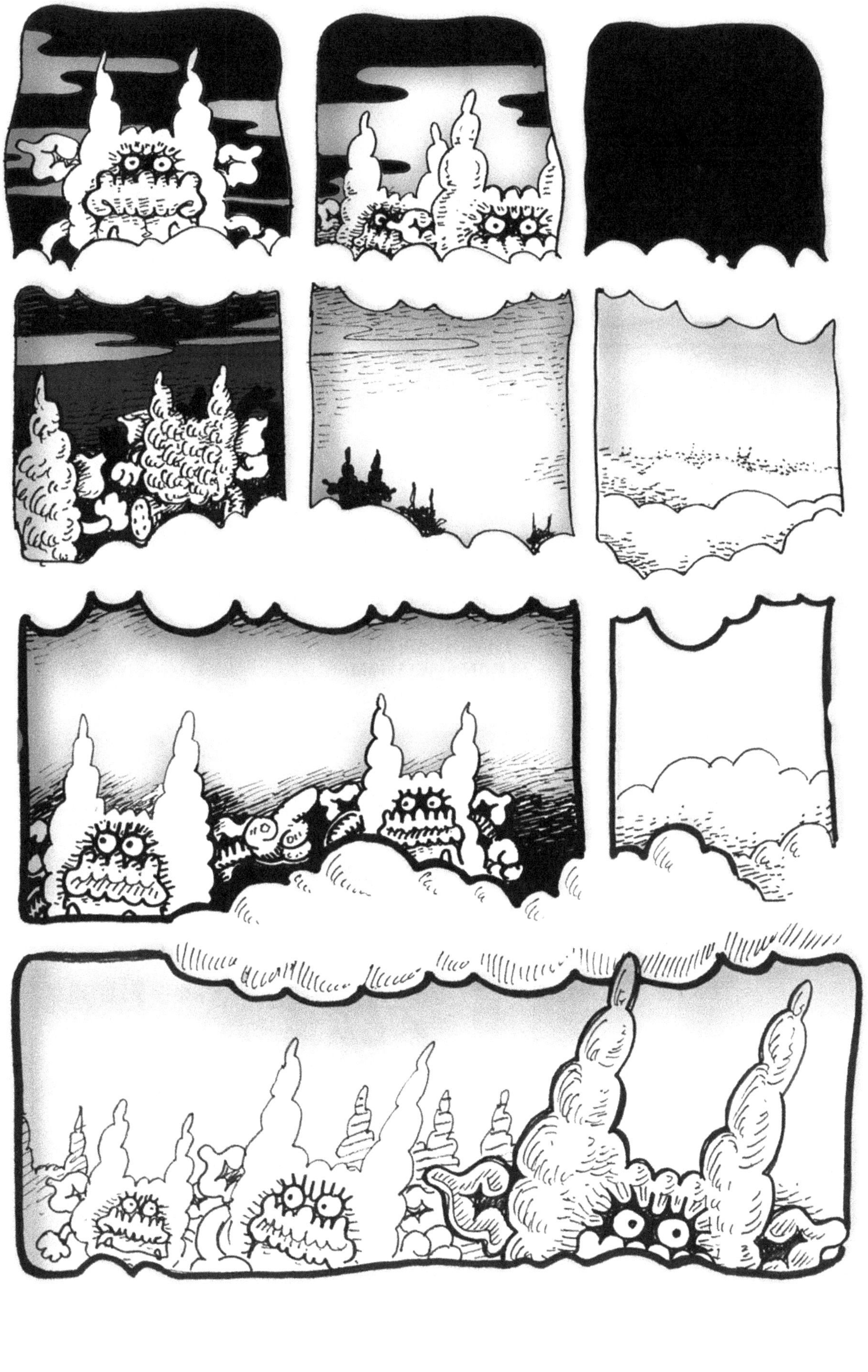

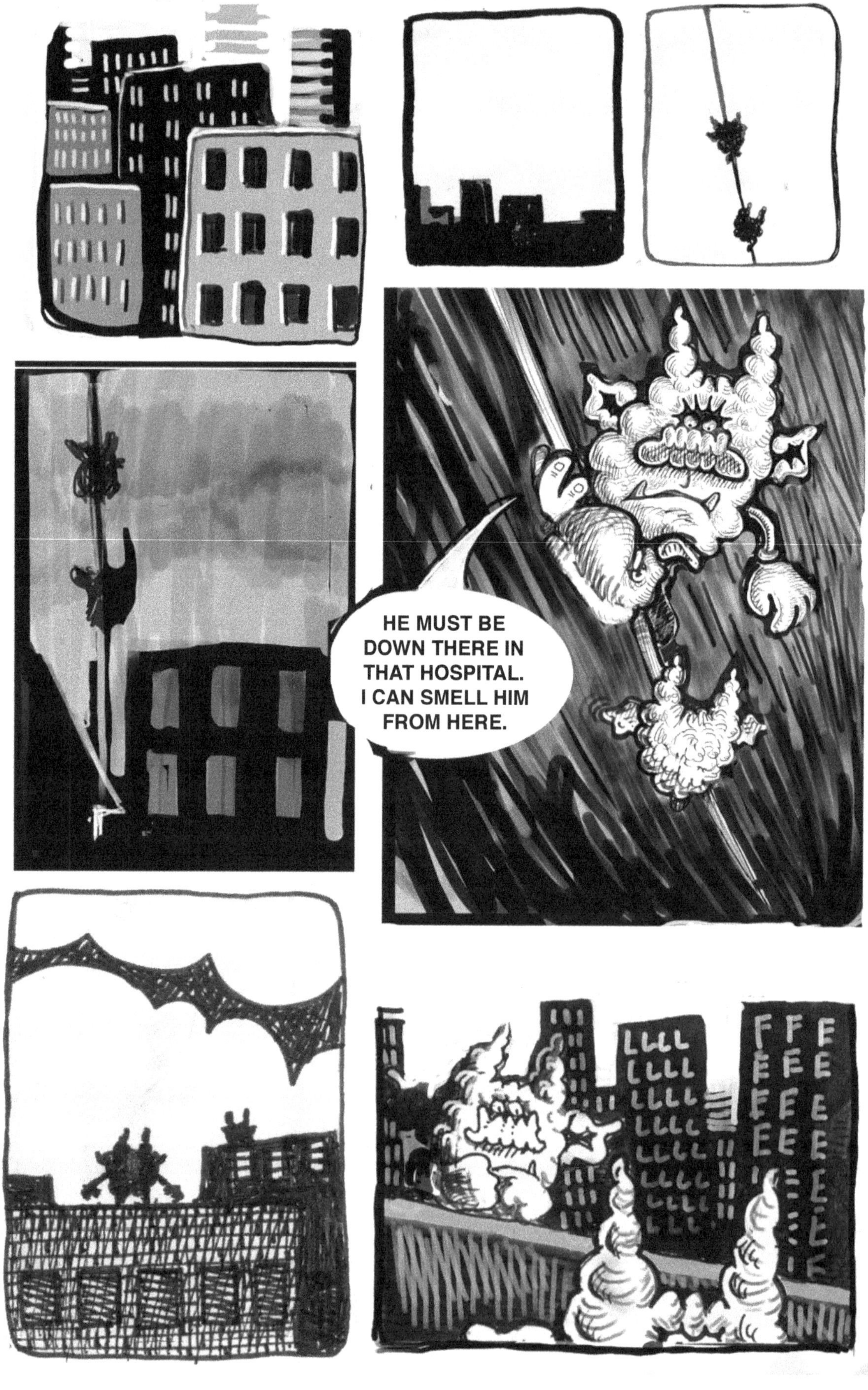
HE MUST BE DOWN THERE IN THAT HOSPITAL. I CAN SMELL HIM FROM HERE.

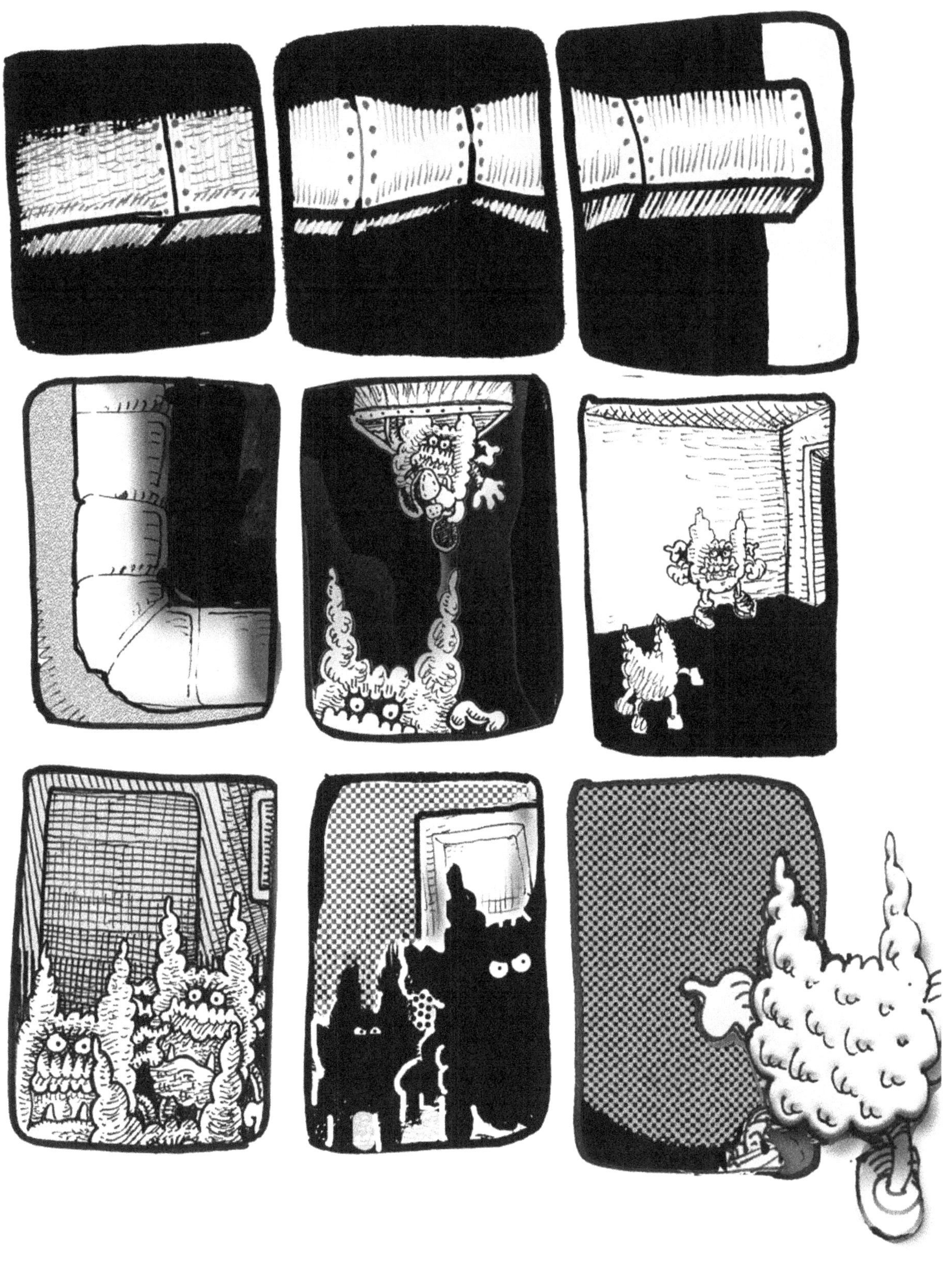

OK, WE'RE CLEAR
DO YOU SMELL COFFEE?
YUP!
GUYS LOOK!

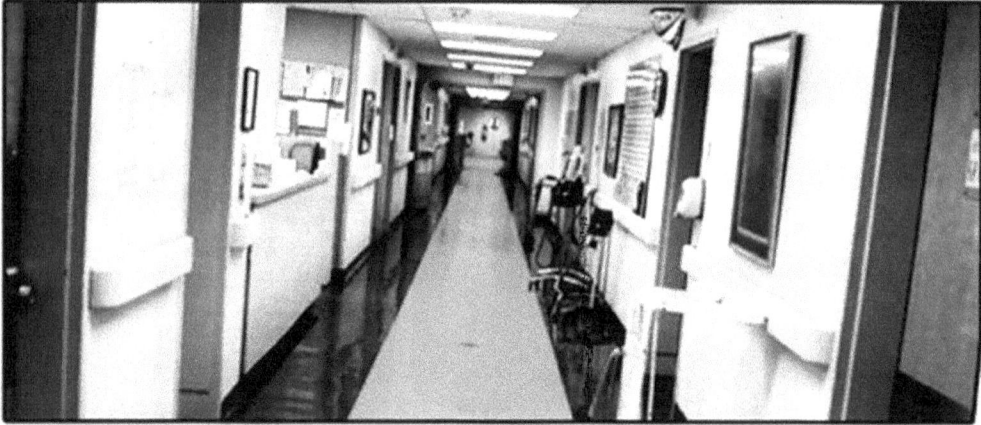

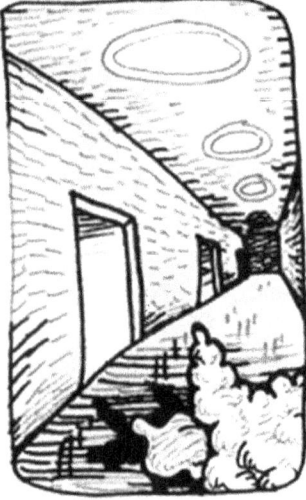

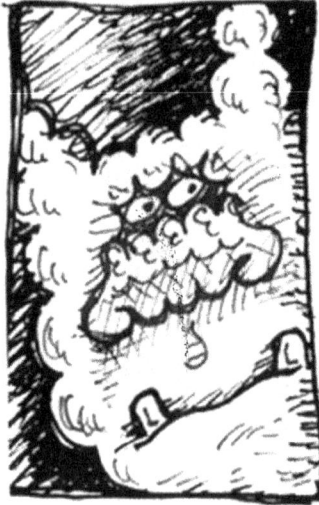

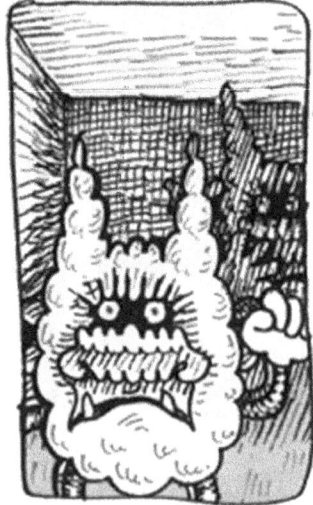

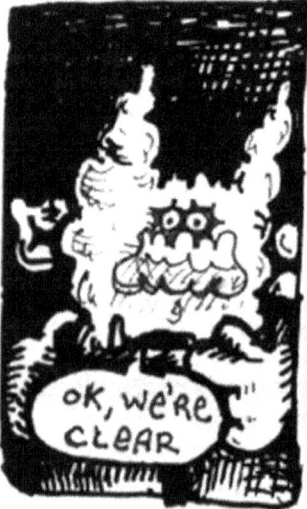

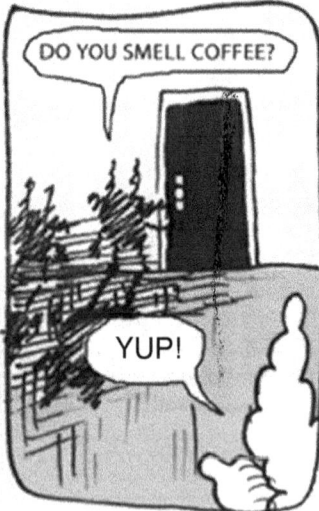

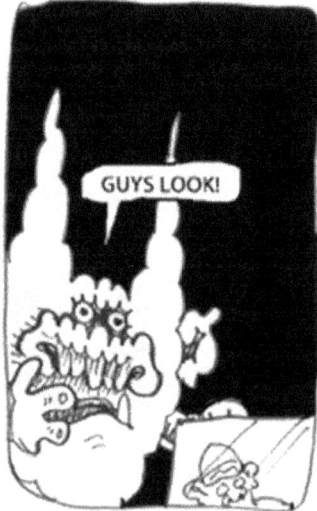

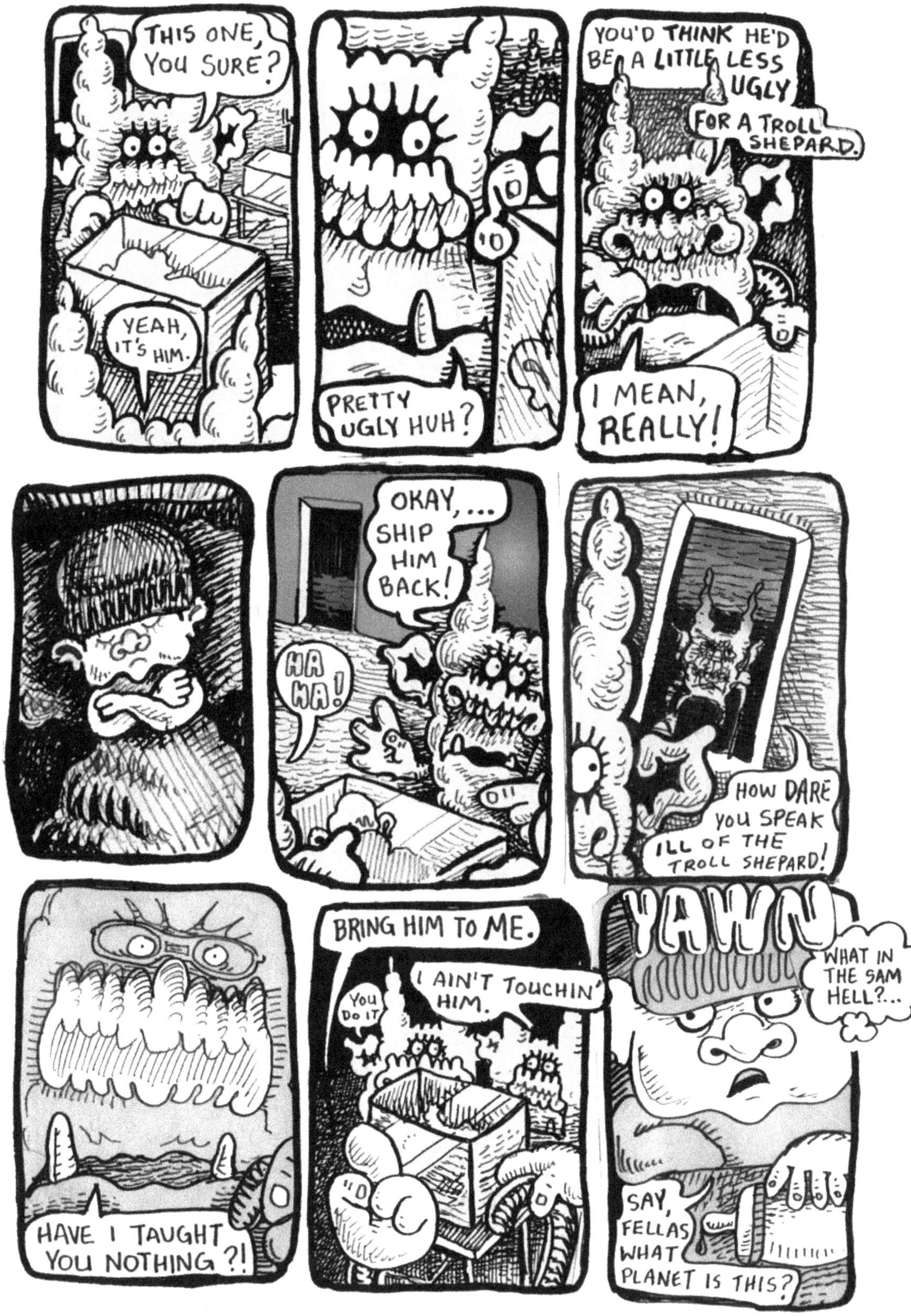
THIS ONE, YOU SURE?
YEAH, IT'S HIM.
PRETTY UGLY HUH?
YOU'D THINK HE'D BE A LITTLE LESS UGLY
FOR A TROLL SHEPARD.
I MEAN, REALLY!
OKAY, ... SHIP HIM BACK!
HA HA!
HOW DARE YOU SPEAK ILL OF THE TROLL SHEPARD!
HAVE I TAUGHT YOU NOTHING ?!
BRING HIM TO ME.
YOU DO IT
I AIN'T TOUCHIN' HIM.
YAWN
WHAT IN THE SAM HELL?...
SAY, FELLAS WHAT PLANET IS THIS?

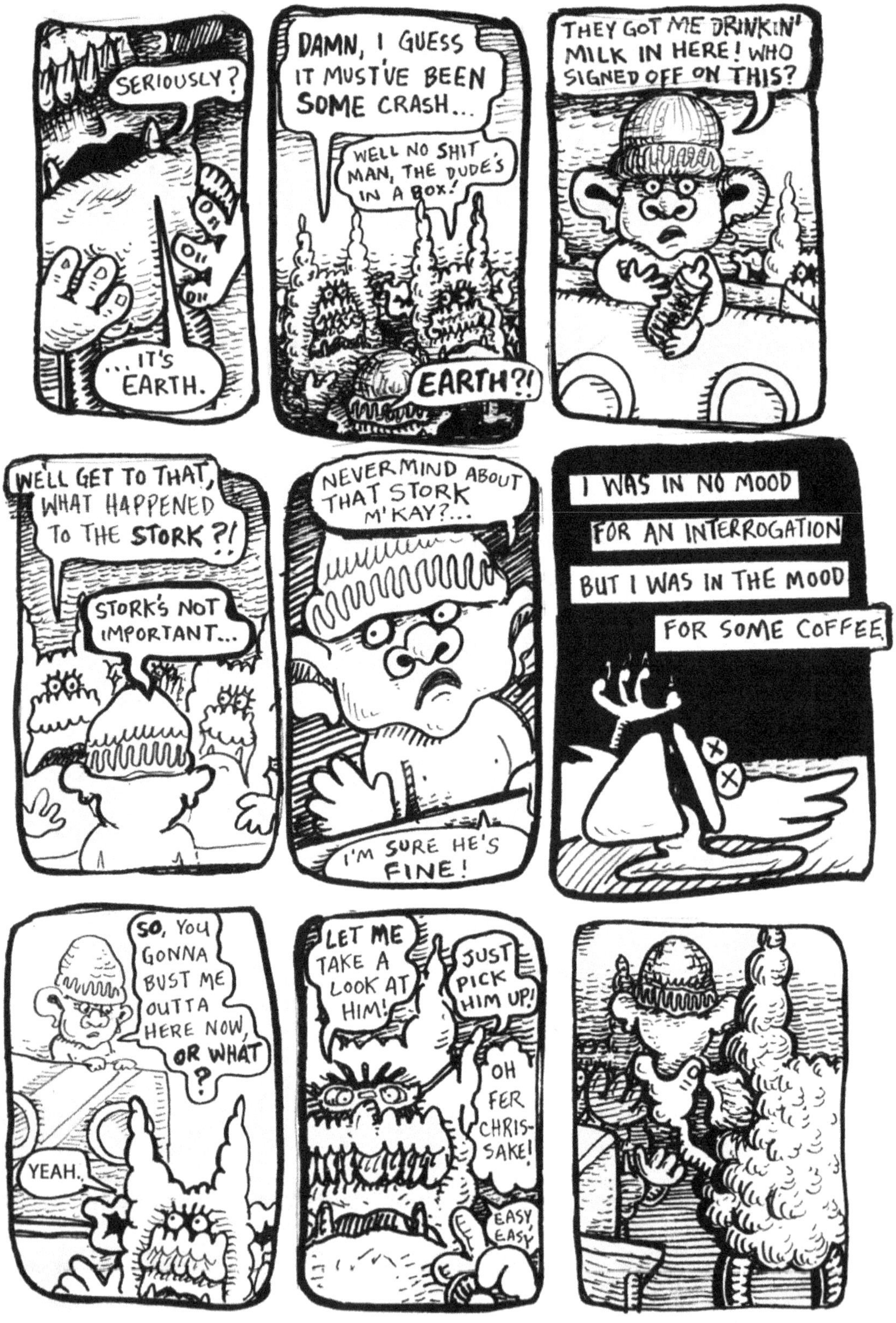
SERIOUSLY?
...IT'S EARTH.
DAMN, I GUESS IT MUST'VE BEEN SOME CRASH...
WELL NO SHIT MAN, THE DUDE'S IN A BOX!
EARTH?!
THEY GOT ME DRINKIN' MILK IN HERE! WHO SIGNED OFF ON THIS?
WE'LL GET TO THAT, WHAT HAPPENED TO THE STORK?!
STORK'S NOT IMPORTANT...
NEVERMIND ABOUT THAT STORK M'KAY?...
I'M SURE HE'S FINE!
I WAS IN NO MOOD
FOR AN INTERROGATION
BUT I WAS IN THE MOOD
FOR SOME COFFEE
SO, YOU GONNA BUST ME OUTTA HERE NOW, OR WHAT?
YEAH.
LET ME TAKE A LOOK AT HIM!
JUST PICK HIM UP!
OH FER CHRIS-SAKE!
EASY, EASY

HOT
COFFEE
SEE `CAUSE WHEN I WAS BORN, SHIT... I WAS COLD AS ICE

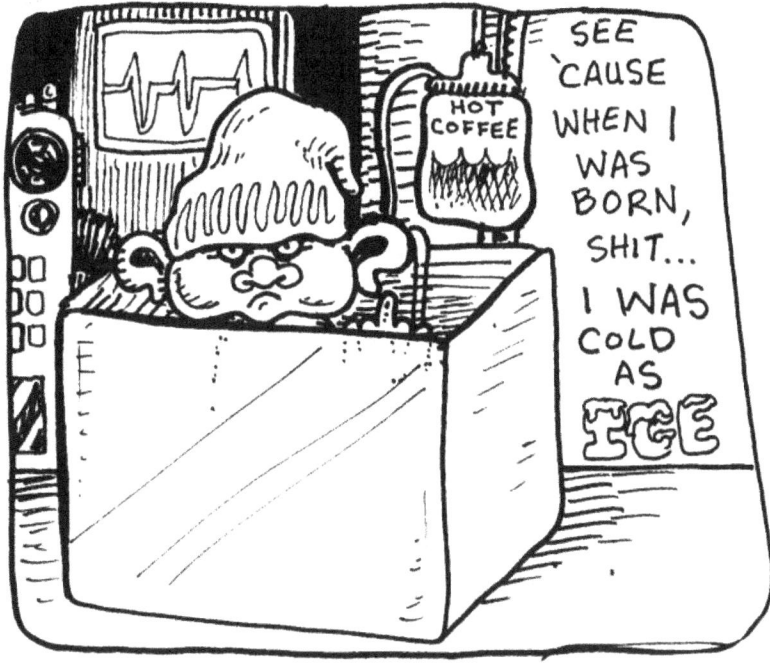

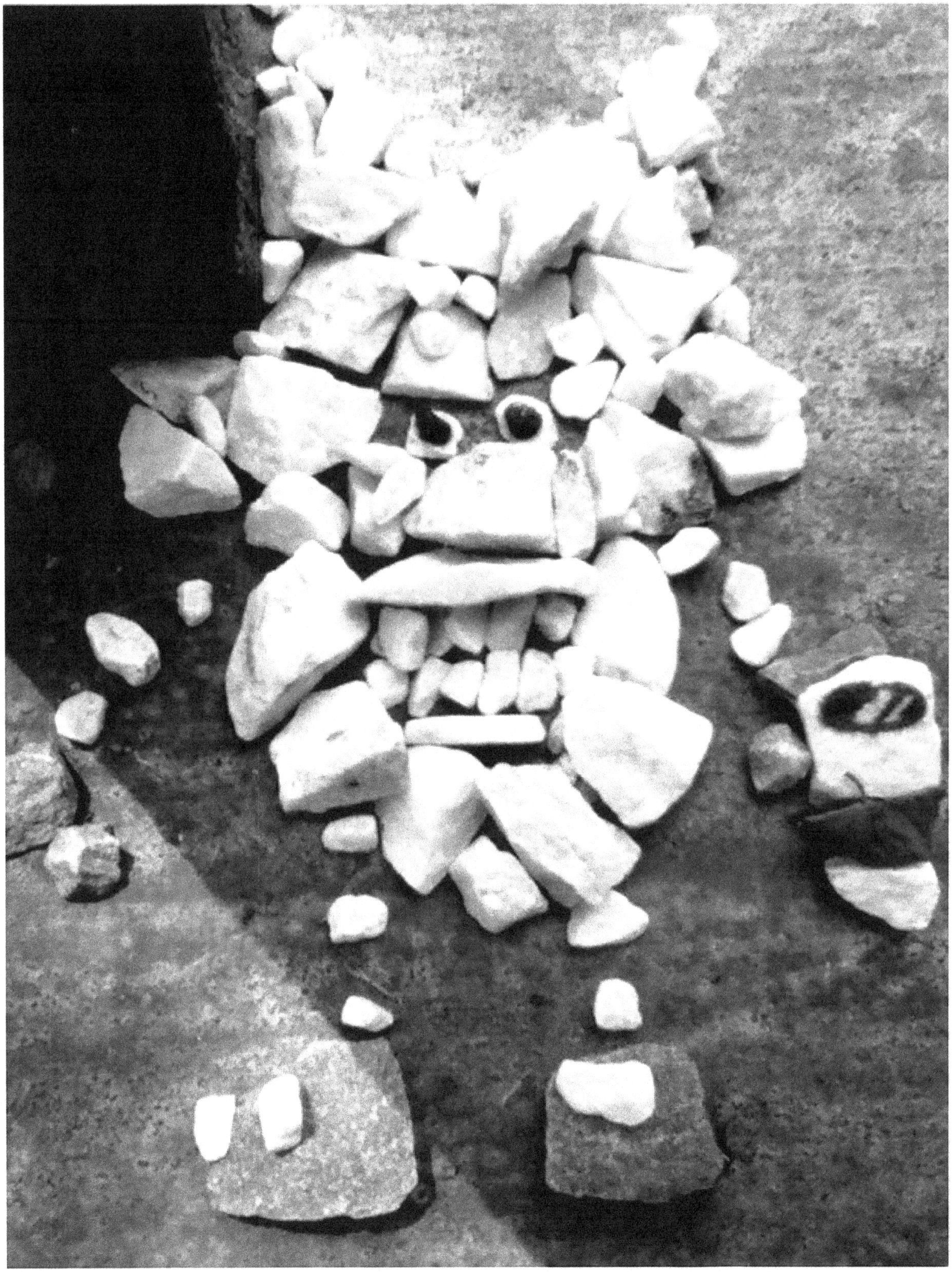

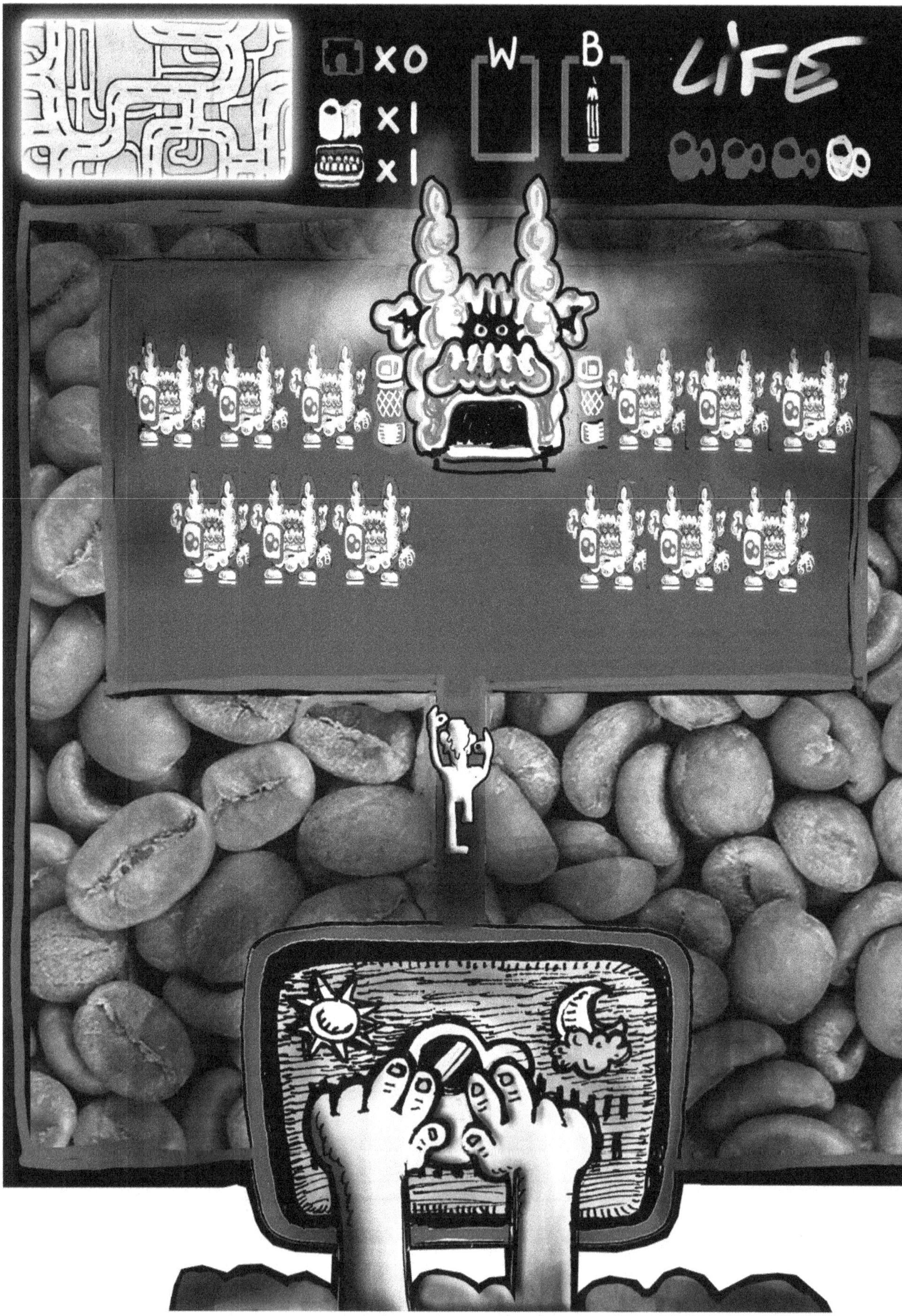
x0
x1
x1
W
B
LIFE

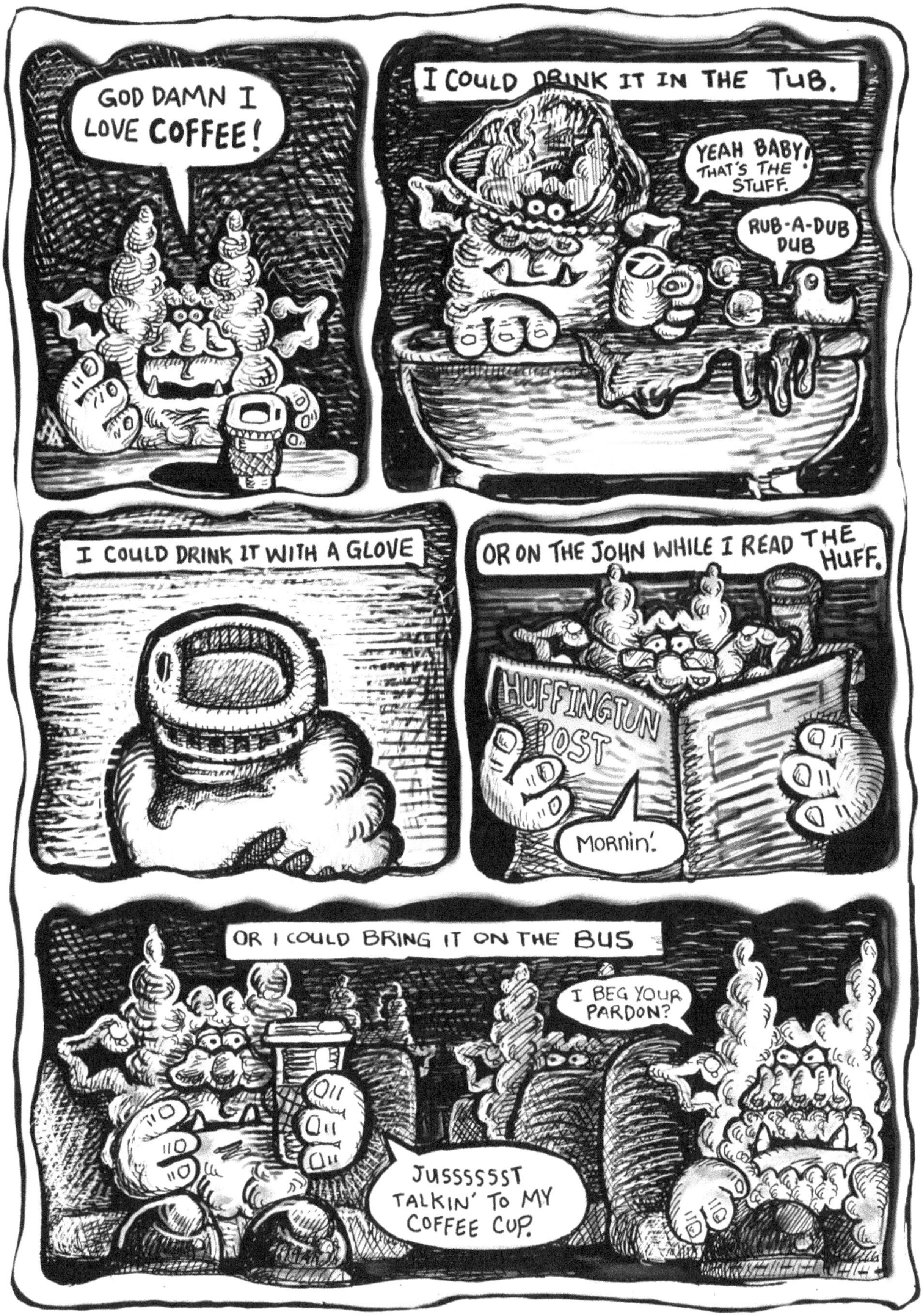
GOD DAMN I LOVE COFFEE!
I COULD DRINK IT IN THE TUB.
YEAH BABY! THAT'S THE STUFF.
RUB-A-DUB DUB
I COULD DRINK IT WITH A GLOVE
OR ON THE JOHN WHILE I READ THE HUFF.
HUFFINGTUN POST
Mornin'.
OR I COULD BRING IT ON THE BUS
I BEG YOUR PARDON?
JUSSSSSST TALKIN' TO MY COFFEE CUP.

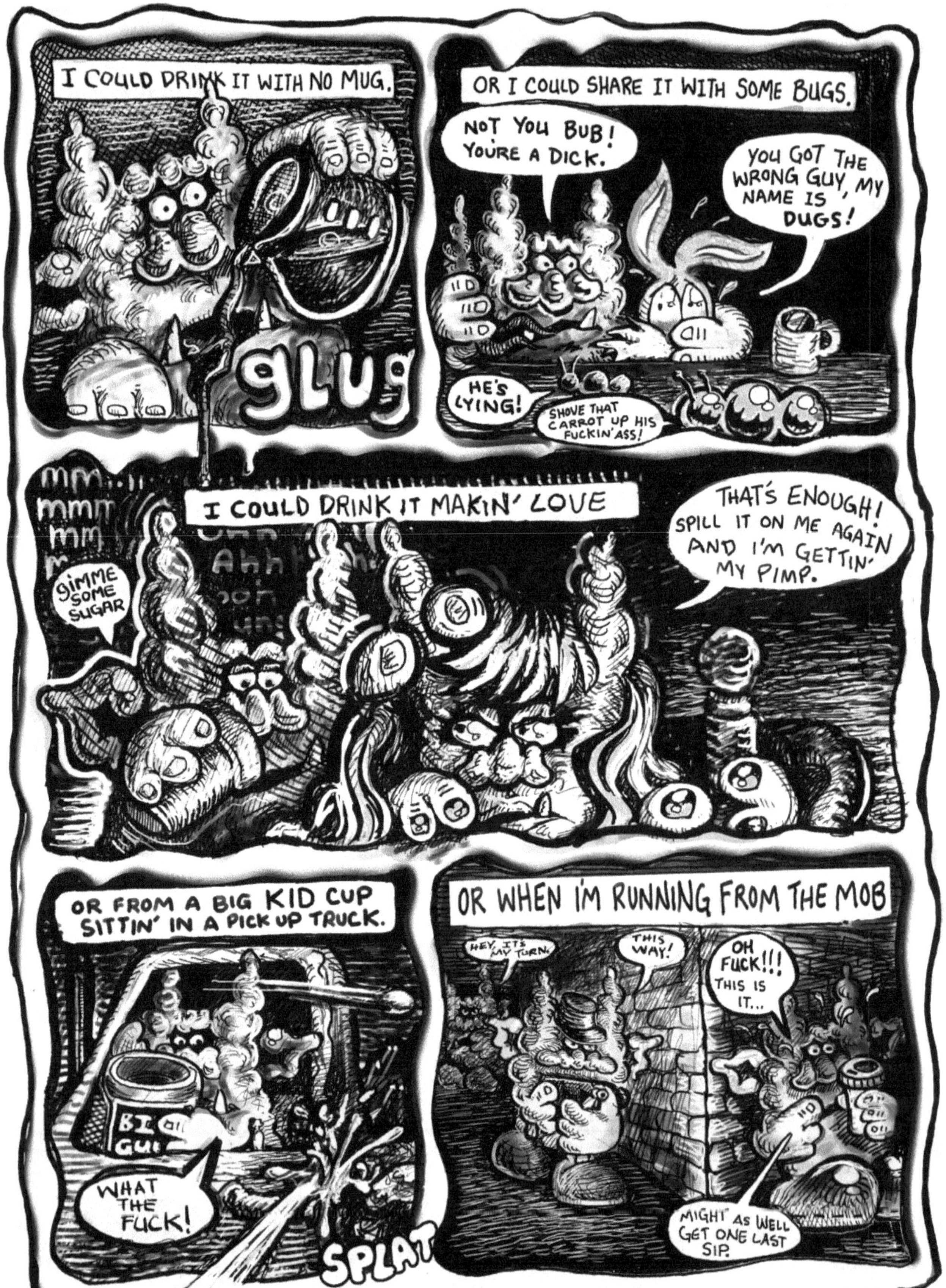
I COULD DRINK IT WITH NO MUG.
glug
OR I COULD SHARE IT WITH SOME BUGS.
NOT YOU BUB! YOU'RE A DICK.
YOU GOT THE WRONG GUY, MY NAME IS DUGS!
HE'S LYING!
SHOVE THAT CARROT UP HIS FUCKIN' ASS!
I COULD DRINK IT MAKIN' LOVE
gimme some sugar
THAT'S ENOUGH! SPILL IT ON ME AGAIN AND I'M GETTIN' MY PIMP.
OR FROM A BIG KID CUP SITTIN' IN A PICK UP TRUCK.
WHAT THE FUCK!
SPLAT
OR WHEN I'M RUNNING FROM THE MOB
HEY, ITS MY TURN.
THIS WAY!
OH FUCK!!! THIS IS IT...
MIGHT AS WELL GET ONE LAST SIP.

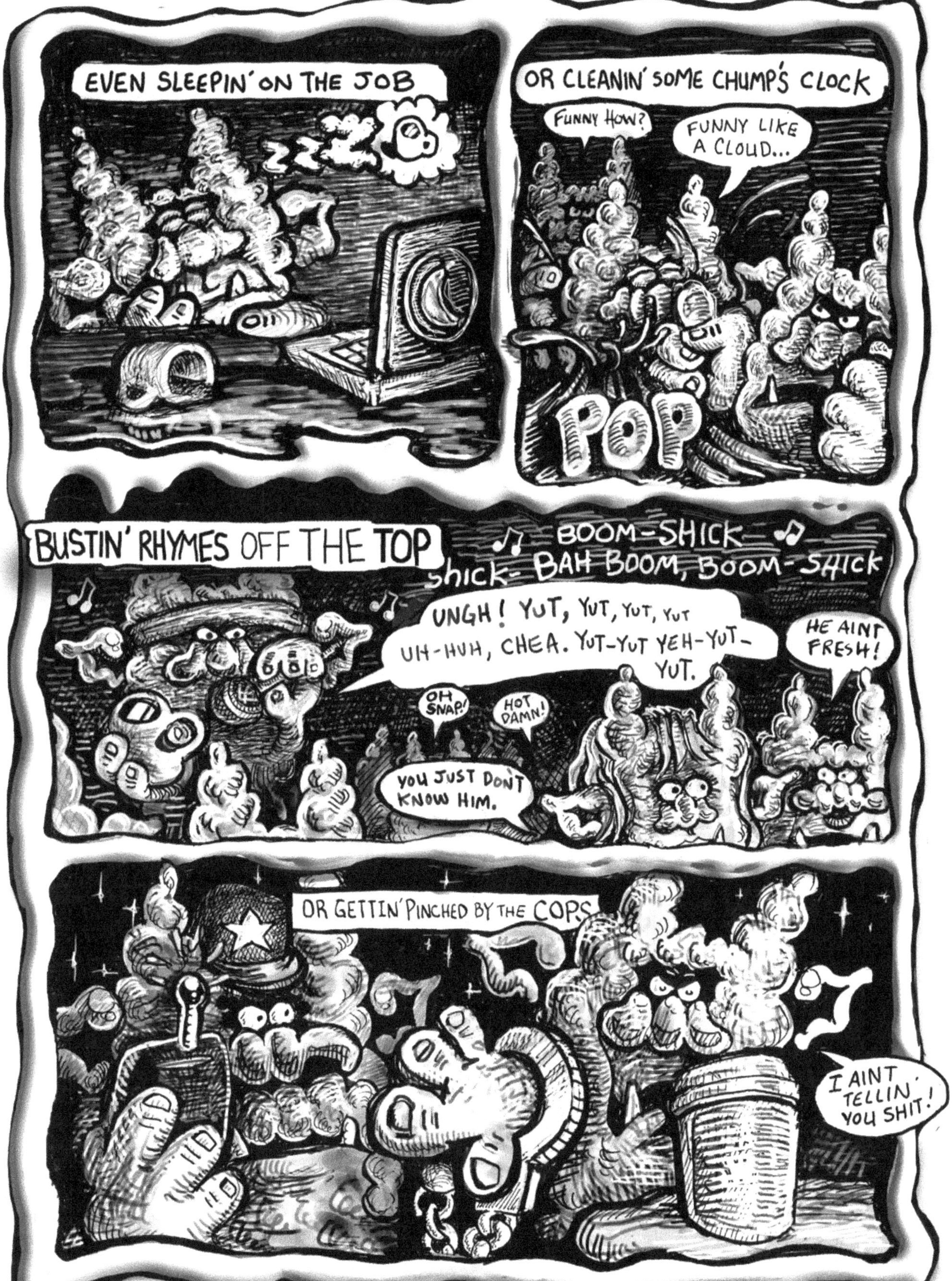

EVEN SLEEPIN' ON THE JOB
OR CLEANIN' SOME CHUMP'S CLOCK
FUNNY HOW?
FUNNY LIKE A CLOUD...
POP
BUSTIN' RHYMES OFF THE TOP
BOOM-SHICK
SHICK- BAH BOOM, BOOM-SHICK
UNGH! YUT, YUT, YUT, YUT
UH-HUH, CHEA. YUT-YUT YEH-YUT-YUT.
HE AINT FRESH!
OH SNAP!
HOT DAMN!
YOU JUST DON'T KNOW HIM.
OR GETTIN' PINCHED BY THE COPS
I AINT TELLIN' YOU SHIT!

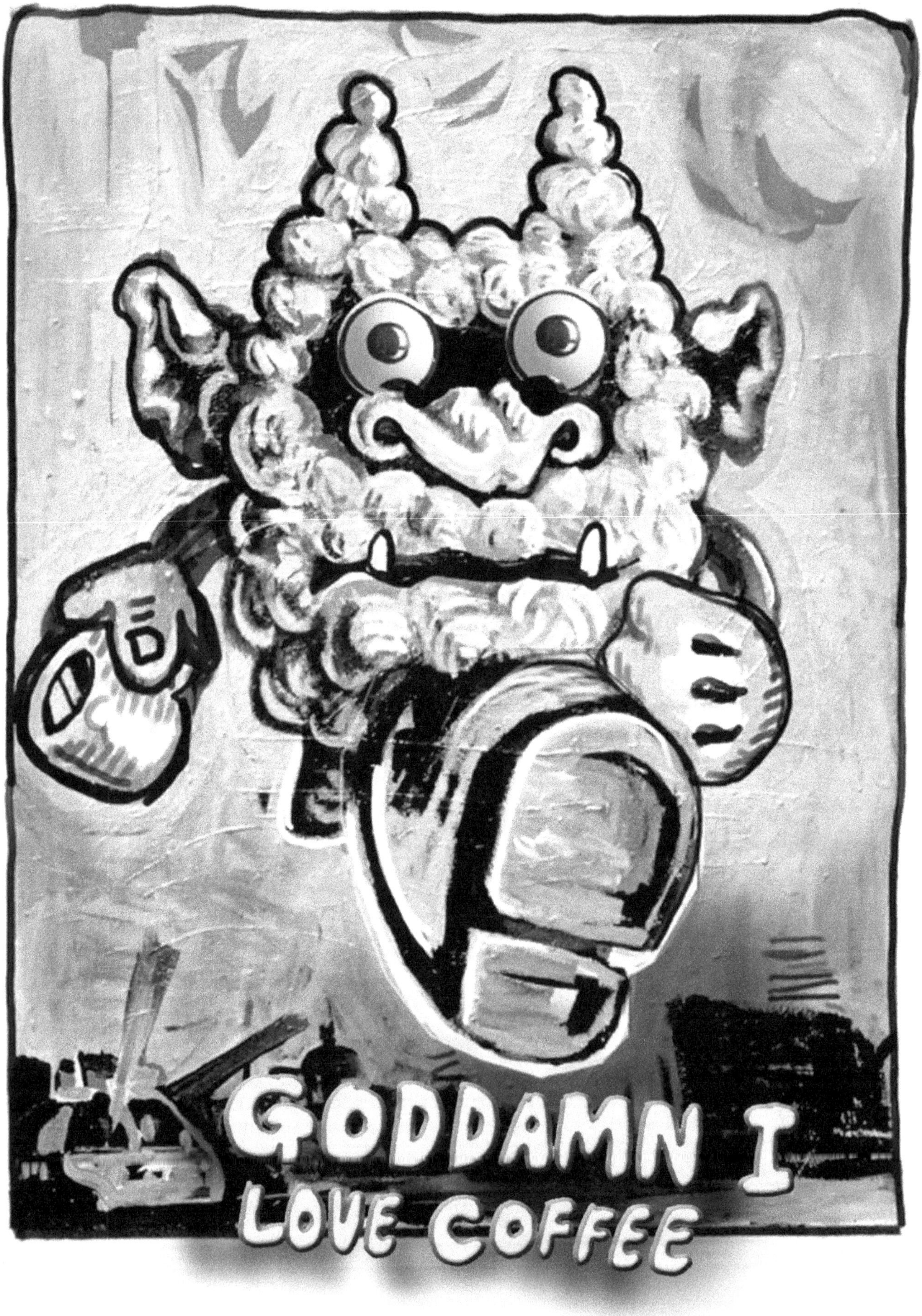
GODDAMN I LOVE COFFEE

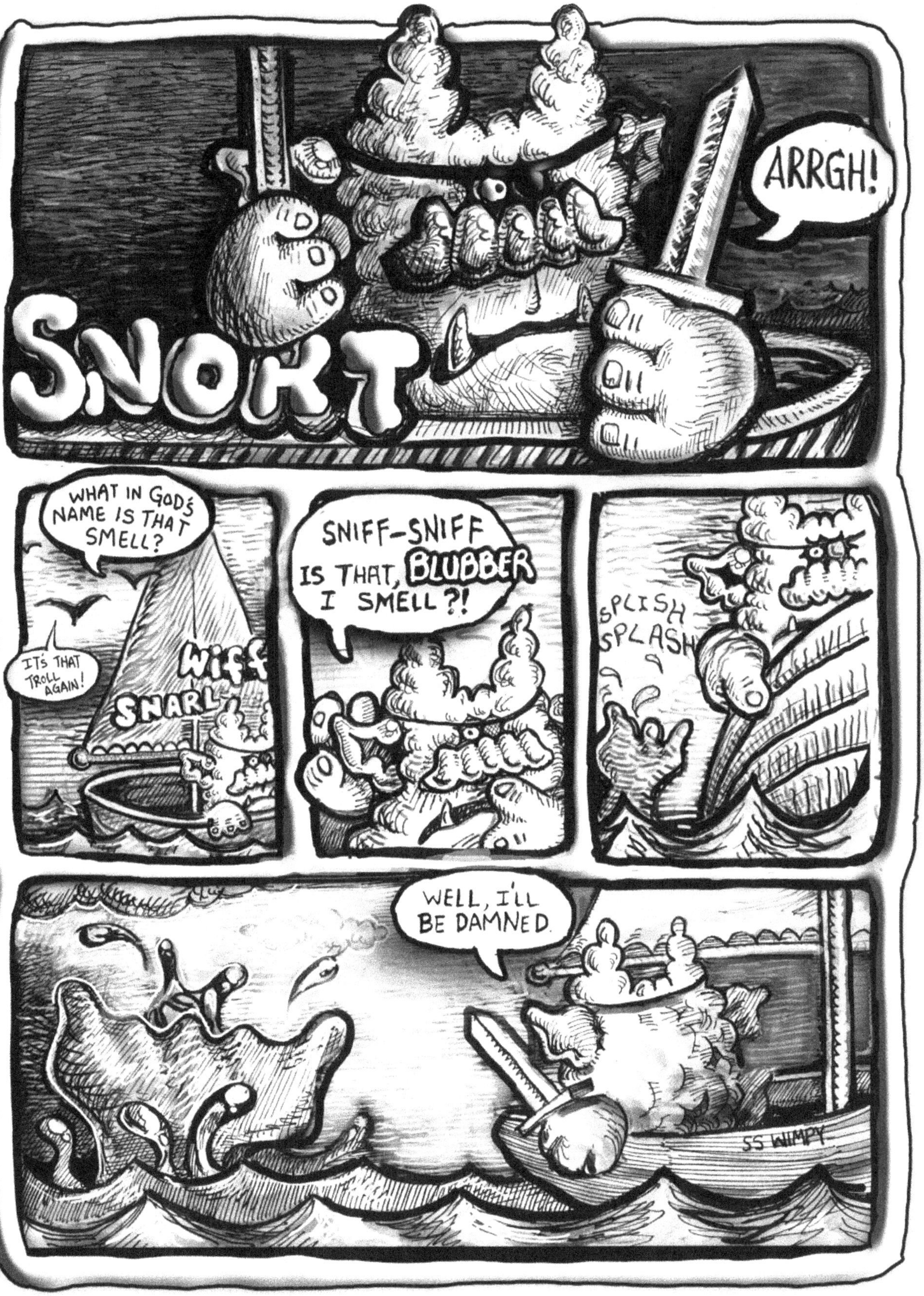
ARRGH!
SNORT
WHAT IN GOD'S NAME IS THAT SMELL?
IT'S THAT TROLL AGAIN!
WIFF
SNARL
SNIFF-SNIFF IS THAT, BLUBBER I SMELL?!
SPLISH SPLASH
WELL, I'LL BE DAMNED.
SS WIMPY

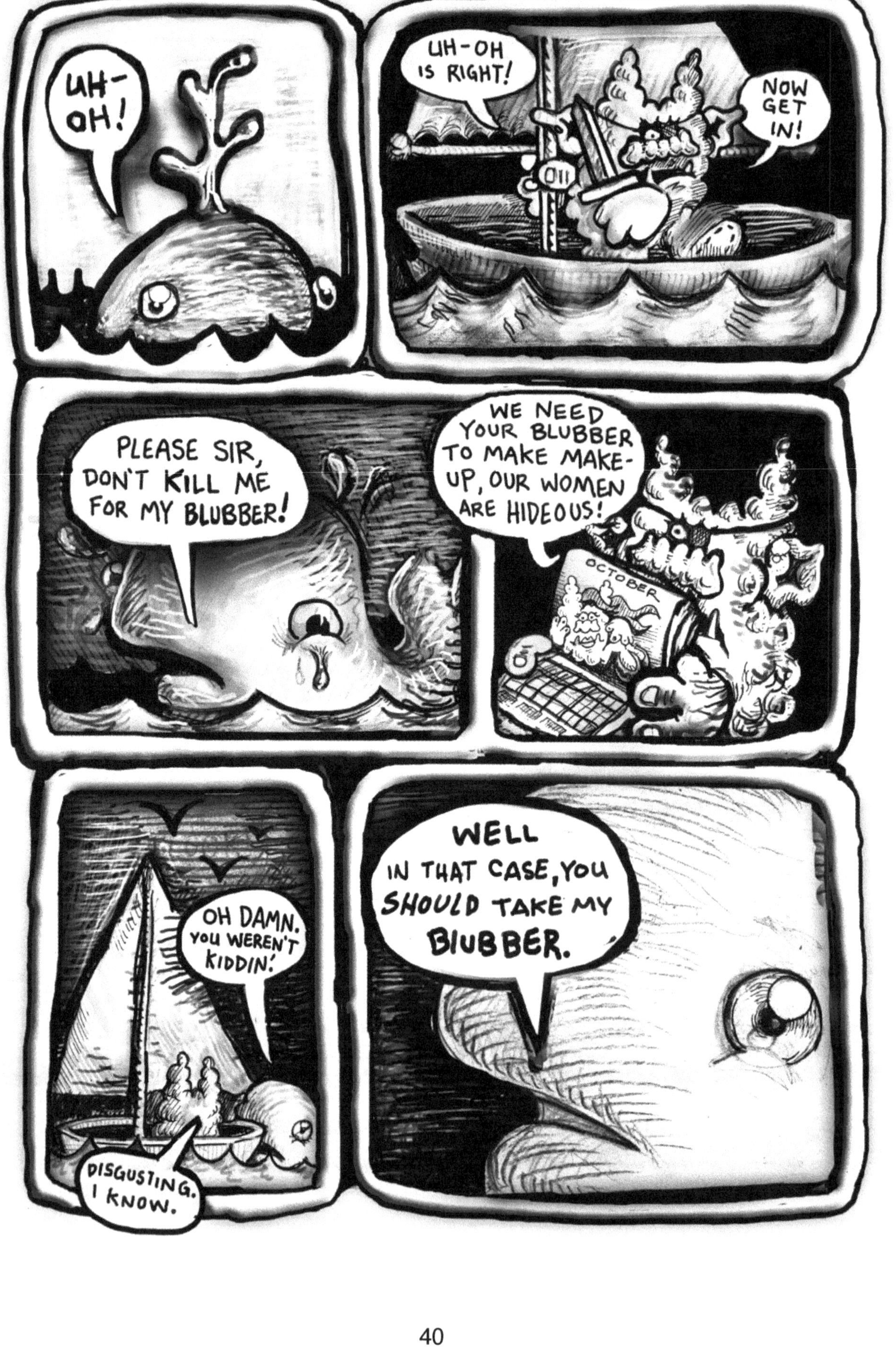
UH-OH!
UH-OH IS RIGHT!
NOW GET IN!
PLEASE SIR, DON'T KILL ME FOR MY BLUBBER!
WE NEED YOUR BLUBBER TO MAKE MAKE-UP, OUR WOMEN ARE HIDEOUS!
OCTOBER
OH DAMN. YOU WEREN'T KIDDIN'!
DISGUSTING. I KNOW.
WELL IN THAT CASE, YOU SHOULD TAKE MY BlUBBER.

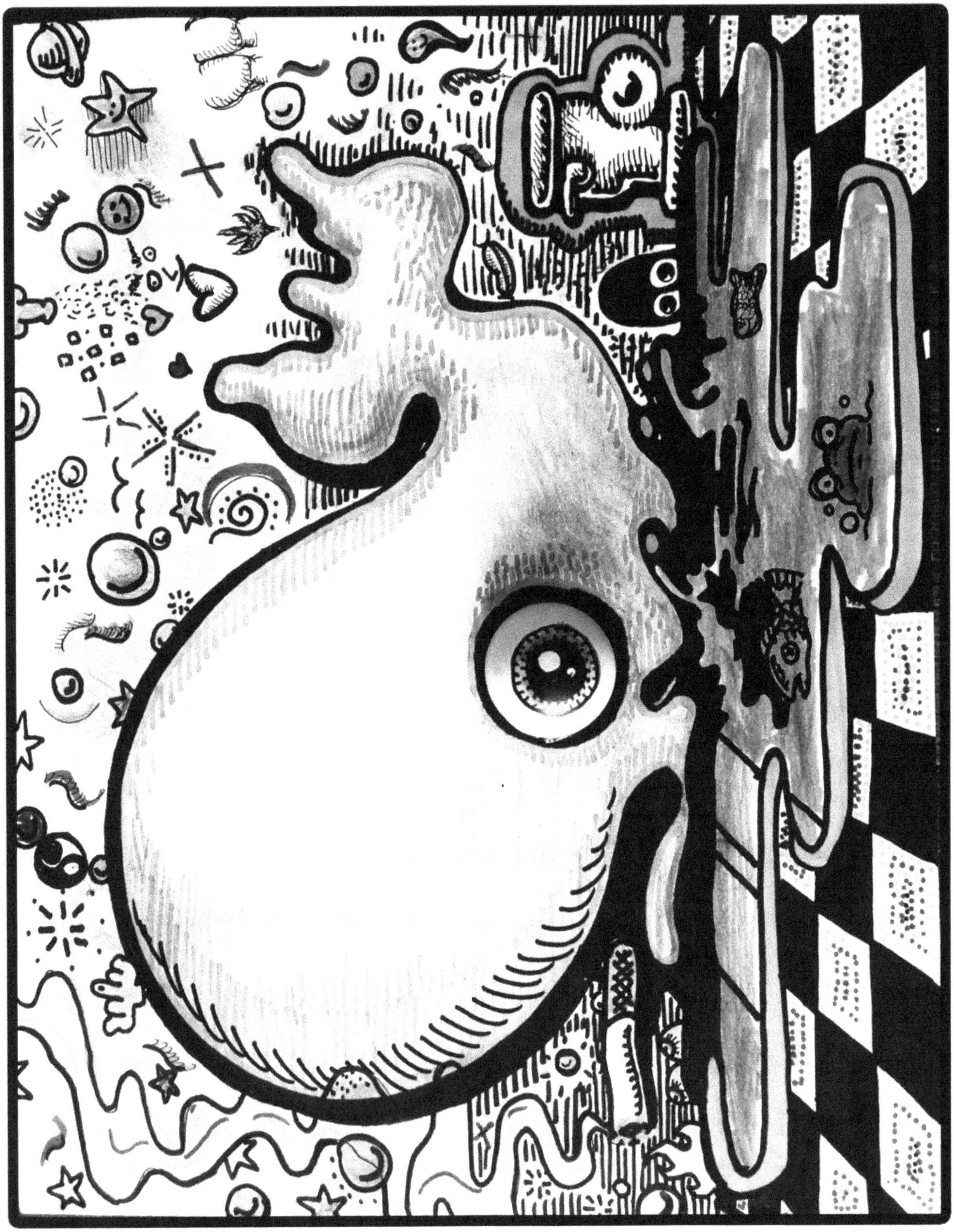

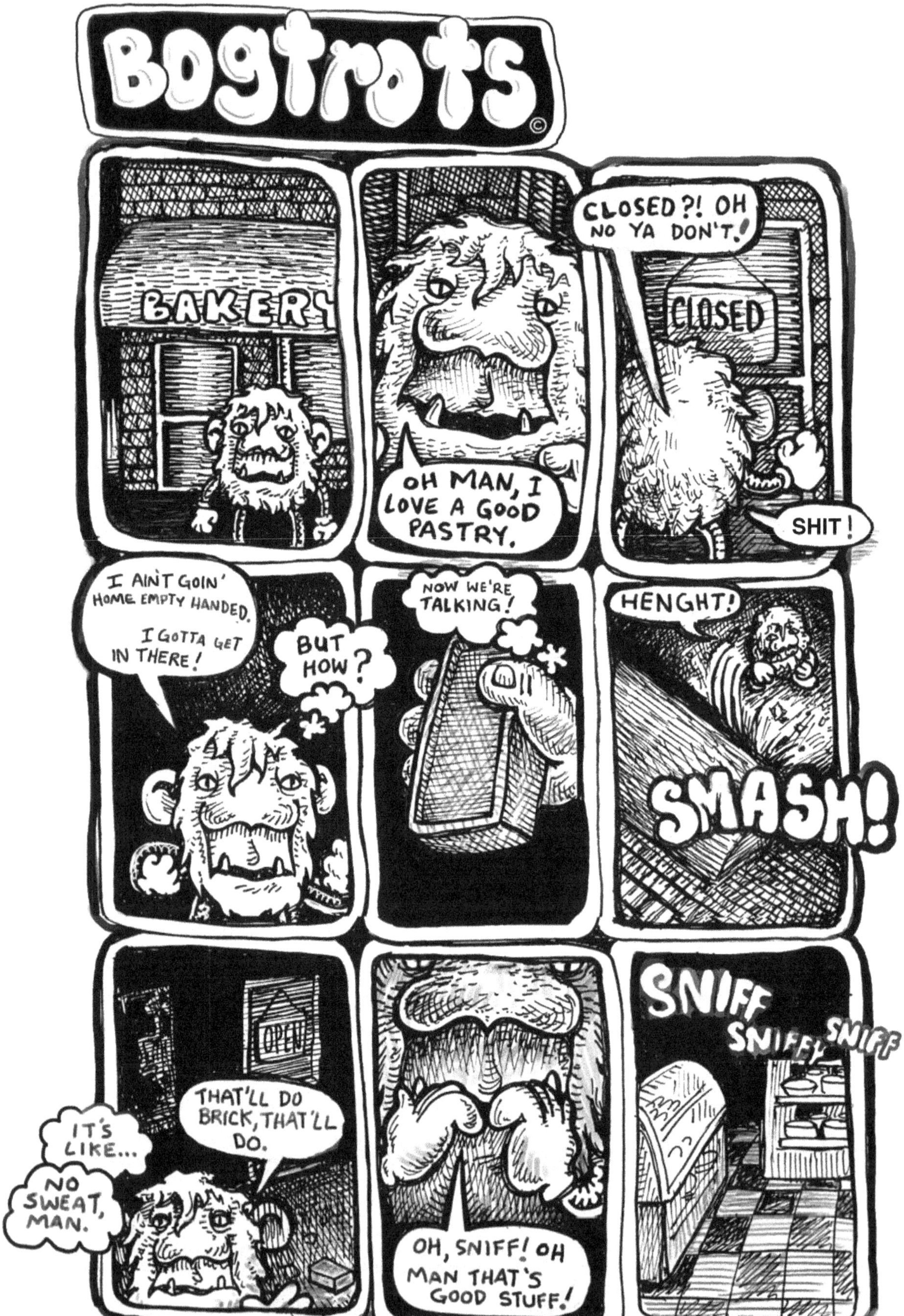
Bogtrots ©
BAKERY
OH MAN, I LOVE A GOOD PASTRY.
CLOSED?! OH NO YA DON'T!
CLOSED
SHIT!
I AIN'T GOIN' HOME EMPTY HANDED.
I GOTTA GET IN THERE!
BUT HOW?
NOW WE'RE TALKING!
HENGHT!
SMASH!
OPEN
THAT'LL DO BRICK, THAT'LL DO.
IT'S LIKE...
NO SWEAT, MAN.
OH, SNIFF! OH MAN THAT'S GOOD STUFF!
SNIFF
SNIFF
SNIFF
SNIFF

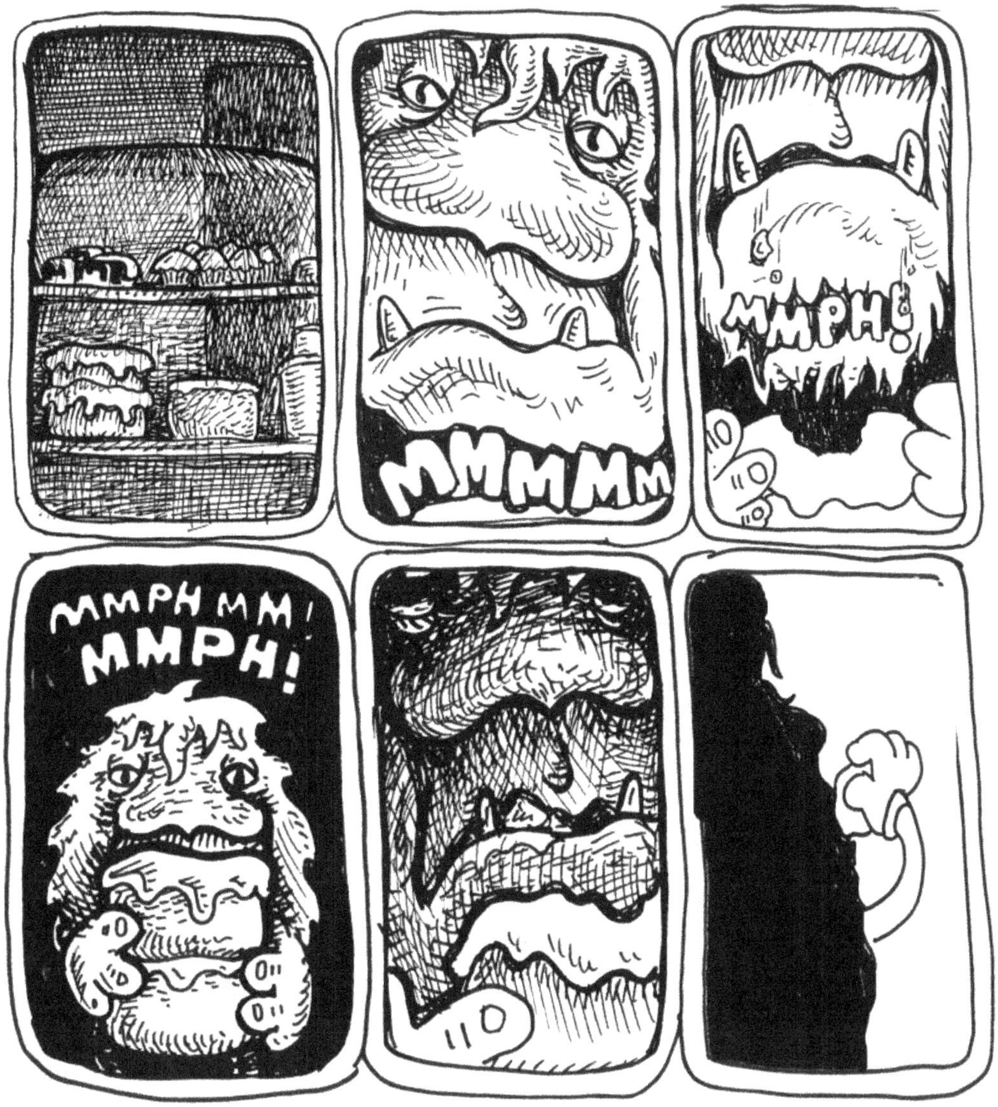
MMMMMM
MMPH!
MMPH MM!
MMPH!

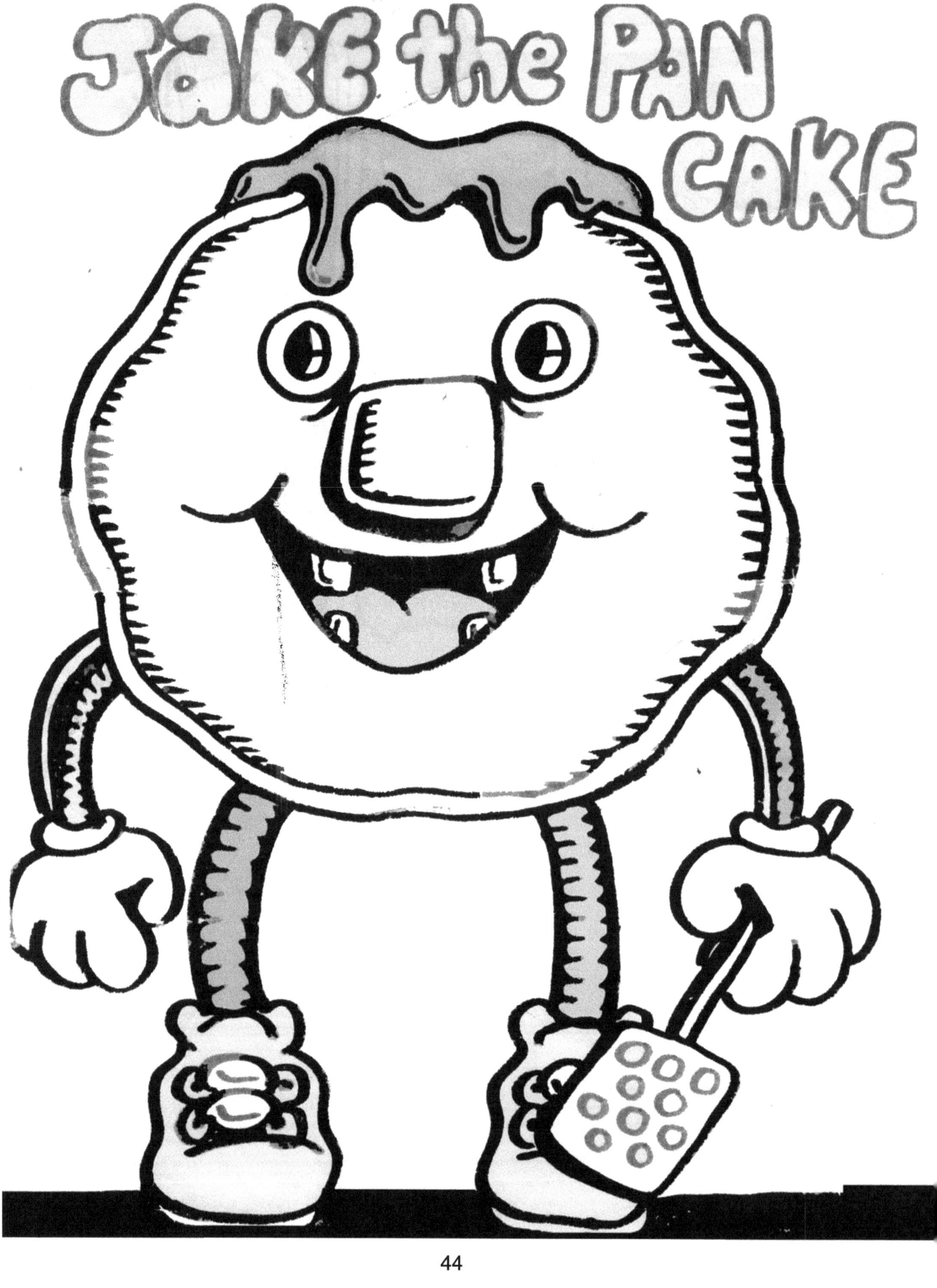
JAKE the PAN
CAKE

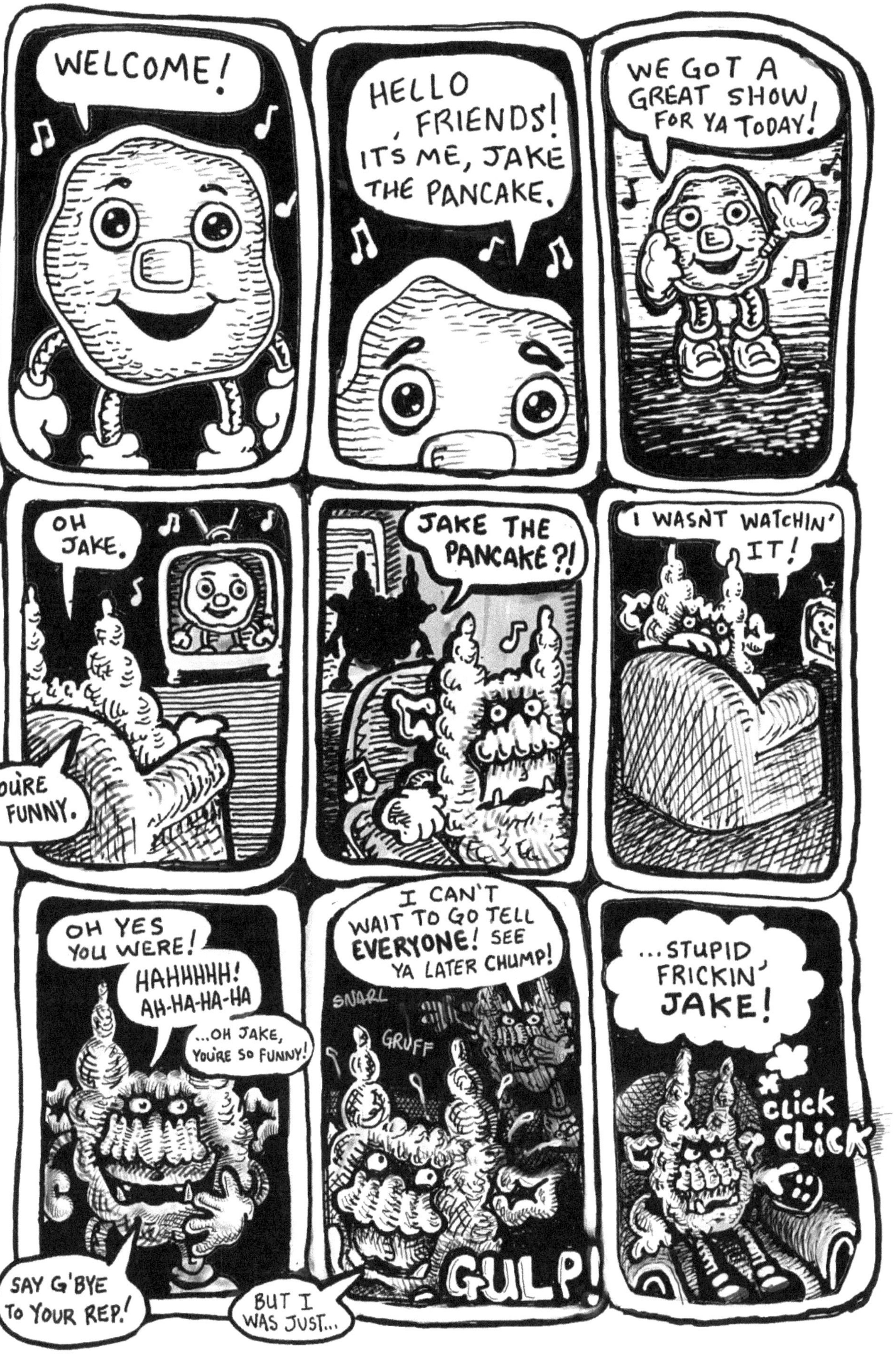
WELCOME!
HELLO, FRIENDS! IT'S ME, JAKE THE PANCAKE.
WE GOT A GREAT SHOW FOR YA TODAY!
OH JAKE.
YOU'RE SO FUNNY.
JAKE THE PANCAKE?!
I WASN'T WATCHIN' IT!
OH YES YOU WERE!
HAHHHHH! AH-HA-HA-HA
...OH JAKE, YOU'RE SO FUNNY!
SAY G'BYE TO YOUR REP!
I CAN'T WAIT TO GO TELL EVERYONE! SEE YA LATER CHUMP!
SNARL
GRUFF
BUT I WAS JUST...
GULP!
...STUPID FRICKIN' JAKE!
* CLICK CLICK

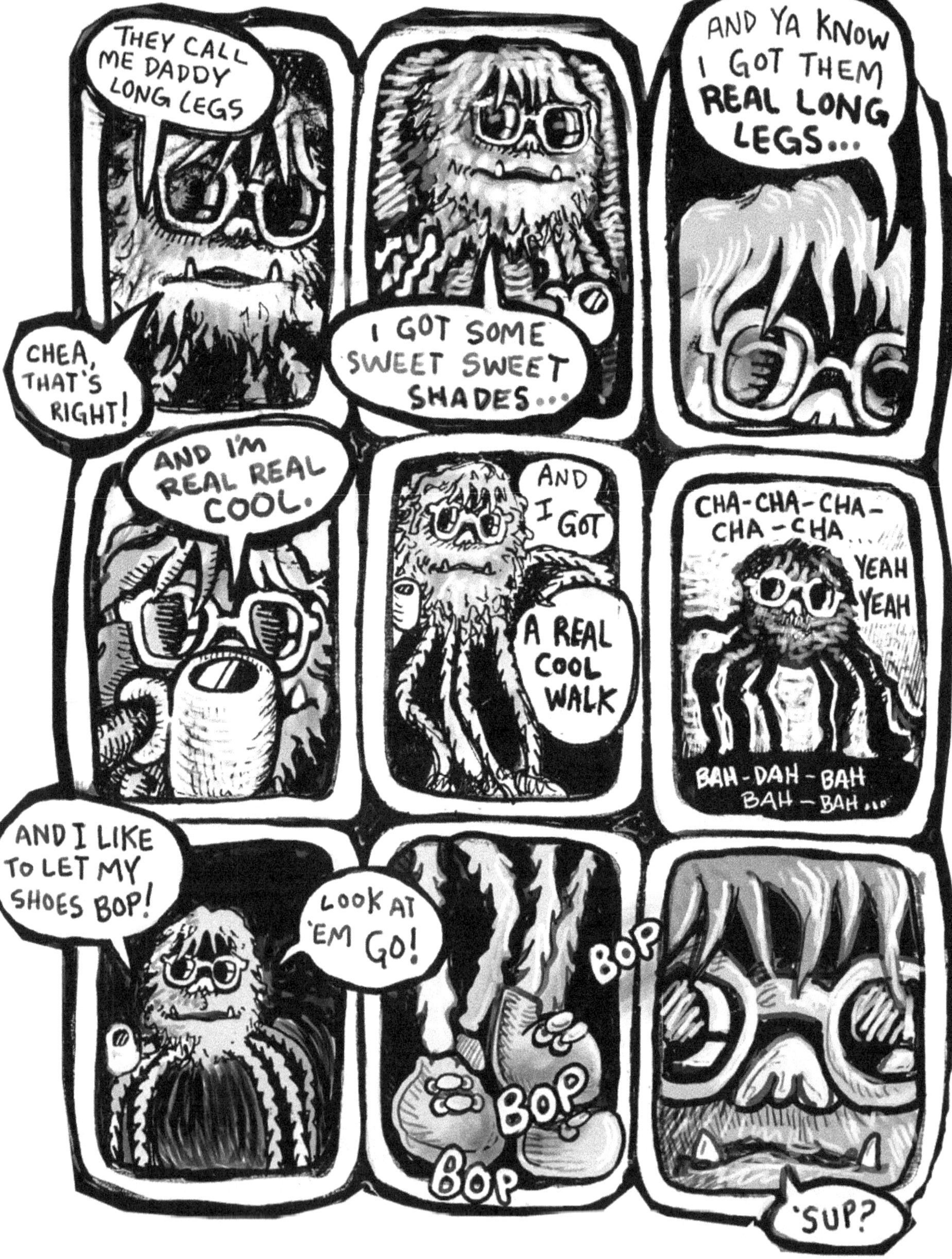
THEY CALL ME DADDY LONG LEGS
CHEA, THAT'S RIGHT!
I GOT SOME SWEET SWEET SHADES...
AND YA KNOW I GOT THEM REAL LONG LEGS...
AND I'M REAL REAL COOL.
AND I GOT
A REAL COOL WALK
CHA-CHA-CHA-CHA-CHA...
YEAH YEAH
BAH-DAH-BAH BAH-BAH...
AND I LIKE TO LET MY SHOES BOP!
LOOK AT 'EM GO!
BOP
BOP
BOP
'SUP?

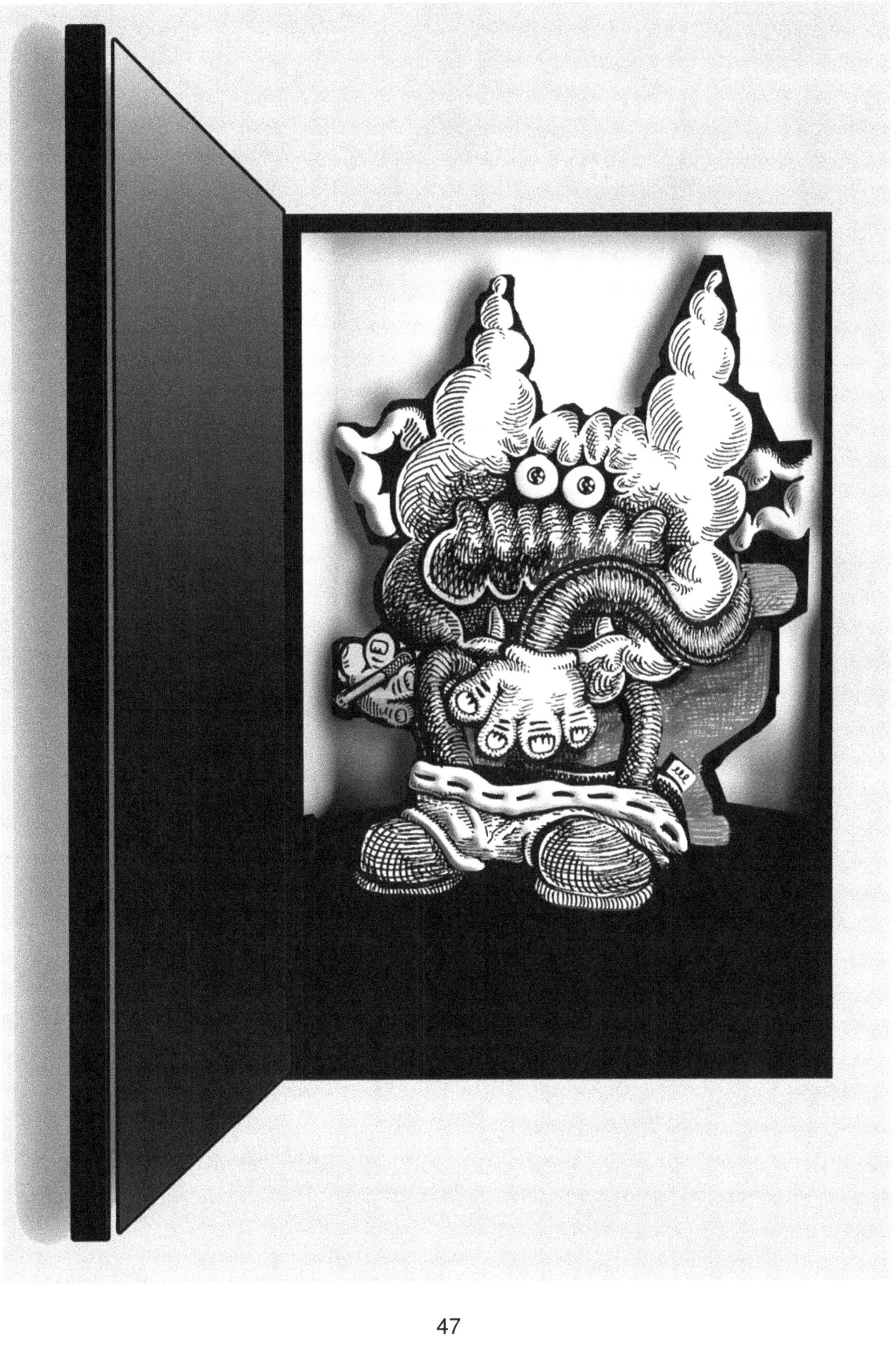

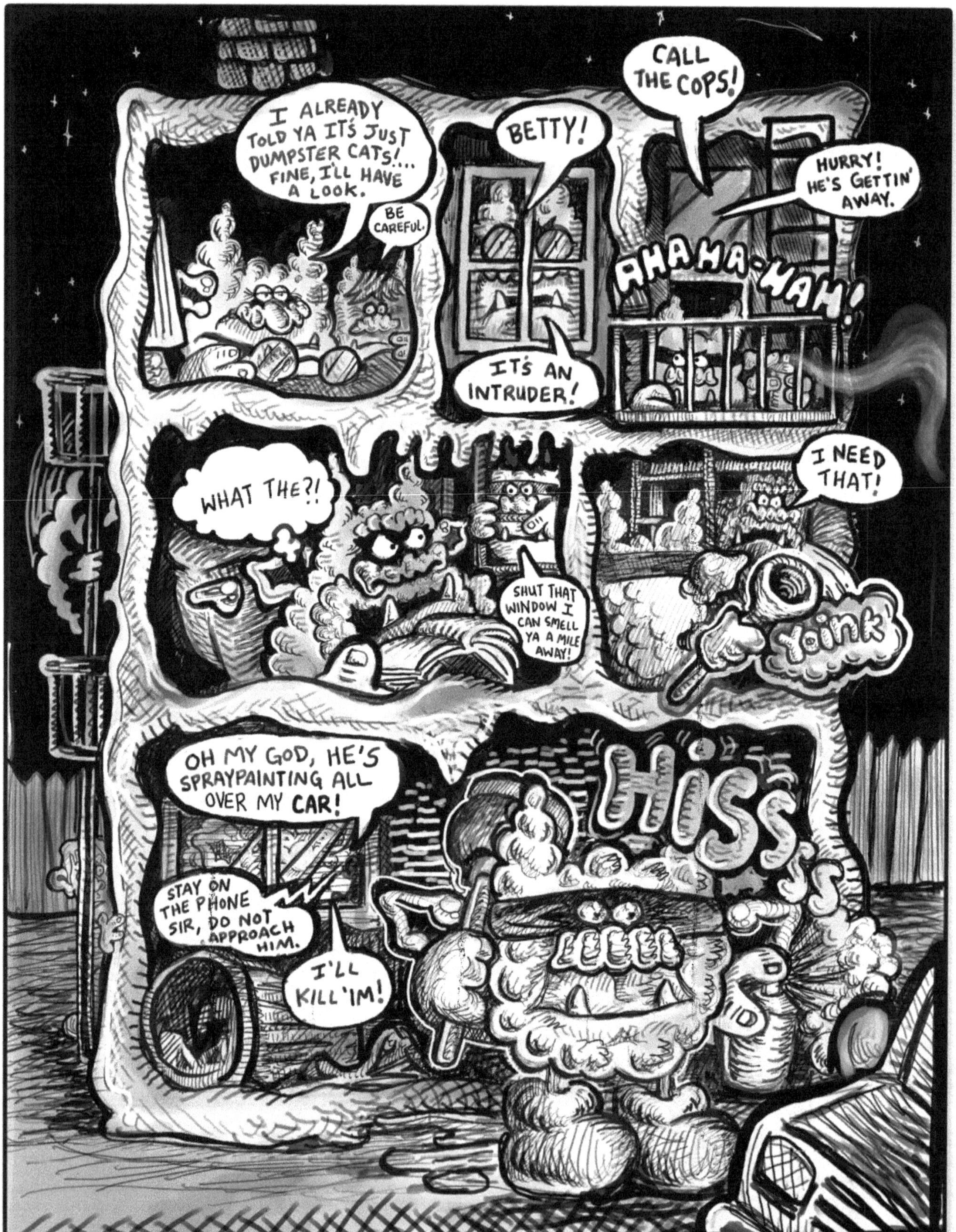
I ALREADY TOLD YA IT'S JUST DUMPSTER CATS!... FINE, I'LL HAVE A LOOK.
BE CAREFUL.
BETTY!
IT'S AN INTRUDER!
CALL THE COPS!
HURRY! HE'S GETTIN' AWAY.
AHAHA-HAH!
WHAT THE?!
SHUT THAT WINDOW I CAN SMELL YA A MILE AWAY!
I NEED THAT!
YOINK
OH MY GOD, HE'S SPRAYPAINTING ALL OVER MY CAR!
STAY ON THE PHONE SIR, DO NOT APPROACH HIM.
I'LL KILL 'IM!
HISS

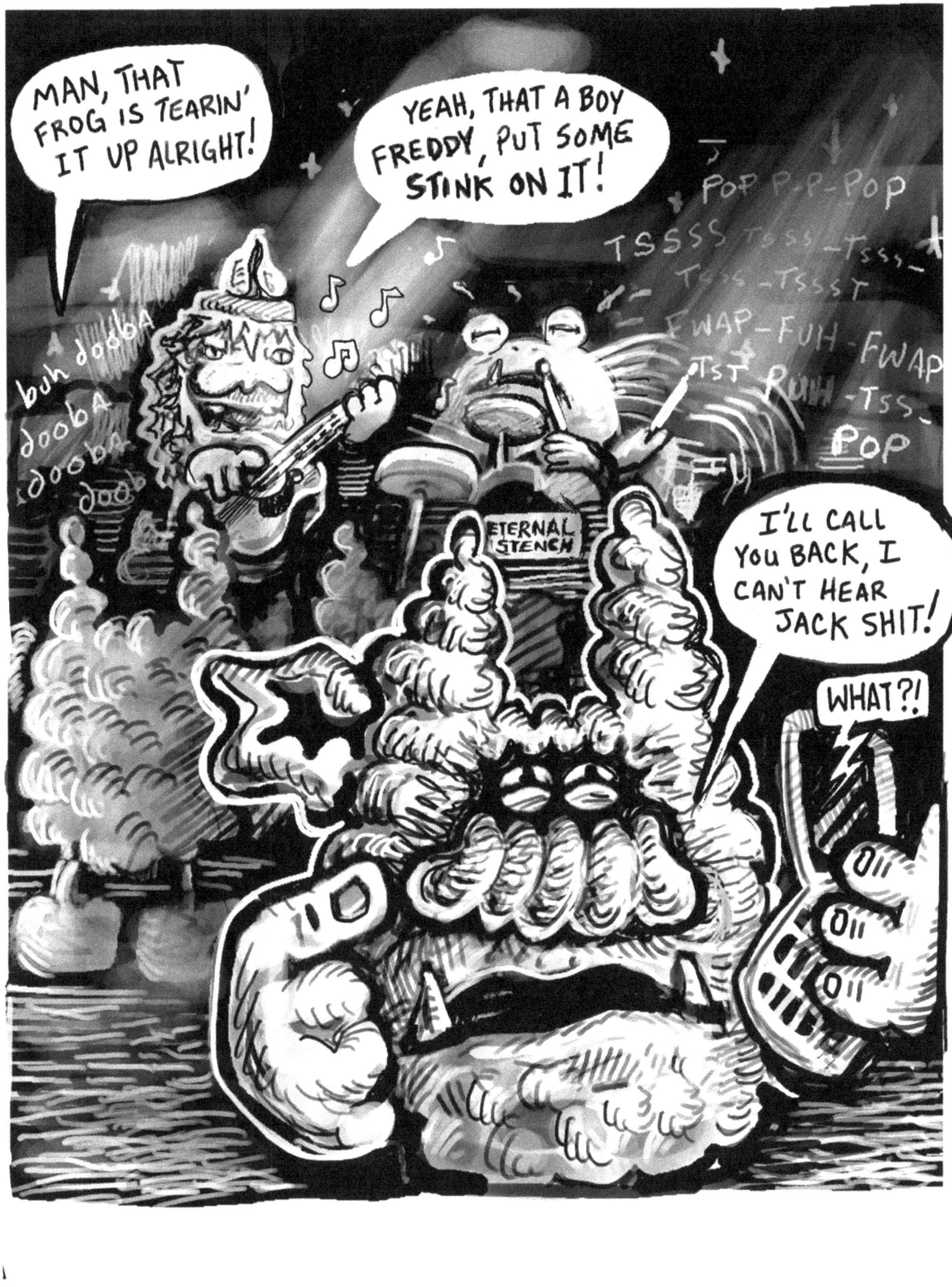
MAN, THAT FROG IS TEARIN' IT UP ALRIGHT!
YEAH, THAT A BOY FREDDY, PUT SOME STINK ON IT!
POP P-P-POP
TSSSS-TSSS-TSSS-
TSSS-TSSST
FWAP-FUH-FWAP
TST
-TSS-
POP
buh dooba
dooba
dooba
doob
ETERNAL STENCH
I'LL CALL YOU BACK, I CAN'T HEAR JACK SHIT!
WHAT?!

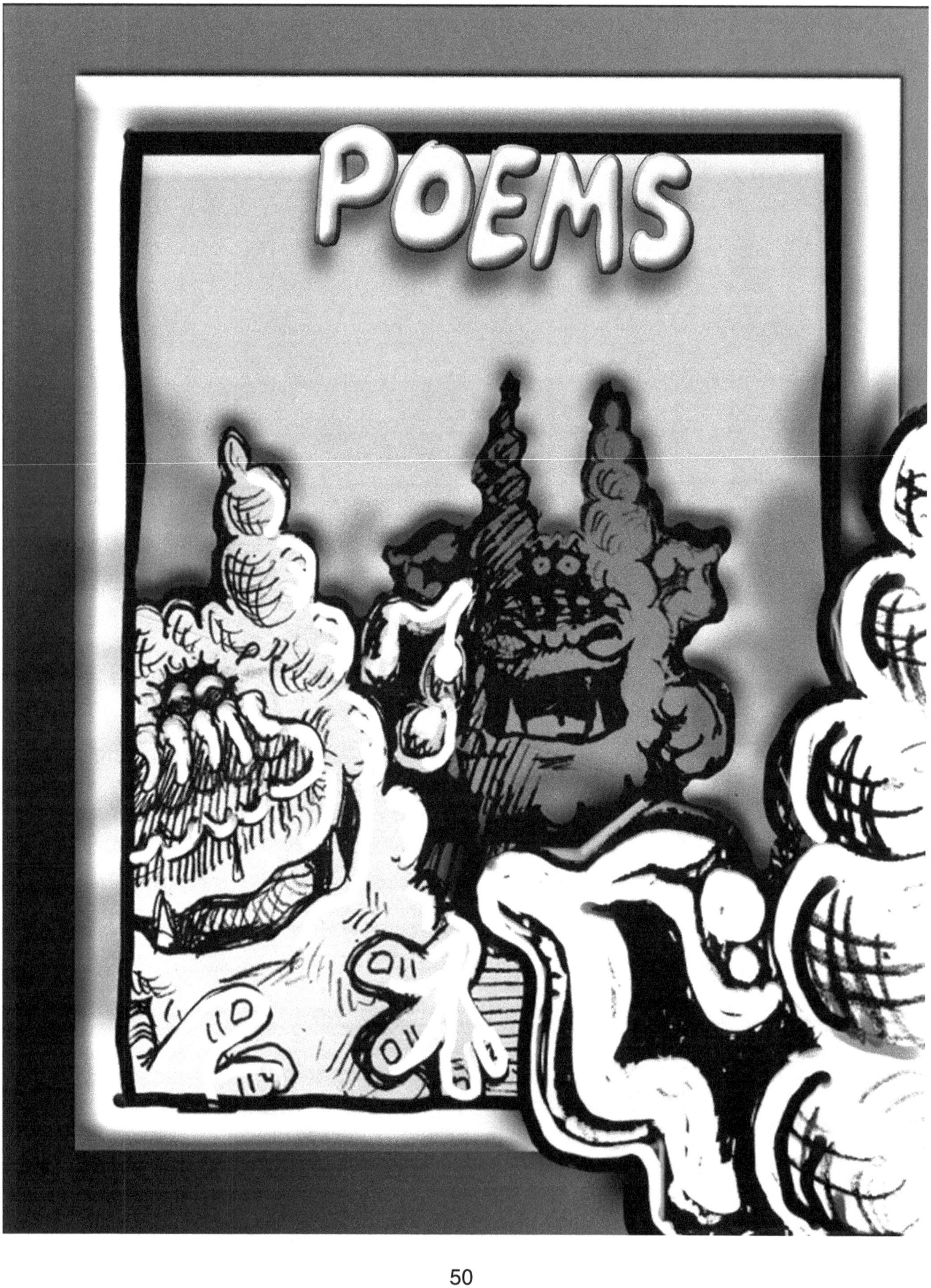
POEMS

To whom it may concern,

Whomsoever this Mr. Welcome is,

Consider this a paper jam. Consider this…a test.
Consider this: i'm fresh. Now, bring it in.
You know what time it is.
Look bud, oun't care who owns this place M'Kay?
Oun't give a rip.
'Way I see it, I'm doing YOU a favor keeping this thing brief!
Which brings me to my main point:
I want that goddamn job, and I want it right-the-fuck NOW!
(Seriously though, man to man, i'm not kidding.)

 ((if not a "man" please add a "wo" to the front of the second "man"
back there for me, I'm getting sick of writing this stupid cover letter
and I don't have time to go back over something silly like that, y'know?
'Mean I'm a busy man… got more important things to do.))

Look, just call me when you get this so we can start talking salary,
pension, 401k, company cars, shit like that, and also,
be sure to visit the P.S. section below for accommodations/requirements
for my upcoming "interview." Just so you're aware, I don't take kindly
to prolonged waiting and I will be timing you, so I suggest you get a
 move on.

Sincerely,

Wild Bernie

MR. Wild Bernie
(emphasis on the Mister)
P.S.

MR. is of course not my first name, but it IS however, what you should
address me as during and after my upcoming "interview."
Please be sure to do so at all times.

P.S.S.

Be sure to eliminate any unpleasant smells and sounds from the air
(ex: old people smells, mouth breathers, shit like that.).

Should I feel the need to relieve myself, I will also require that your
facilities be at all times be sparkling clean and unoccupied
(For several hours prior to, as well as throughout the entire duration of my stay.)

Last but not least, upon my arrival please be sure to have a very comfortable
chair waiting for me with wheels on it, should I get bored or feel the need to
slide around on the floors/ in hallways at my leisure. I'll be able to give you a
more detailed list of accommodations which will be required, once I pick out
which office I want.

PISS, YES PISS.
I'M PISSED, *YEAH* PISSED.
SO PISSED, SO...*PISSED*,
SCREW THIS, I'M PISSED*!*
AND IF I HAD A NICKEL
FOR EVERY TIME
I GOT PISSED OFF...
I'D BE RICH,
AND I'M NOT,
...SO I'M PISSED.

F-book connected to the, Overload.

Overload connected to the,Mainstream.

Mainstream connected to the, Brainwash.

Brainwash connected to the, Monopolies

Monopolies connected to the, Fraudulence.

Fraudulence connected to the, Secrecy.

Oh those skeleton bones.

Oh mercy how they scare!

"Tough, but Fair"

'S'ain't no time for chit-chat.
'Sain't no frickin' sewing circle.
'Sain't no god-damn Breakfast Club.
'Sain't no day-time-t-v-talk-show,

This is the coffee line.
So stop clogging it up.

Sides,
Nobody wants to hear that sh-
There-there, now.
shhhhhhh.
there-there.

tough, but fair.
Tough…but Fair.

You're goddamn right I'm pissed!
And, I'll bet you're pissed too.
A'Mean, Ay, why shouldn't you be?
Damnit, It's no wonder we're pissed,
what with all that voluptous brainwash and all!

Wake up and smell the coffee!
Oh, here's some now...

Go on, have a sip....that's it, mmm.

little more, little more…
Good…
Mmmmm numb numb numb,
MMMMM NUMB-NUMB-NUMB-NUMMMM
NUMMY-NUM-NUM-NUM!

Guess what? They pissed in that too.

YOUNG COFFEE MAN

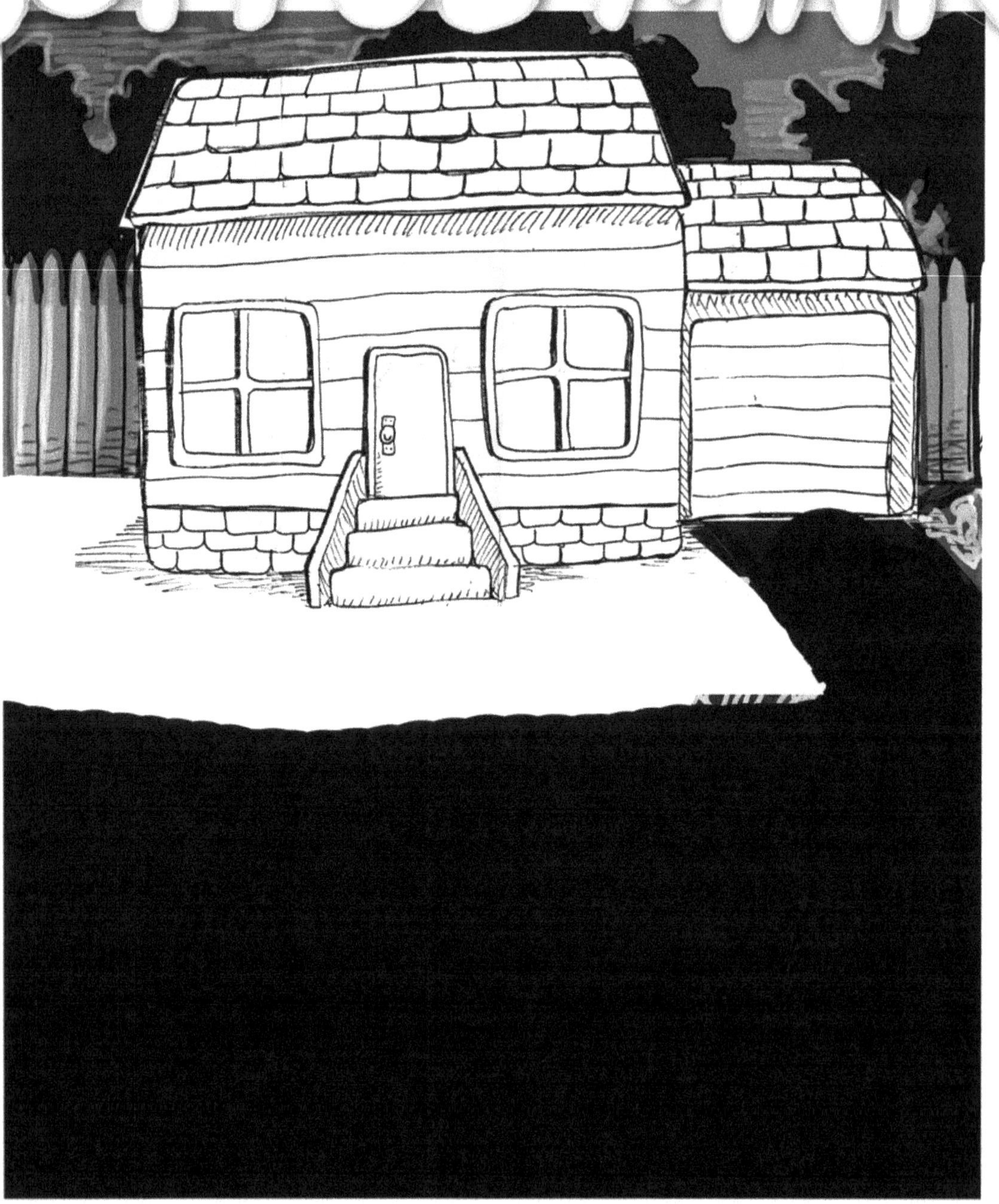

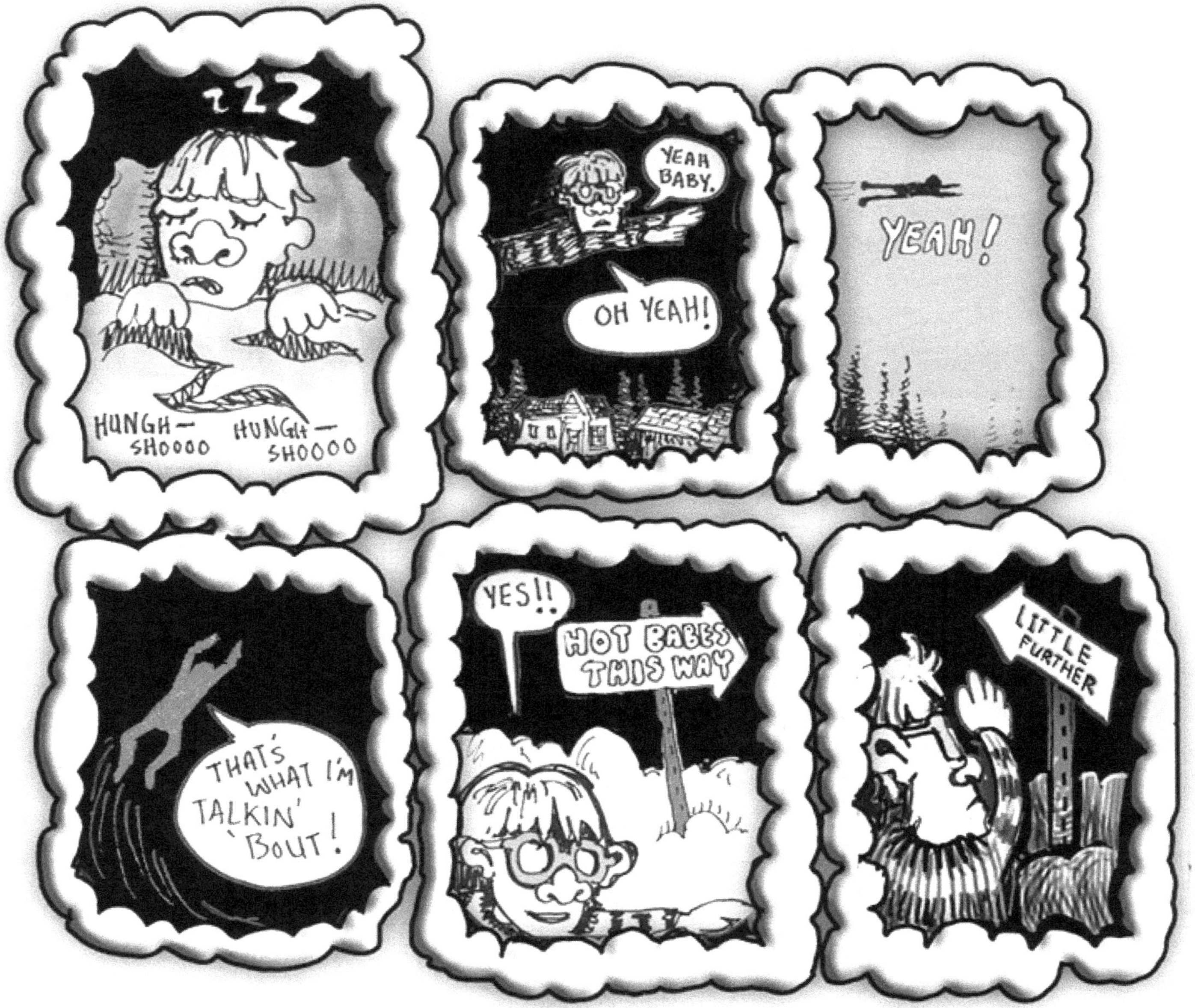
zZZ
HUNGH—SHOOOO HUNGH—SHOOOO
YEAH BABY.
OH YEAH!
YEAH!
THAT'S WHAT I'M TALKIN' 'BOUT!
YES!!
HOT BABES THIS WAY
LITTLE FURTHER

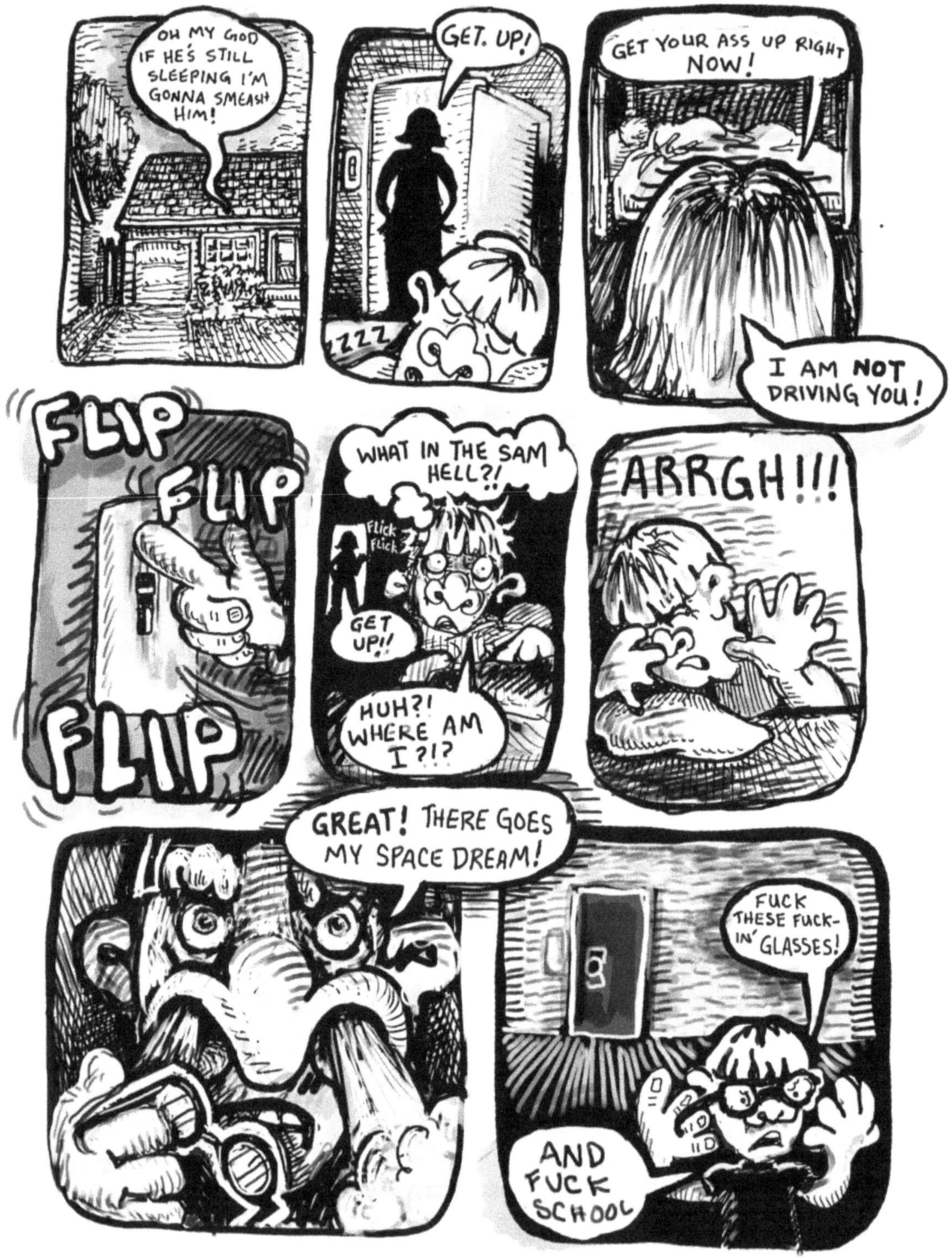
OH MY GOD IF HE'S STILL SLEEPING I'M GONNA SMEASH HIM!
GET. UP!
ZZZZ
GET YOUR ASS UP RIGHT NOW!
I AM NOT DRIVING YOU!
FLIP
FLIP
FLIP
WHAT IN THE SAM HELL?!
Flick Flick
GET UP!!
HUH?! WHERE AM I?!?
ARRGH!!!
GREAT! THERE GOES MY SPACE DREAM!
FUCK THESE FUCK-IN' GLASSES!
AND FUCK SCHOOL

CRUNCH
CRUNCH
CRUNCH
CRUNCH

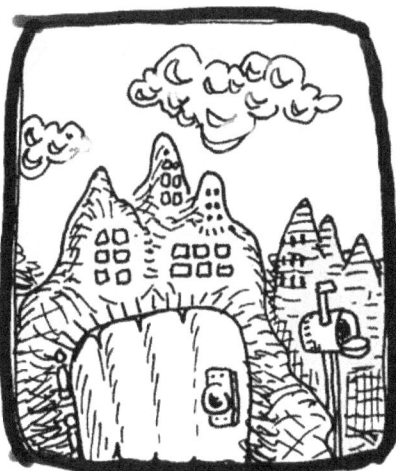

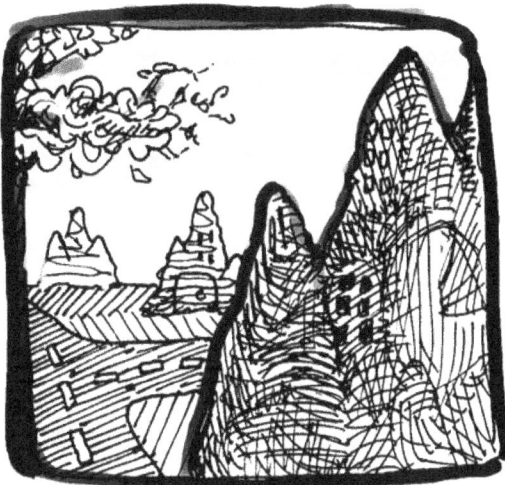

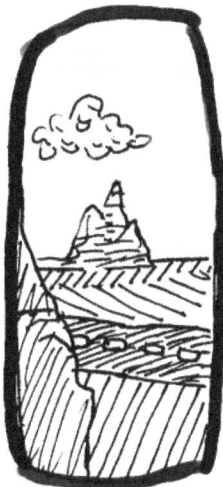

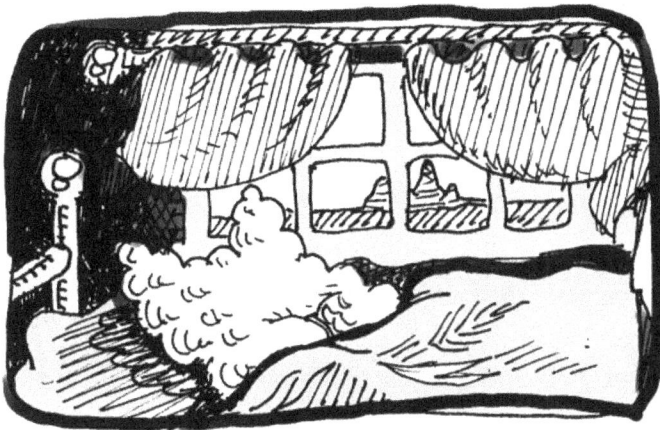

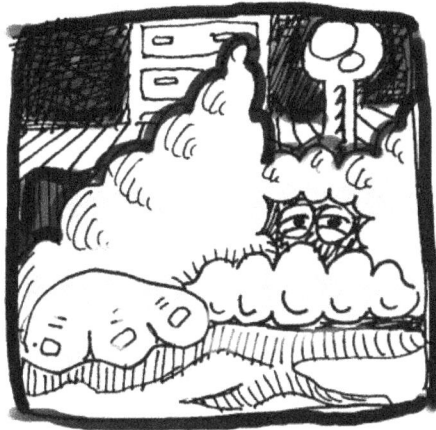

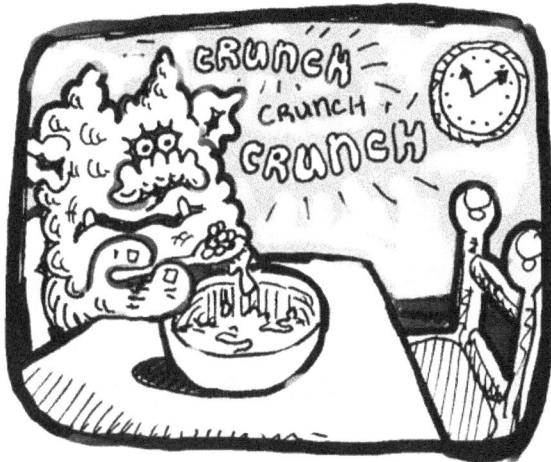

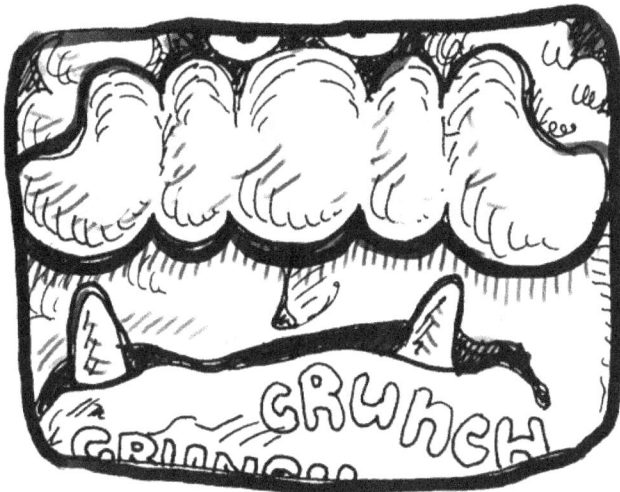

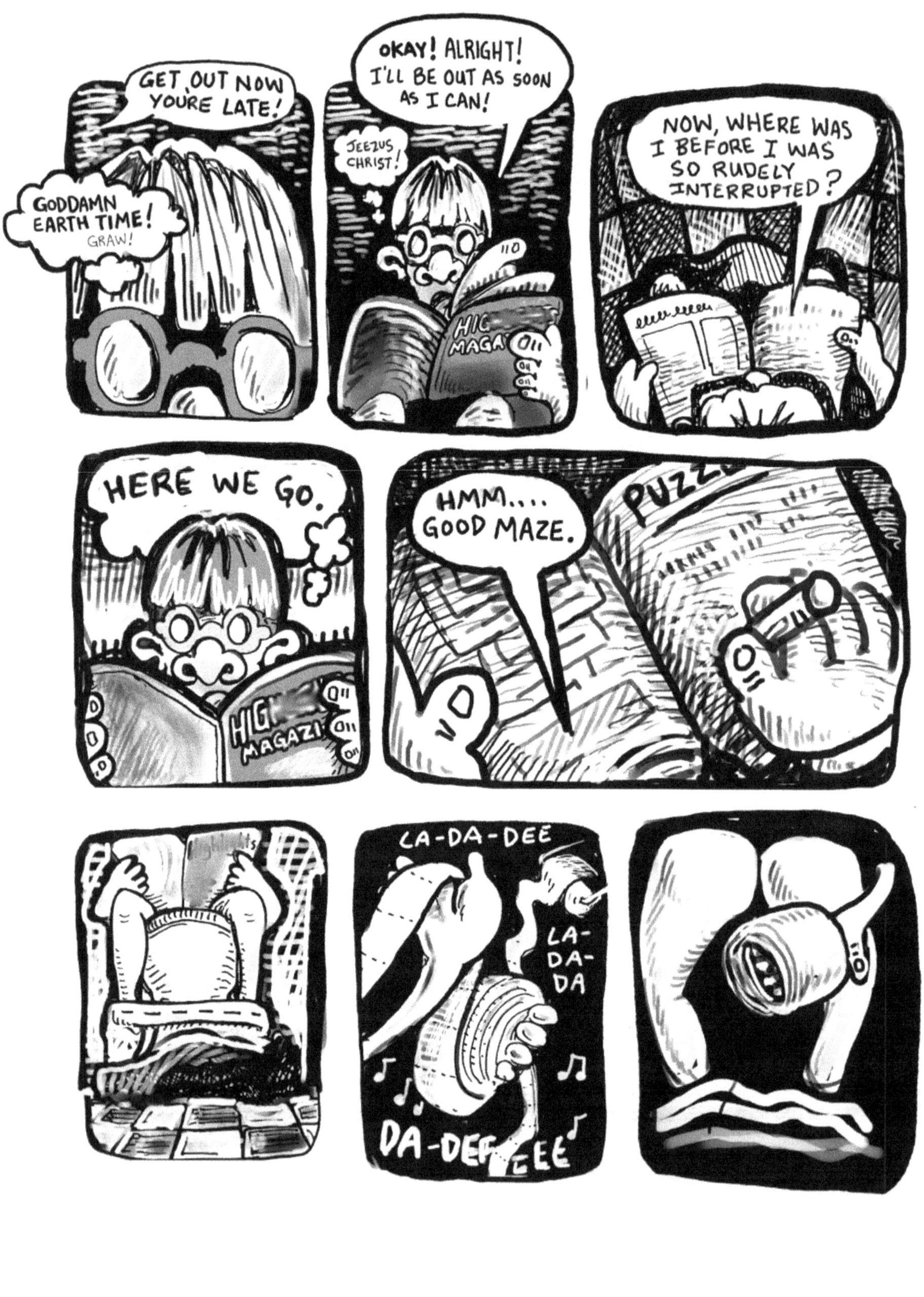
GET OUT NOW YOU'RE LATE!
GODDAMN EARTH TIME!
GRAW!
OKAY! ALRIGHT! I'LL BE OUT AS SOON AS I CAN!
JEEZUS CHRIST!
NOW, WHERE WAS I BEFORE I WAS SO RUDELY INTERRUPTED?
HERE WE GO.
HMM.... GOOD MAZE.
LA-DA-DEE
LA-DA-DA
DA-DEE-EEE

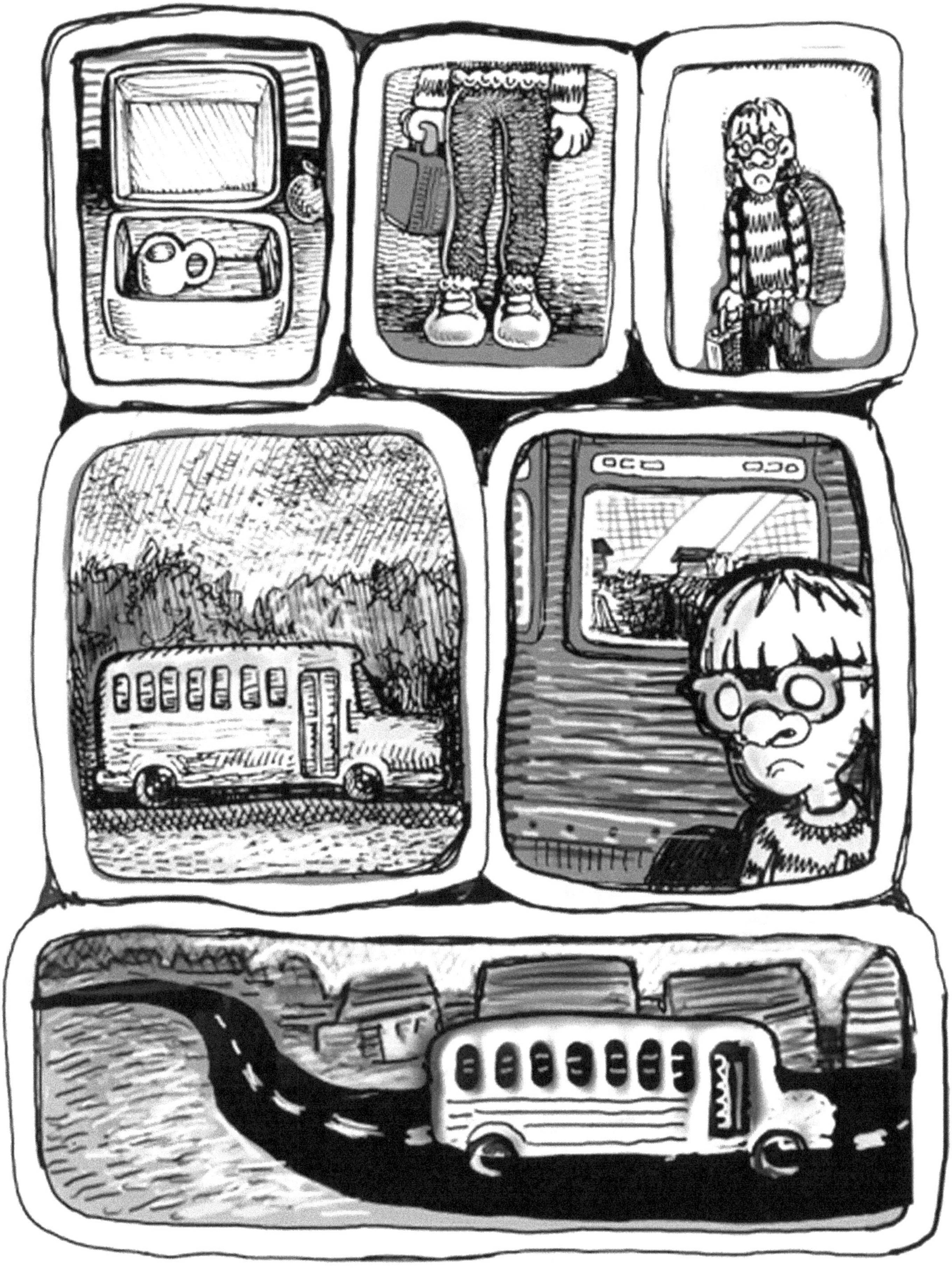

SCANNIES

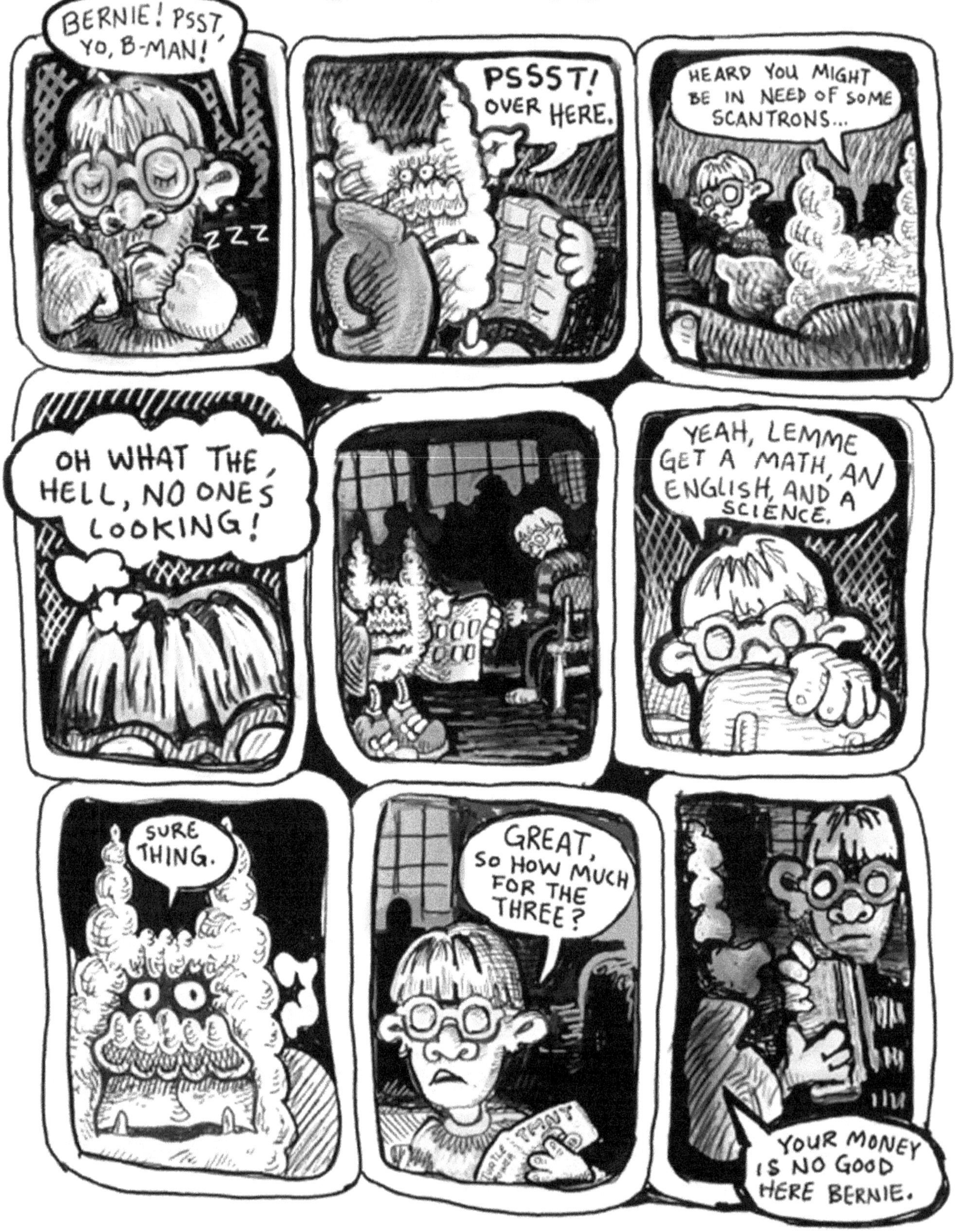
BERNIE! PSST, YO, B-MAN!
ZZZ
PSSST! OVER HERE.
HEARD YOU MIGHT BE IN NEED OF SOME SCANTRONS...
OH WHAT THE HELL, NO ONE'S LOOKING!
YEAH, LEMME GET A MATH, AN ENGLISH, AND A SCIENCE.
SURE THING.
GREAT, SO HOW MUCH FOR THE THREE?
YOUR MONEY IS NO GOOD HERE BERNIE.

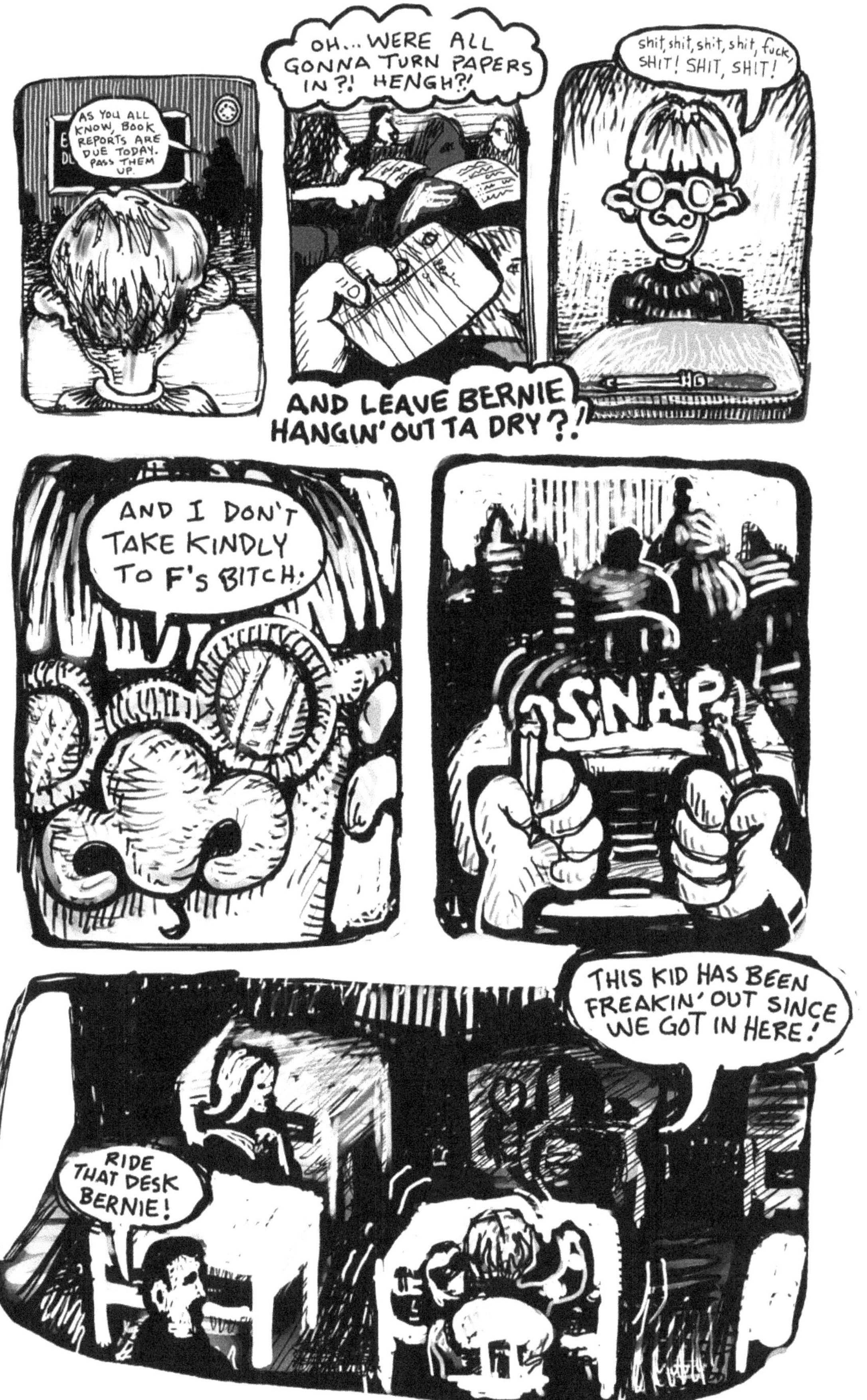

AS YOU ALL KNOW, BOOK REPORTS ARE DUE TODAY. PASS THEM UP.
OH... WERE ALL GONNA TURN PAPERS IN?! HENGH?!
shit, shit, shit, shit, fuck, SHIT! SHIT, SHIT!
AND LEAVE BERNIE HANGIN' OUTTA DRY?!
AND I DON'T TAKE KINDLY TO F's BITCH.
SNAP
THIS KID HAS BEEN FREAKIN' OUT SINCE WE GOT IN HERE!
RIDE THAT DESK BERNIE!

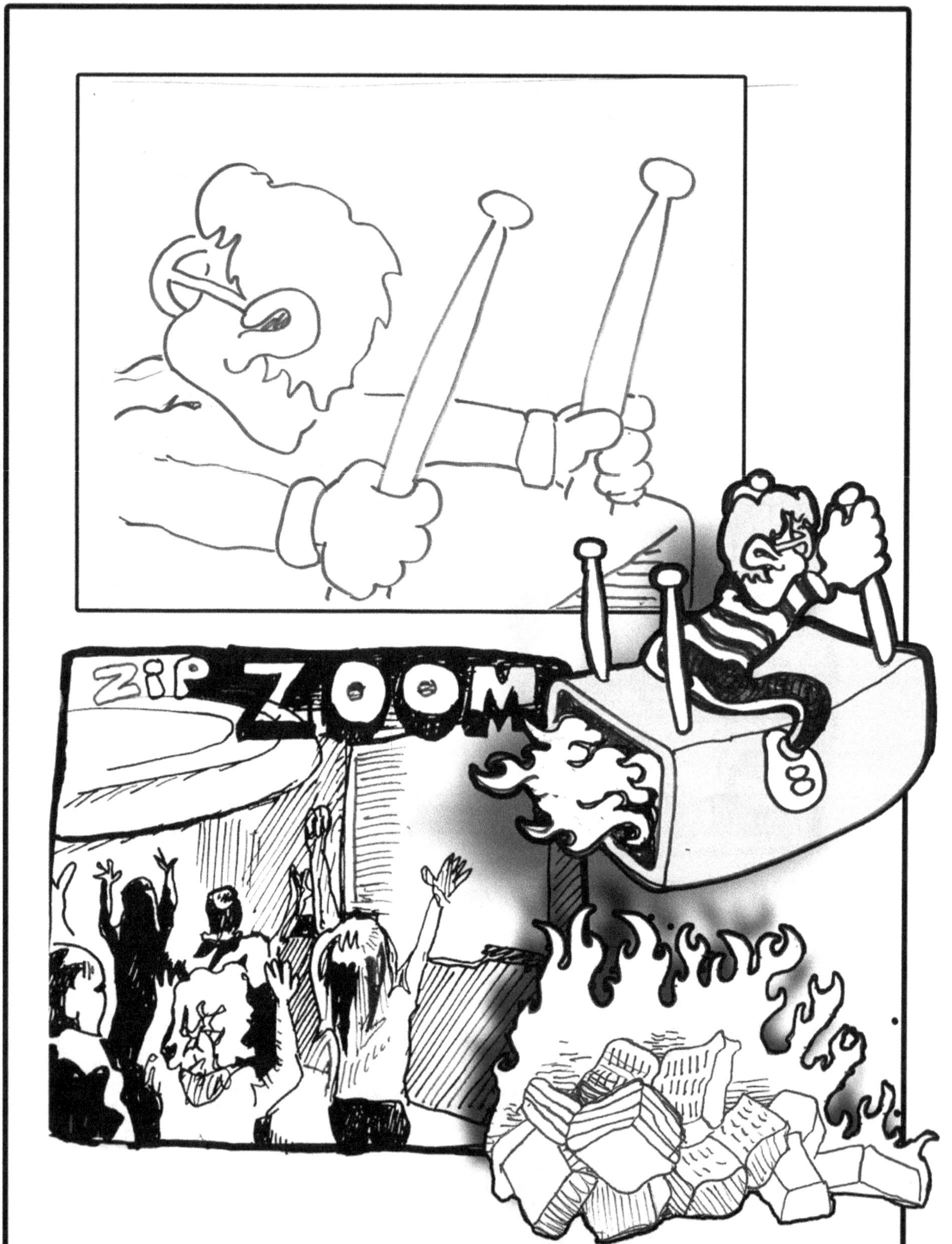
ZIP ZOOM
8

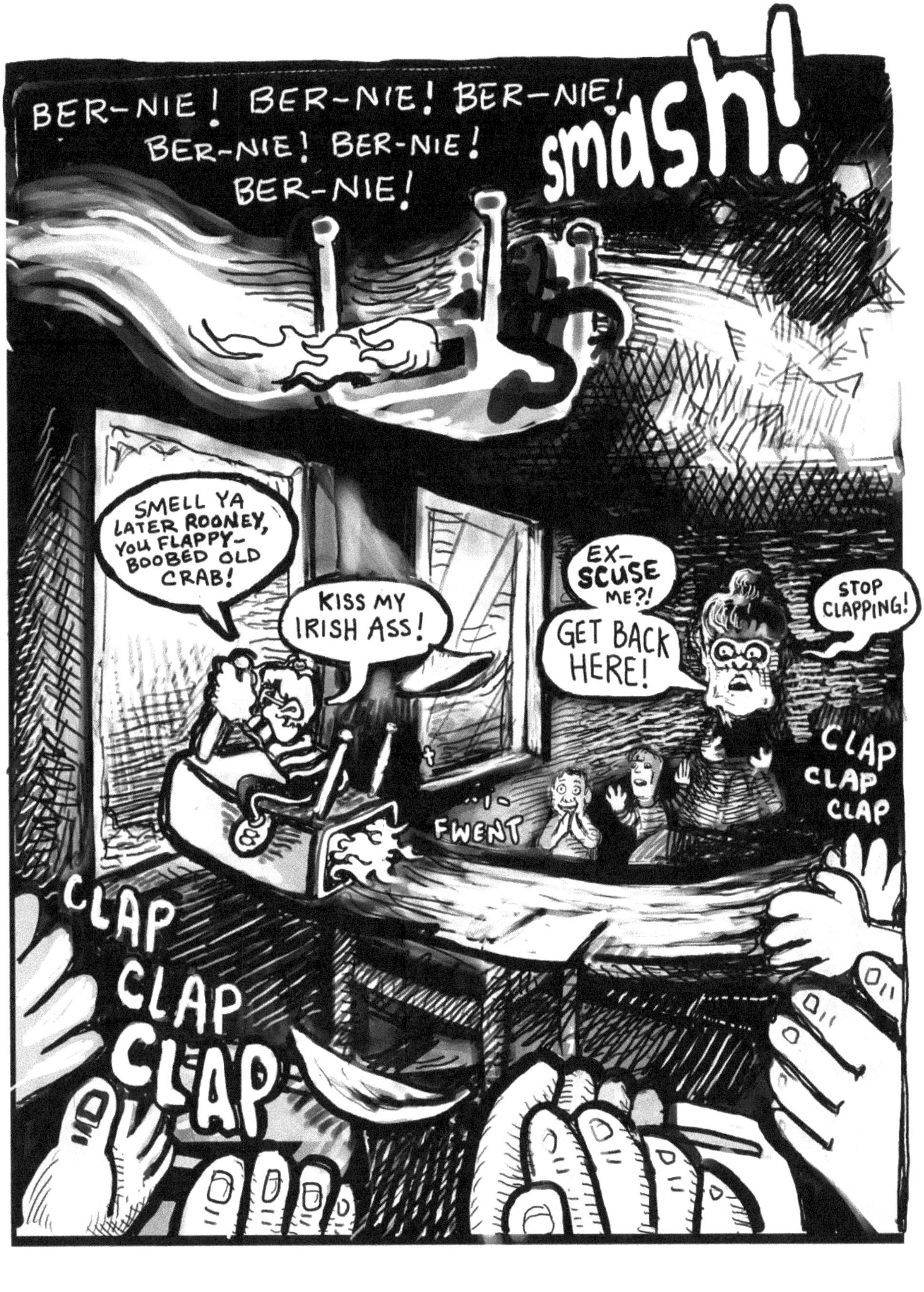
BER-NIE! BER-NIE! BER-NIE!
BER-NIE! BER-NIE!
BER-NIE!
smash!
SMELL YA LATER ROONEY, YOU FLAPPY-BOOBED OLD CRAB!
KISS MY IRISH ASS!
FWENT
EX-SCUSE ME?!
GET BACK HERE!
STOP CLAPPING!
CLAP CLAP CLAP
CLAP CLAP CLAP

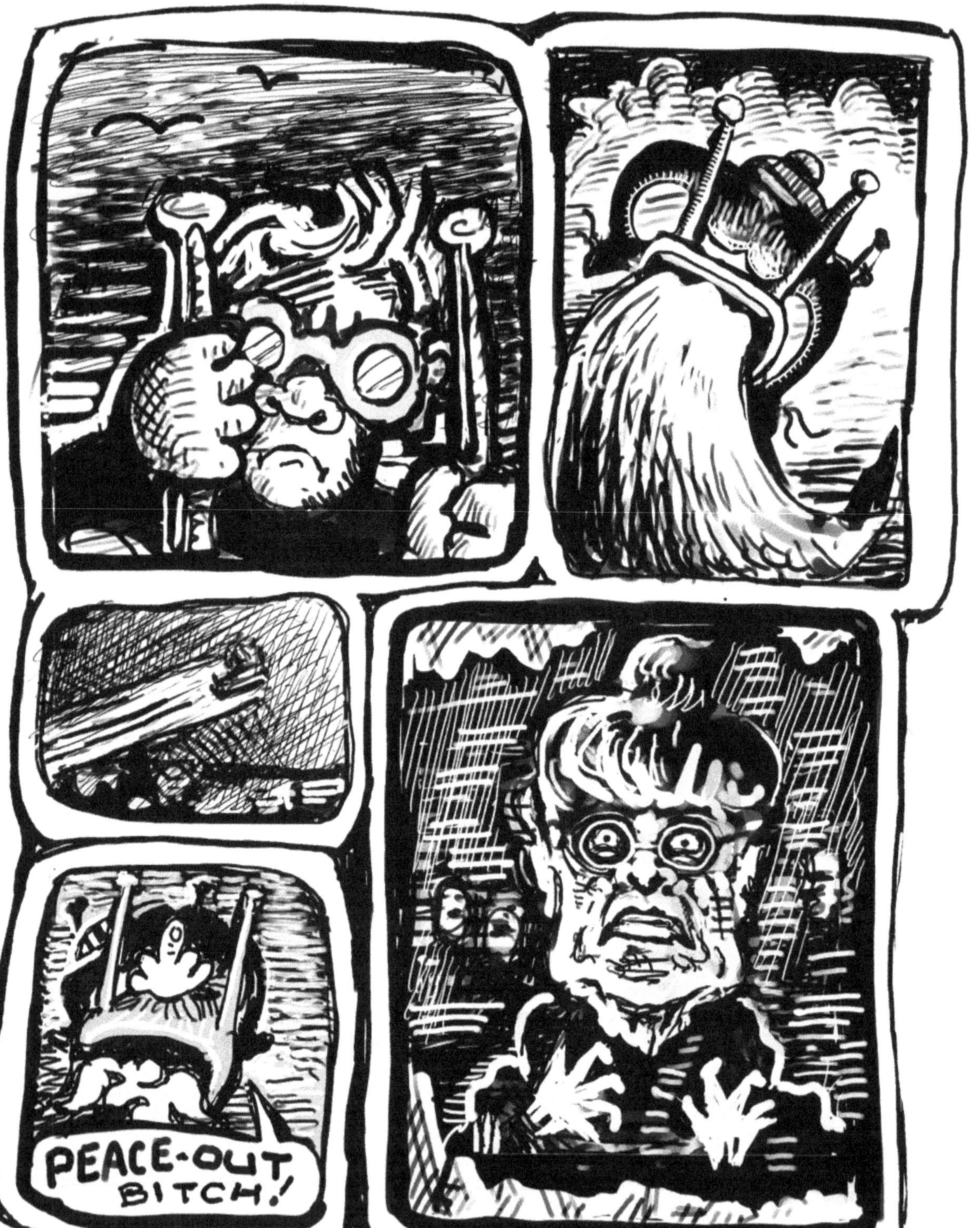
PEACE-OUT, BITCH!

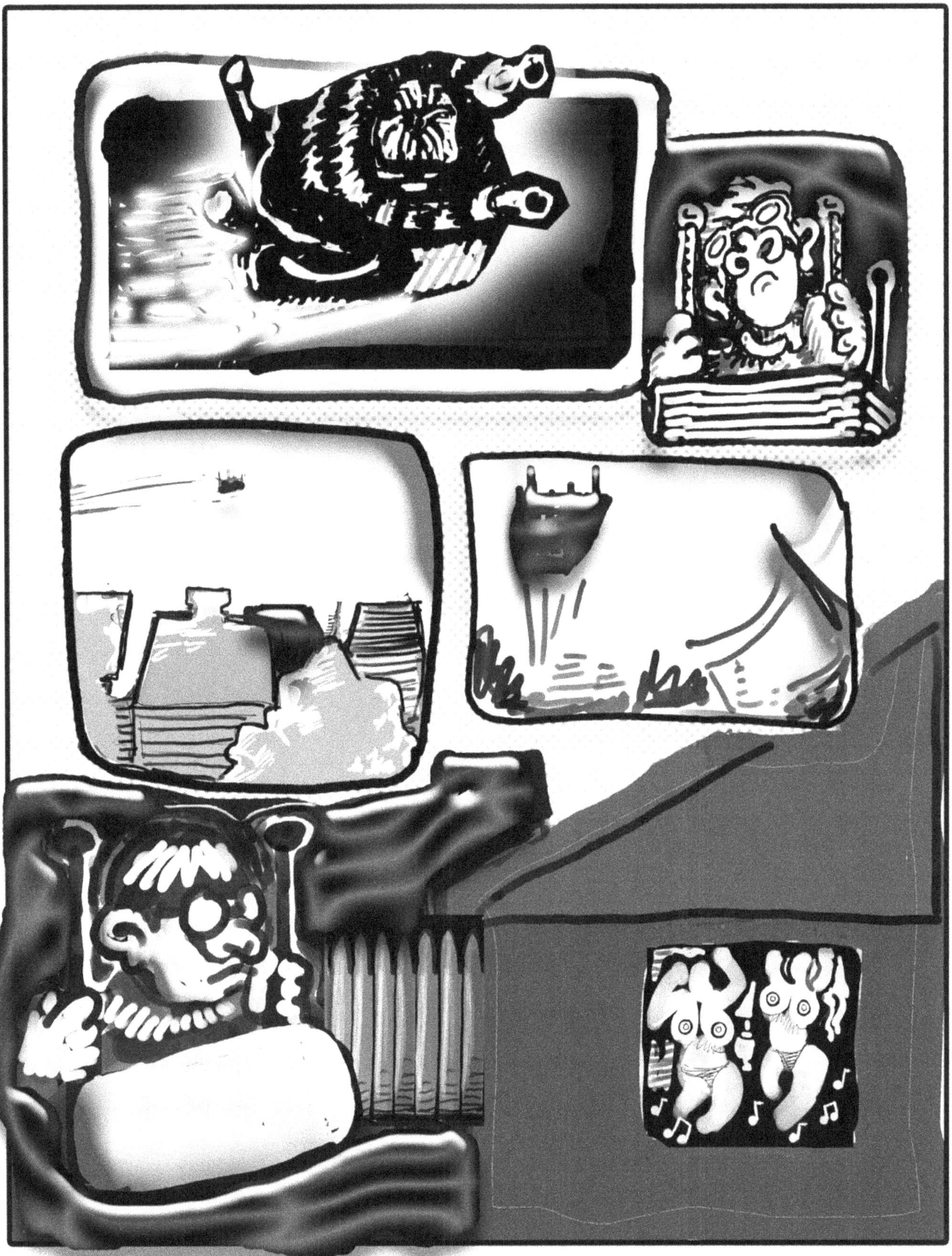

THE BOOK THIEF

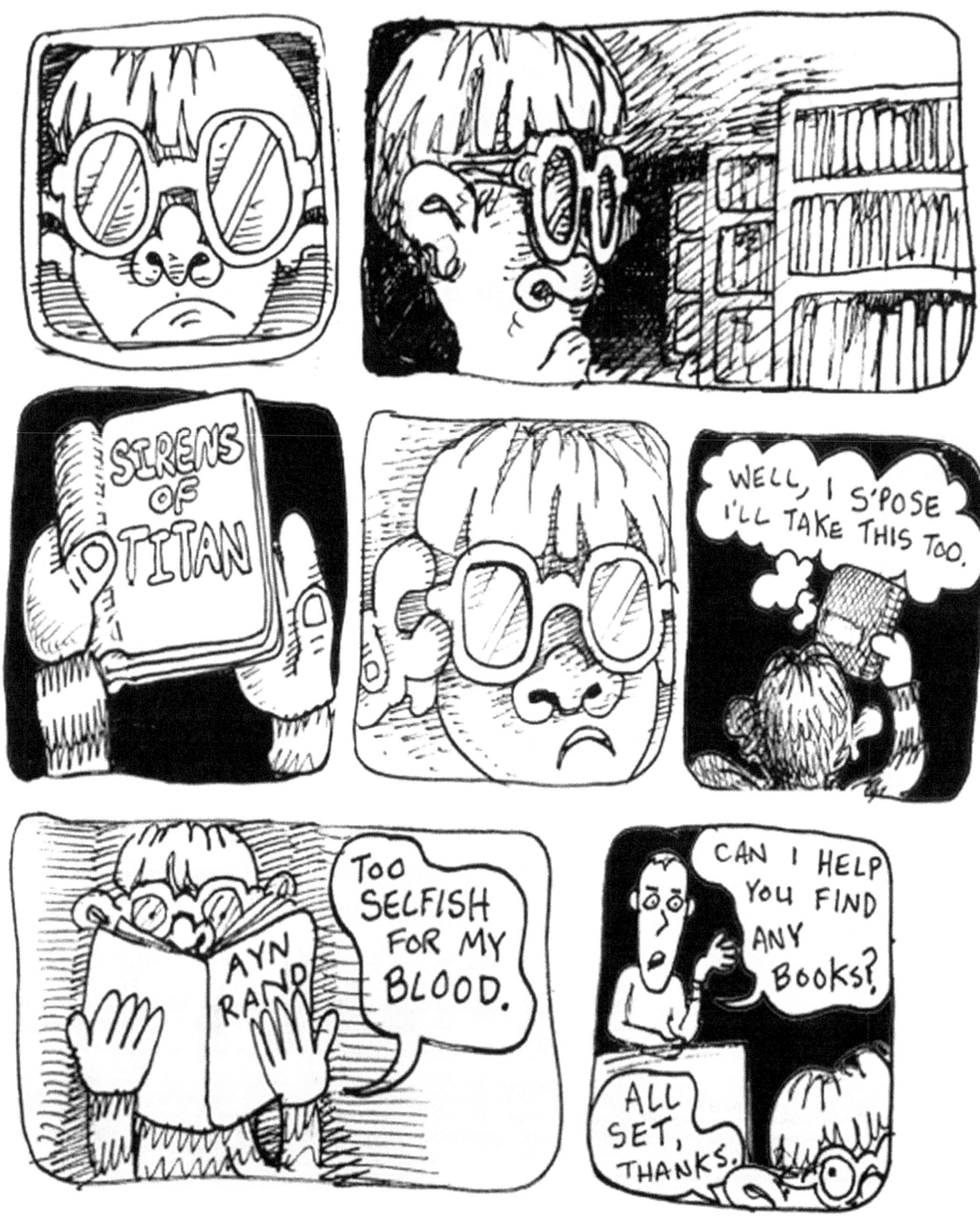
SIRENS OF TITAN
WELL, I S'POSE I'LL TAKE THIS TOO.
AYN RAND
TOO SELFISH FOR MY BLOOD.
CAN I HELP YOU FIND ANY BOOKS?
ALL SET, THANKS.

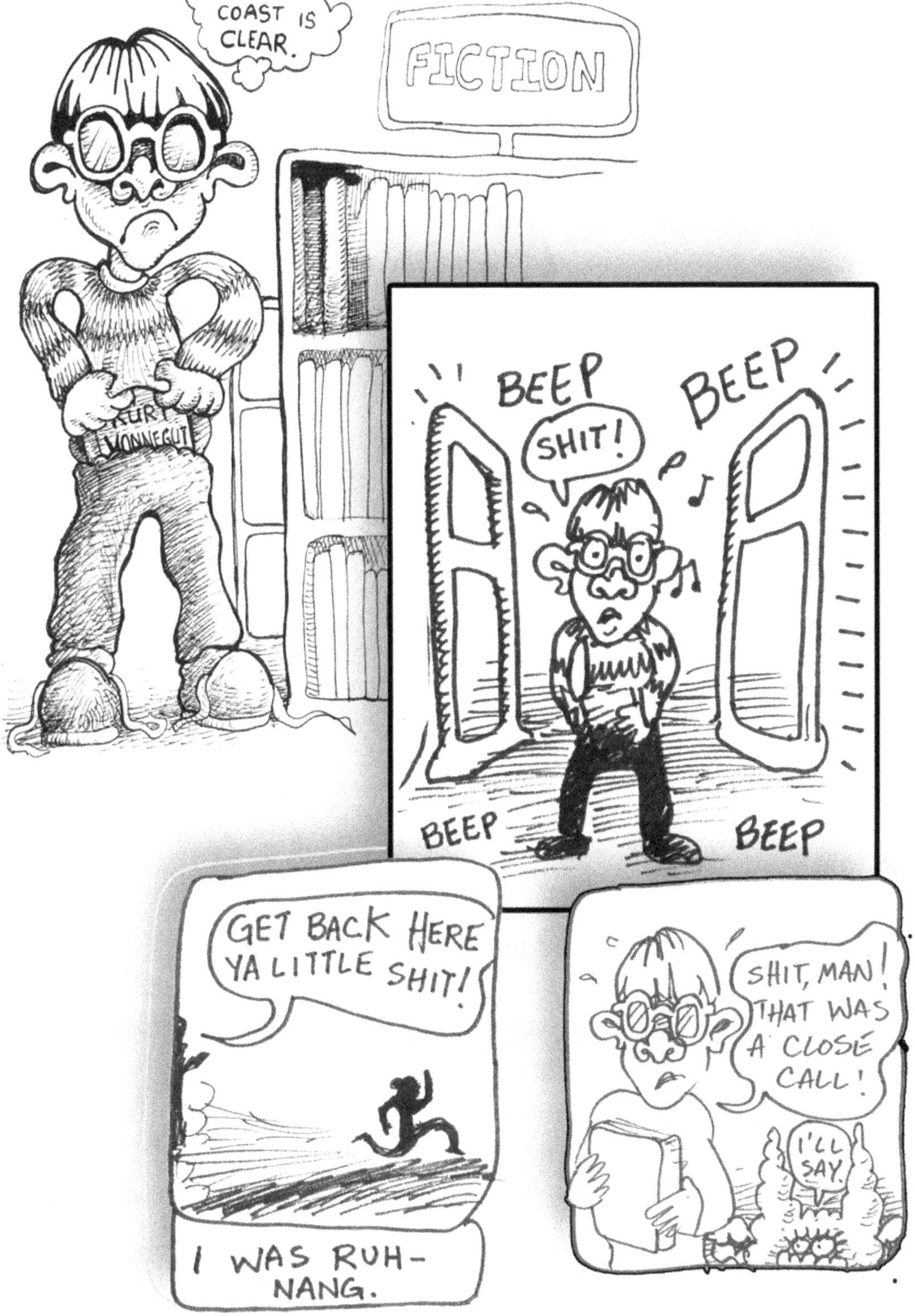
COAST IS CLEAR.
FICTION
KURT VONNEGUT
BEEP
BEEP
SHIT!
BEEP
BEEP
GET BACK HERE YA LITTLE SHIT!
I WAS RUH-NANG.
SHIT, MAN! THAT WAS A CLOSE CALL!
I'LL SAY.

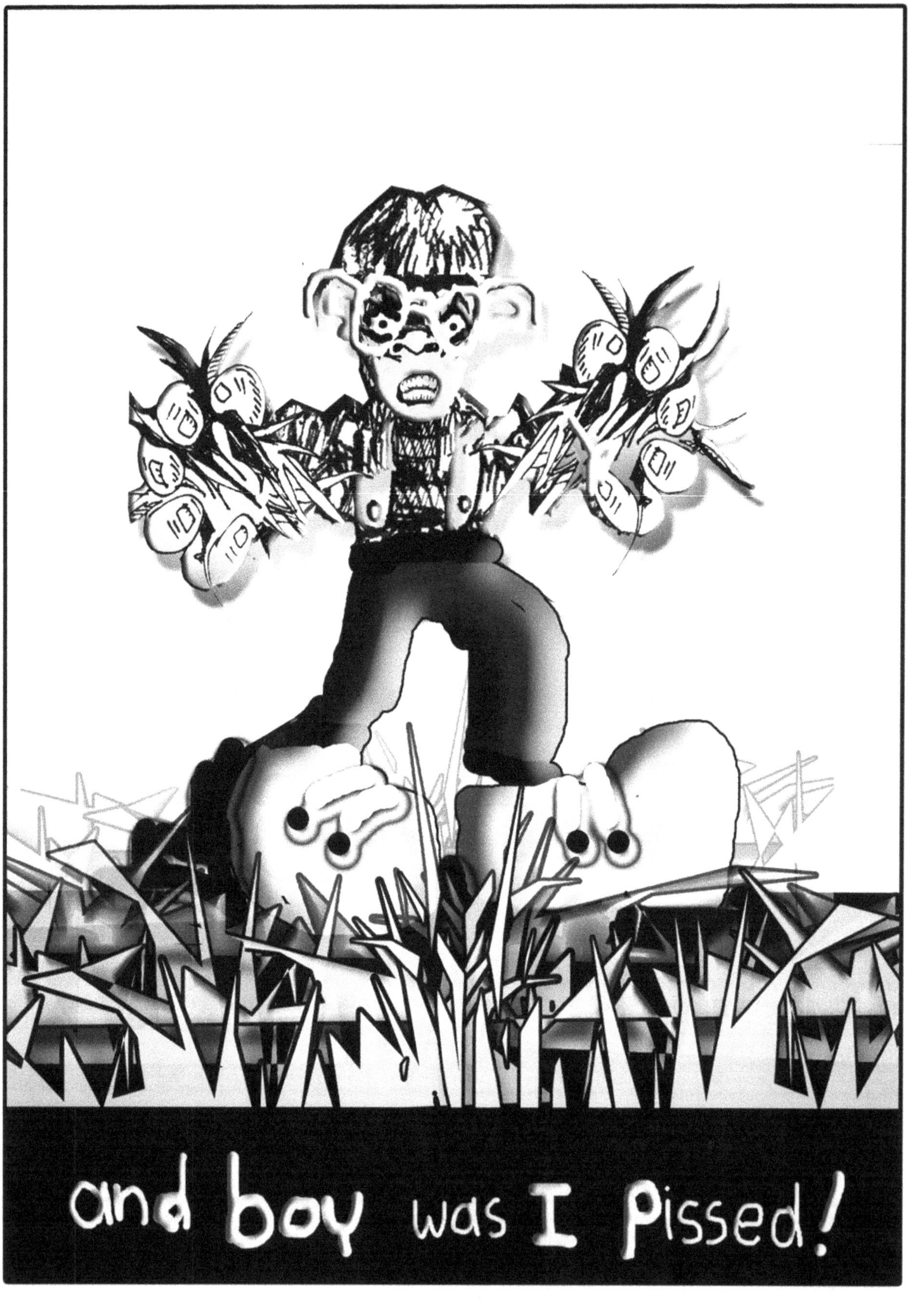
and boy was I pissed!

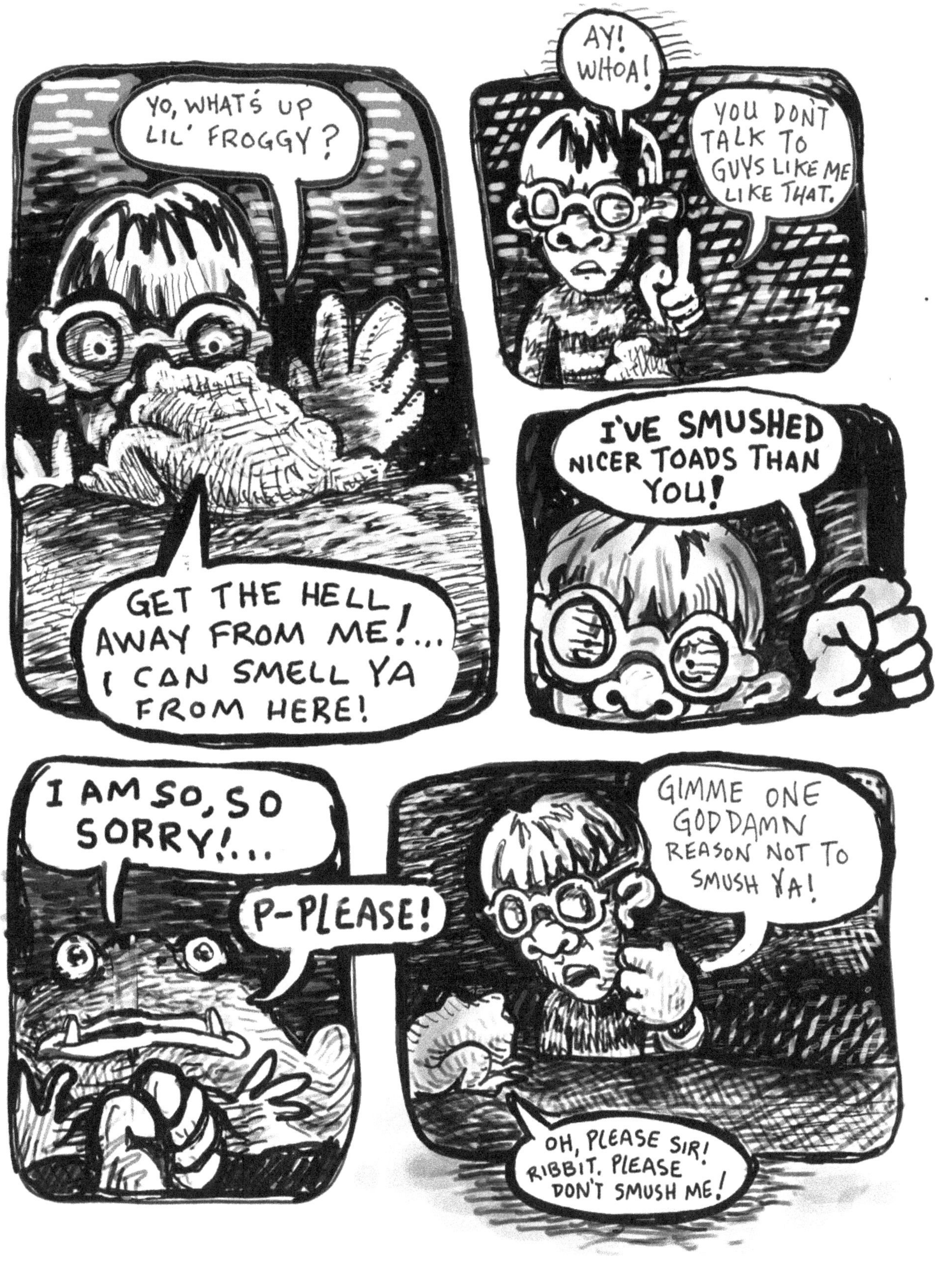

YO, WHAT'S UP LIL' FROGGY?
GET THE HELL AWAY FROM ME!... I CAN SMELL YA FROM HERE!
AY! WHOA!
YOU DON'T TALK TO GUYS LIKE ME LIKE THAT.
I'VE SMUSHED NICER TOADS THAN YOU!
I AM SO, SO SORRY!...
P-PLEASE!
GIMME ONE GODDAMN REASON NOT TO SMUSH YA!
OH, PLEASE SIR! RIBBIT. PLEASE DON'T SMUSH ME!

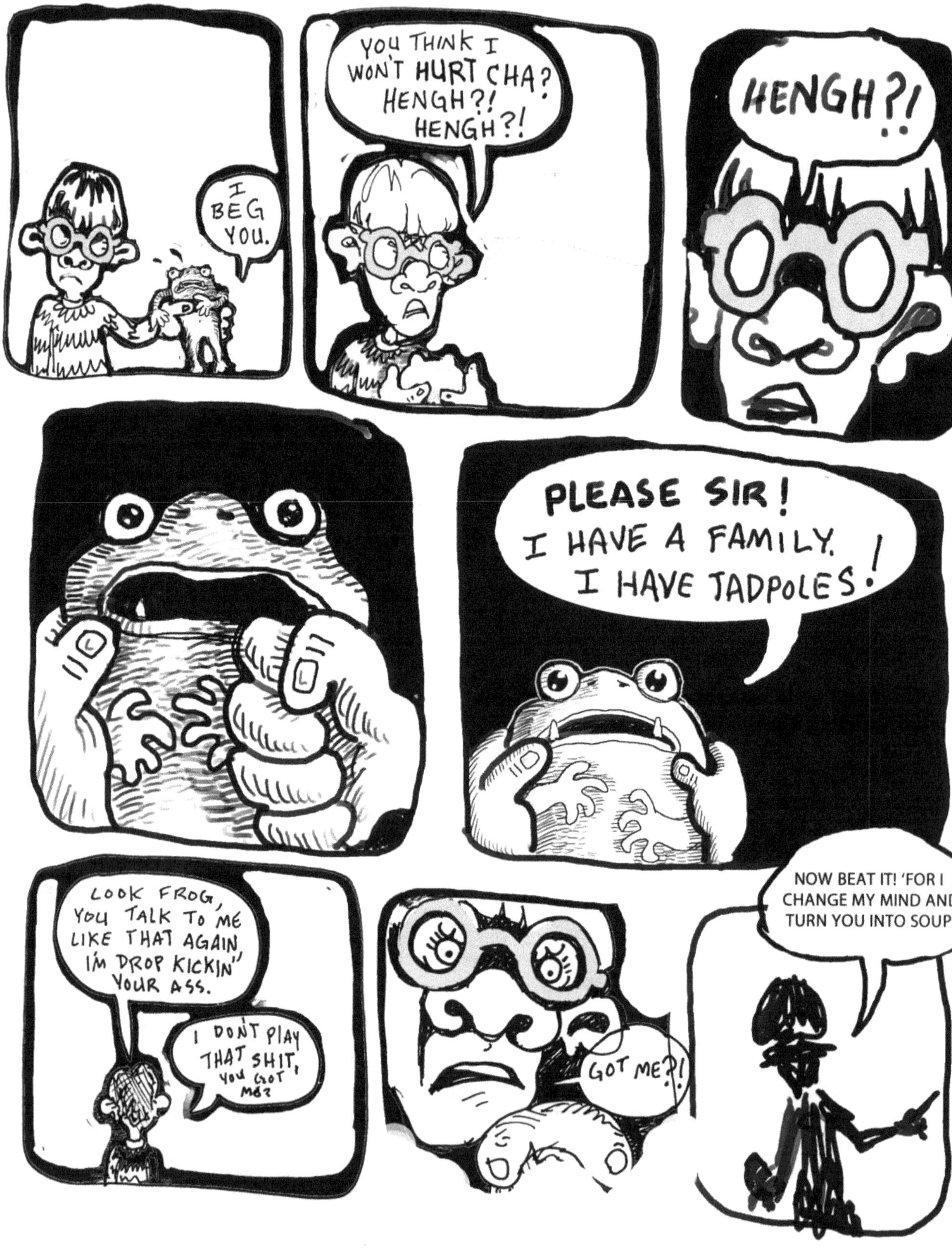
I BEG YOU.
YOU THINK I WON'T HURT CHA? HENGH?! HENGH?!
HENGH?!
PLEASE SIR! I HAVE A FAMILY. I HAVE TADPOLES!
LOOK FROG, YOU TALK TO ME LIKE THAT AGAIN I'M DROP KICKIN'' YOUR ASS.
I DON'T PLAY THAT SHIT, YOU GOT ME?
GOT ME?!
NOW BEAT IT! 'FOR I CHANGE MY MIND AND TURN YOU INTO SOUP!

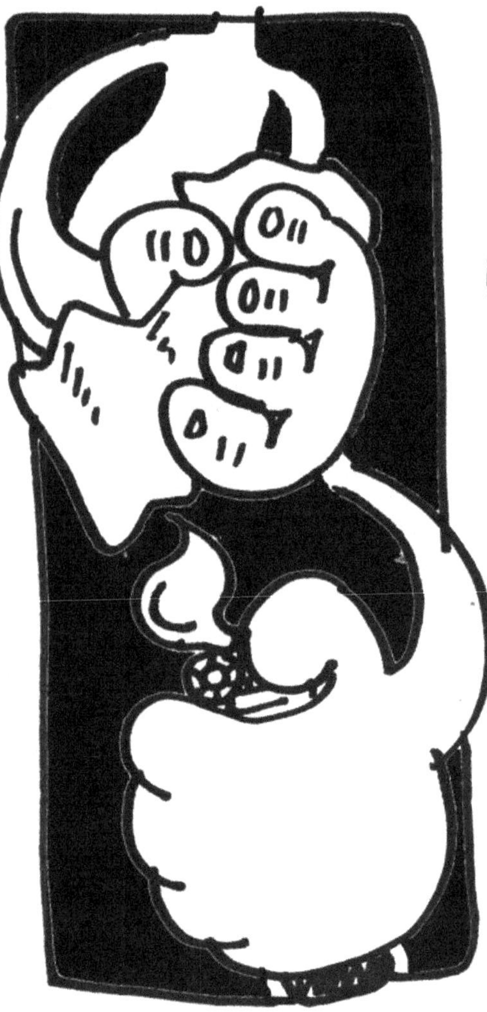

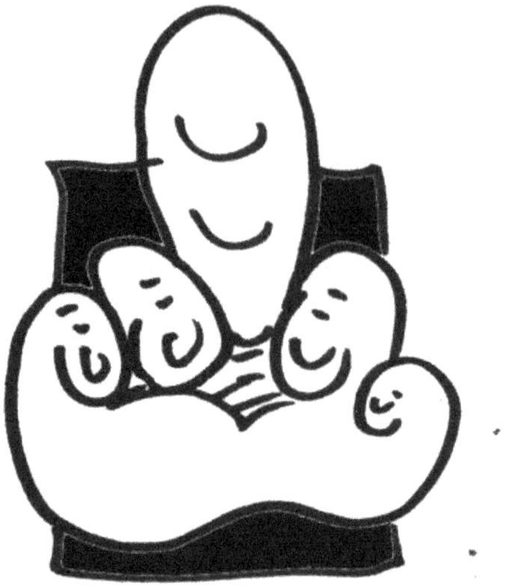

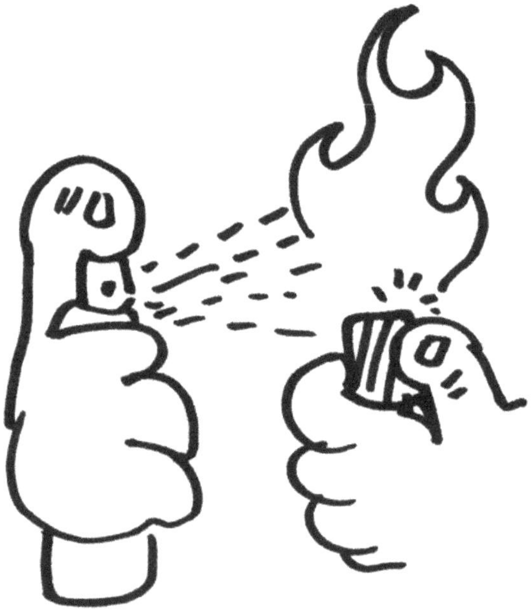

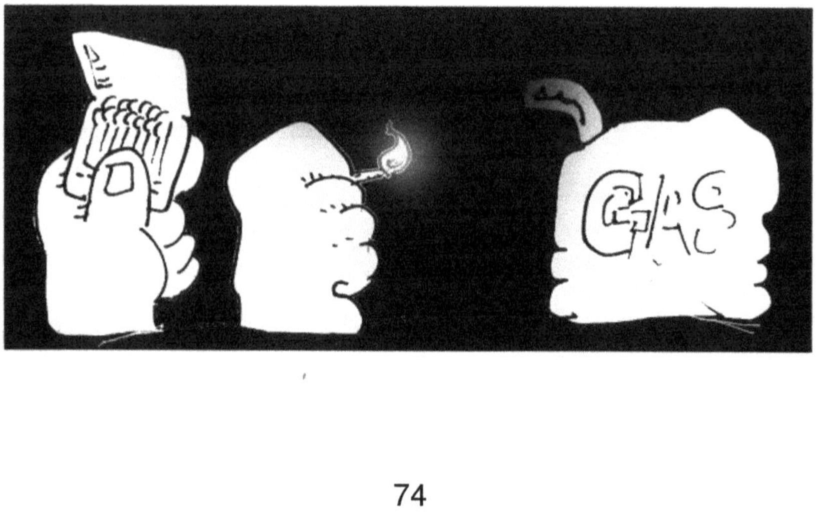
GAS

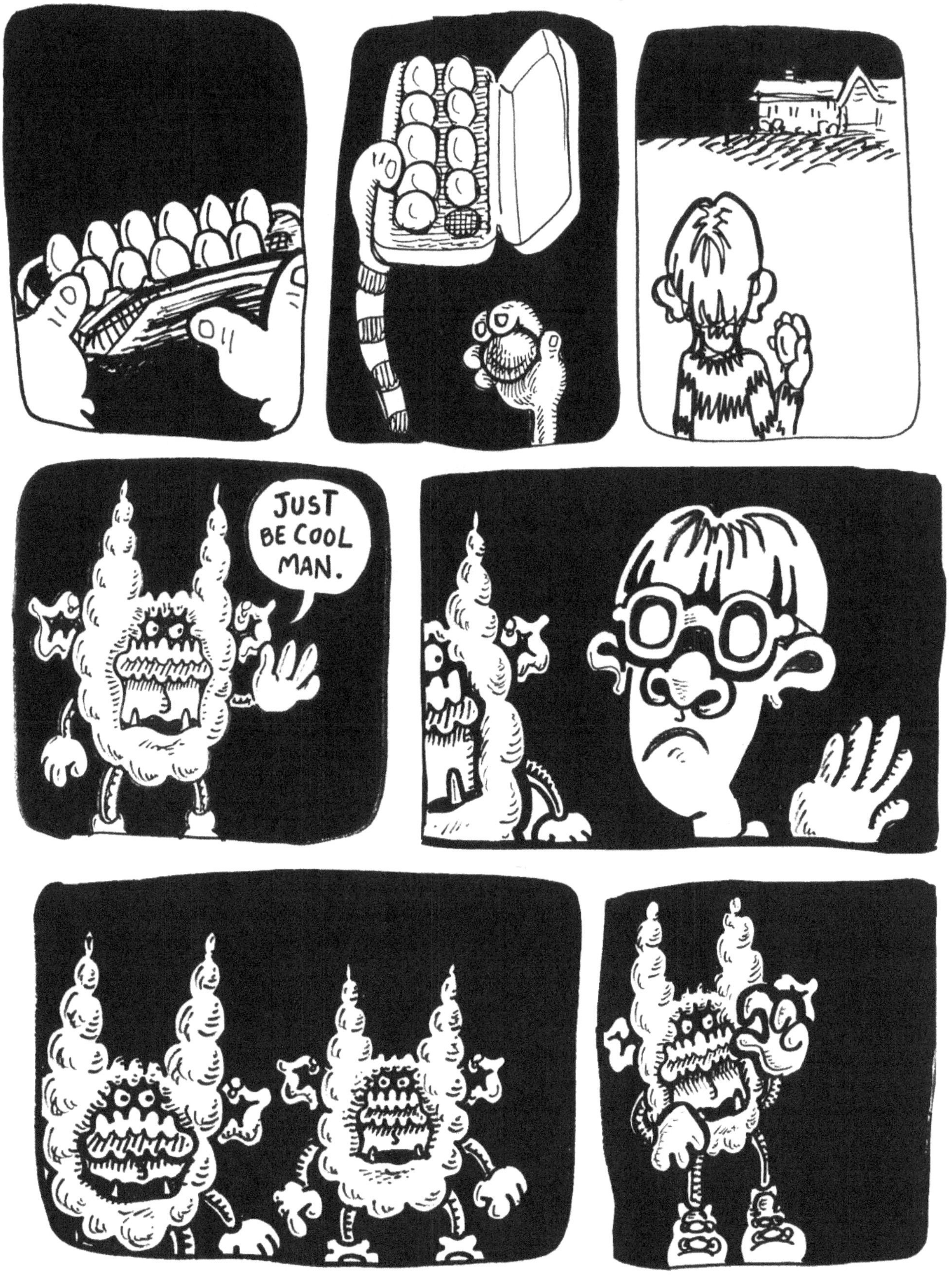
JUST BE COOL MAN.

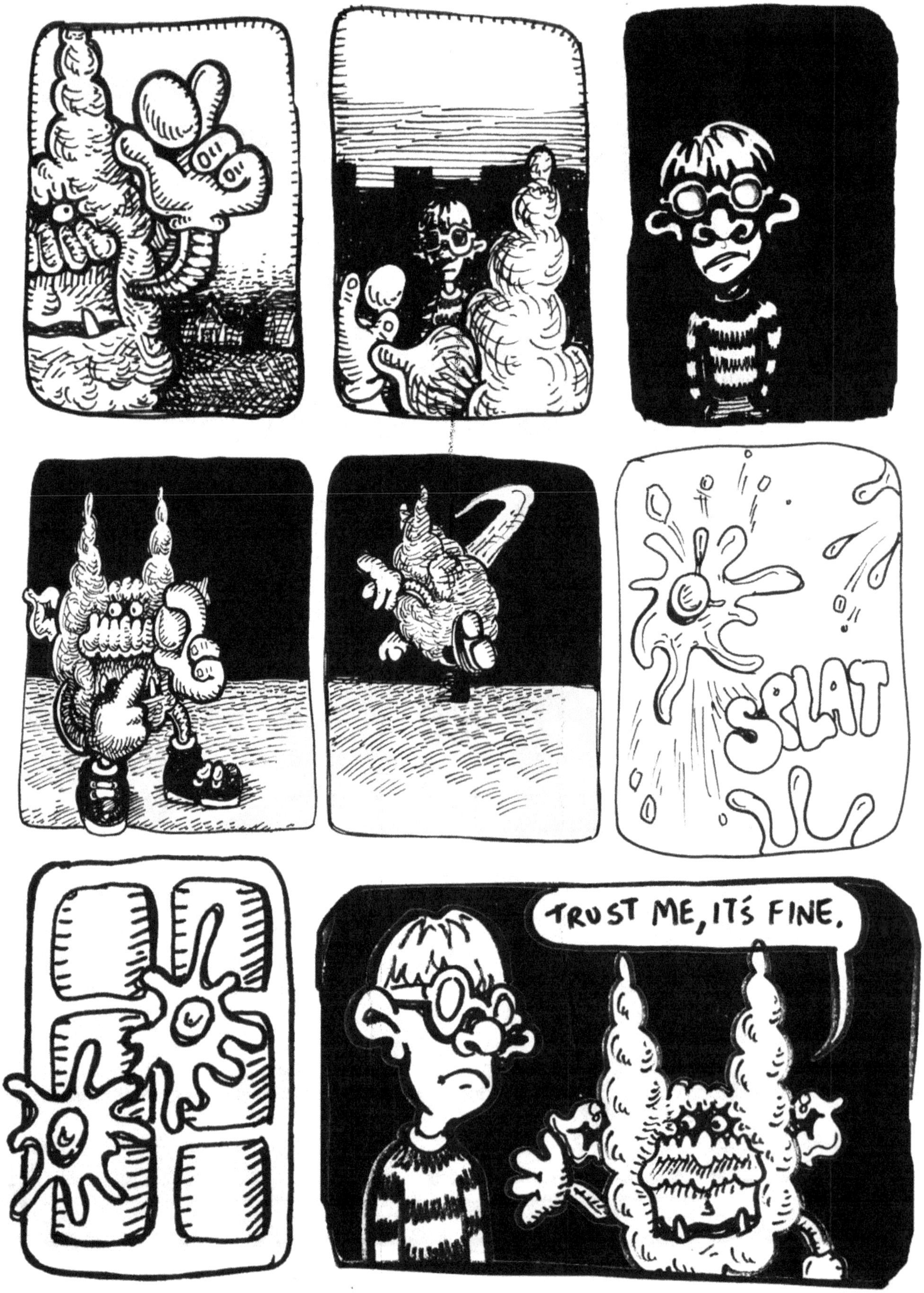
SPLAT
TRUST ME, IT'S FINE.

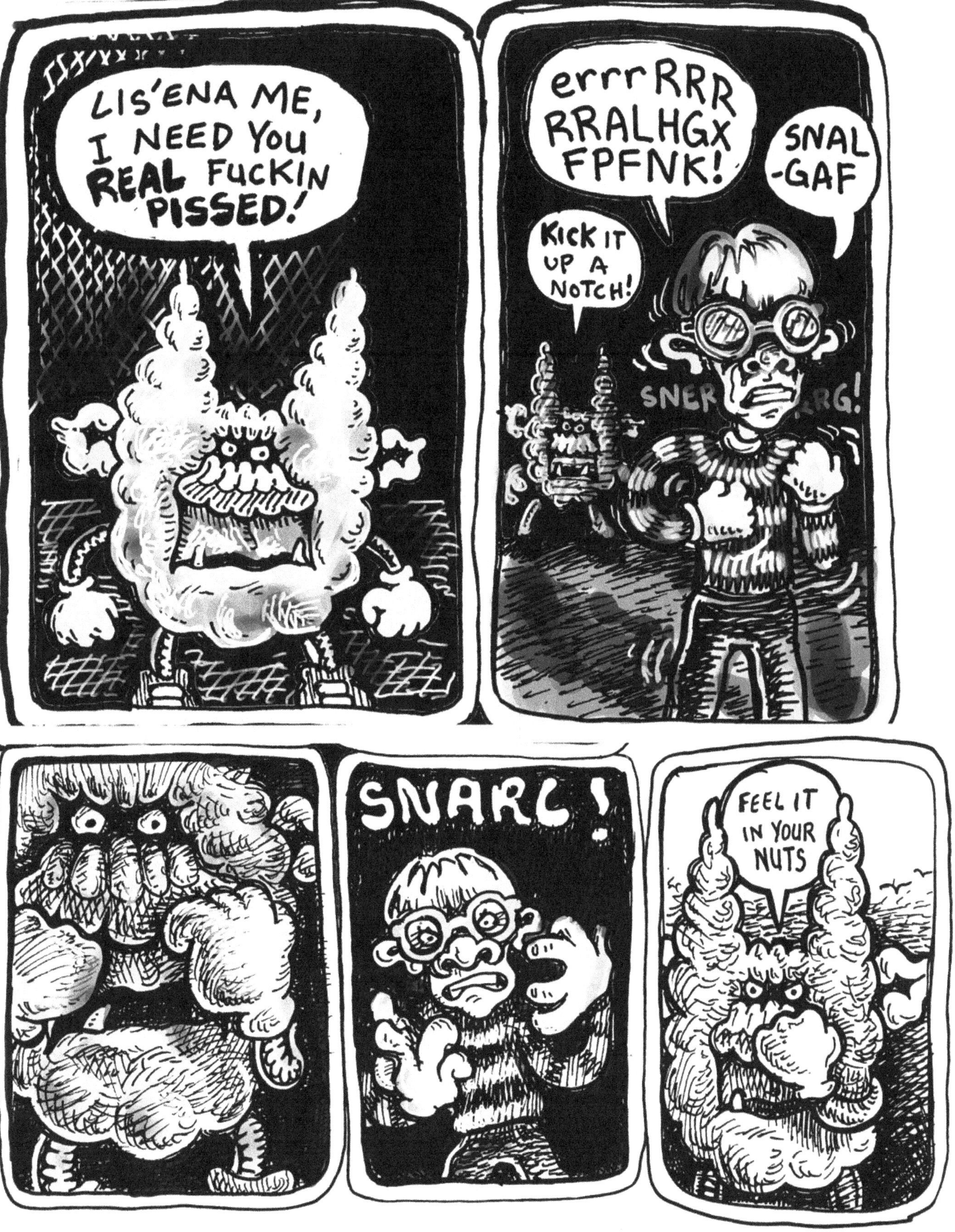
LIS'ENA ME, I NEED YOU REAL FUCKIN PISSED!
errrRRR RRALHGX FPFNK!
SNAL -GAF
KICK IT UP A NOTCH!
SNER
RG!
SNARL!
FEEL IT IN YOUR NUTS

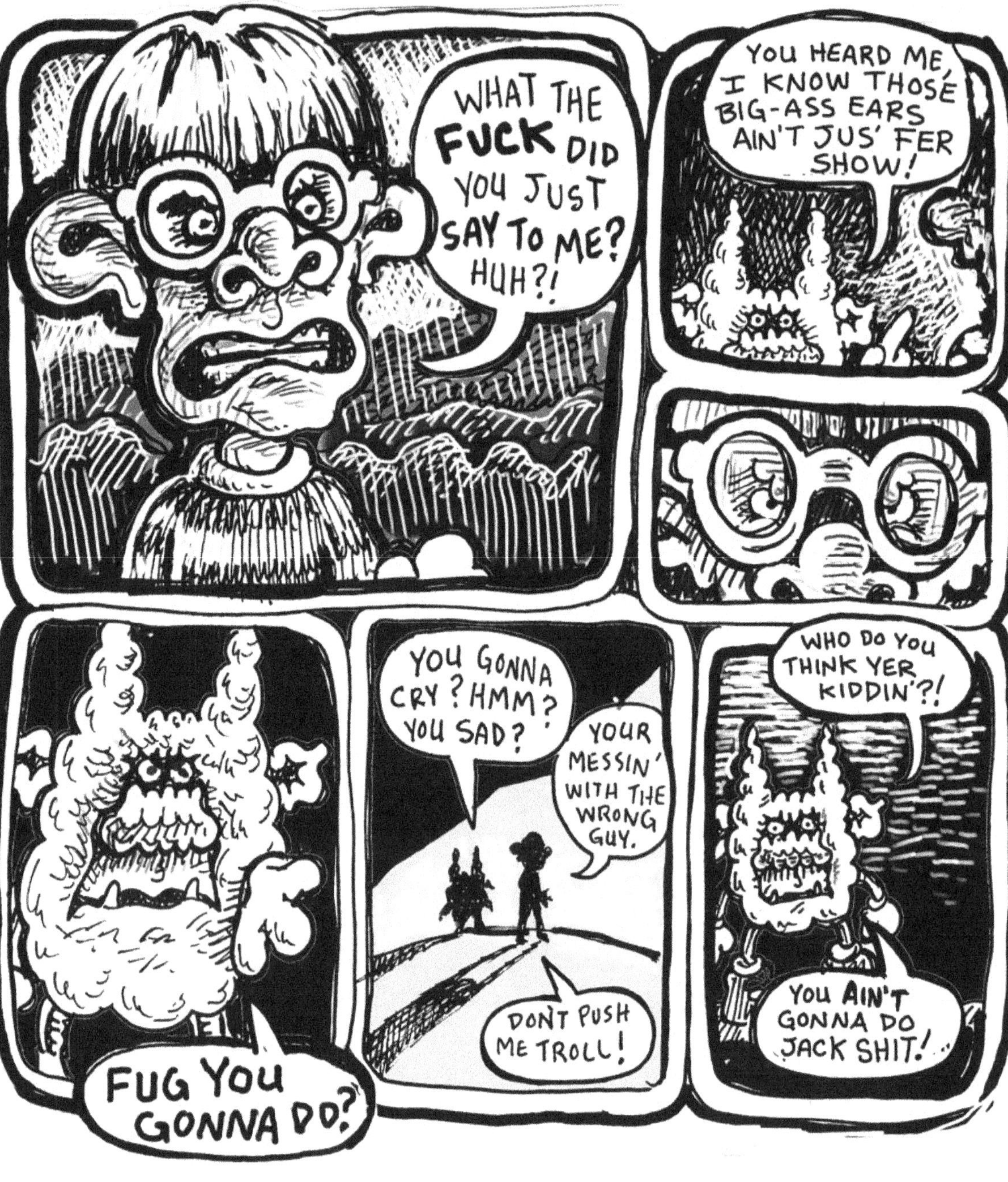
WHAT THE FUCK DID YOU JUST SAY TO ME? HUH?!
YOU HEARD ME, I KNOW THOSE BIG-ASS EARS AIN'T JUS' FER SHOW!
FUG YOU GONNA DO?
YOU GONNA CRY? HMM? YOU SAD?
YOUR MESSIN' WITH THE WRONG GUY.
DON'T PUSH ME TROLL!
WHO DO YOU THINK YER KIDDIN'?!
YOU AIN'T GONNA DO JACK SHIT!

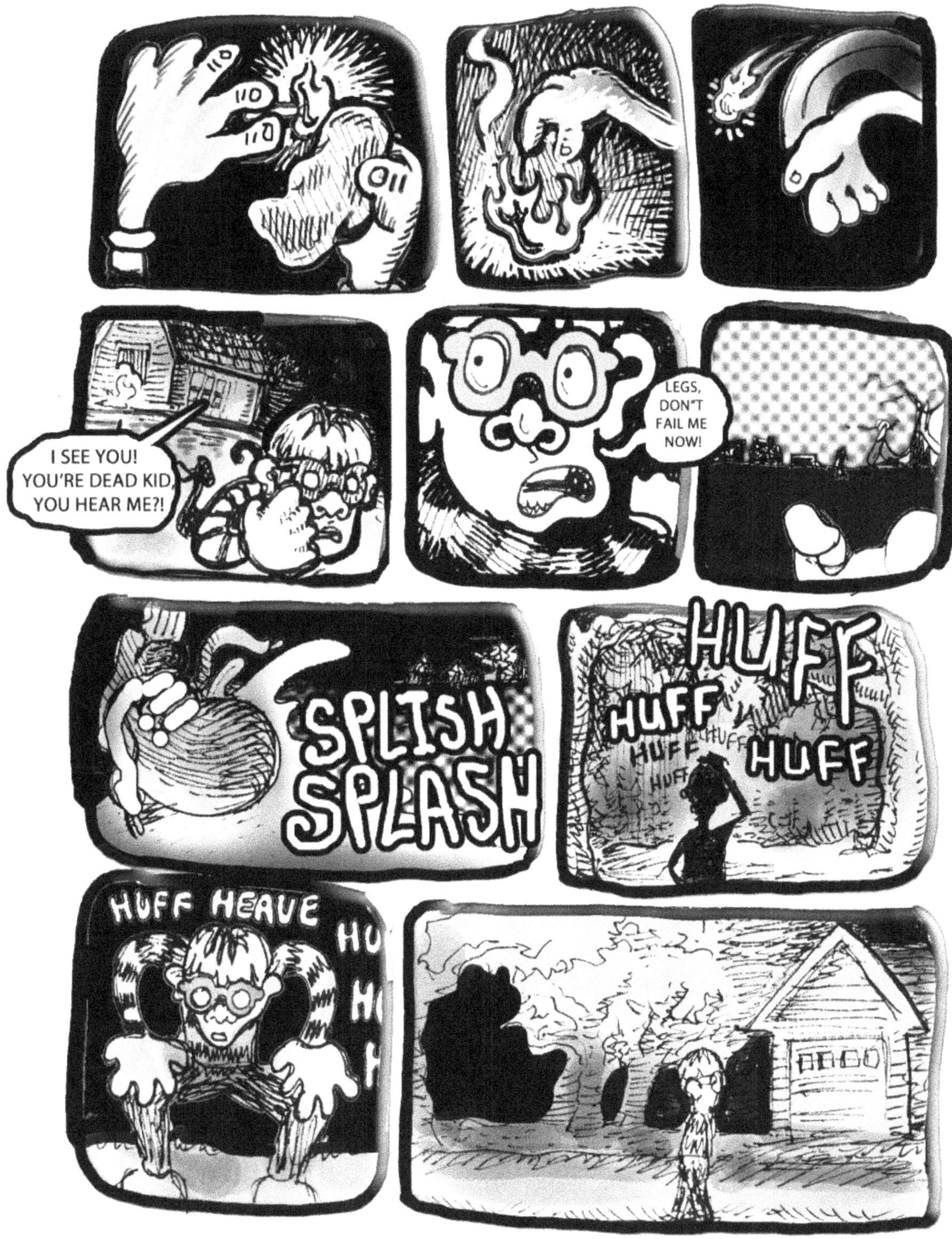
I SEE YOU!
YOU'RE DEAD KID, YOU HEAR ME?!
LEGS, DON'T FAIL ME NOW!
SPLISH SPLASH
HUFF
HUFF
HUFF
HUFF
HUFF
HUFF
HUFF HEAVE

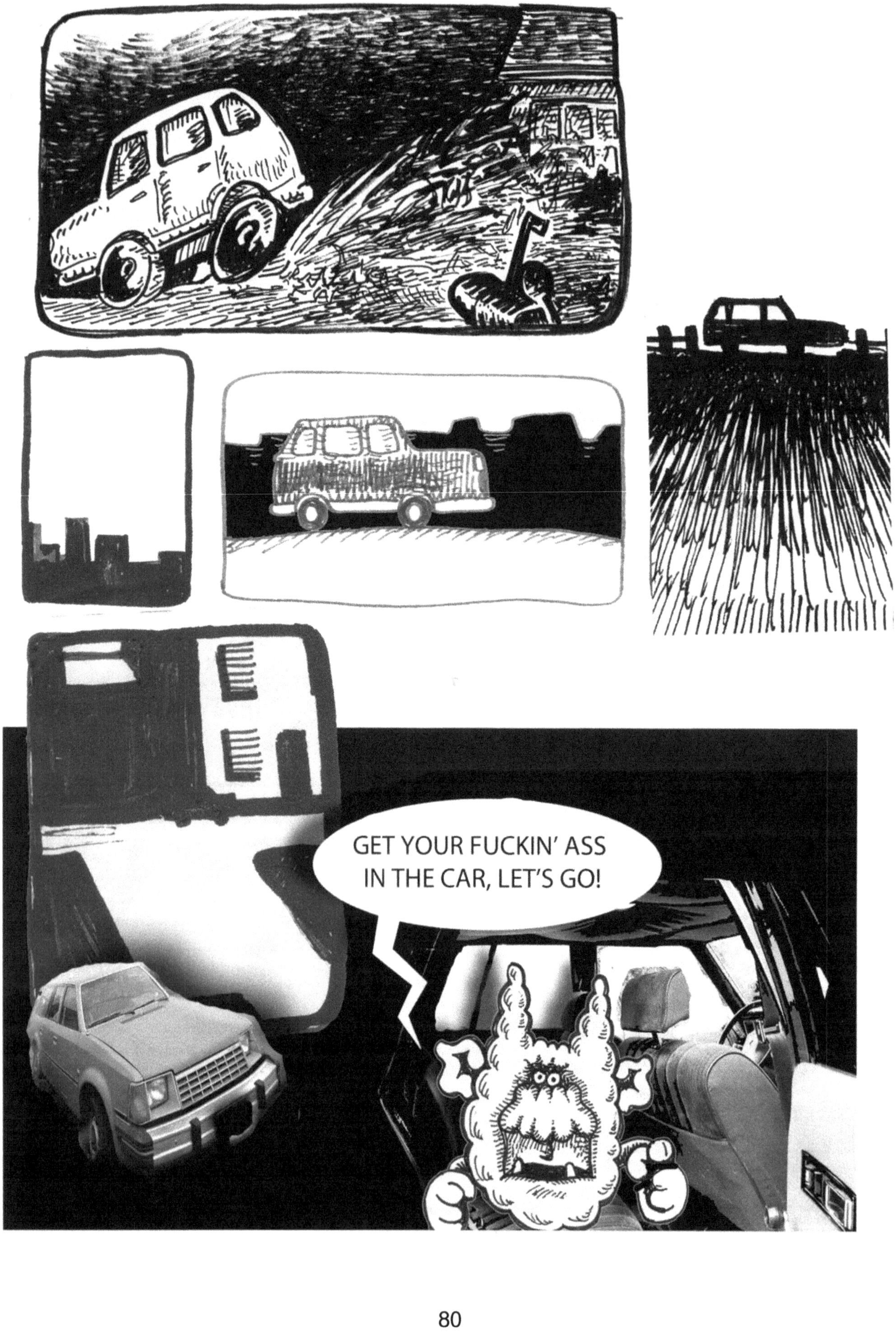
GET YOUR FUCKIN' ASS
IN THE CAR, LET'S GO!

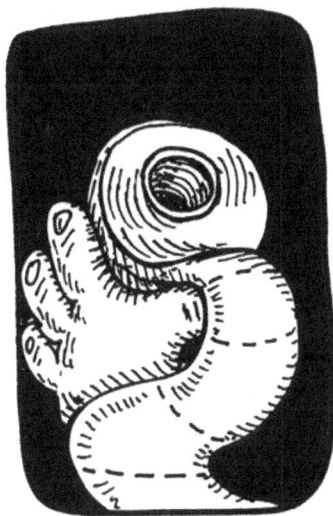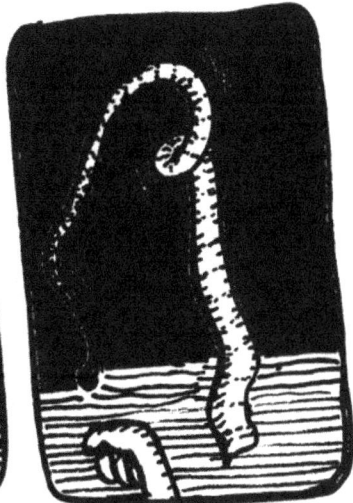

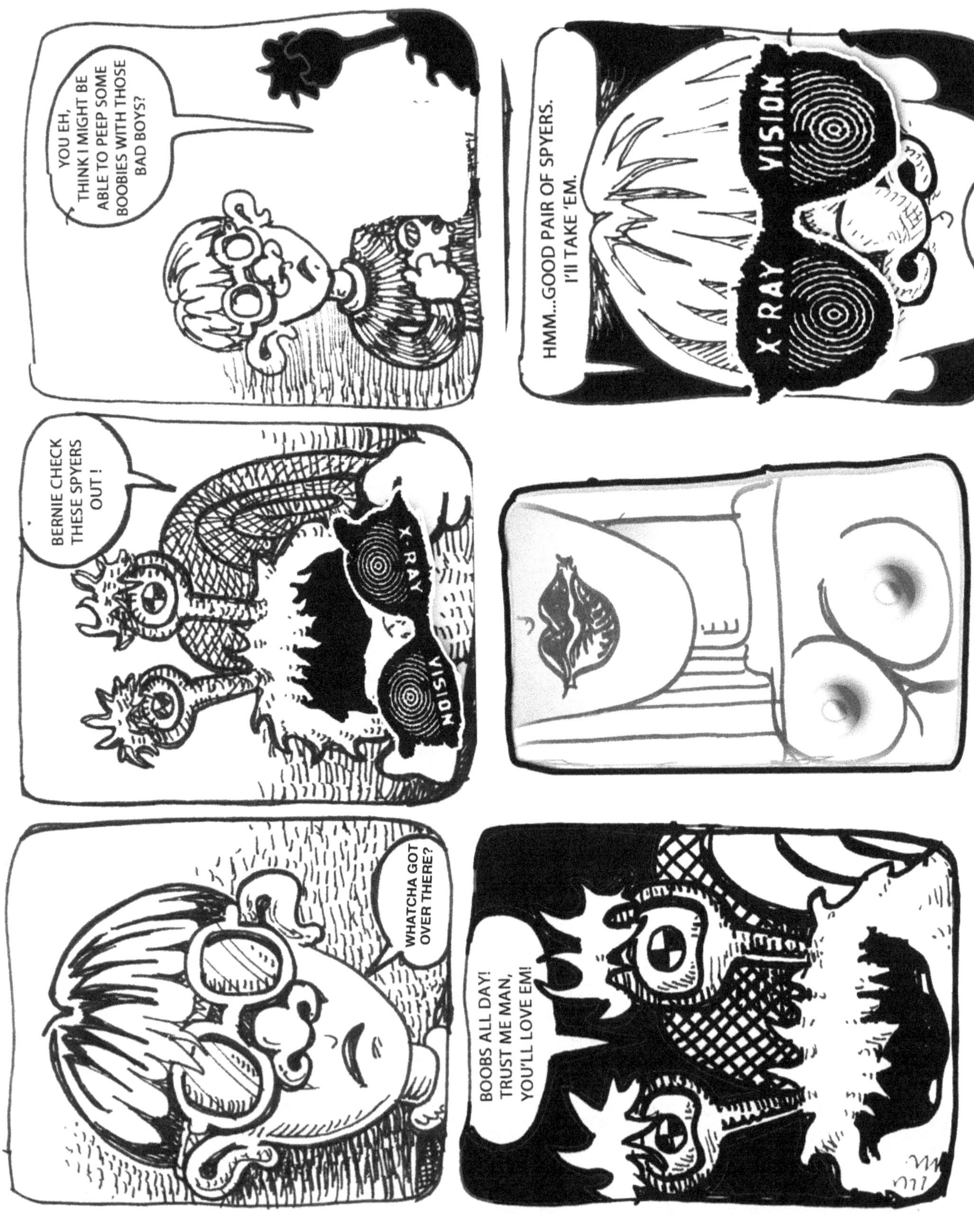

WHATCHA GOT OVER THERE?
BERNIE CHECK THESE SPYERS OUT !
X-RAY VISION
YOU EH, THINK I MIGHT BE ABLE TO PEEP SOME BOOBIES WITH THOSE BAD BOYS?
BOOBS ALL DAY! TRUST ME MAN, YOU'LL LOVE EM!
HMM...GOOD PAIR OF SPYERS. I'll TAKE 'EM.
X-RAY VISION

THE ADVENTURES OF WILD BERNIE

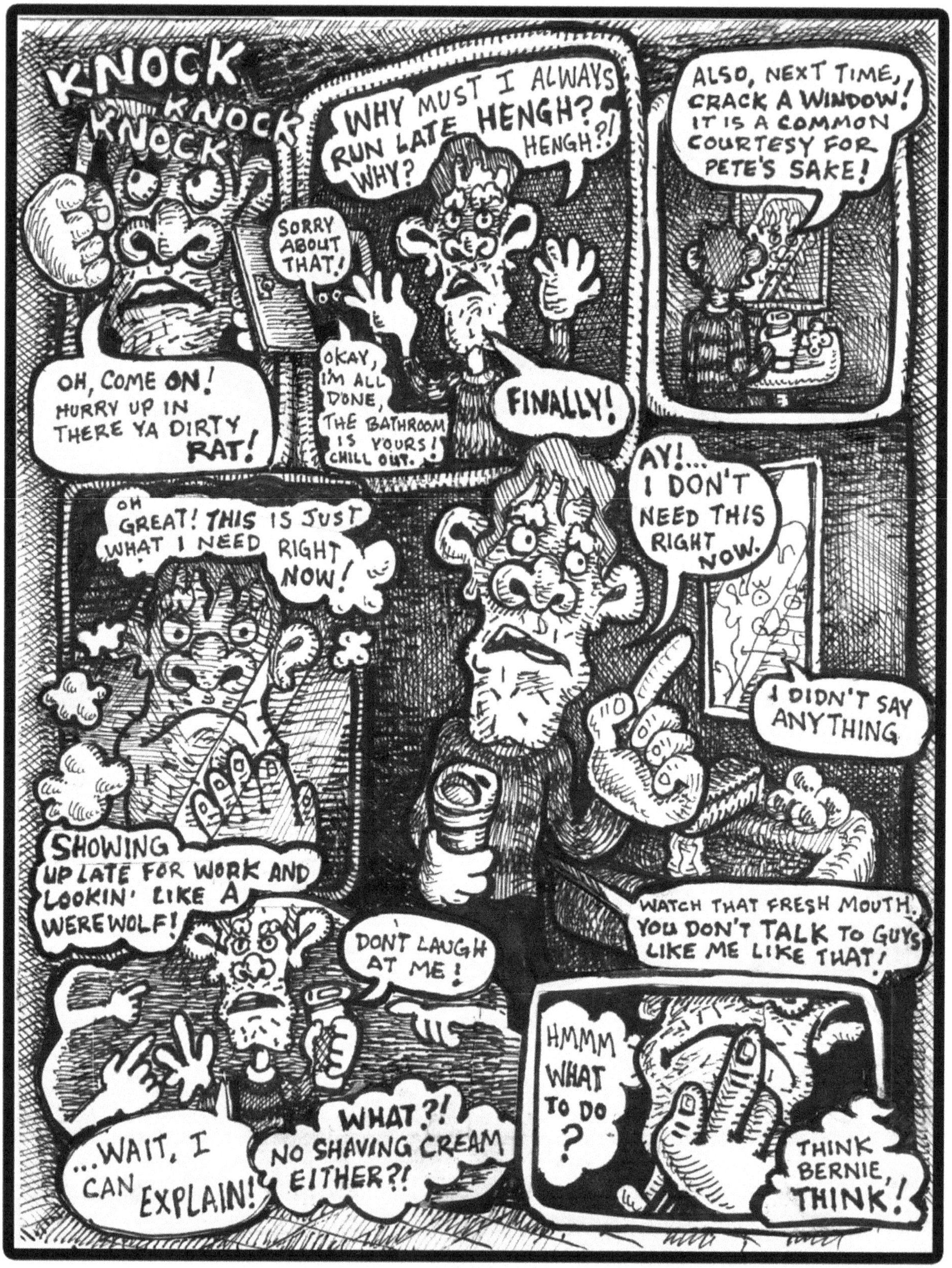
KNOCK KNOCK KNOCK
OH, COME ON! HURRY UP IN THERE YA DIRTY RAT!
WHY MUST I ALWAYS RUN LATE HENGH? WHY? HENGH?!
SORRY ABOUT THAT!
OKAY, I'M ALL DONE, THE BATHROOM IS YOURS! CHILL OUT.
FINALLY!
ALSO, NEXT TIME, CRACK A WINDOW! IT IS A COMMON COURTESY FOR PETE'S SAKE!
OH GREAT! THIS IS JUST WHAT I NEED RIGHT NOW!
AY!... I DON'T NEED THIS RIGHT NOW.
I DIDN'T SAY ANYTHING
SHOWING UP LATE FOR WORK AND LOOKIN' LIKE A WEREWOLF!
DON'T LAUGH AT ME!
WATCH THAT FRESH MOUTH. YOU DON'T TALK TO GUYS LIKE ME LIKE THAT!
...WAIT, I CAN EXPLAIN!
WHAT?! NO SHAVING CREAM EITHER?!
HMMM WHAT TO DO ?
THINK BERNIE, THINK!

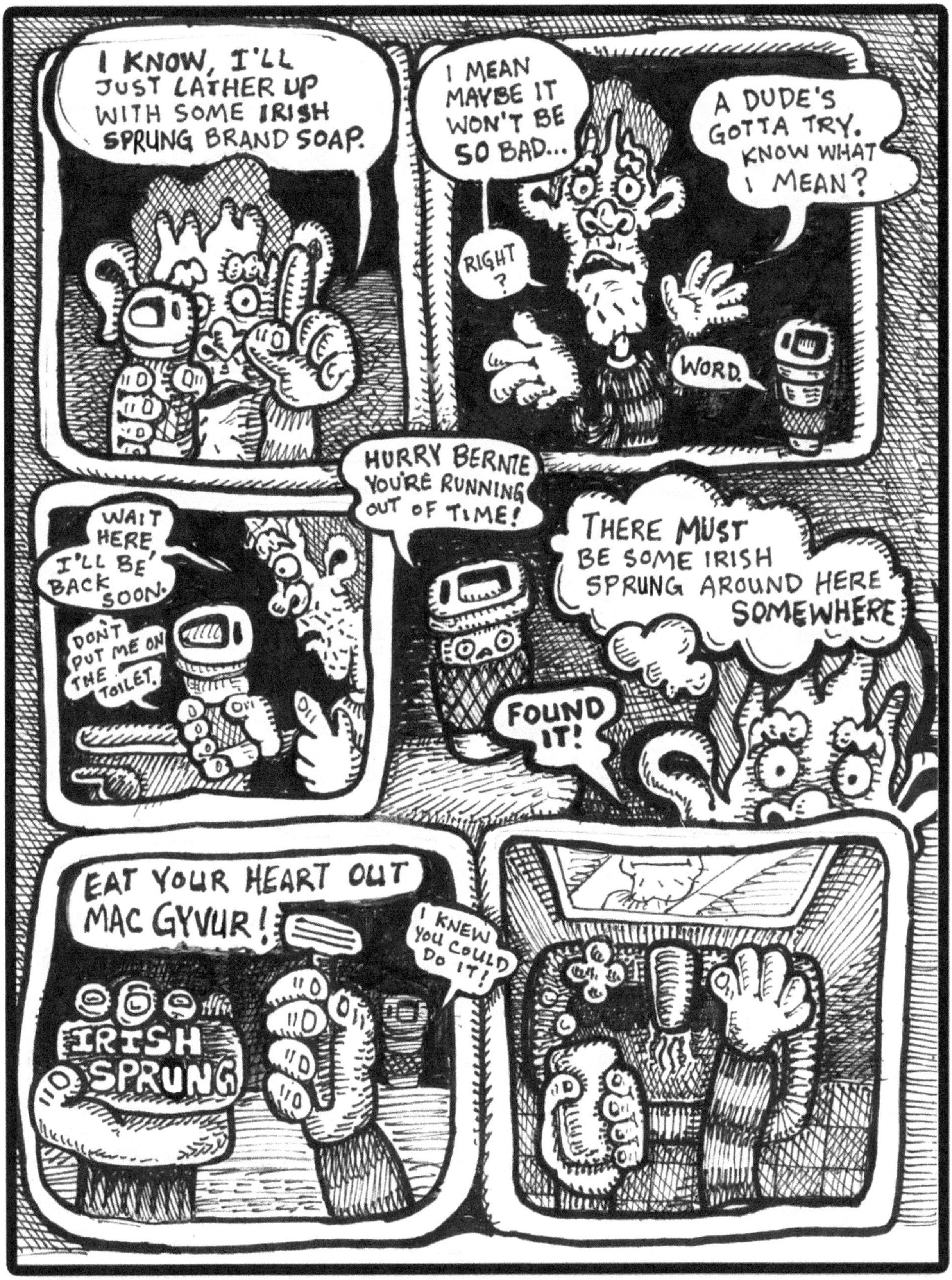
I KNOW, I'LL JUST LATHER UP WITH SOME IRISH SPRUNG BRAND SOAP.
I MEAN MAYBE IT WON'T BE SO BAD...
RIGHT ?
A DUDE'S GOTTA TRY. KNOW WHAT I MEAN?
WORD.
HURRY BERNIE YOU'RE RUNNING OUT OF TIME!
WAIT HERE, I'LL BE BACK SOON.
DON'T PUT ME ON THE TOILET.
THERE MUST BE SOME IRISH SPRUNG AROUND HERE SOMEWHERE
FOUND IT!
EAT YOUR HEART OUT MAC GYVUR!
I KNEW YOU COULD DO IT!
IRISH SPRUNG

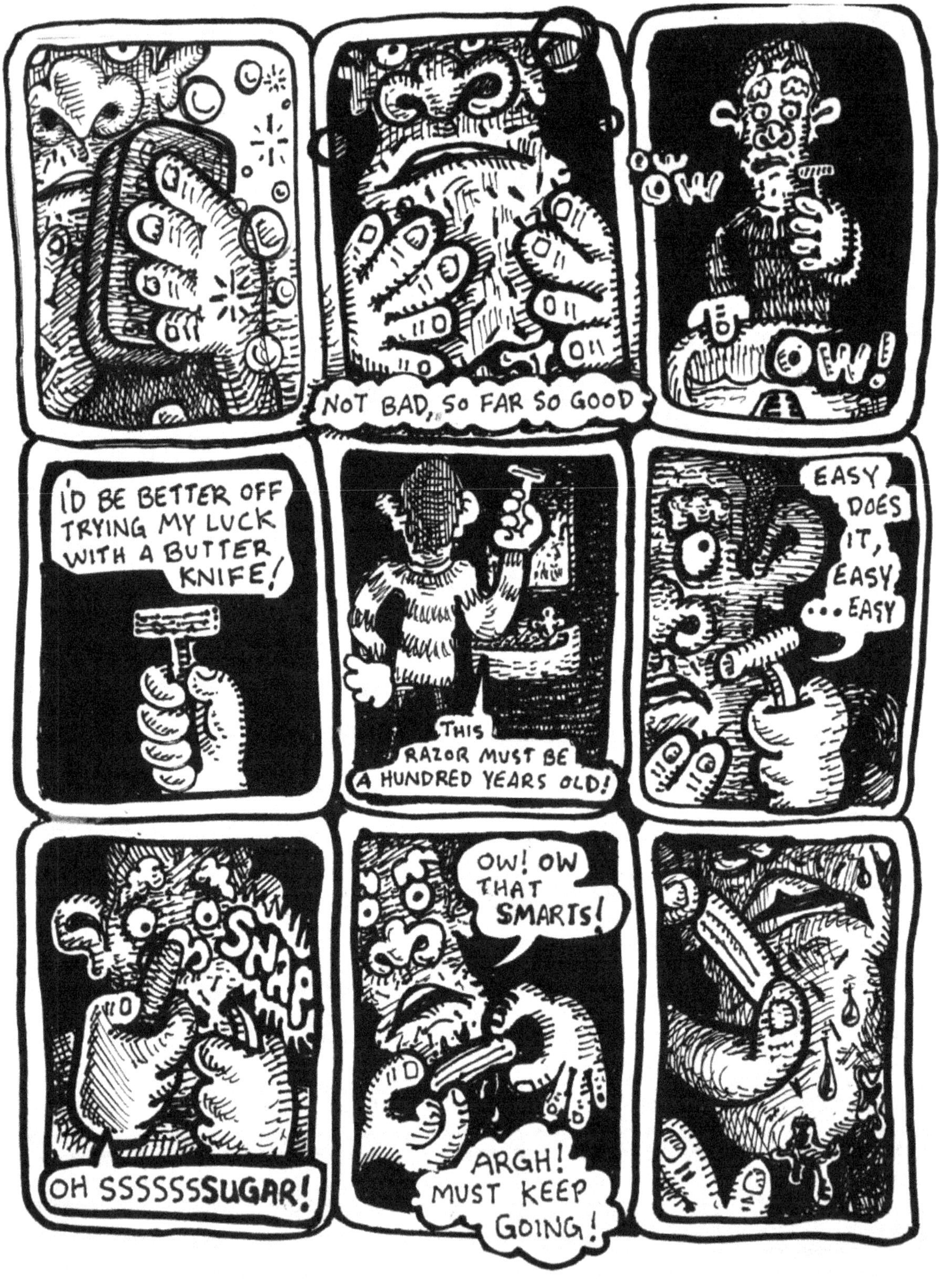
NOT BAD, SO FAR SO GOOD
OW
OW!
I'D BE BETTER OFF TRYING MY LUCK WITH A BUTTER KNIFE!
THIS RAZOR MUST BE A HUNDRED YEARS OLD!
EASY DOES IT, EASY ...EASY
SNAP
OH SSSSSSSUGAR!
OW! OW THAT SMARTS!
ARGH! MUST KEEP GOING!

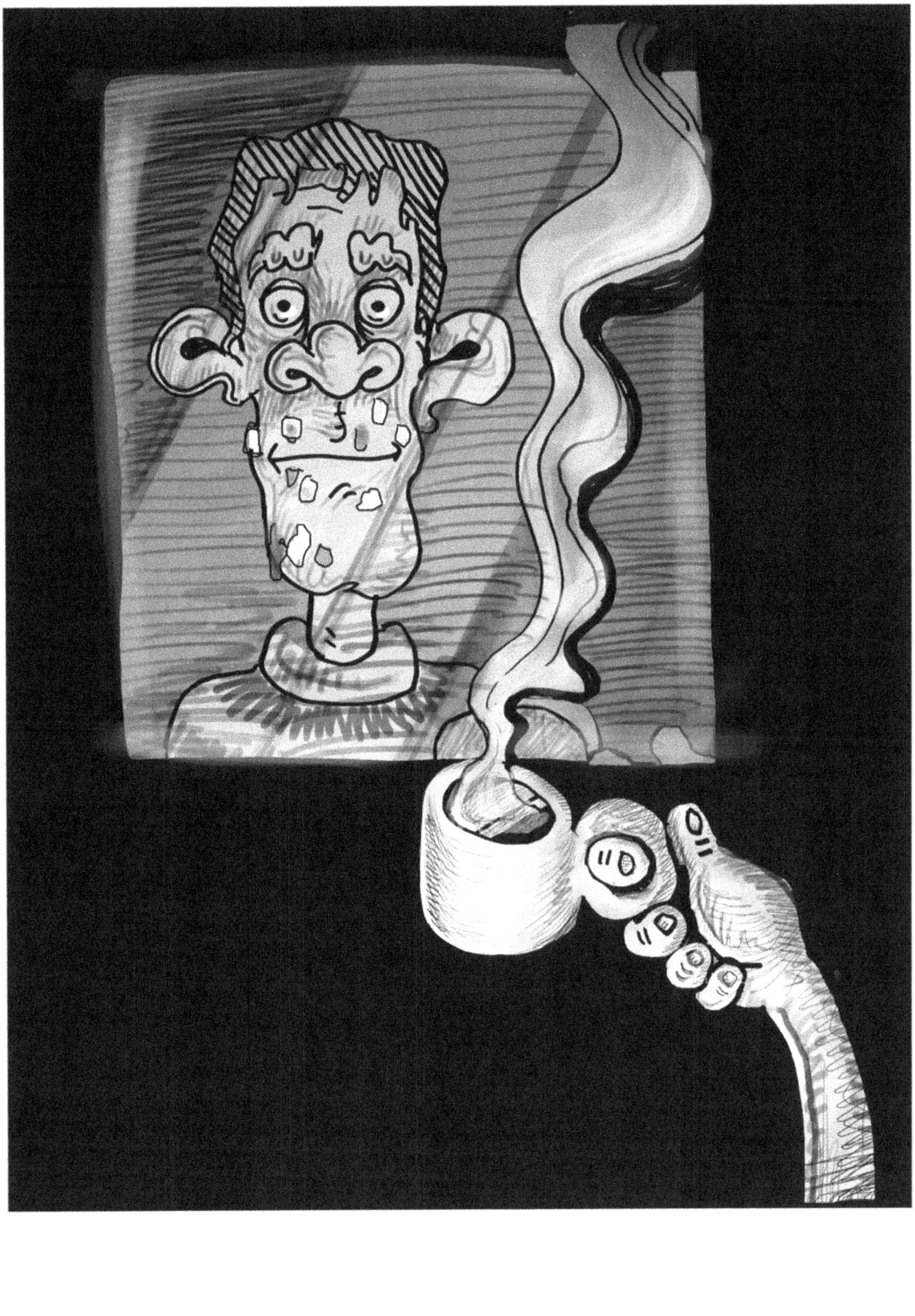

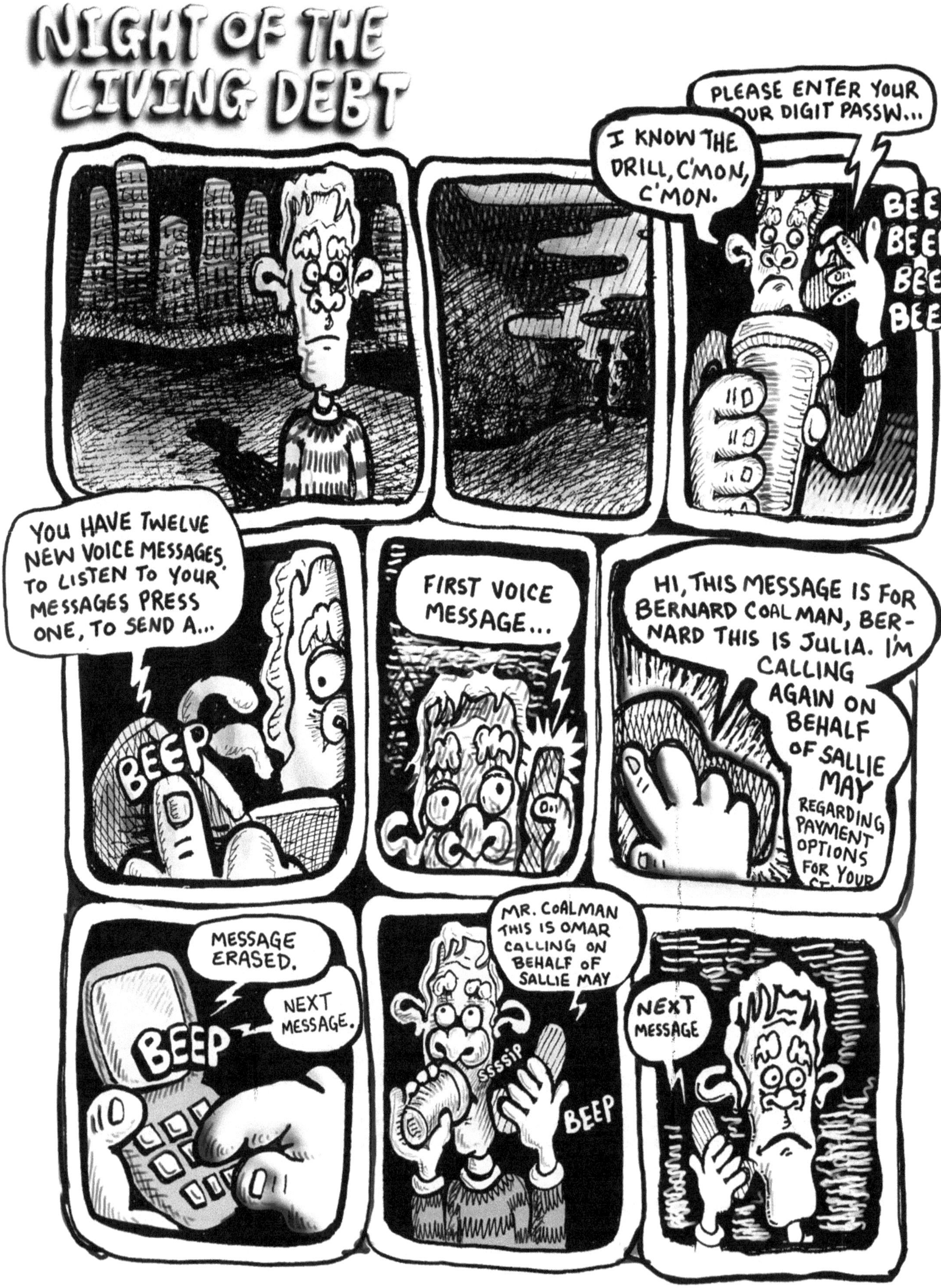

NIGHT OF THE LIVING DEBT
PLEASE ENTER YOUR OUR DIGIT PASSW...
I KNOW THE DRILL, C'MON, C'MON.
BEEP BEEP BEEP BEEP
YOU HAVE TWELVE NEW VOICE MESSAGES. TO LISTEN TO YOUR MESSAGES PRESS ONE, TO SEND A...
BEEP
FIRST VOICE MESSAGE...
HI, THIS MESSAGE IS FOR BERNARD COALMAN, BERNARD THIS IS JULIA. I'M CALLING AGAIN ON BEHALF OF SALLIE MAY REGARDING PAYMENT OPTIONS FOR YOUR
MESSAGE ERASED.
BEEP
NEXT MESSAGE.
MR. COALMAN THIS IS OMAR CALLING ON BEHALF OF SALLIE MAY
SSSSIP
BEEP
NEXT MESSAGE

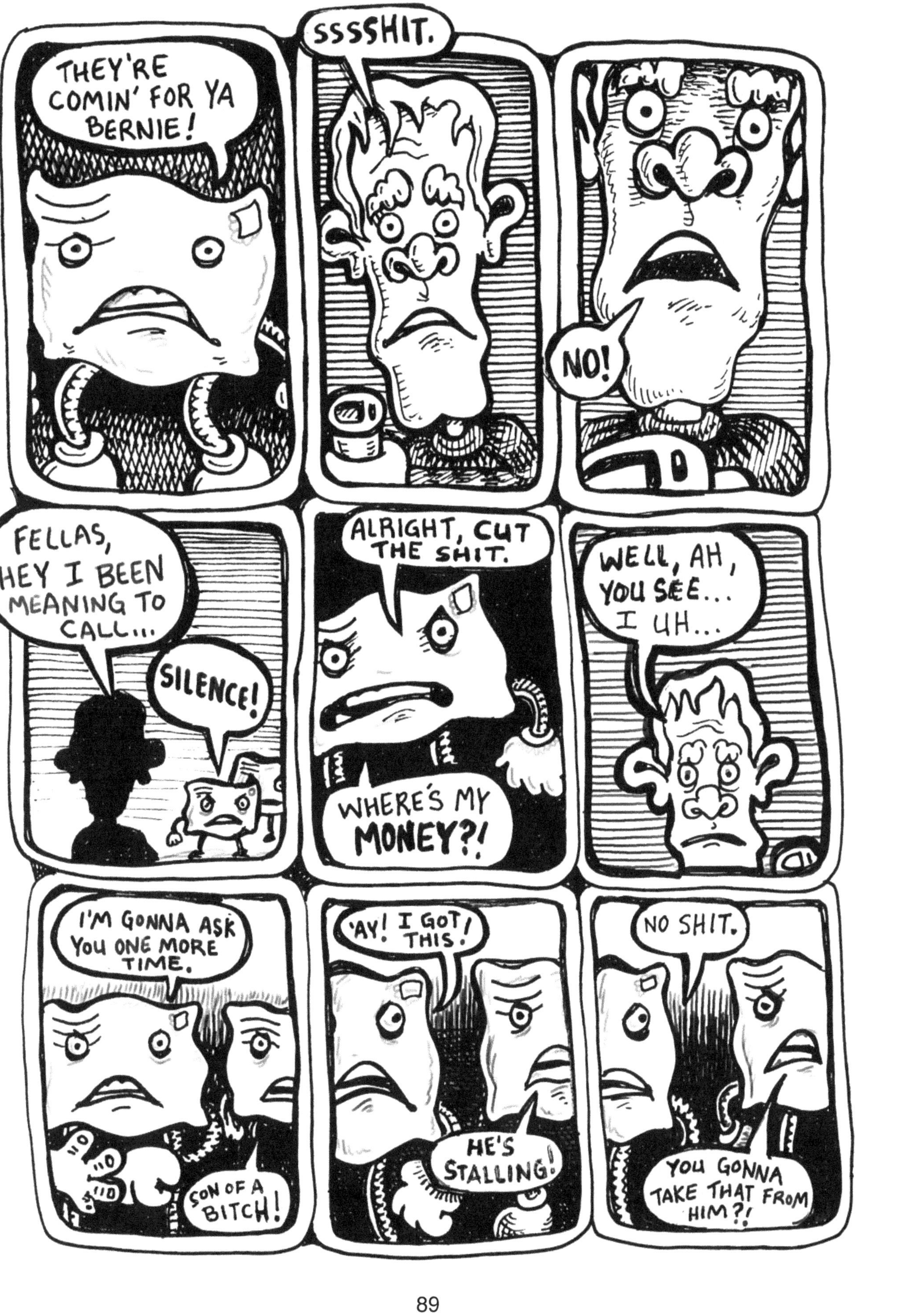
THEY'RE COMIN' FOR YA BERNIE!
SSSSHIT.
NO!
FELLAS, HEY I BEEN MEANING TO CALL...
SILENCE!
ALRIGHT, CUT THE SHIT.
WHERE'S MY MONEY?!
WELL, AH, YOU SEE... I UH...
I'M GONNA ASK YOU ONE MORE TIME.
SON OF A BITCH!
'AY! I GOT THIS!
HE'S STALLING!
NO SHIT.
YOU GONNA TAKE THAT FROM HIM?!

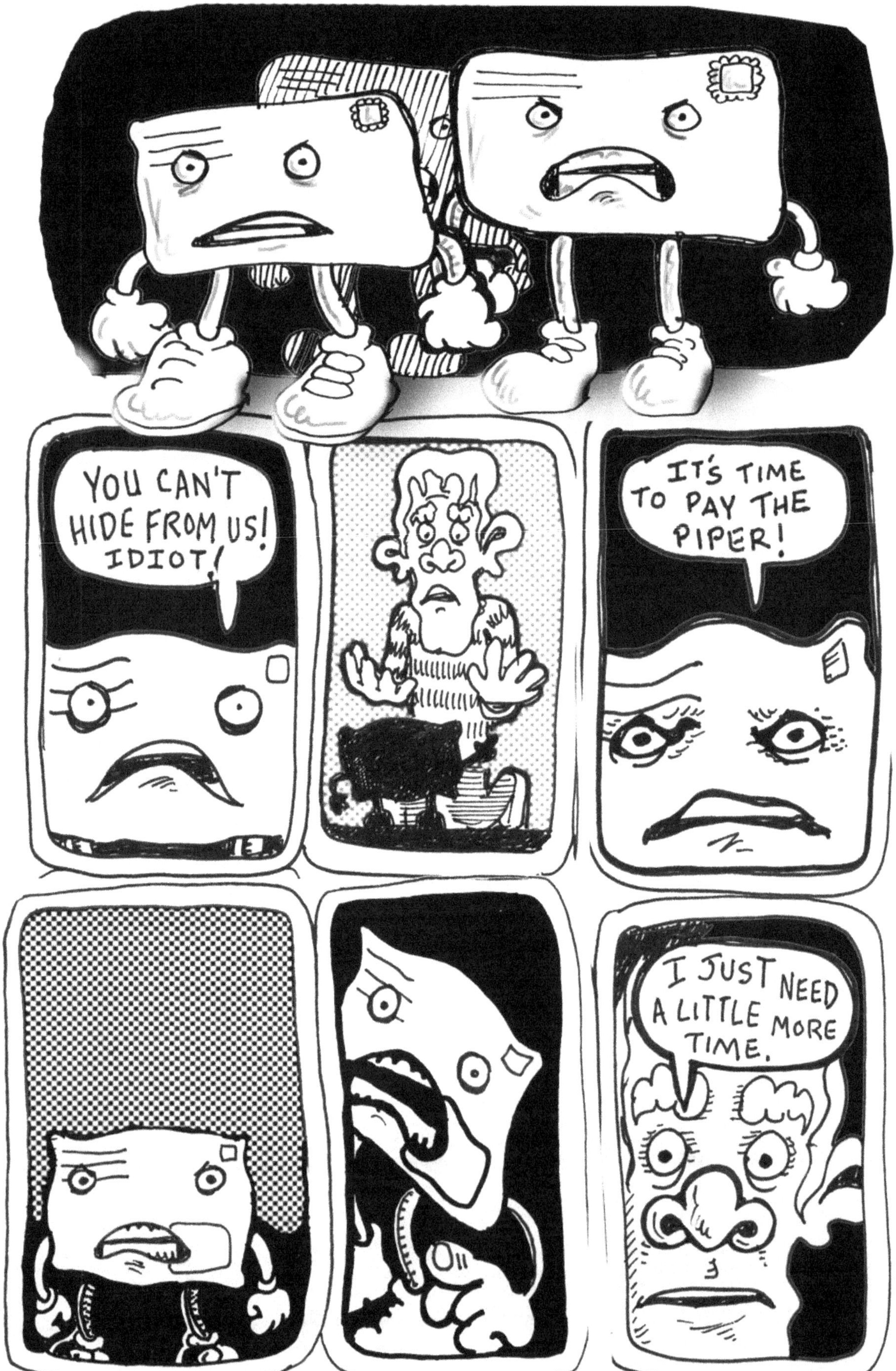
YOU CAN'T HIDE FROM US! IDIOT!
IT'S TIME TO PAY THE PIPER!
I JUST NEED A LITTLE MORE TIME.

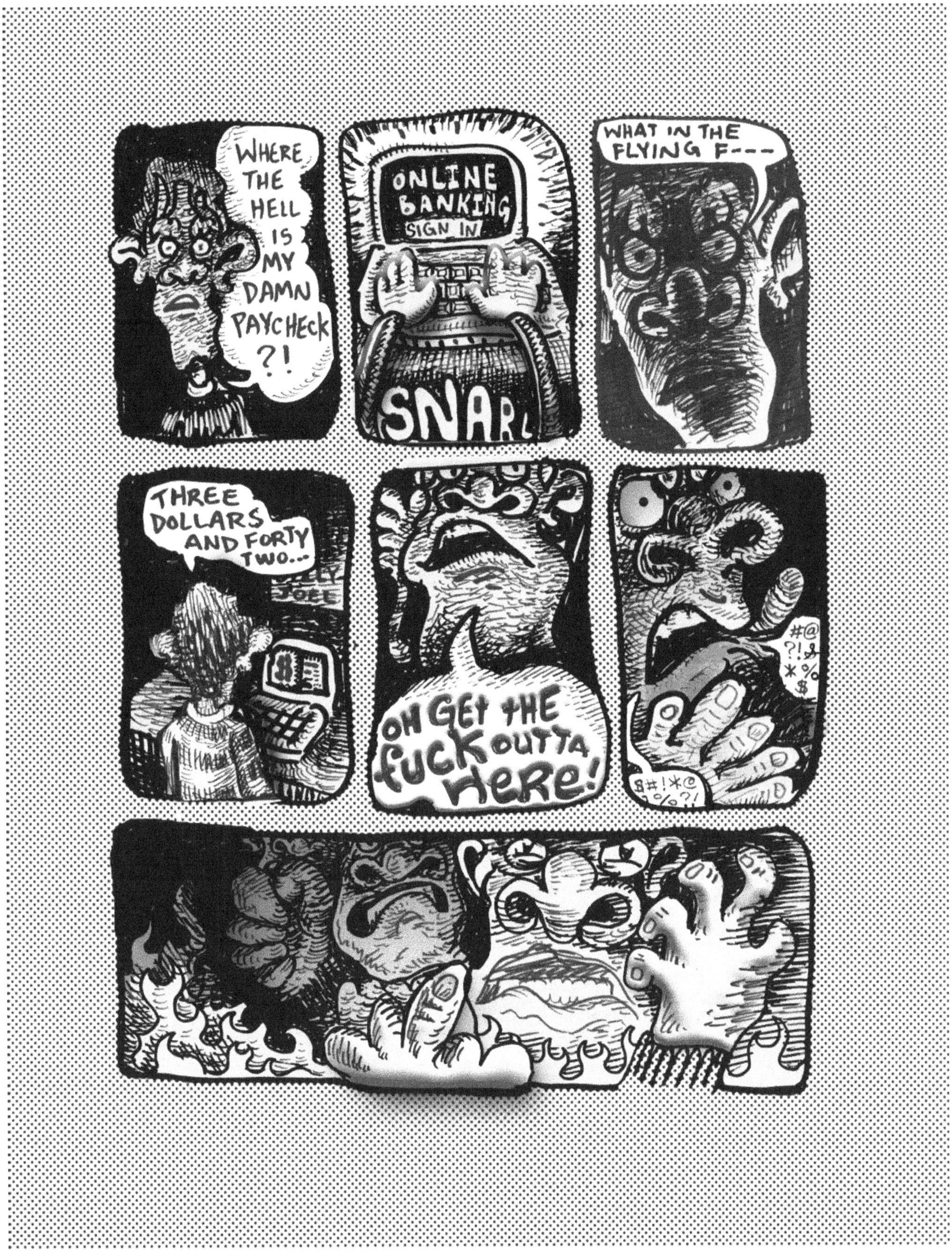
WHERE THE HELL IS MY DAMN PAYCHECK ?!
ONLINE BANKING
SIGN IN
SNARL
WHAT IN THE FLYING F---
THREE DOLLARS AND FORTY TWO...
OH GET THE FUCK OUTTA HERE!
#@ ?!& *% $
$#!*@ ?%?!

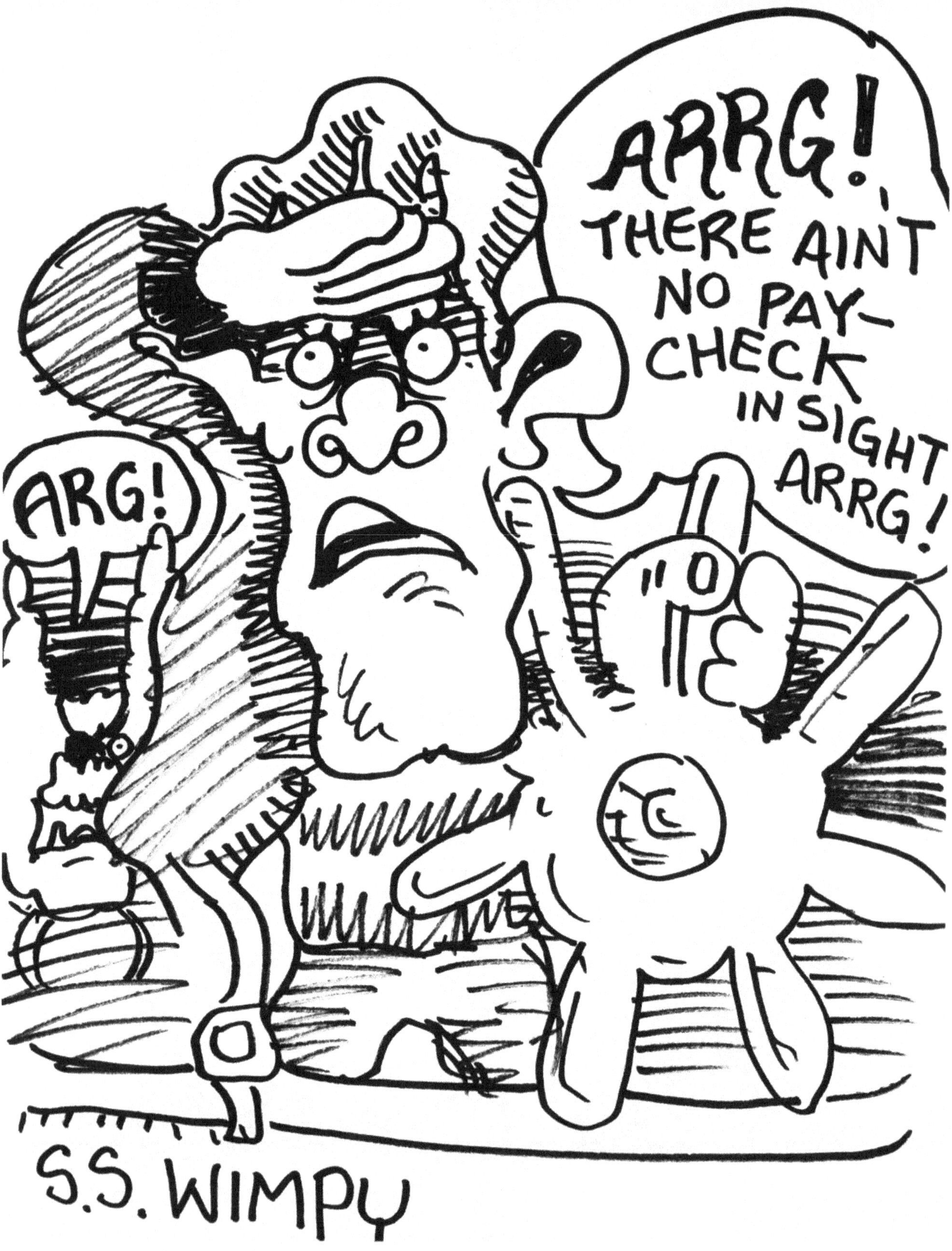
ARRG! THERE AINT NO PAY-CHECK IN SIGHT ARRG!
ARG!
S.S. WIMPY

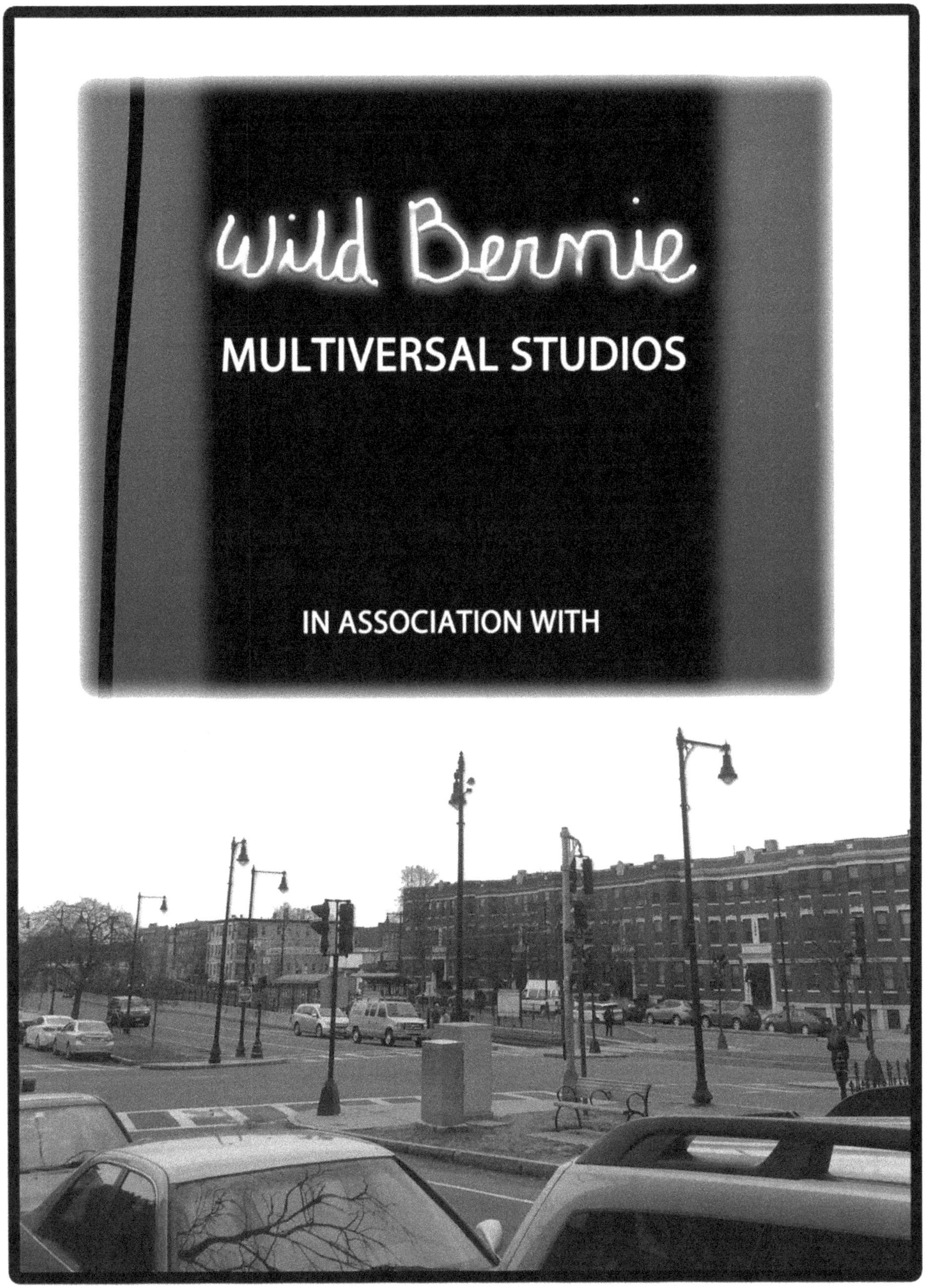
Wild Bernie
MULTIVERSAL STUDIOS
IN ASSOCIATION WITH

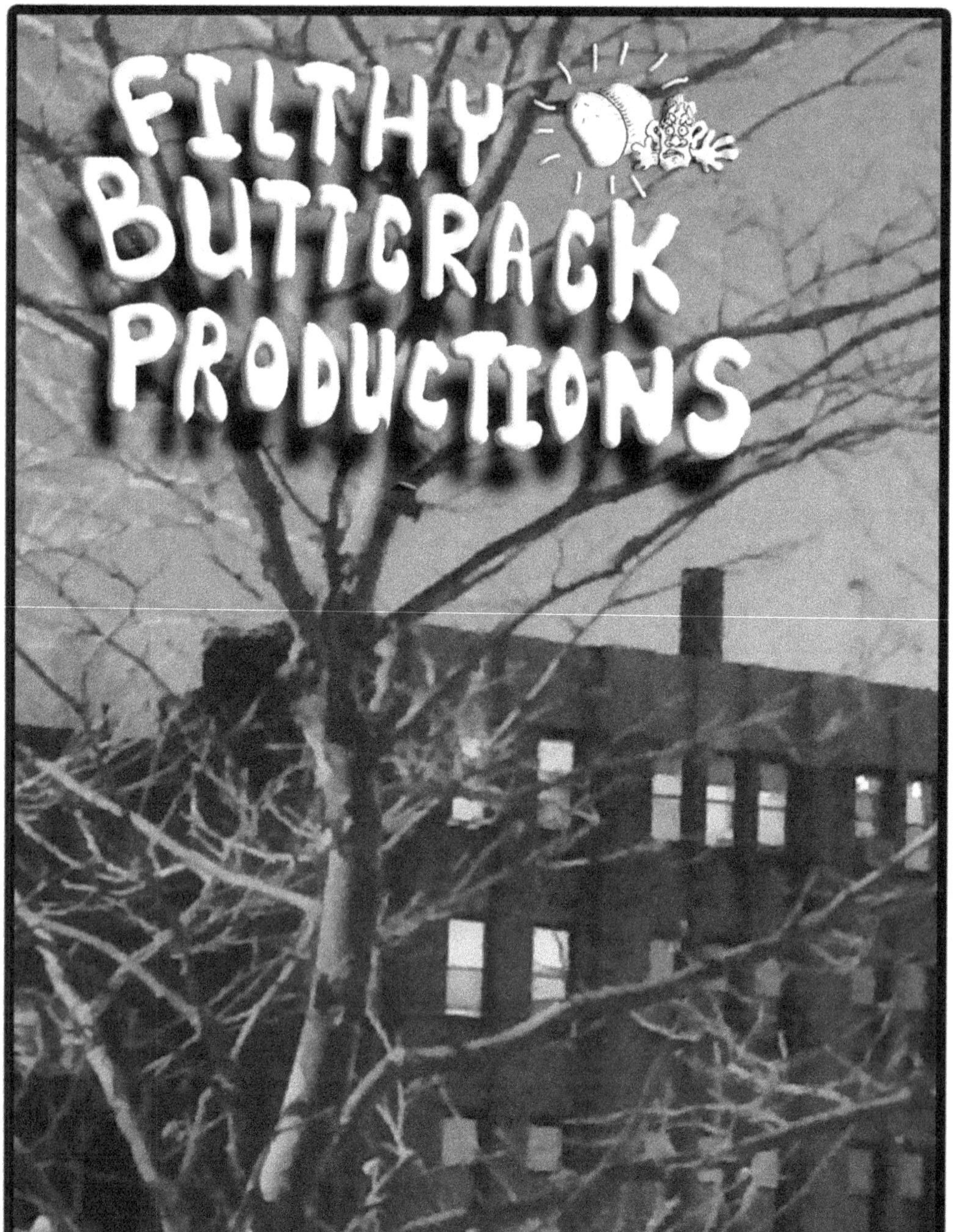
FILTHY
BUTTCRACK
PRODUCTIONS

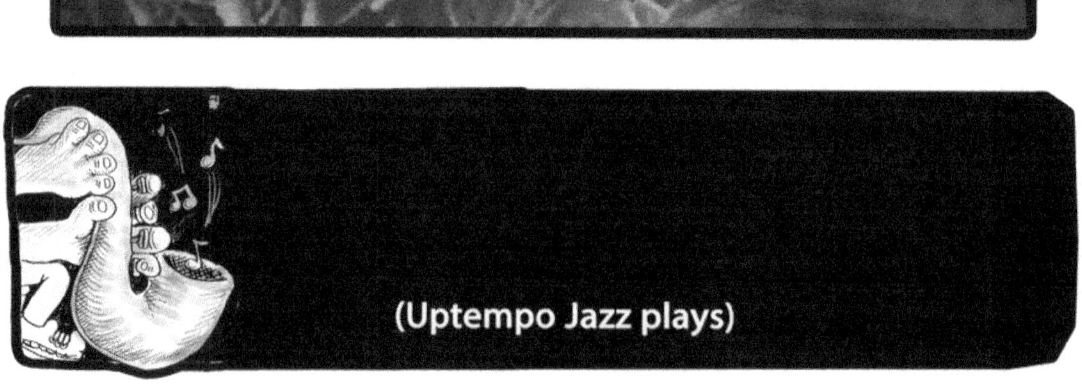
(Uptempo Jazz plays)

The ADVENTURES of WILD BERNIE

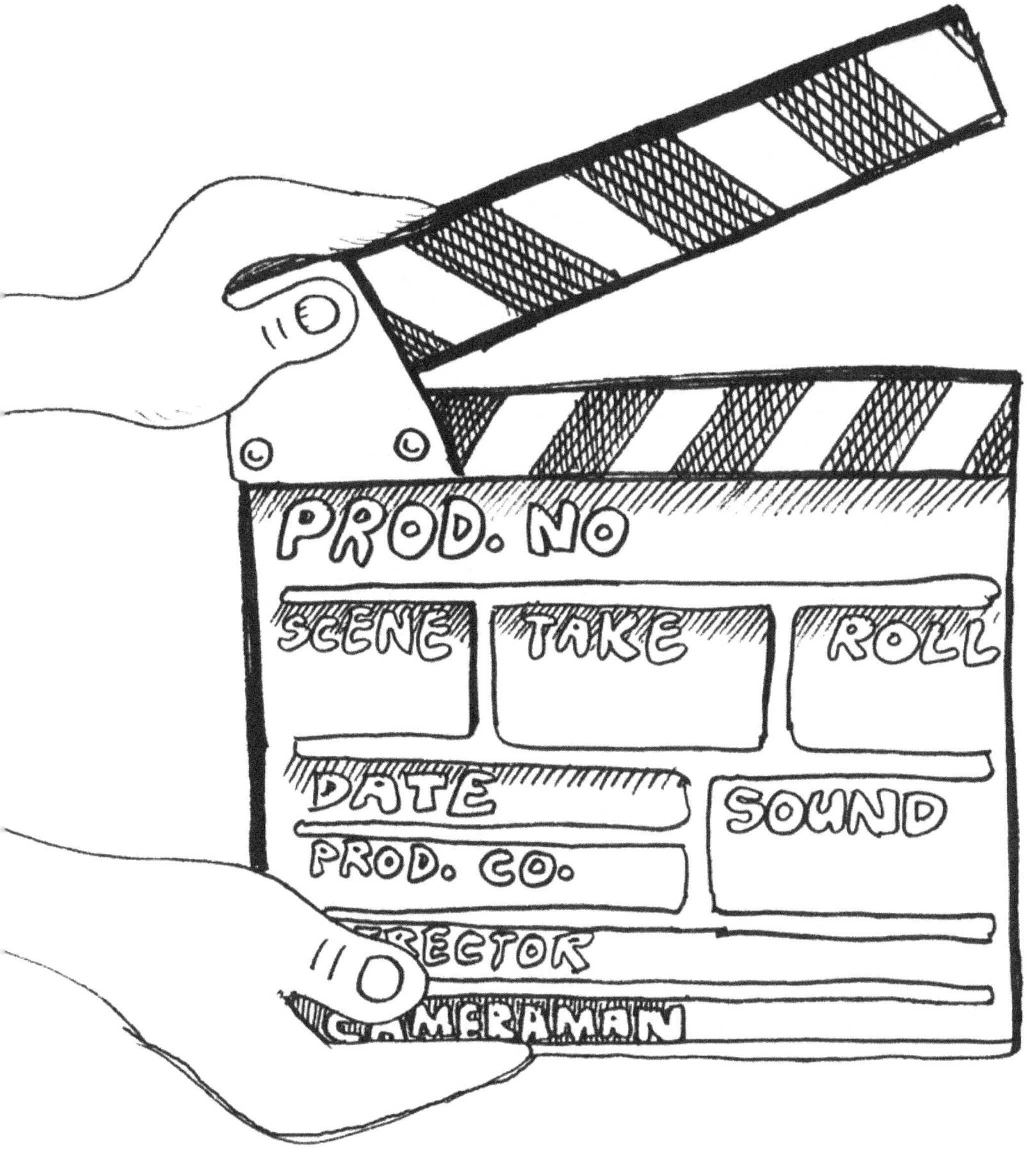

PROD. NO
SCENE
TAKE
ROLL
DATE
SOUND
PROD. CO.

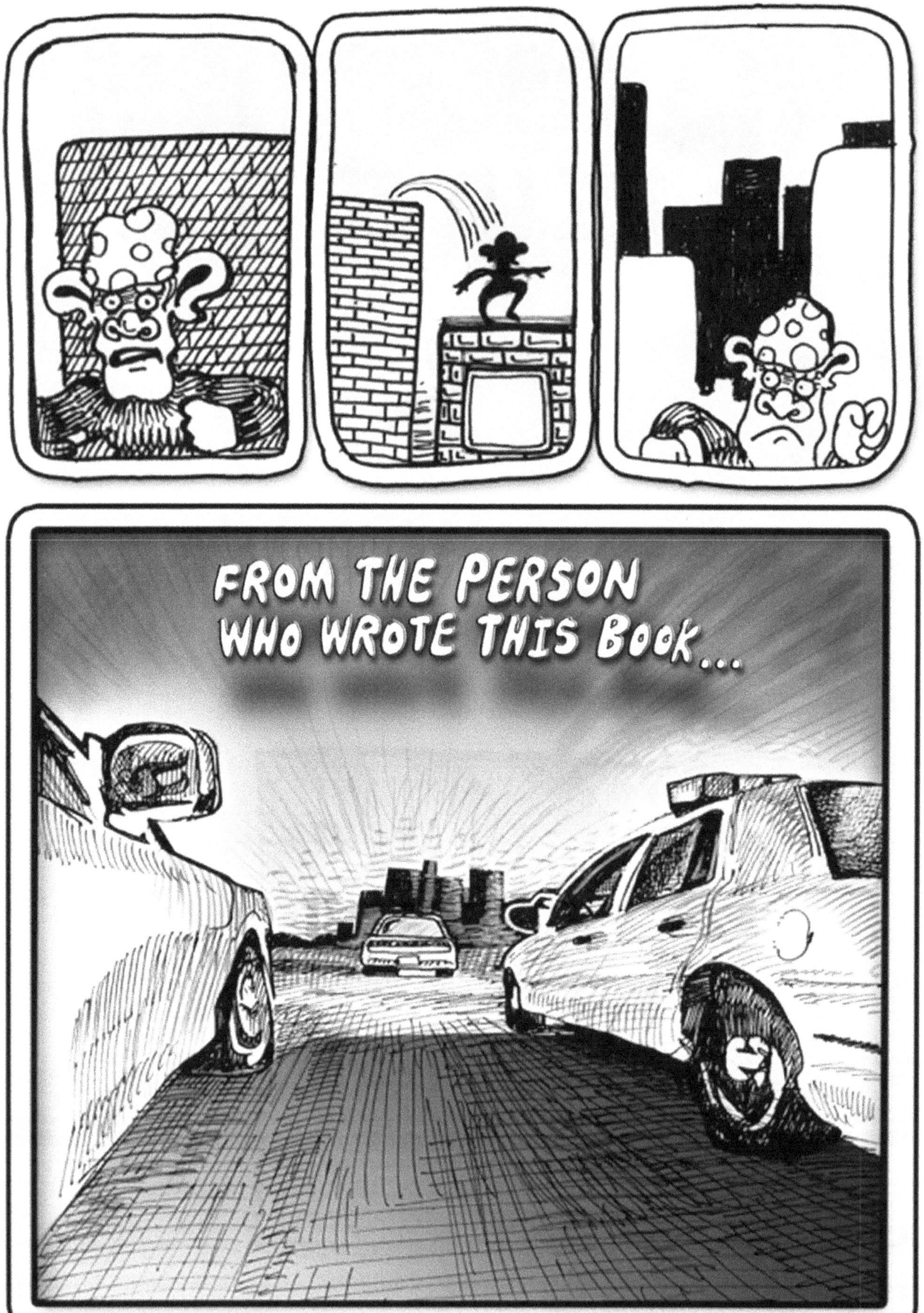
FROM THE PERSON
WHO WROTE THIS BOOK...

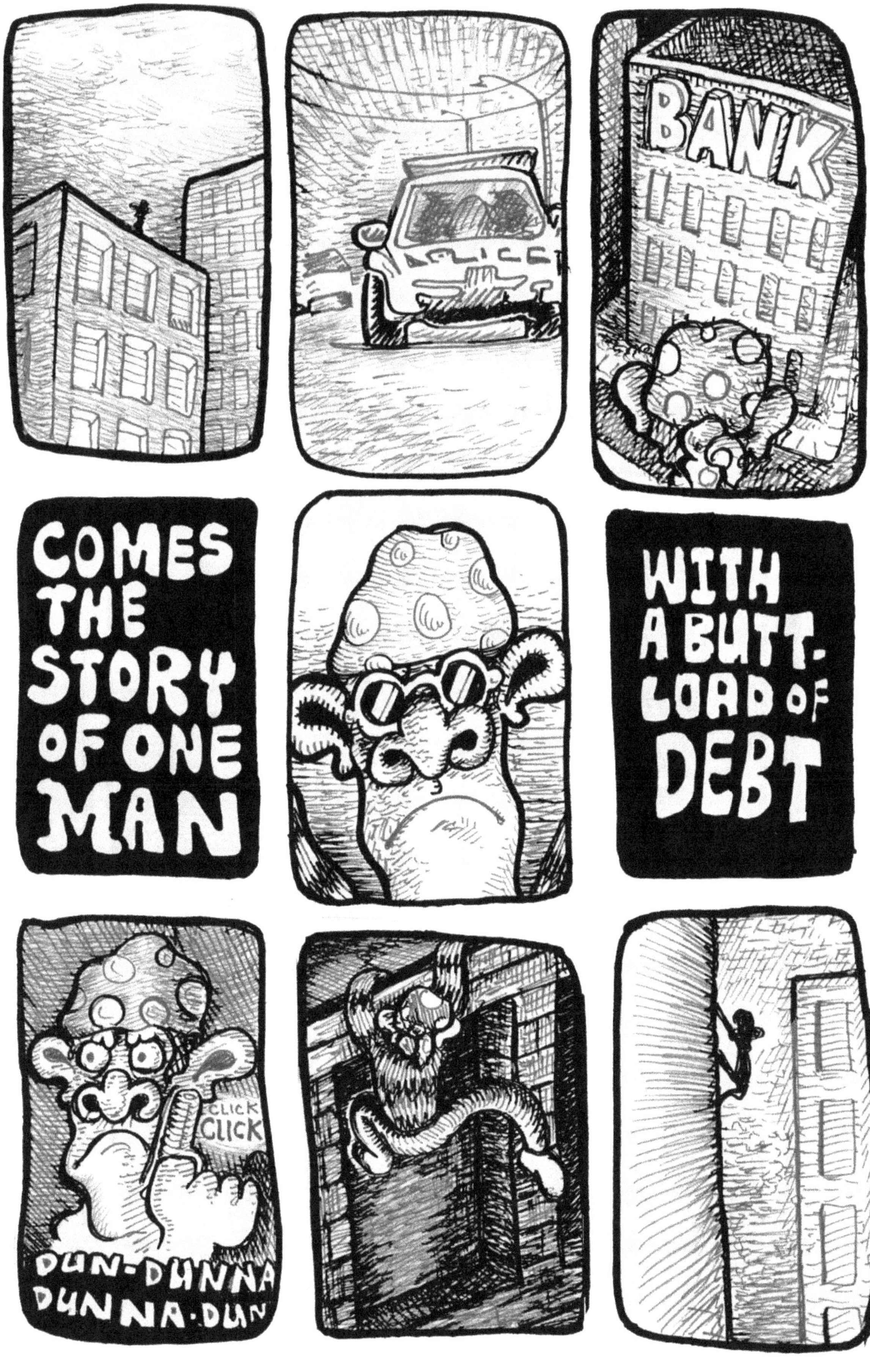
BANK
COMES THE STORY OF ONE MAN
WITH A BUTT-LOAD OF DEBT
CLICK
CLICK
DUN-DUNNA
DUNNA-DUN

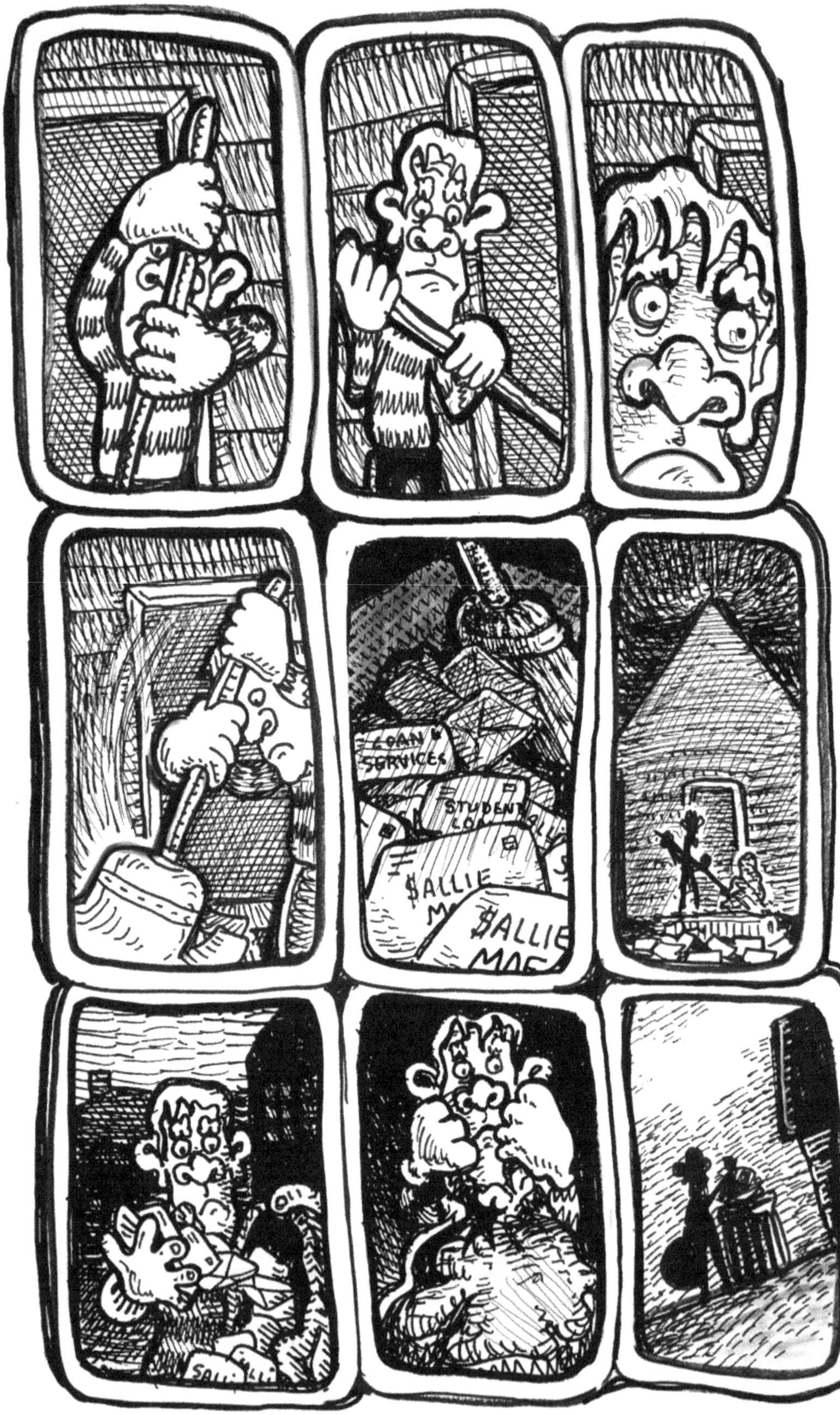
LOAN SERVICES
STUDENT
$ALLIE
$ALLIE

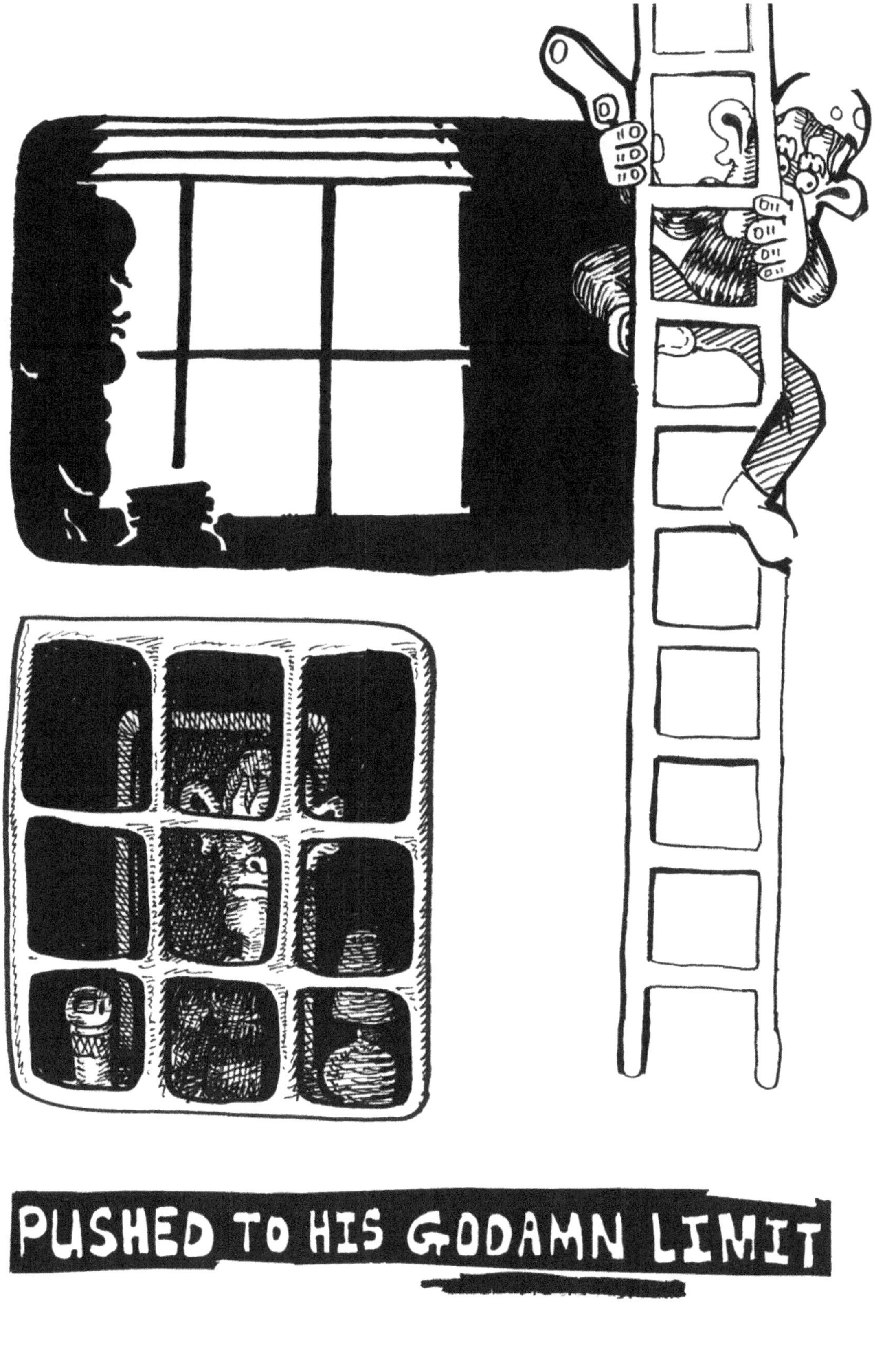
PUSHED TO HIS GODAMN LIMIT

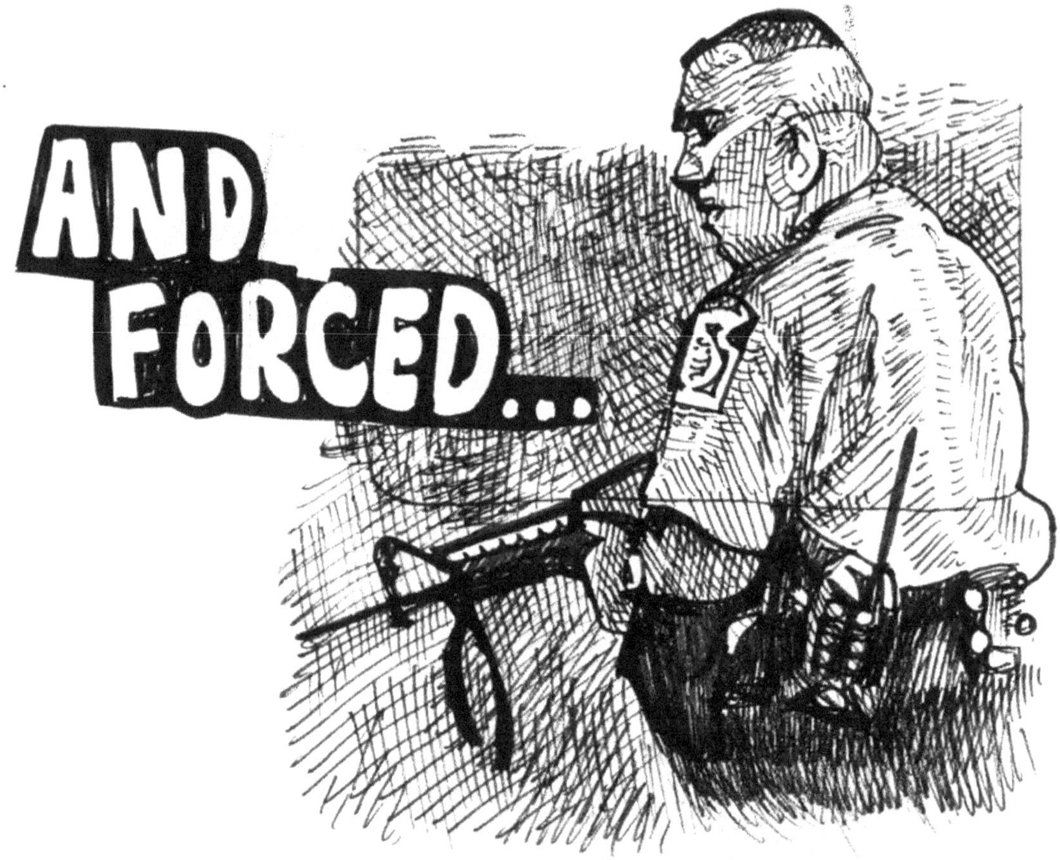
AND
FORCED...

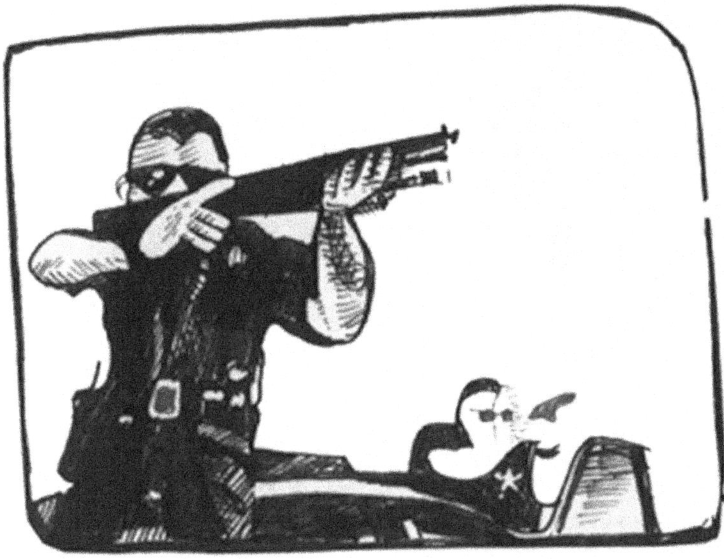

TO

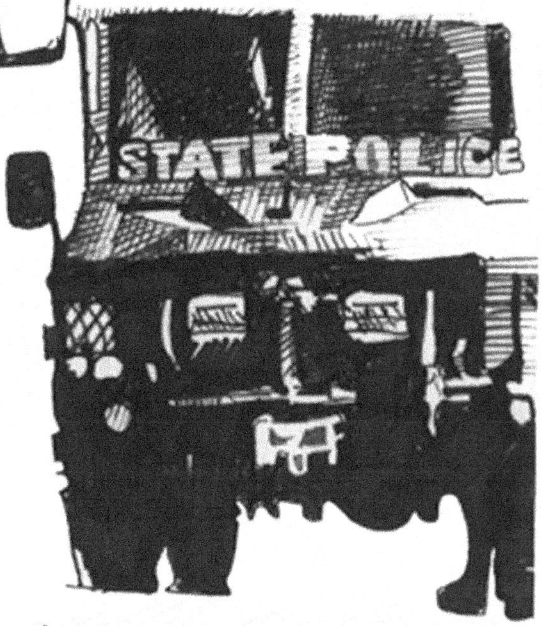
STATE POLICE

RUN

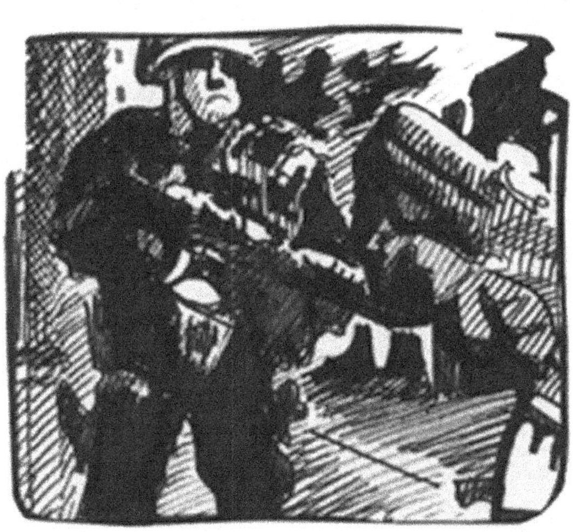

WILD!

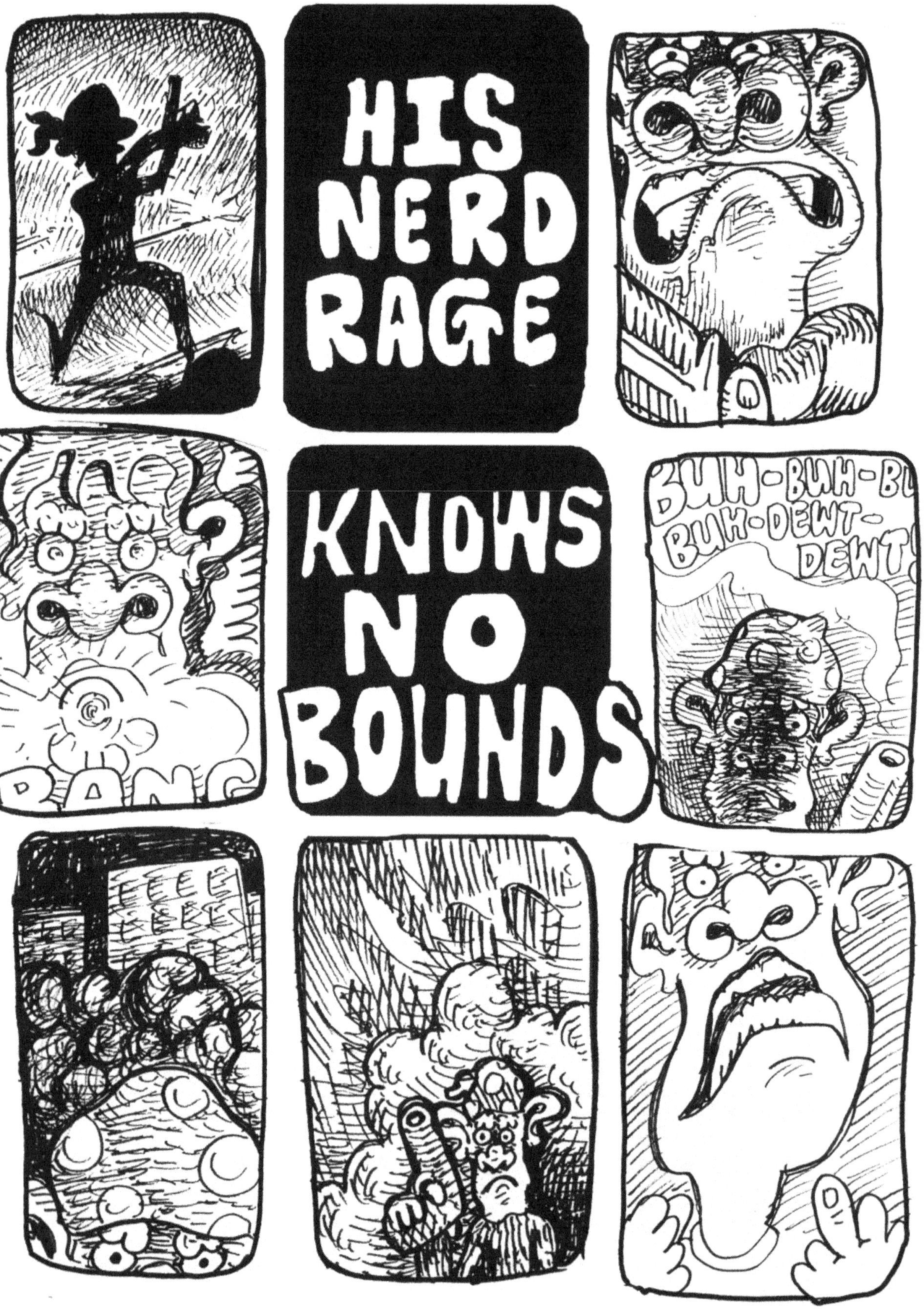
HIS NERD RAGE
BANG
KNOWS NO BOUNDS
BUH-BUH-BU
BUH-DEWT-
DEWT

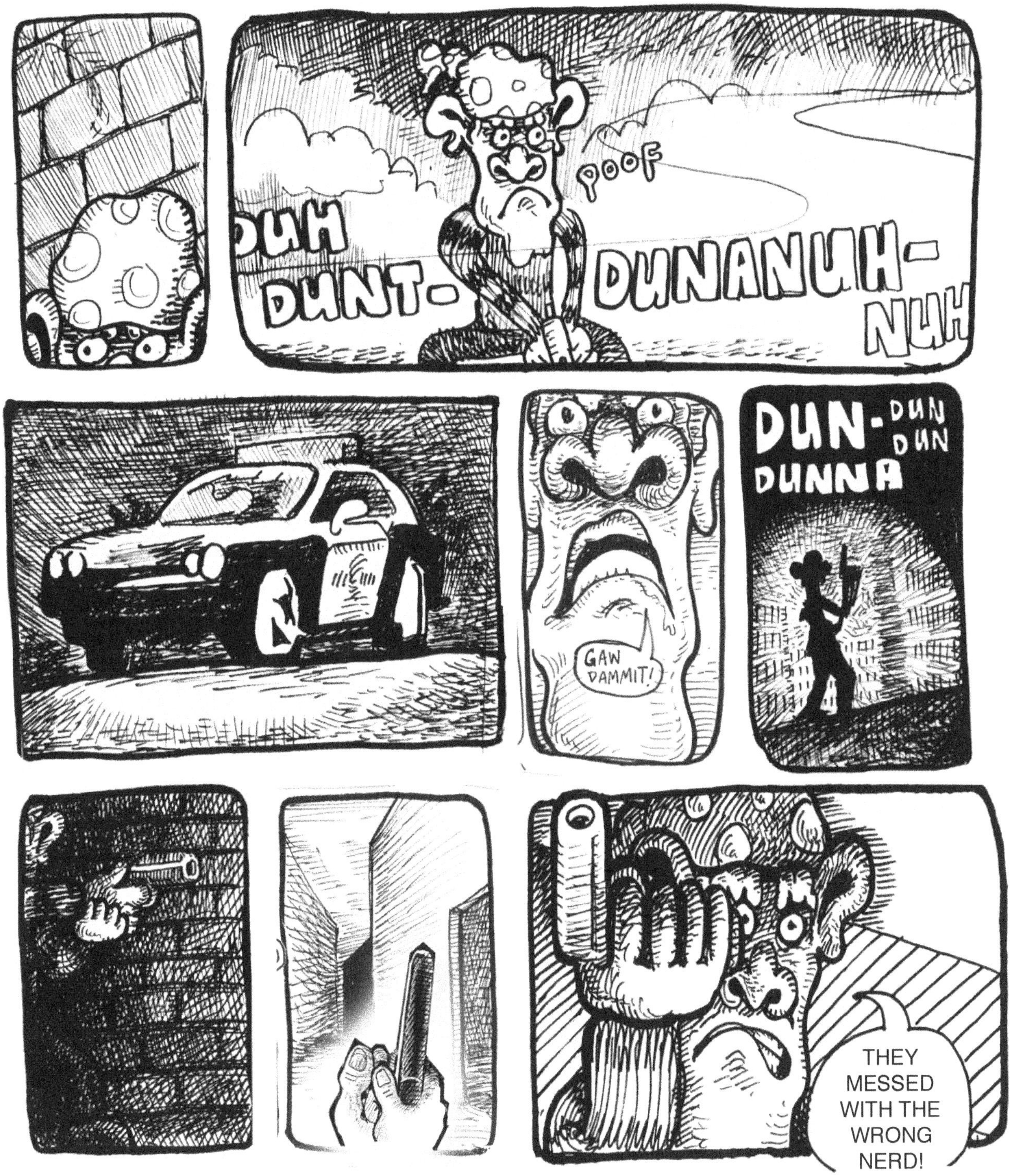
DUH DUNT-
DUNANUH-NUH
poof
DUN-DUN DUN DUNNA
GAW DAMMIT!
THEY MESSED WITH THE WRONG NERD!

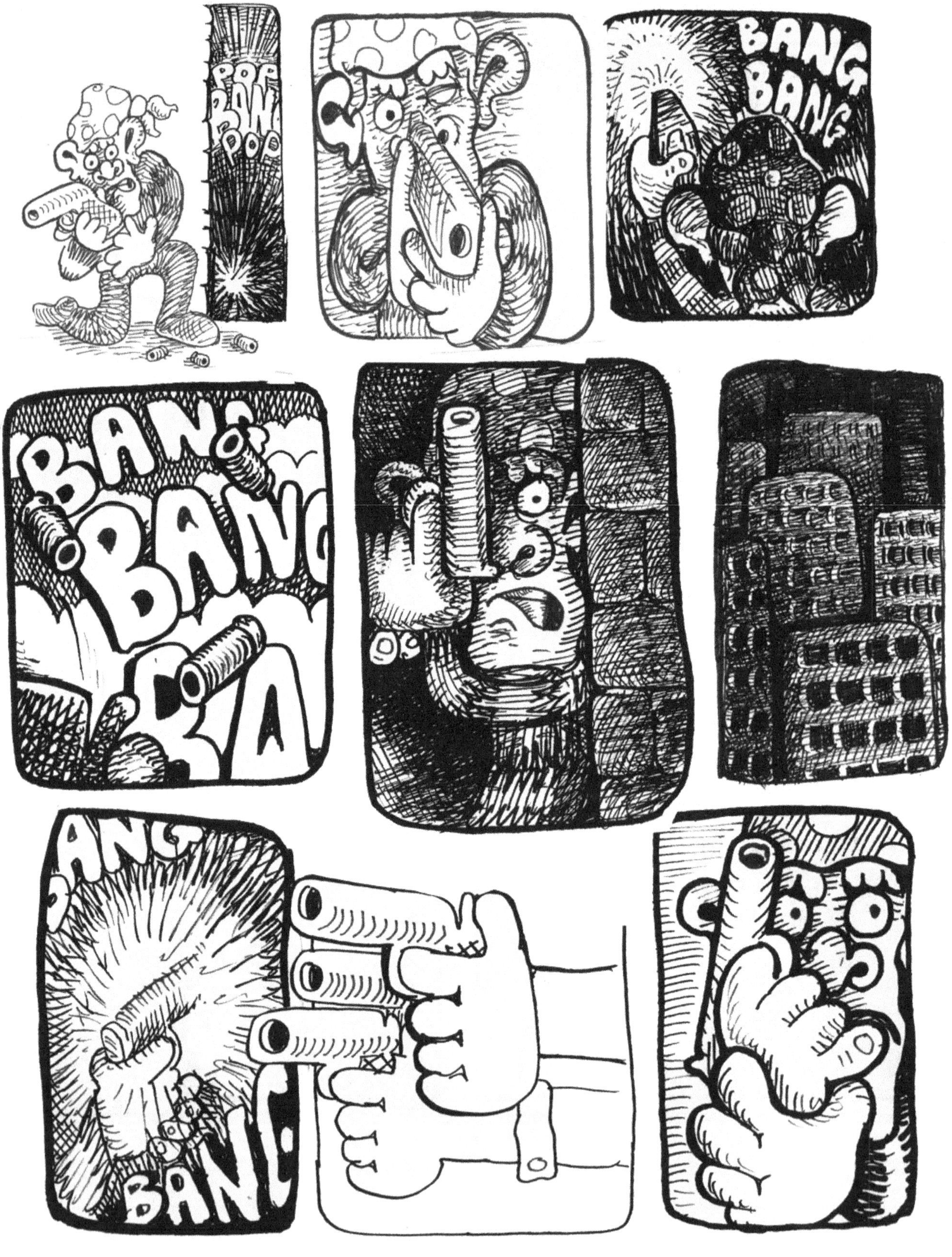
POP
BANG
POP
BANG
BANG
BANG
BANG

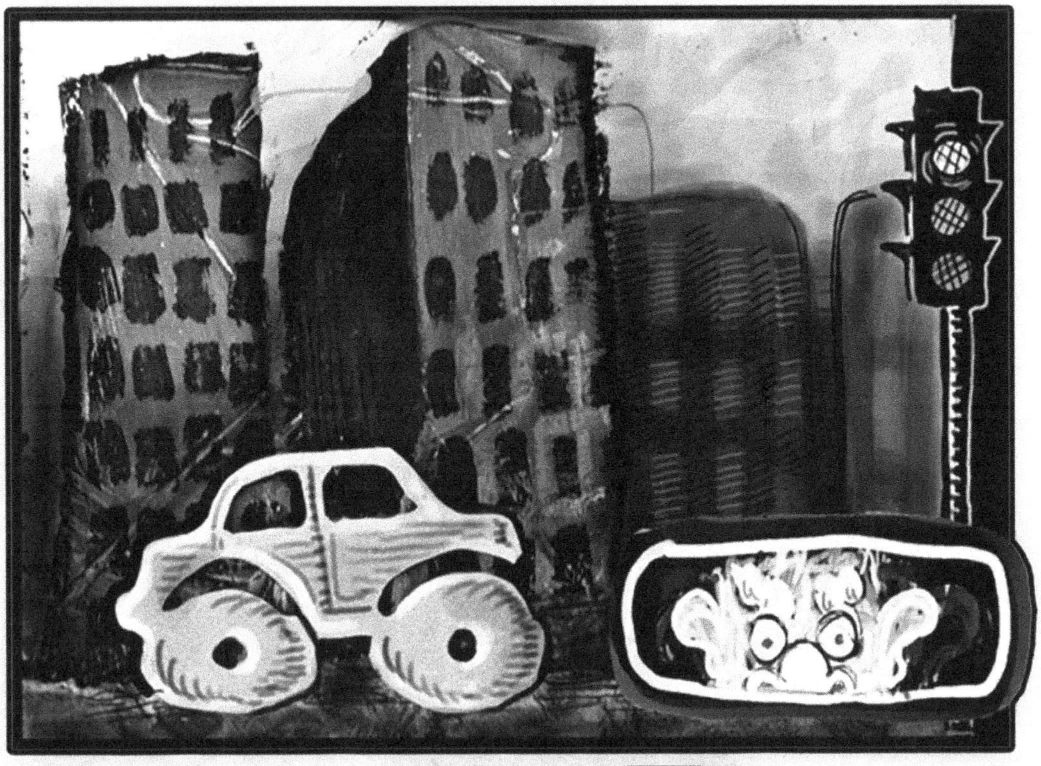

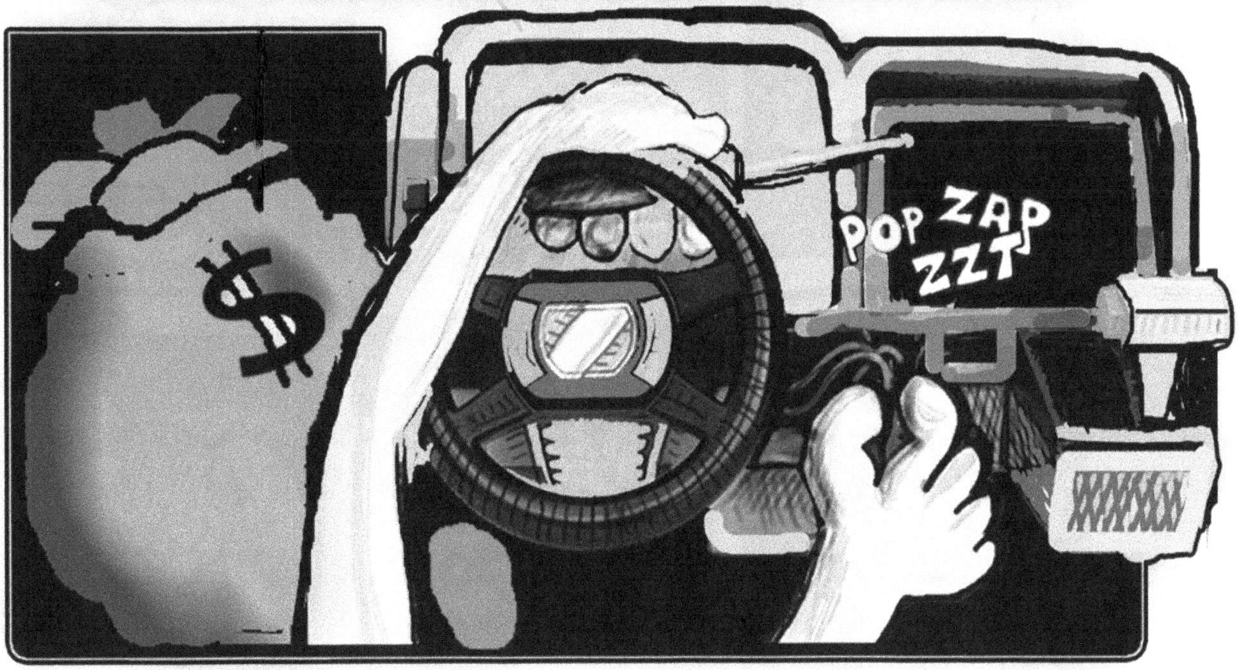
POP ZAP
ZZT

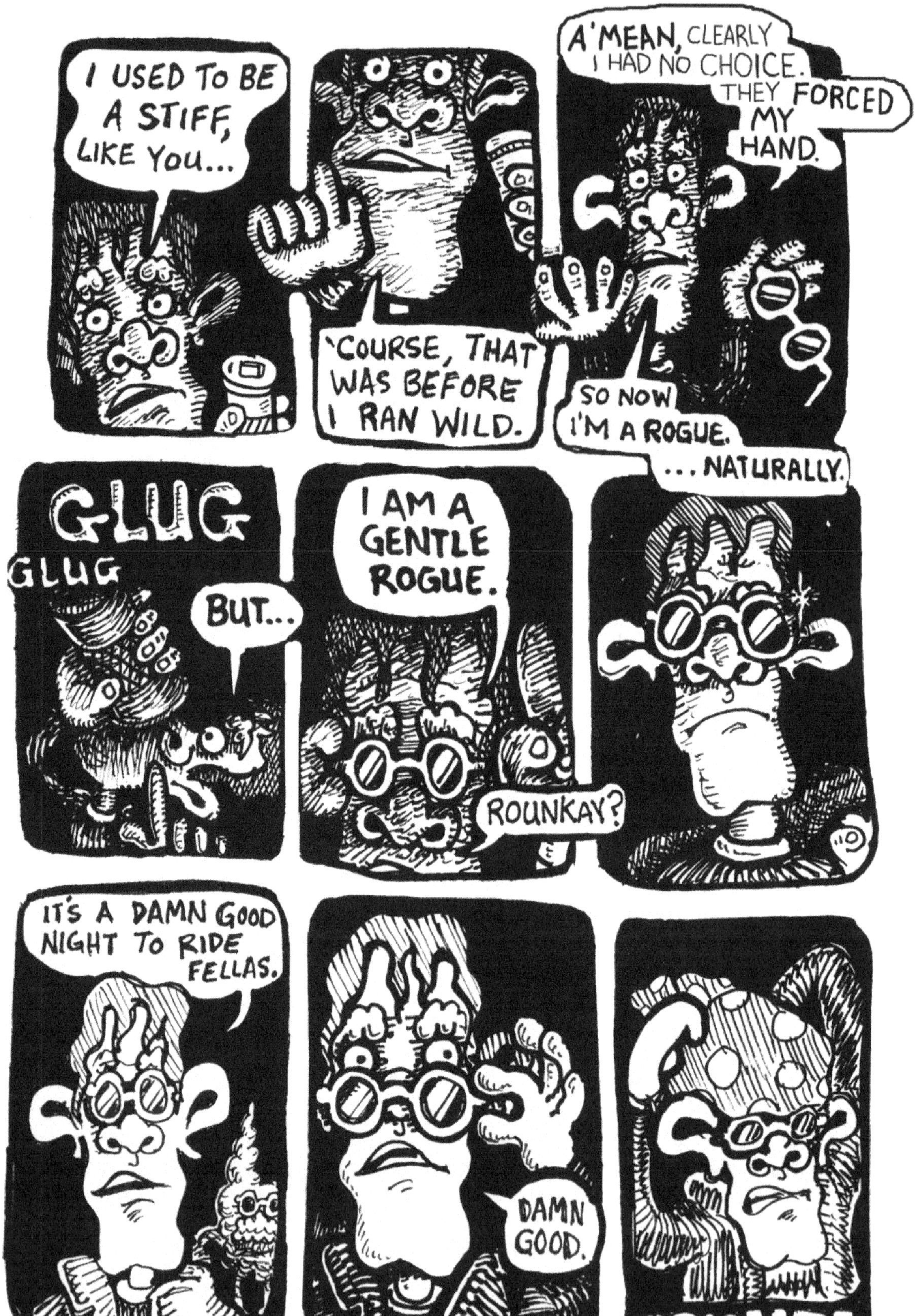
I USED TO BE A STIFF, LIKE YOU...
`COURSE, THAT WAS BEFORE I RAN WILD.
A'MEAN, CLEARLY I HAD NO CHOICE.
THEY FORCED MY HAND.
SO NOW I'M A ROGUE.
... NATURALLY.
GLUG
GLUG
BUT...
I AM A GENTLE ROGUE.
ROUNKAY?
IT'S A DAMN GOOD NIGHT TO RIDE FELLAS.
DAMN GOOD.
GRUNT!

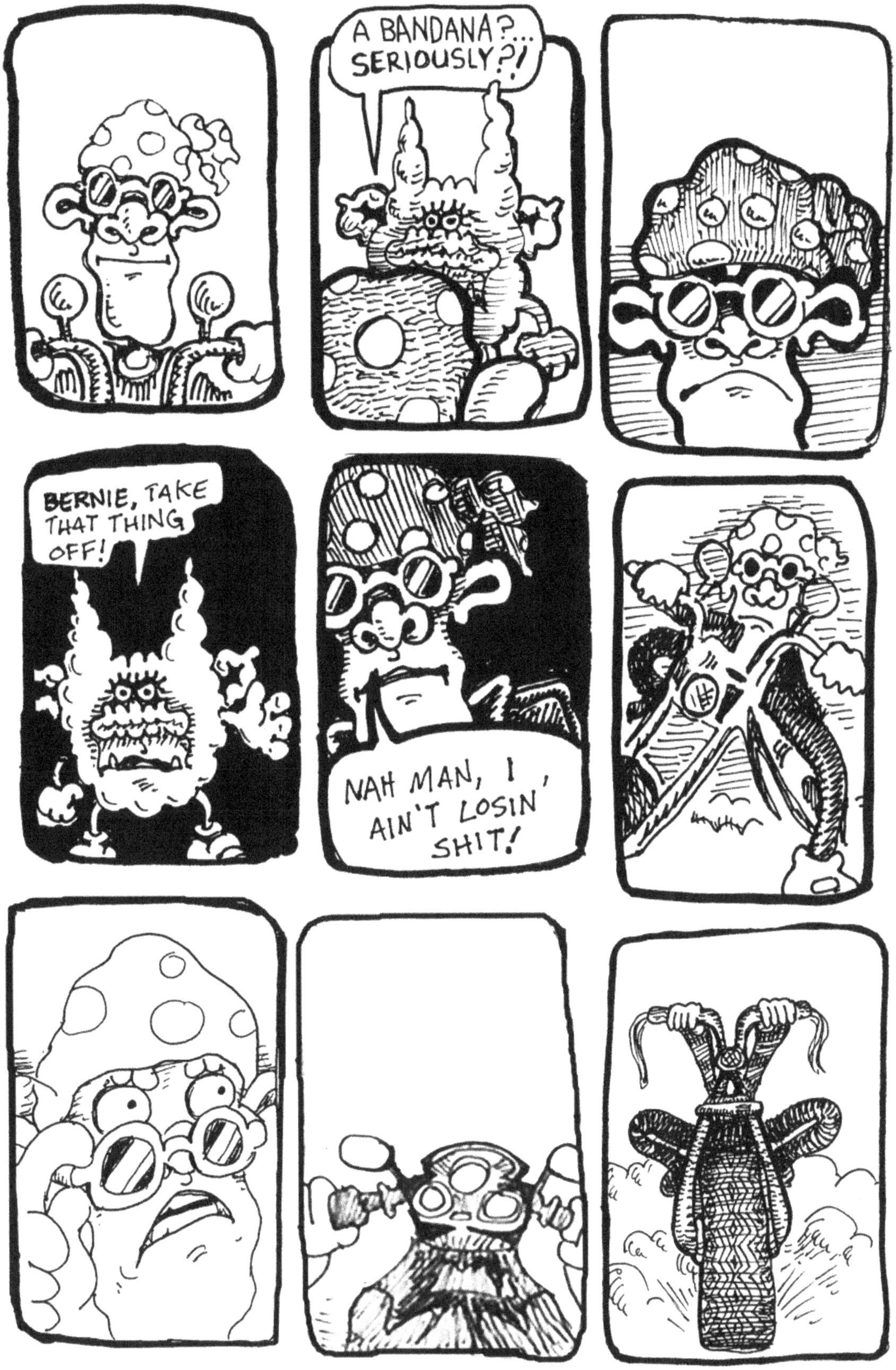
A BANDANA?... SERIOUSLY?!
BERNIE, TAKE THAT THING OFF!
NAH MAN, I AIN'T LOSIN' SHIT!

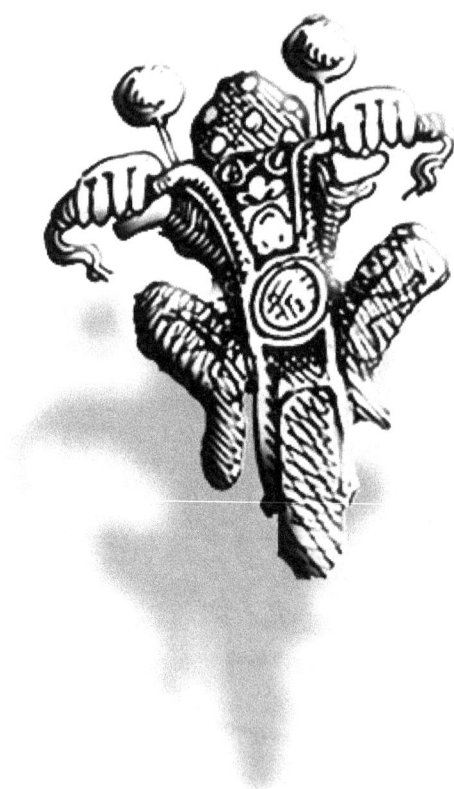

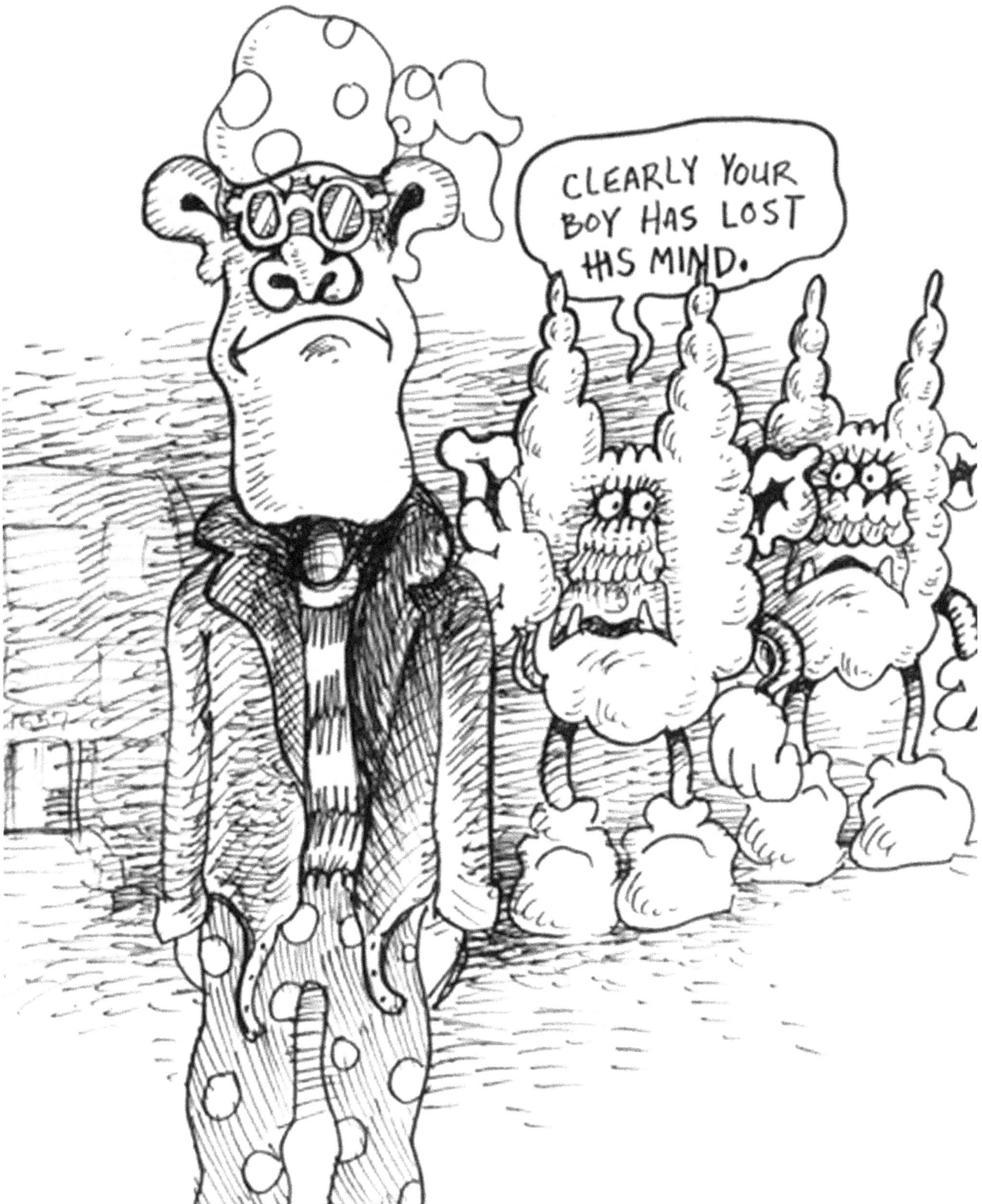
CLEARLY YOUR BOY HAS LOST HIS MIND.

UH-OH.
WE SHOULD KEEP HIM OUTTA SIGHT FOR A WHILE...
...I MEAN WE CAN'T HAVE HIM WALKIN' AROUND IN GIRLS' PAJAMAS AND FUCKIN SUNGLASSES!
WHY? I LIKE THE PAJAMAS.

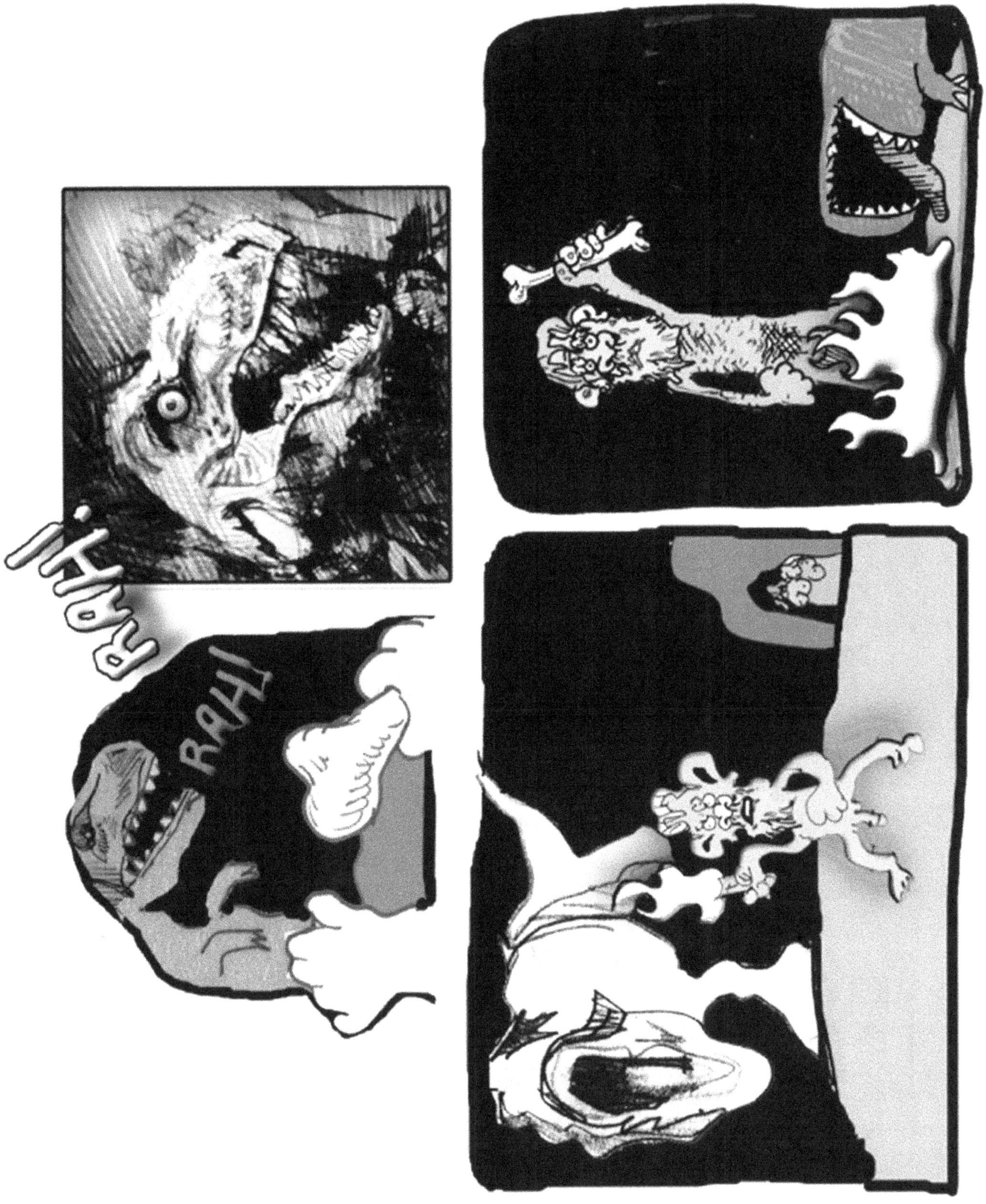
RAH!
RAAH!

GRANWOLF

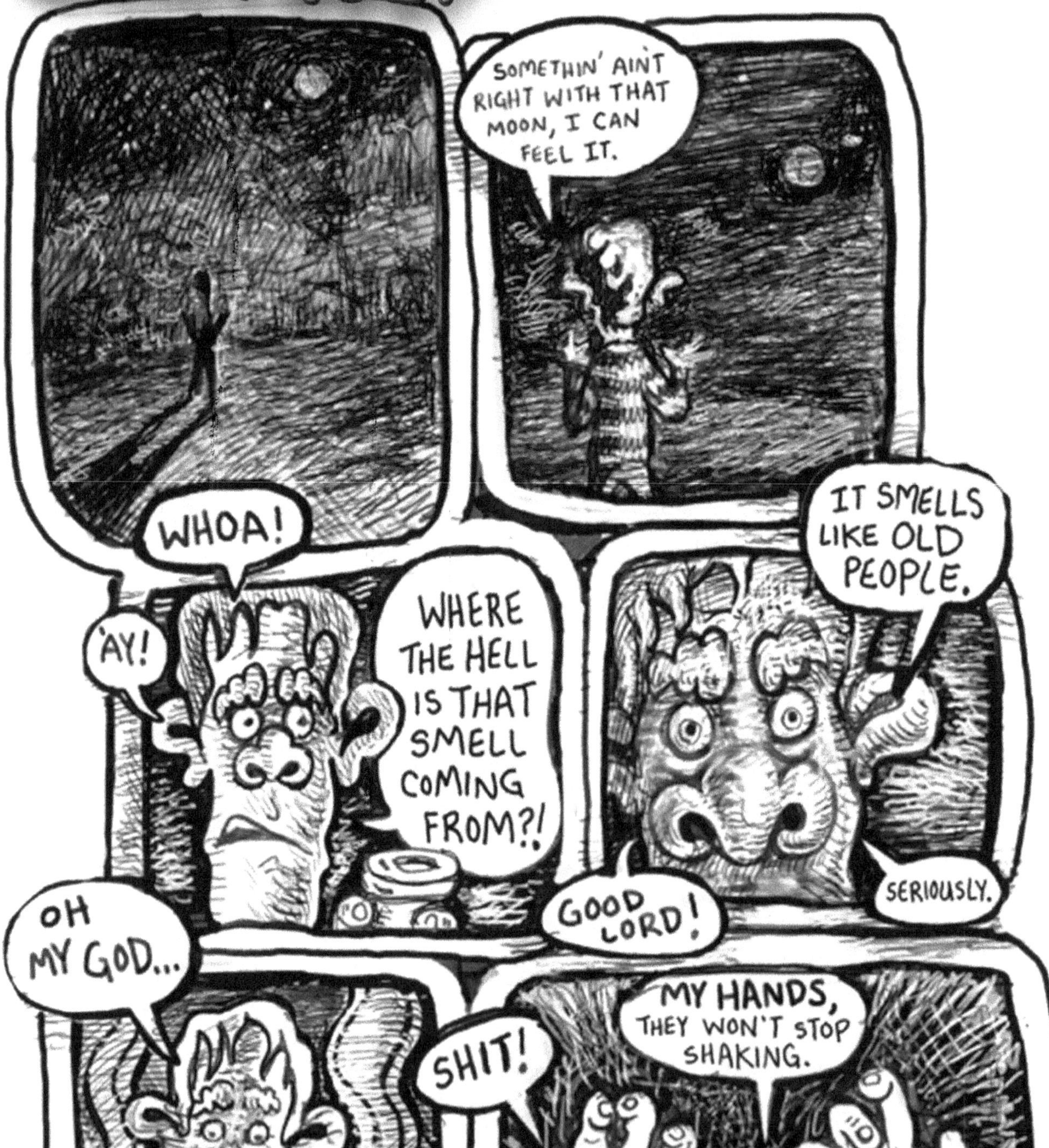

SOMETHIN' AIN'T RIGHT WITH THAT MOON, I CAN FEEL IT.
WHOA!
'AY!
WHERE THE HELL IS THAT SMELL COMING FROM?!
IT SMELLS LIKE OLD PEOPLE.
GOOD LORD!
SERIOUSLY.
OH MY GOD...
IS THAT... ME?!
SHIT!
MY HANDS, THEY WON'T STOP SHAKING.

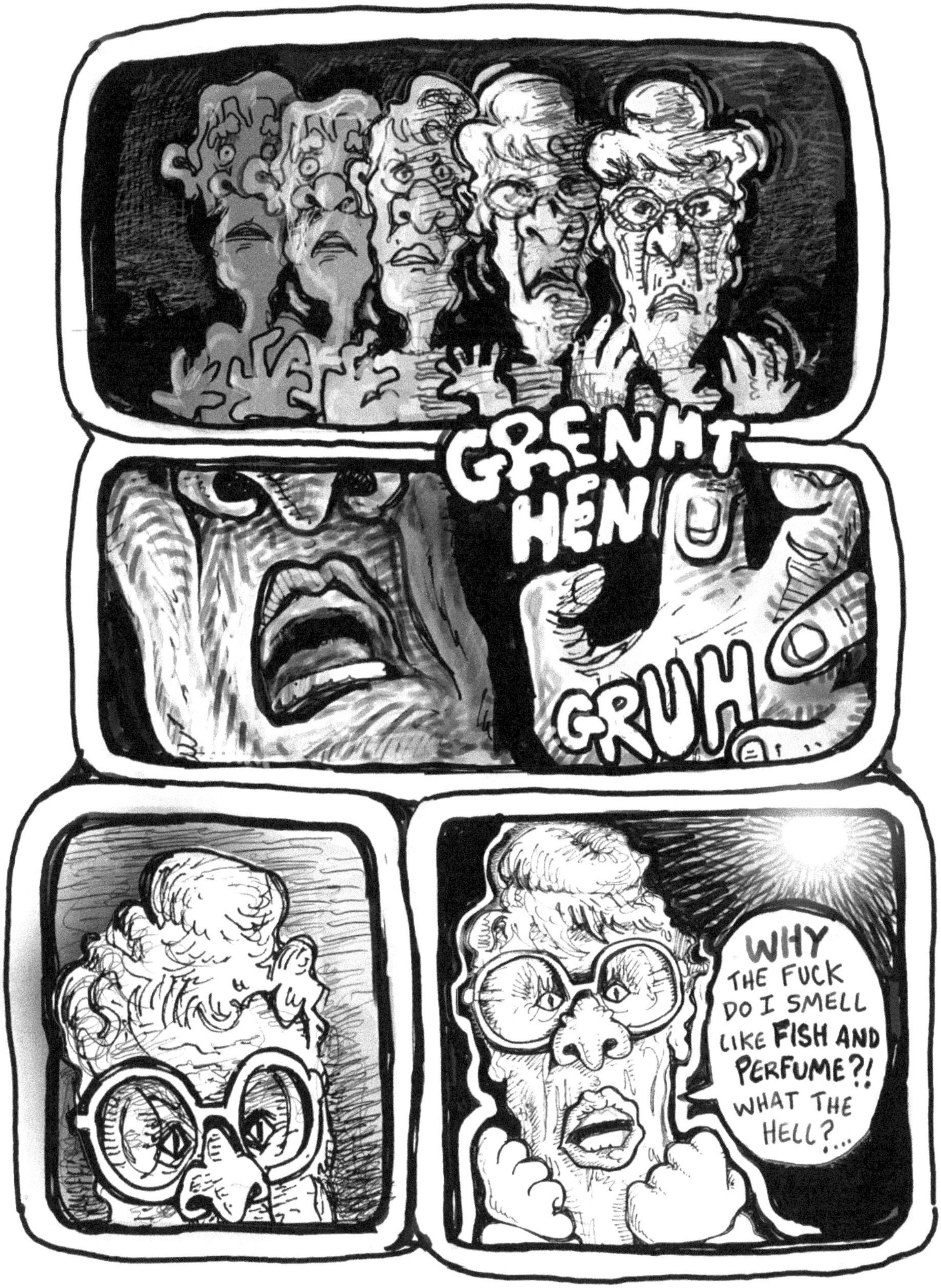
GRENHT HEN
GRUH
WHY THE FUCK DO I SMELL LIKE FISH AND PERFUME?! WHAT THE HELL?...

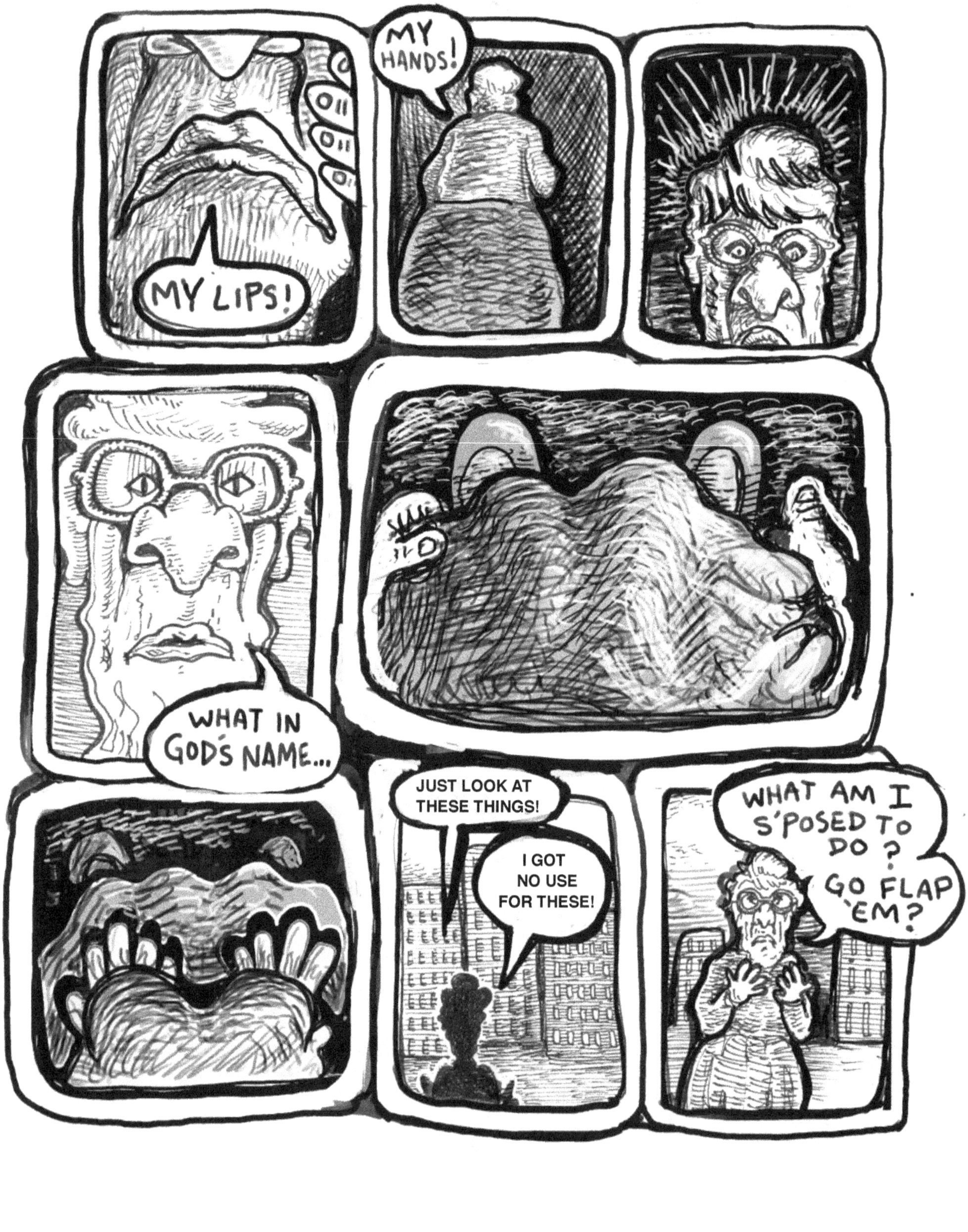
MY LIPS!
MY HANDS!
WHAT IN GOD'S NAME...
JUST LOOK AT THESE THINGS!
I GOT NO USE FOR THESE!
WHAT AM I S'POSED TO DO ?
GO FLAP 'EM?

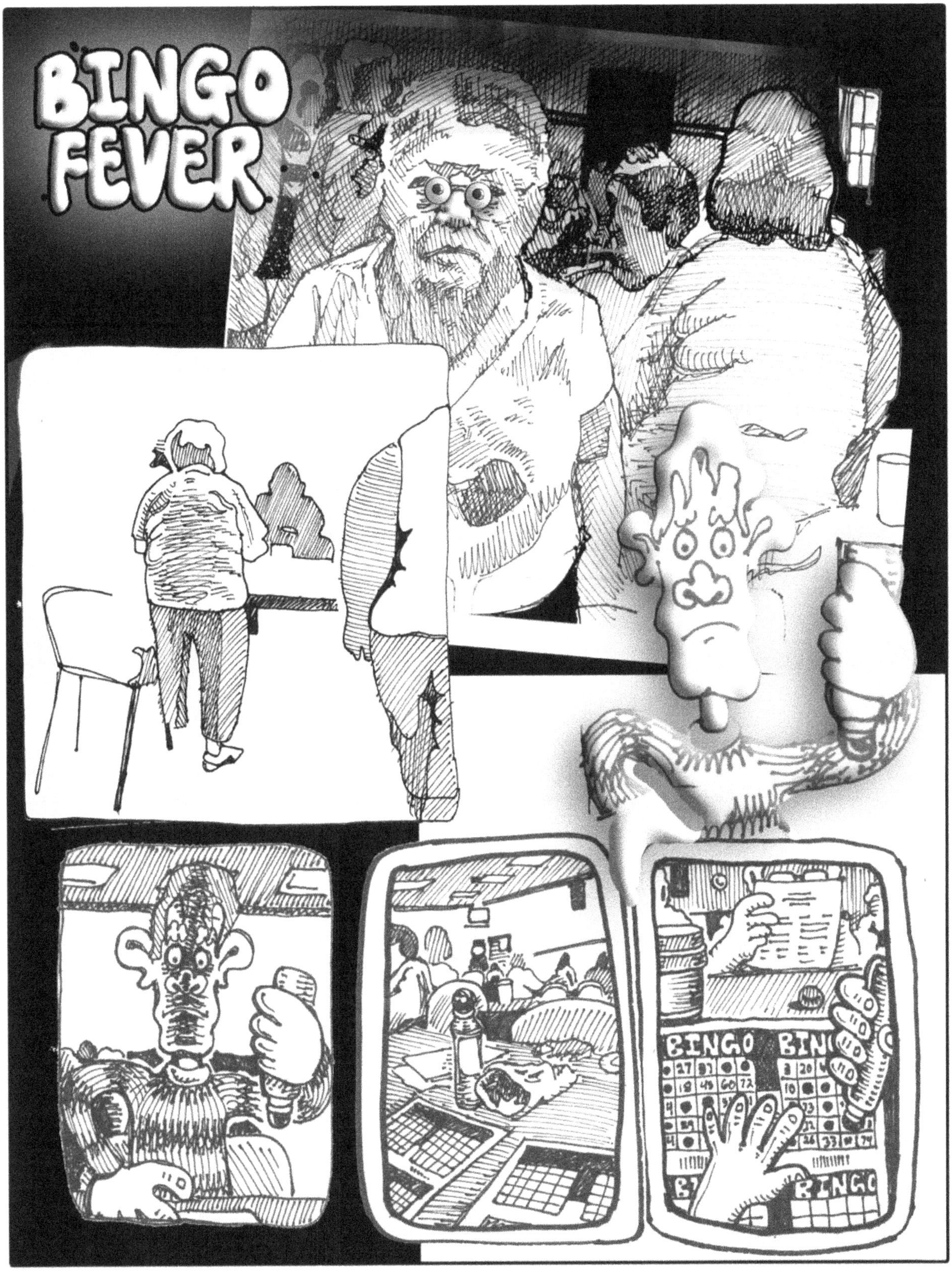
BINGO FEVER
BINGO
BIN
BINGO

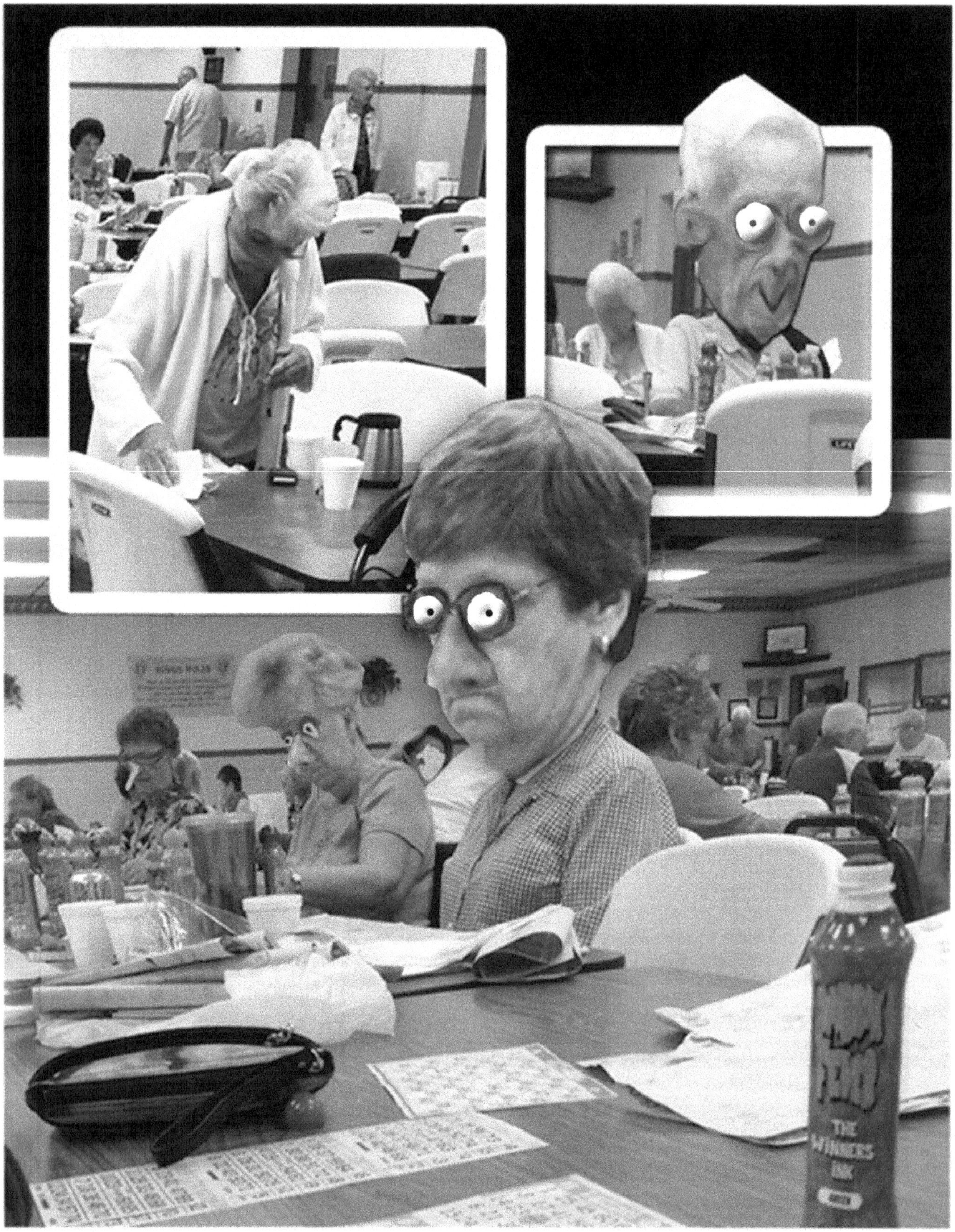
THE
WINNERS
INK

ON HOLD

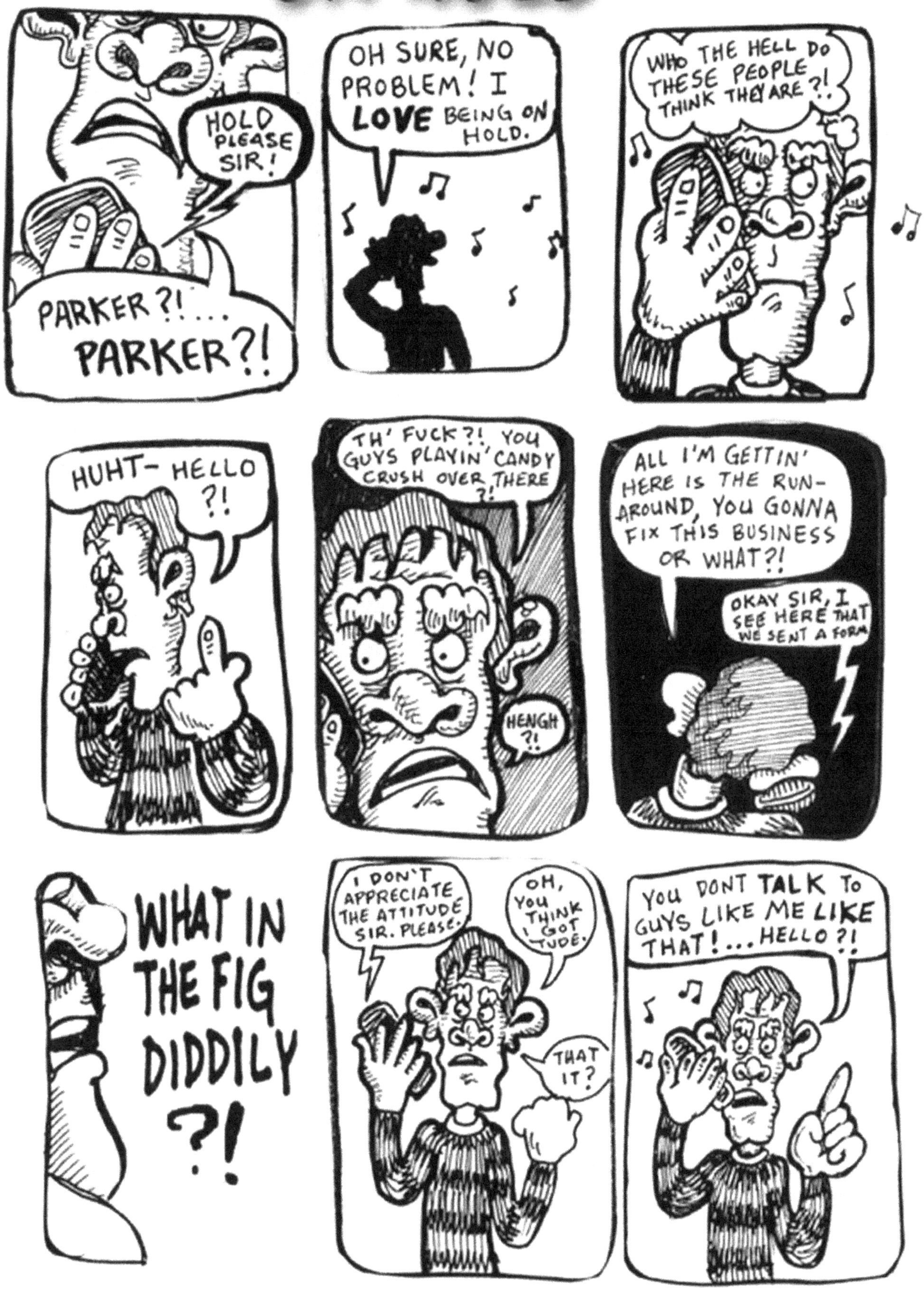
HOLD PLEASE SIR!
PARKER?!.... PARKER?!
OH SURE, NO PROBLEM! I LOVE BEING ON HOLD.
WHO THE HELL DO THESE PEOPLE THINK THEY ARE?!
HUHT- HELLO ?!
TH' FUCK?! YOU GUYS PLAYIN' CANDY CRUSH OVER THERE ?!
HENGH ?!
ALL I'M GETTIN' HERE IS THE RUN-AROUND, YOU GONNA FIX THIS BUSINESS OR WHAT?!
OKAY SIR, I SEE HERE THAT WE SENT A FORM
WHAT IN THE FIG DIDDILY ?!
I DON'T APPRECIATE THE ATTITUDE SIR. PLEASE.
OH, YOU THINK I GOT TUDE.
THAT IT?
YOU DONT TALK TO GUYS LIKE ME LIKE THAT!... HELLO?!

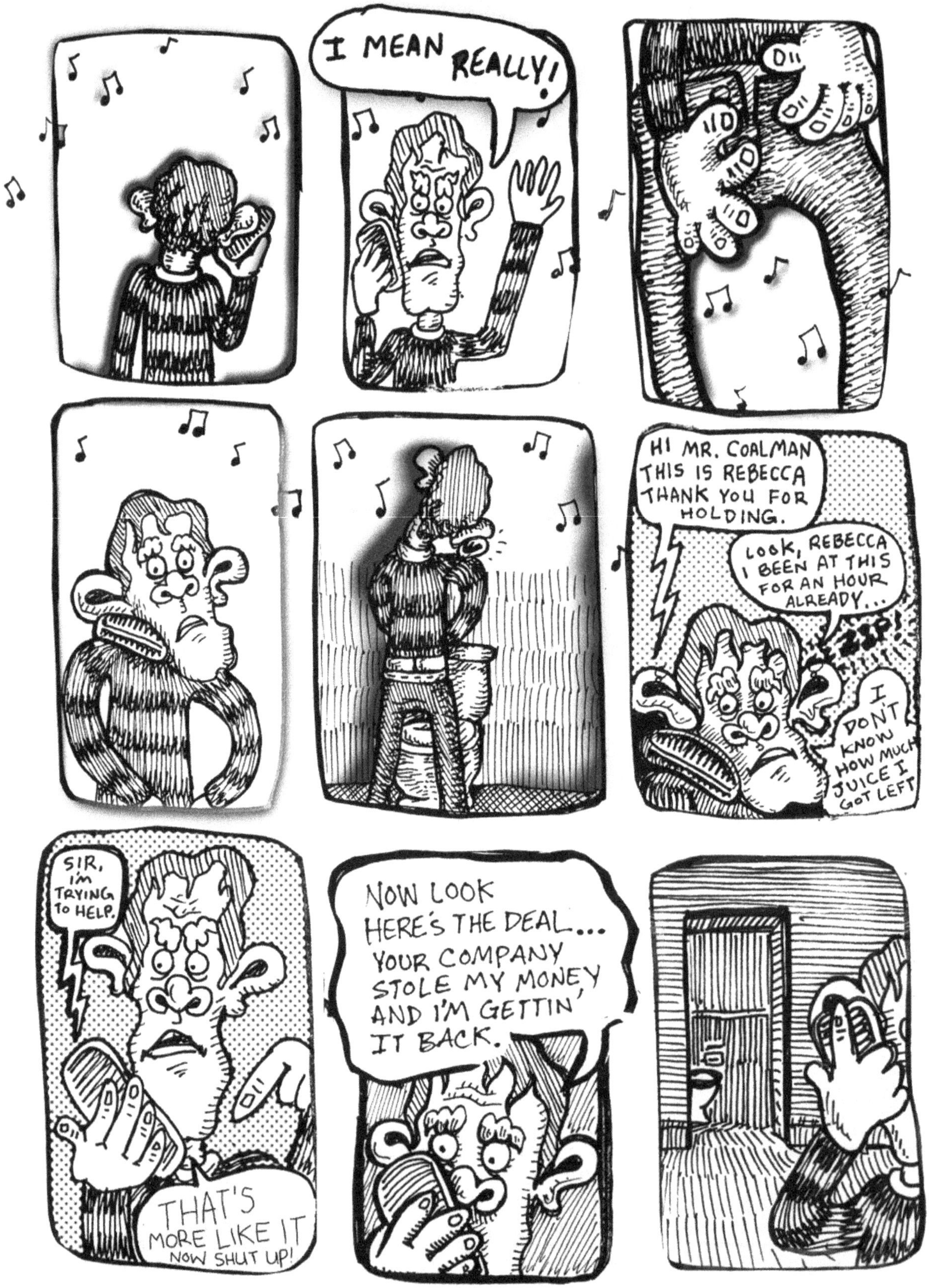
I MEAN REALLY!
HI MR. COALMAN THIS IS REBECCA THANK YOU FOR HOLDING.
LOOK, REBECCA I BEEN AT THIS FOR AN HOUR ALREADY...
ZZP!
I DON'T KNOW HOW MUCH JUICE I GOT LEFT
SIR, I'M TRYING TO HELP.
THAT'S MORE LIKE IT NOW SHUT UP!
NOW LOOK HERE'S THE DEAL... YOUR COMPANY STOLE MY MONEY AND I'M GETTIN' IT BACK.

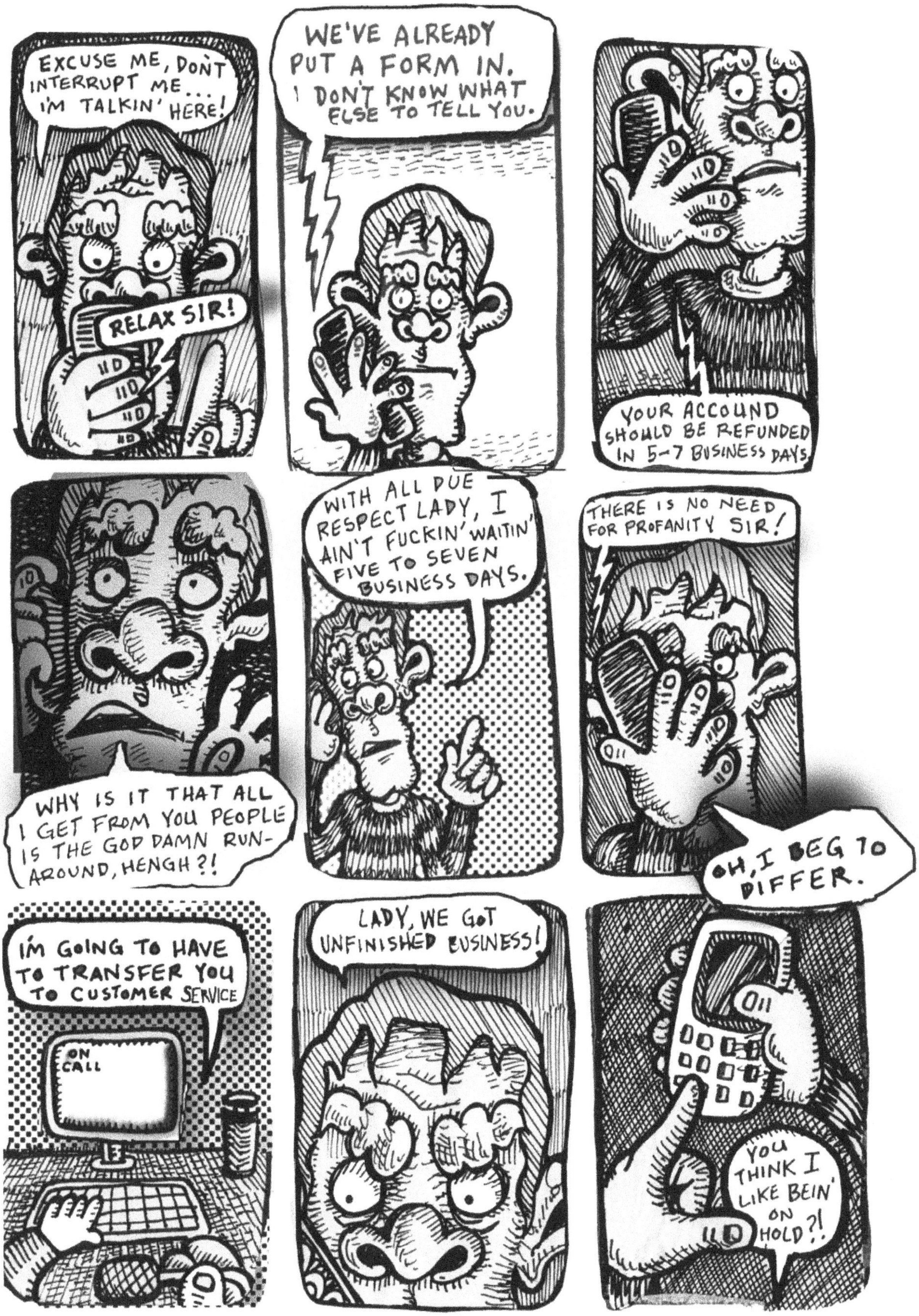
EXCUSE ME, DON'T INTERRUPT ME... I'M TALKIN' HERE!
RELAX SIR!
WE'VE ALREADY PUT A FORM IN. I DON'T KNOW WHAT ELSE TO TELL YOU.
YOUR ACCOUND SHOULD BE REFUNDED IN 5-7 BUSINESS DAYS
WHY IS IT THAT ALL I GET FROM YOU PEOPLE IS THE GOD DAMN RUN-AROUND, HENGH?!
WITH ALL DUE RESPECT LADY, I AIN'T FUCKIN' WAITIN' FIVE TO SEVEN BUSINESS DAYS.
THERE IS NO NEED FOR PROFANITY SIR!
OH, I BEG TO DIFFER.
I'M GOING TO HAVE TO TRANSFER YOU TO CUSTOMER SERVICE
ON CALL
LADY, WE GOT UNFINISHED BUSINESS!
YOU THINK I LIKE BEIN' ON HOLD?!

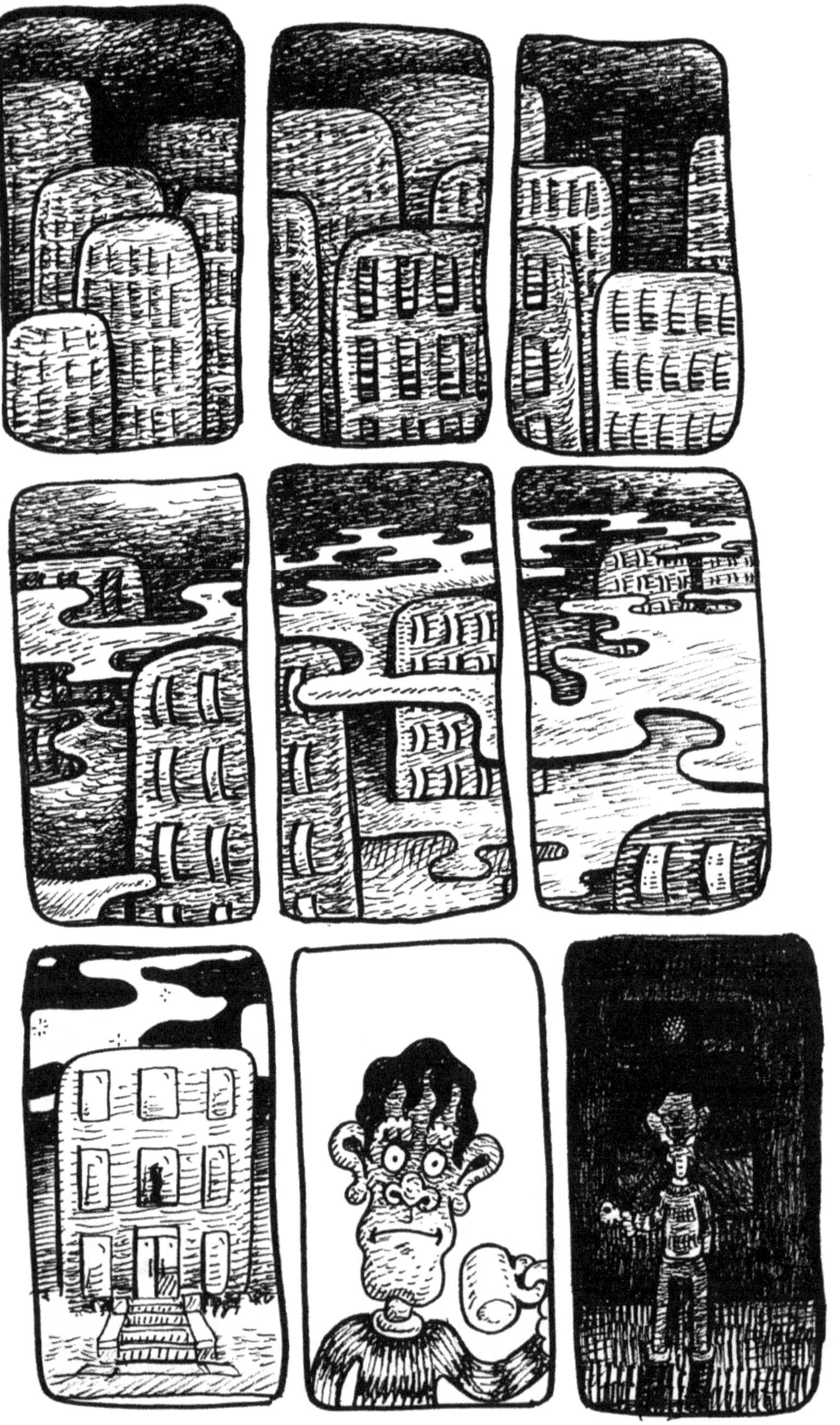

ARG!
IF I CAN'T, JOIN EM I'LL BEAT EM!

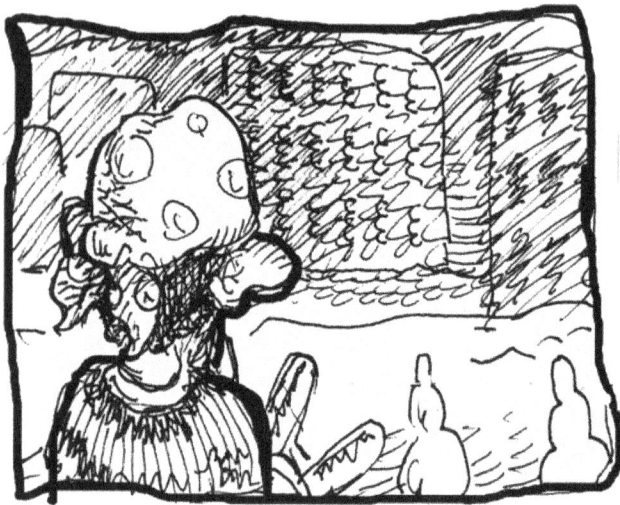

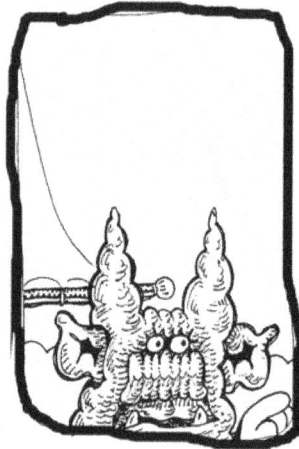

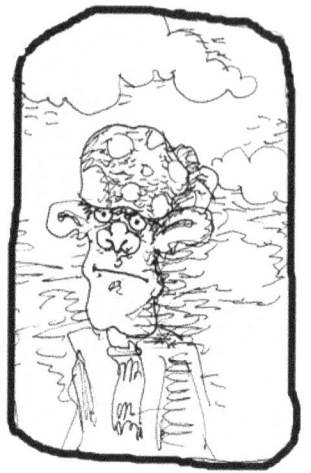

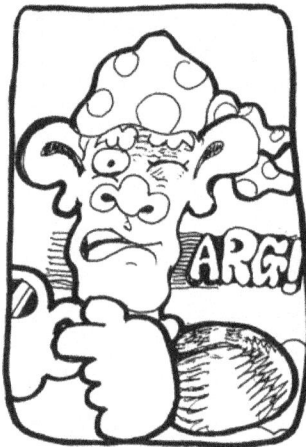

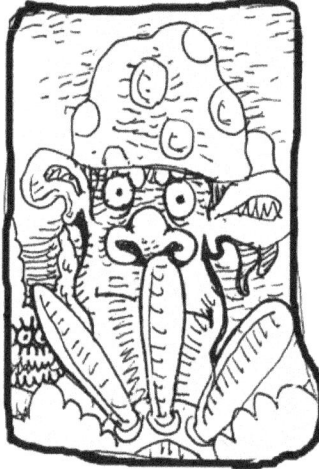

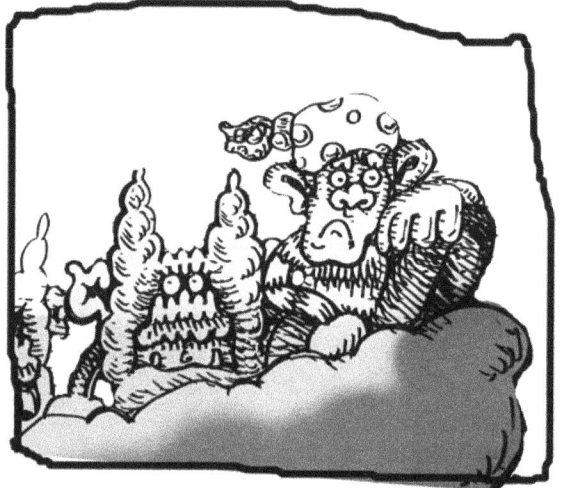

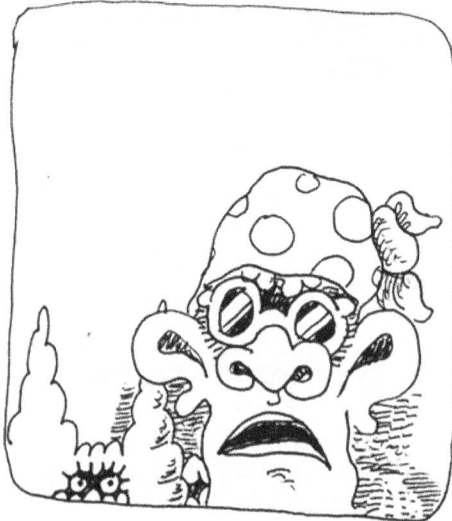

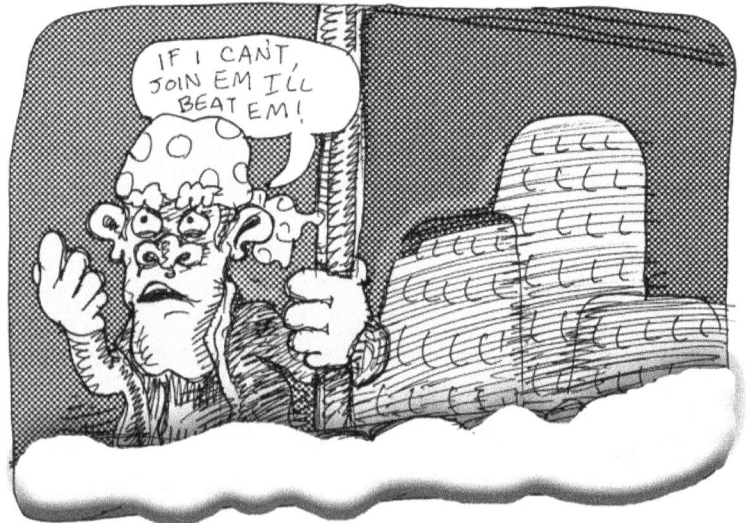

LOST AND FOUND

Panel 1: LAST STOP SIR. PLEASE EXIT THE BUS.

SOMEONE MUST'VE FORGOT THEIR GLASSES. WHAT A SHAME TOO...

Panel 2: IT'S PROLLY RARE FOR A NERD OF MY CALLIBER TO RESORT TO THIS BUT...

Panel 3: I'LL TAKE 'EM!

LORD KNOWS I COULD SURE USE 'EM!

Panel 4: THESE ARE SOME HI-STRENGTH OLD LADY GLASSES... FAR OUT MAN!

A NERD LIKE ME COULD REALLY GO PLACES WITH GLASSES LIKE THESE!

Panel 6: AH, FUCK! MY KNEE!

WATCH WHERE YOU'RE GOIN!

SMASH!

Panel 7: I BETTER GET BACK TO MY SECRET NERD LAIR!

123

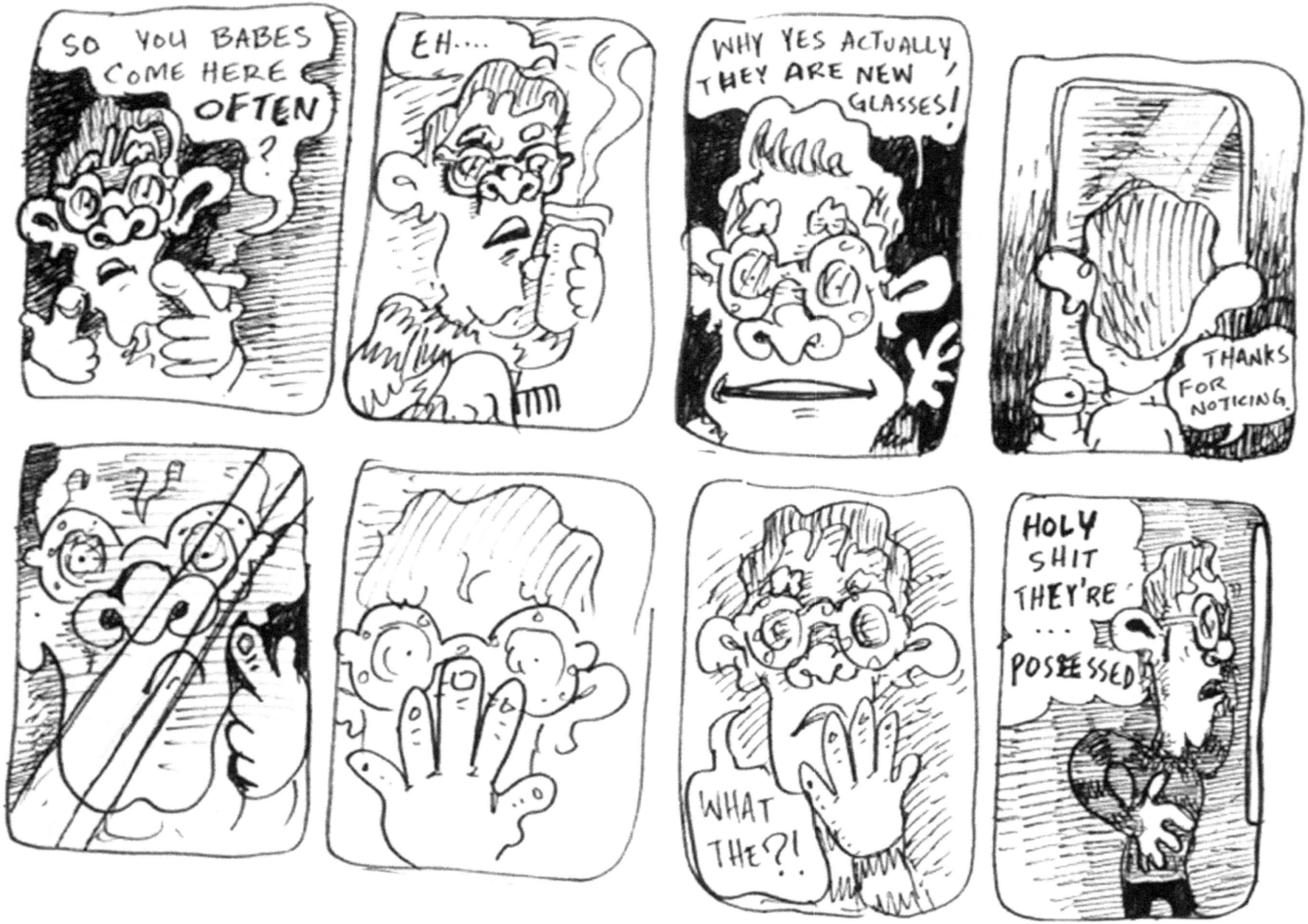
SO YOU BABES COME HERE OFTEN?
EH....
WHY YES ACTUALLY, THEY ARE NEW GLASSES!
THANKS FOR NOTICING.
WHAT THE?!
HOLY SHIT THEY'RE ... POSSESSED

THE BOX HUMPER

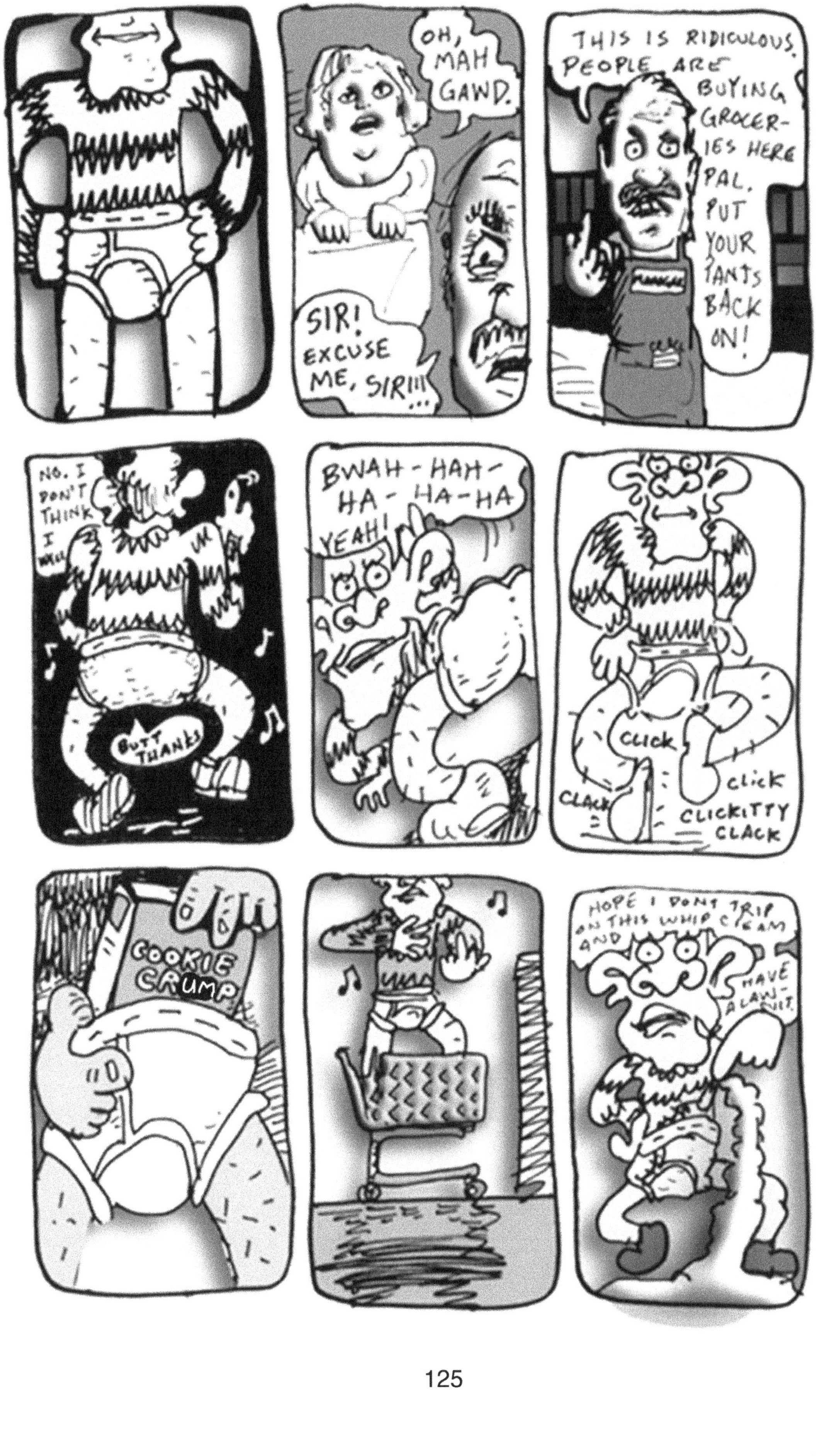

OH, MAH GAWD.
SIR! EXCUSE ME, SIR!!!...
THIS IS RIDICULOUS. PEOPLE ARE BUYING GROCER-IES HERE PAL. PUT YOUR PANTS BACK ON!
NO. I DON'T THINK I
BUTT THANKS
BWAH-HAH-HA-HA-HA
YEAH!
CLICK
CLICK
CLACK
CLICKITTY CLACK
COOKIE CRUMP
HOPE I DONT TRIP ON THIS WHIP CREAM AND HAVE A LAWSUIT.

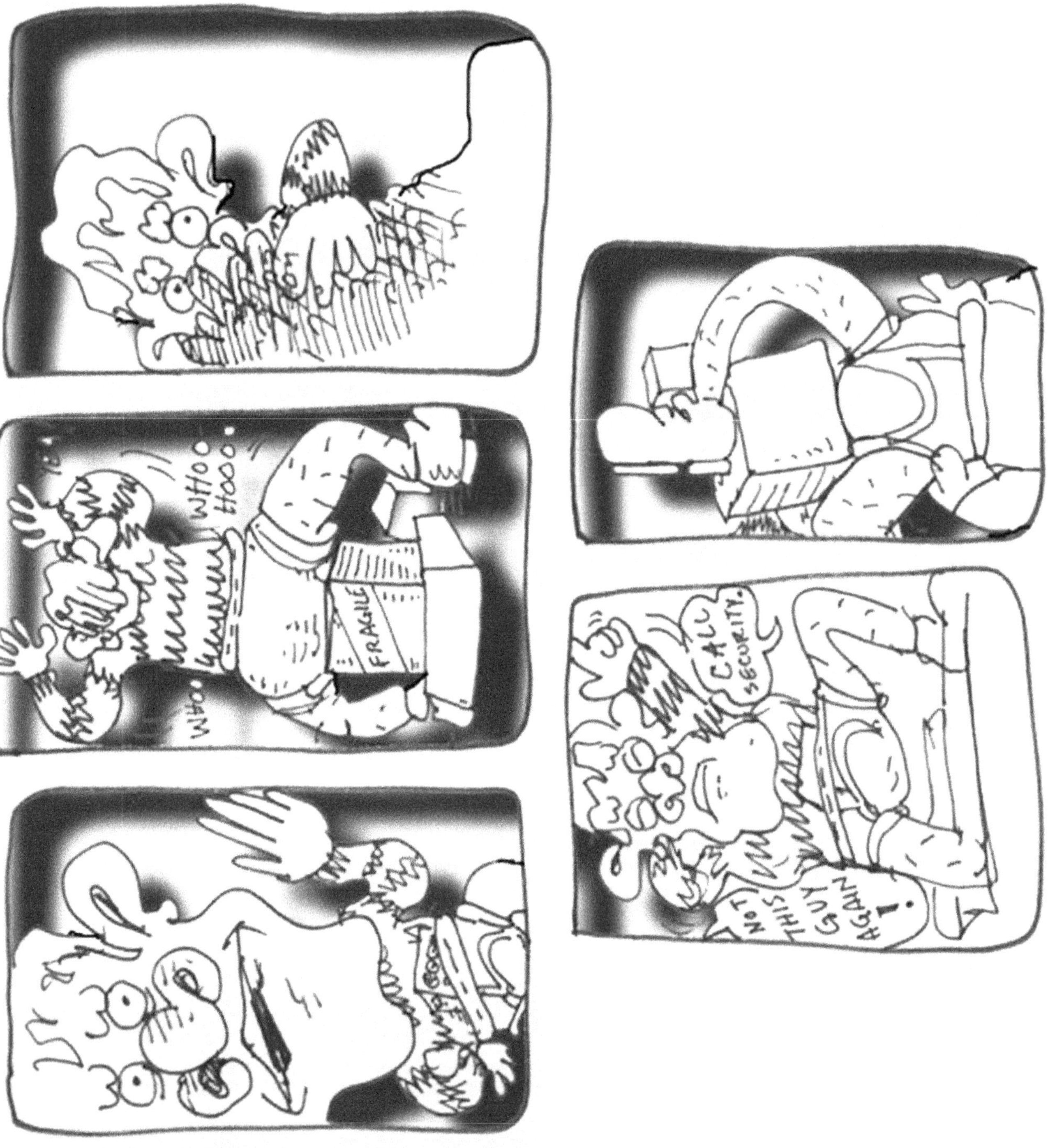
CALL SECURITY.
NOT THIS GUY AGAIN!
WHOO WHOO HOOO...
FRAGILE

YOU STILL GOT THAT HEADACHE MAN?
AH! SHIT
SHIT.
HA.
GOD DAMN HEADACHE!
BUT MY HEADACHE JUST GOT WORSE, AND WORSE, AND WORSE.
GOD DAMN HEADACHE!

DAMN IT, AT THIS RATE I AIN'T NEVER GETTIN' THIS BOOK DONE!
HOLY SHIT MAN, YOU CRYIN'?!
HEY THIS GUY IS CRYIN' AGAIN, BWAH-HAH-HA LOOK!
WHAT?!
NO I'M NOT!
SHUT THE FUCK UP!
I'M YOUR GODDAMN TROLL SHEPARD AND I DESERVE RESPECT!
DON'T GIMME THAT FUCKIN' LOOK!
YOU LITTLE SHIT!

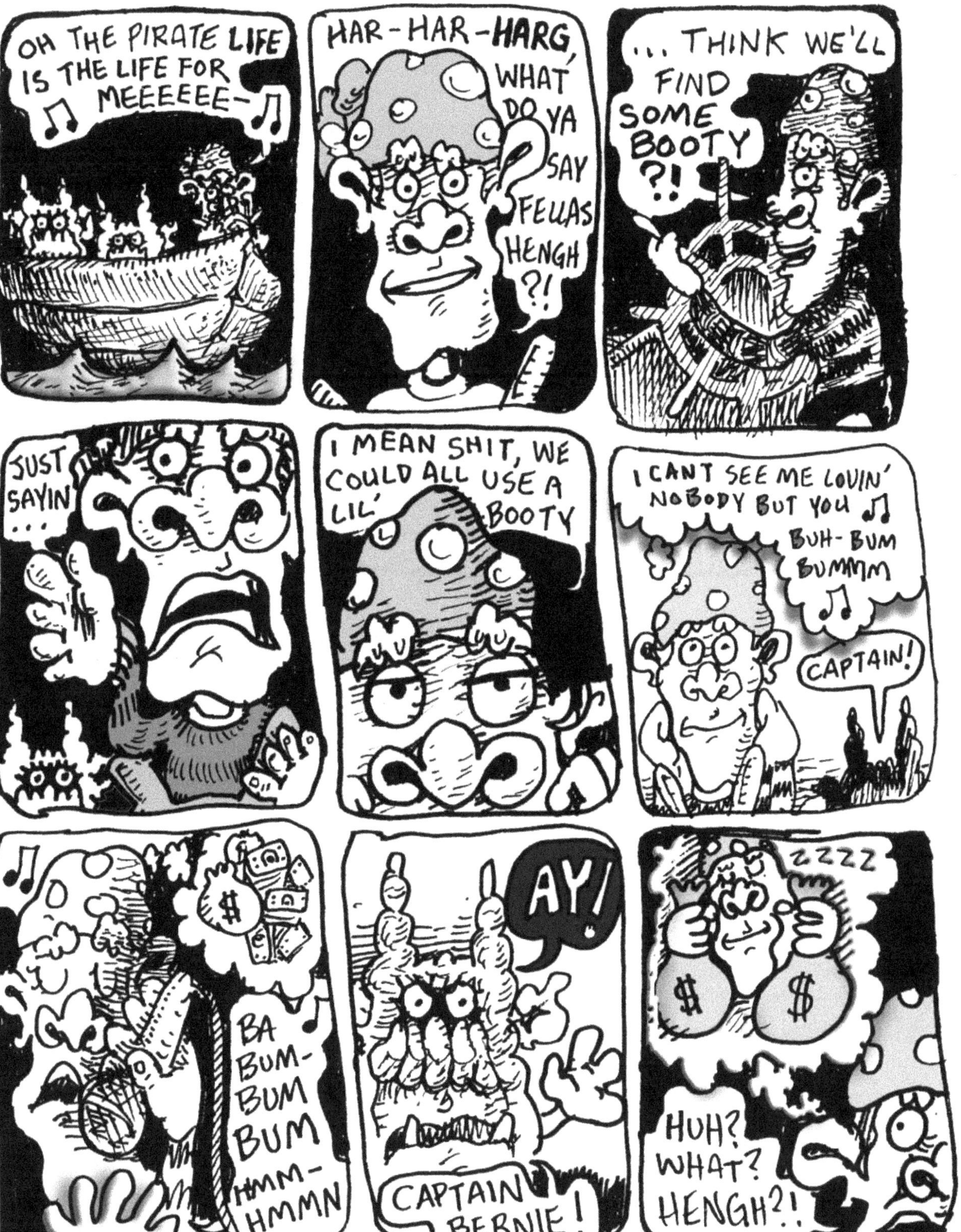
OH THE PIRATE LIFE IS THE LIFE FOR MEEEEEE-
HAR-HAR-HARG, WHAT DO YA SAY FELLAS HENGH ?!
... THINK WE'LL FIND SOME BOOTY ?!
JUST SAYIN ...
I MEAN SHIT, WE COULD ALL USE A LIL' BOOTY
I CANT SEE ME LOVIN' NOBODY BUT YOU
BUH-BUM BUMMM
CAPTAIN!
BA BUM-BUM BUM HMM-HMMN
AY!
CAPTAIN BERNIE!
ZZZZ
HUH? WHAT? HENGH?!

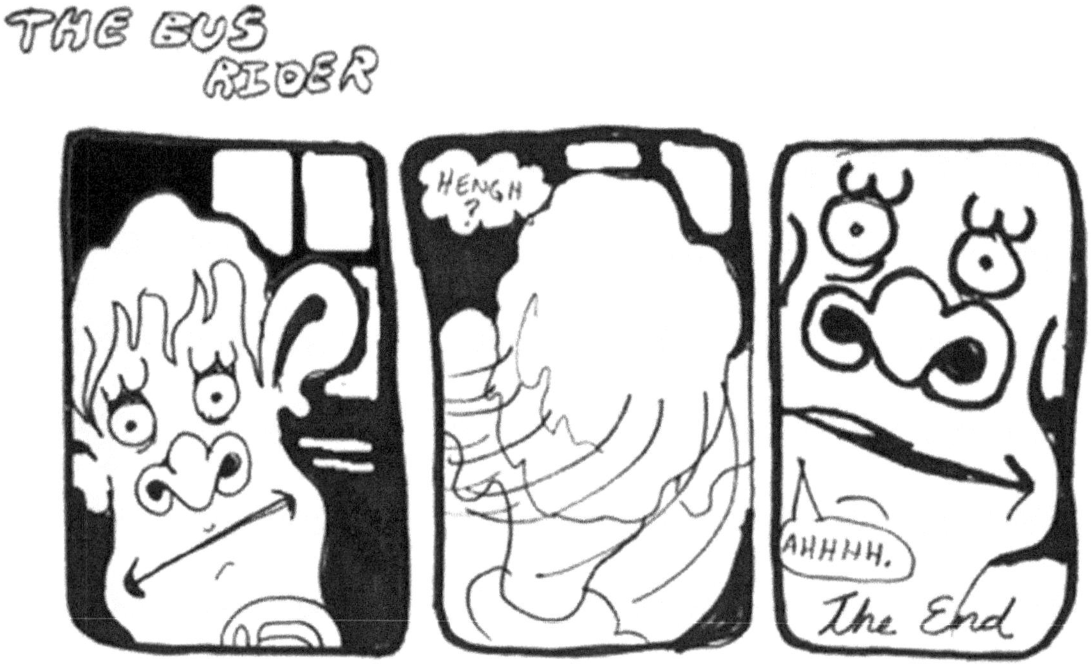
THE BUS RIDER
HENGH ?
AHHHH.
The End

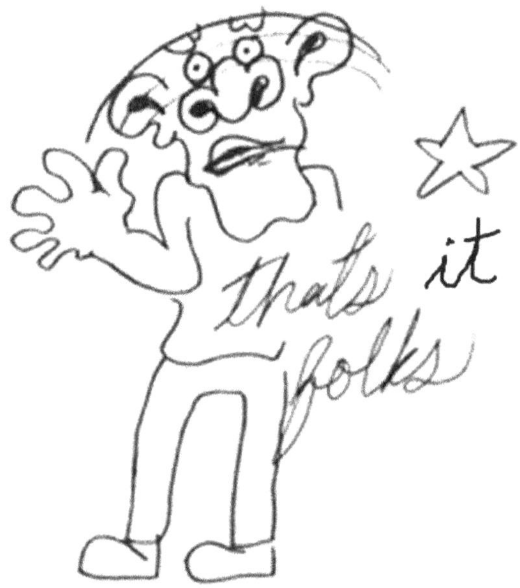
thats it folks

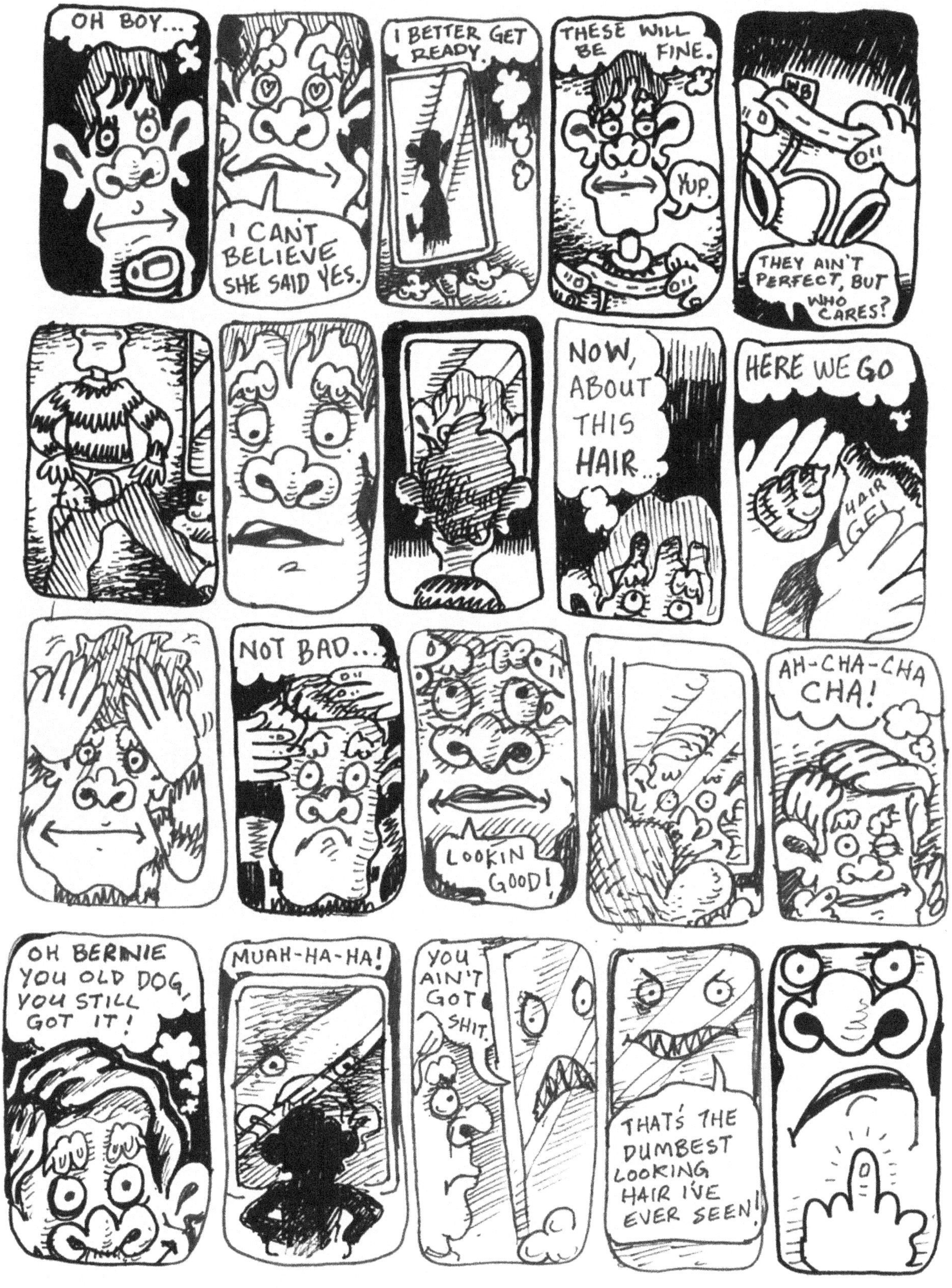
OH BOY...
I CAN'T BELIEVE SHE SAID YES.
I BETTER GET READY.
THESE WILL BE FINE.
YUP.
THEY AIN'T PERFECT, BUT WHO CARES?
NOW, ABOUT THIS HAIR...
HERE WE GO
HAIR GEL
NOT BAD...
LOOKIN GOOD!
AH-CHA-CHA CHA!
OH BERNIE YOU OLD DOG, YOU STILL GOT IT!
MUAH-HA-HA!
YOU AIN'T GOT SHIT.
THAT'S THE DUMBEST LOOKING HAIR I'VE EVER SEEN!

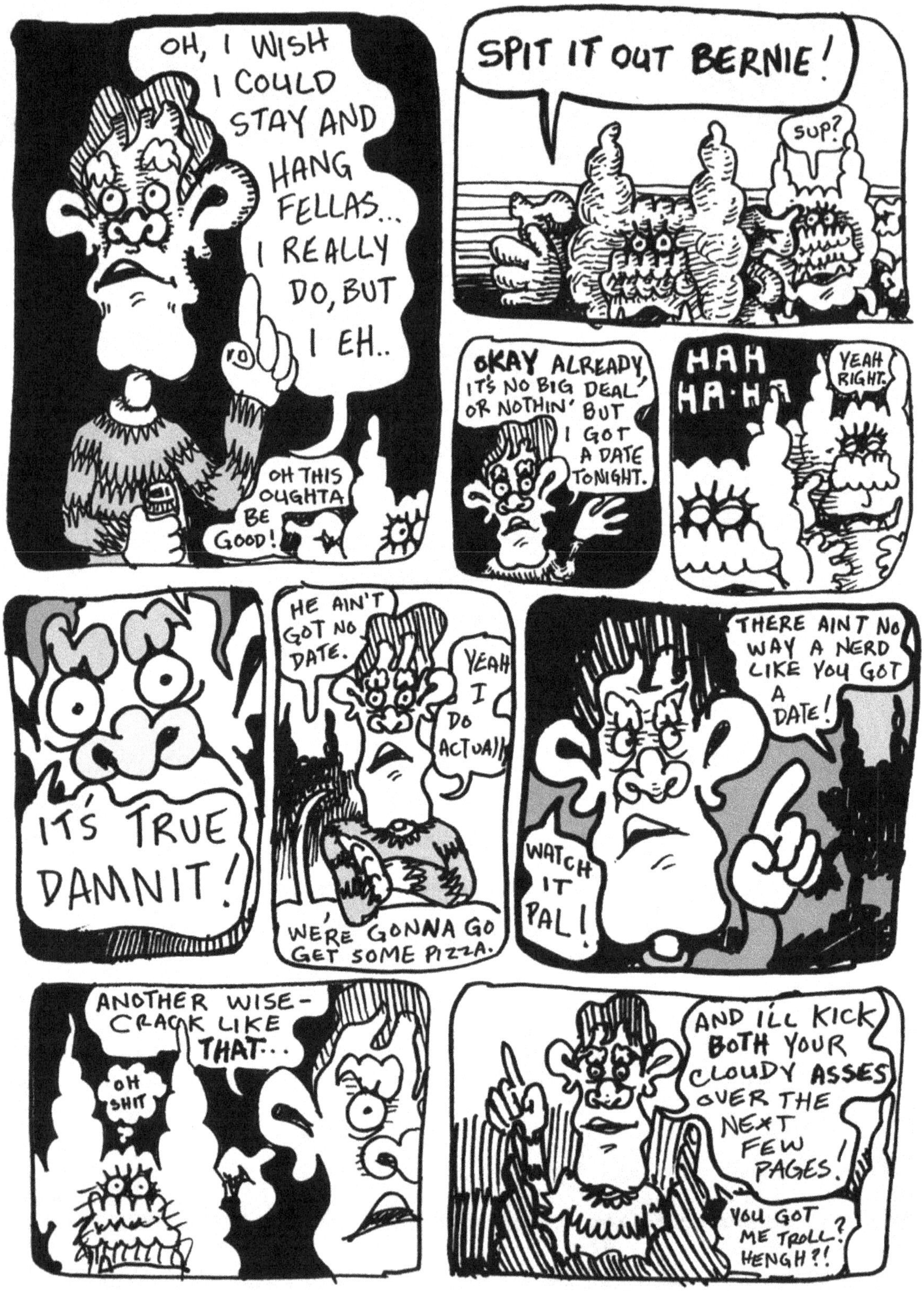

OH, I WISH I COULD STAY AND HANG FELLAS... I REALLY DO, BUT I EH..
OH THIS OUGHTA BE GOOD!
SPIT IT OUT BERNIE!
SUP?
OKAY ALREADY, IT'S NO BIG DEAL OR NOTHIN' BUT I GOT A DATE TONIGHT.
HAH HA·HA
YEAH RIGHT.
IT'S TRUE DAMNIT!
HE AIN'T GOT NO DATE.
YEAH I DO ACTUAll
WE'RE GONNA GO GET SOME PIZZA.
THERE AINT NO WAY A NERD LIKE YOU GOT A DATE!
WATCH IT PAL!
ANOTHER WISE-CRACK LIKE THAT...
OH SHIT
AND I'LL KICK BOTH YOUR CLOUDY ASSES OVER THE NEXT FEW PAGES!
YOU GOT ME TROLL? HENGH?!

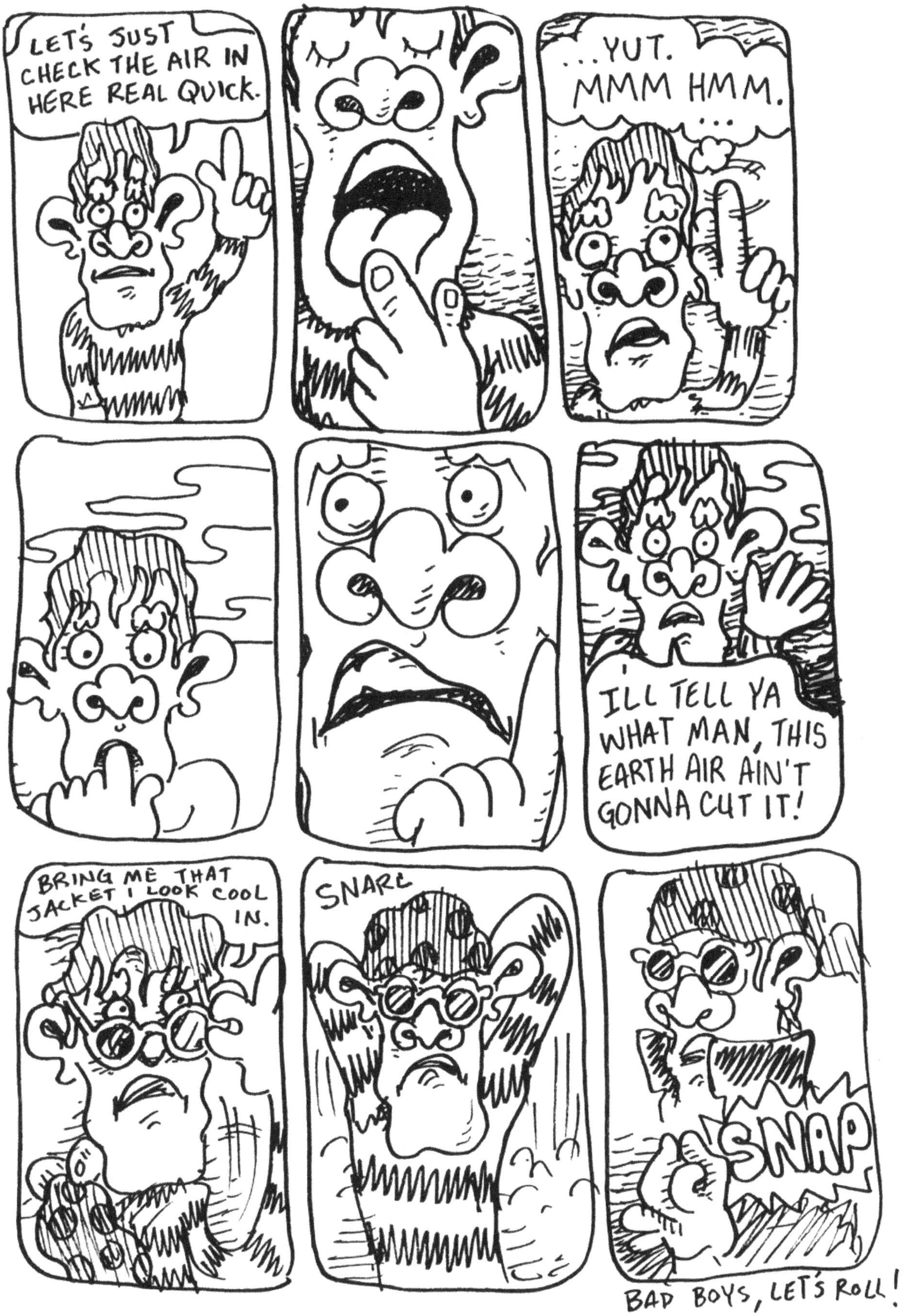

LET'S JUST CHECK THE AIR IN HERE REAL QUICK.
...YUT. MMM HMM. ...
I'LL TELL YA WHAT MAN, THIS EARTH AIR AIN'T GONNA CUT IT!
BRING ME THAT JACKET I LOOK COOL IN.
SNARL
SNAP
BAD BOYS, LET'S ROLL!

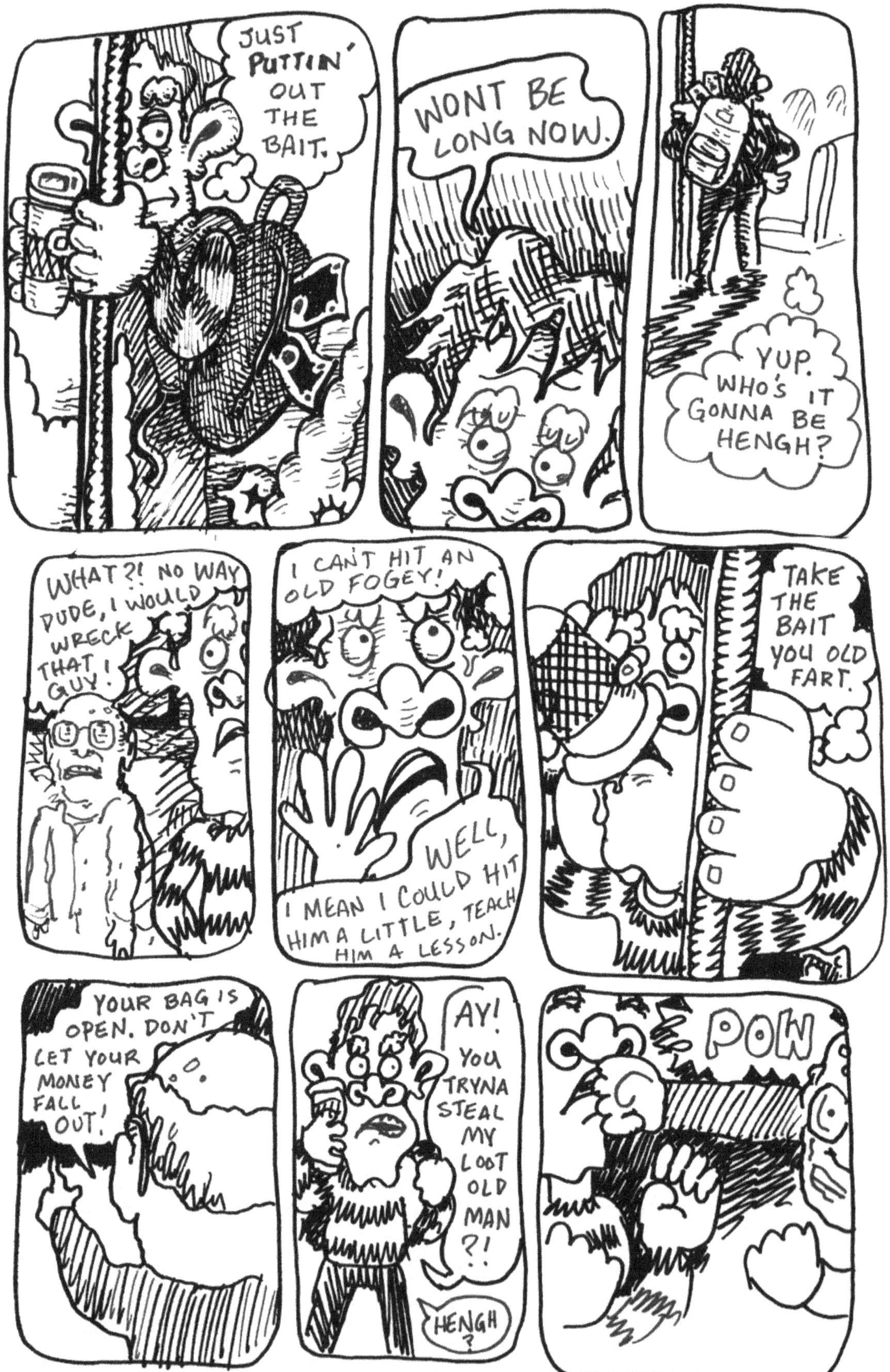
JUST PUTTIN' OUT THE BAIT.
WONT BE LONG NOW.
YUP. WHO'S IT GONNA BE HENGH?
WHAT?! NO WAY DUDE, I WOULD WRECK THAT GUY!
I CAN'T HIT AN OLD FOGEY!
WELL, I MEAN I COULD HIT HIM A LITTLE, TEACH HIM A LESSON.
TAKE THE BAIT YOU OLD FART.
YOUR BAG IS OPEN. DON'T LET YOUR MONEY FALL OUT!
AY! YOU TRYNA STEAL MY LOOT OLD MAN?!
HENGH?
POW

BERNSCOUTS OF AMERICA

XXX

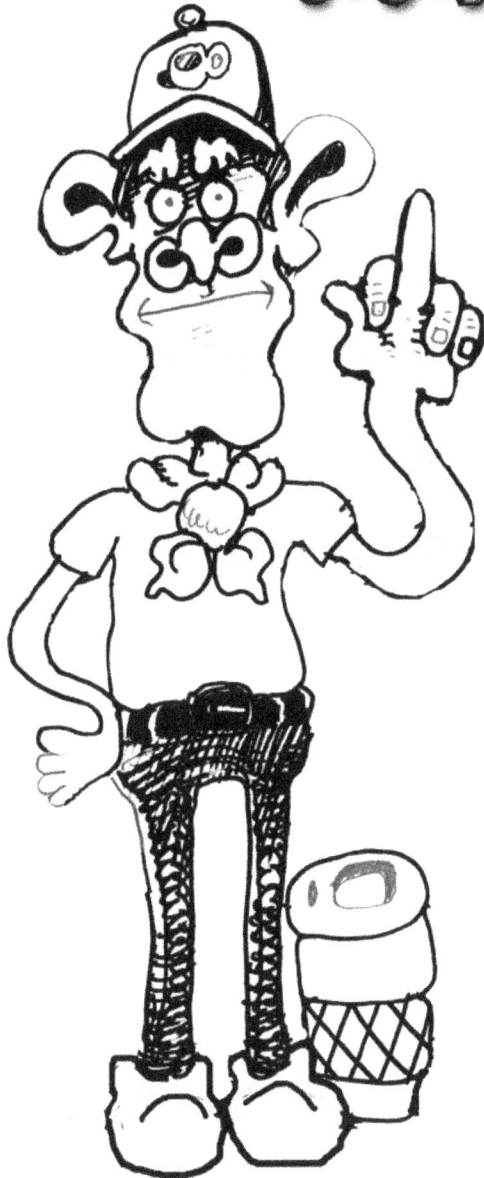

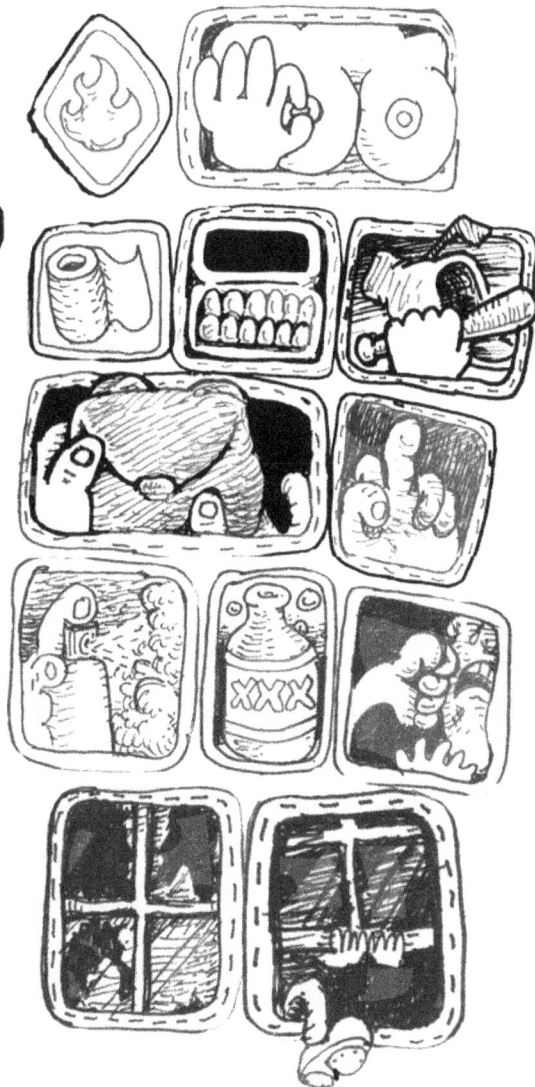

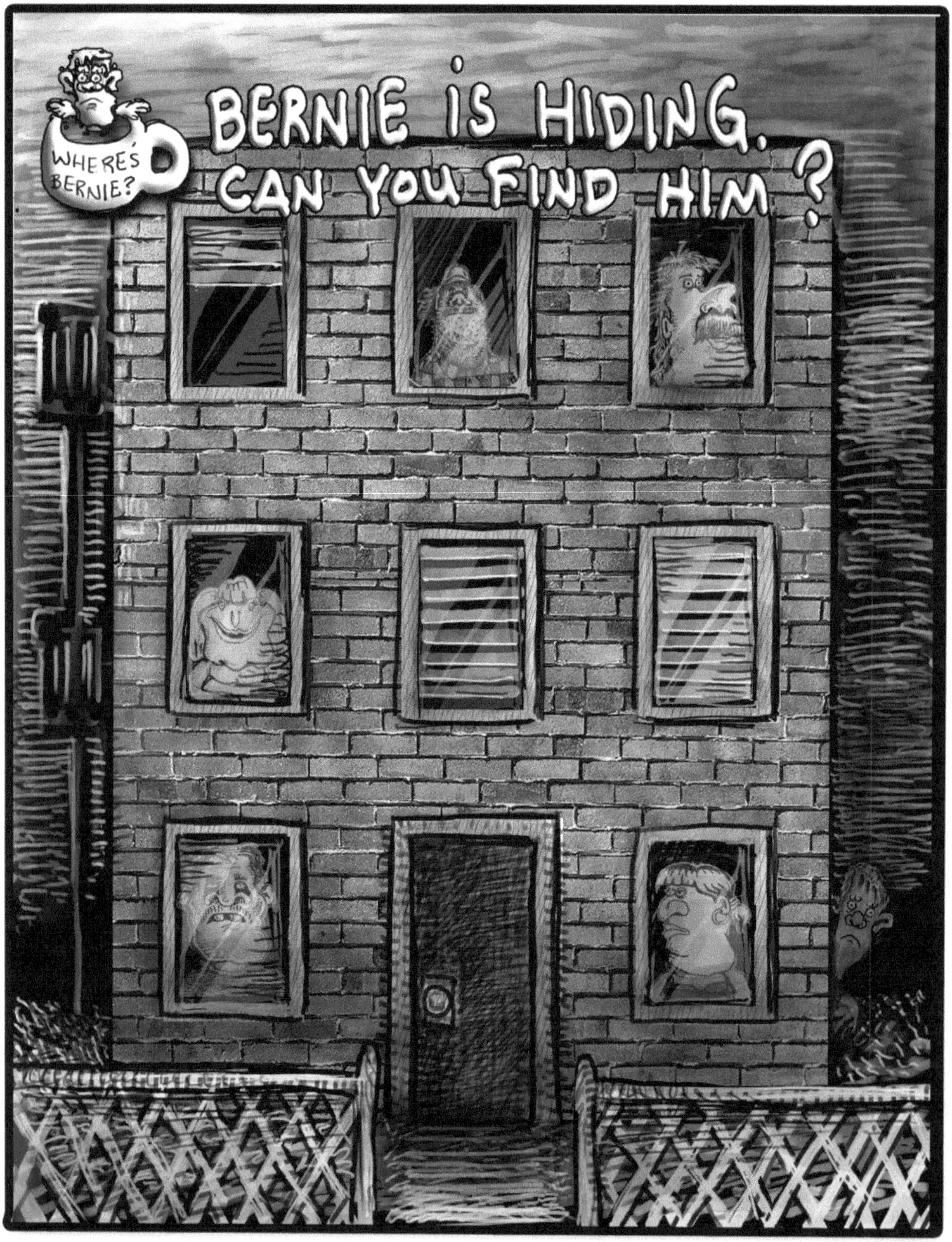
WHERE'S BERNIE?
BERNIE IS HIDING. CAN YOU FIND HIM?

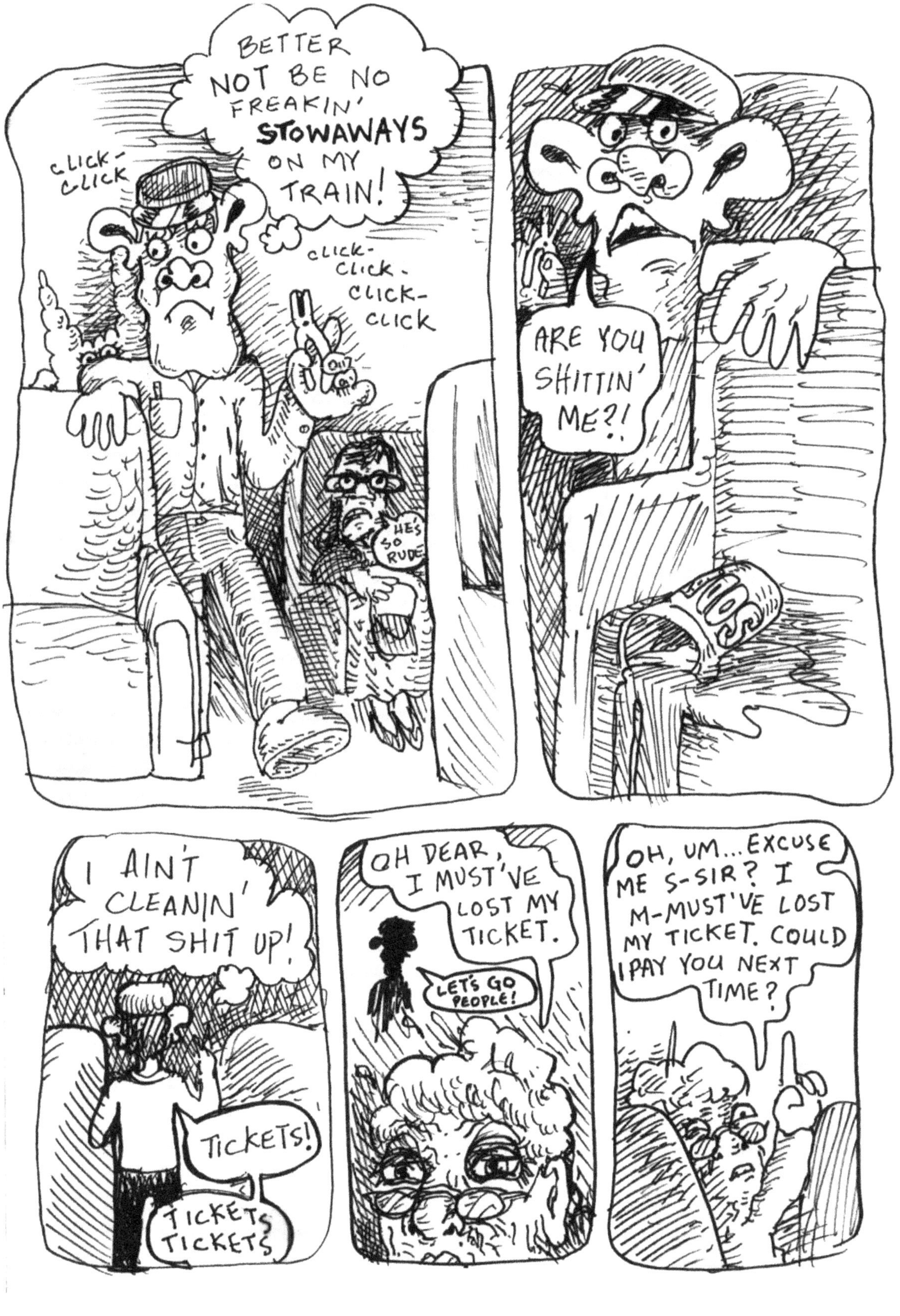

CLICK-CLICK
BETTER NOT BE NO FREAKIN' STOWAWAYS ON MY TRAIN!
CLICK-CLICK-CLICK-CLICK
HE'S SO RUDE
ARE YOU SHITTIN' ME?!
I AIN'T CLEANIN' THAT SHIT UP!
TICKETS!
TICKETS TICKETS
OH DEAR, I MUST'VE LOST MY TICKET.
LET'S GO PEOPLE!
OH, UM... EXCUSE ME S-SIR? I M-MUST'VE LOST MY TICKET. COULD I PAY YOU NEXT TIME?

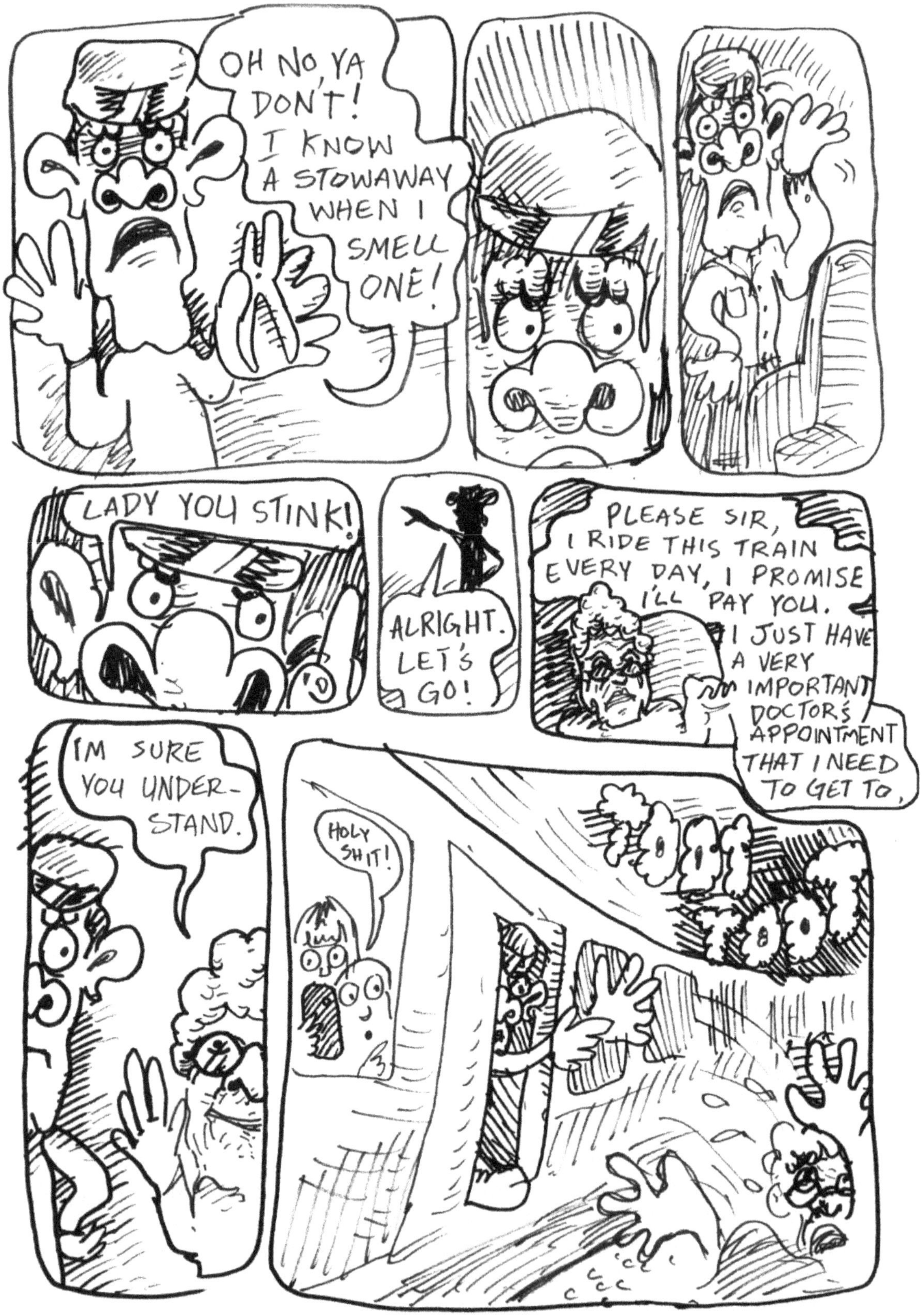
OH NO, YA DON'T! I KNOW A STOWAWAY WHEN I SMELL ONE!
LADY YOU STINK!
ALRIGHT. LET'S GO!
PLEASE SIR, I RIDE THIS TRAIN EVERY DAY, I PROMISE I'LL PAY YOU. I JUST HAVE A VERY IMPORTANT DOCTOR'S APPOINTMENT THAT I NEED TO GET TO.
I'M SURE YOU UNDERSTAND.
HOLY SHIT!

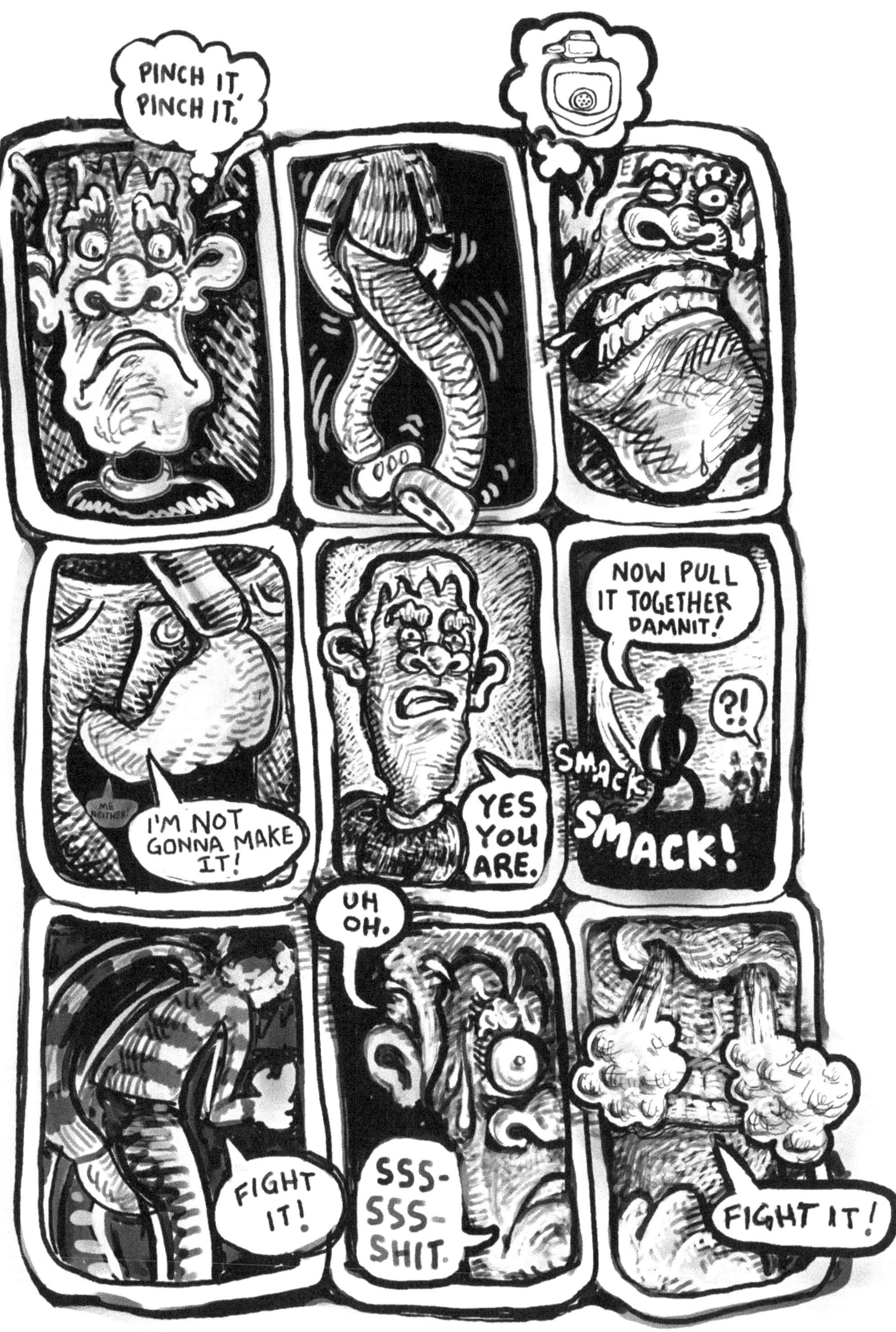
PINCH IT, PINCH IT.
ME NEITHER!
I'M NOT GONNA MAKE IT!
YES YOU ARE.
NOW PULL IT TOGETHER DAMNIT!
?!
SMACK
SMACK!
FIGHT IT!
UH OH.
SSS-SSS-SHIT.
FIGHT IT!

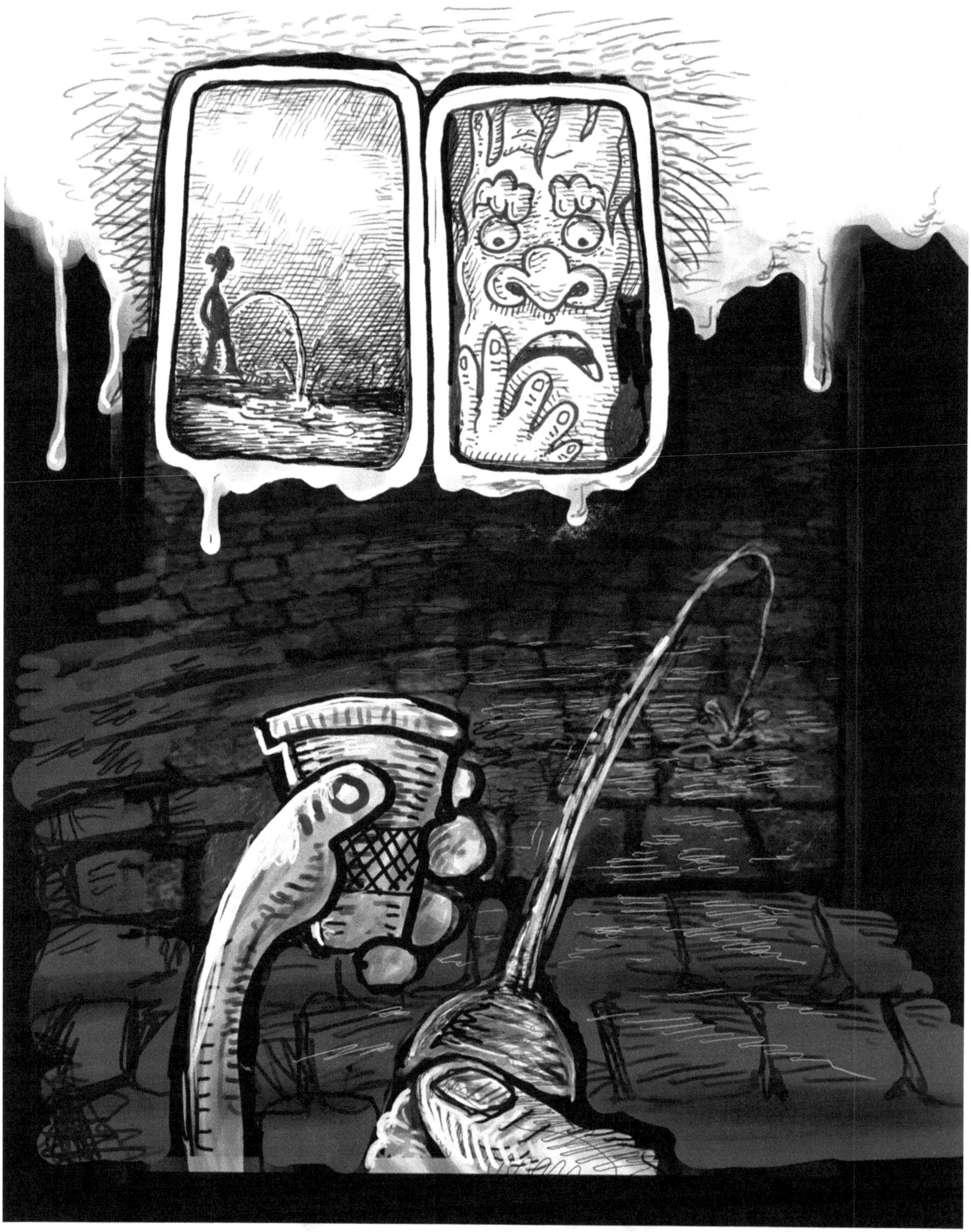

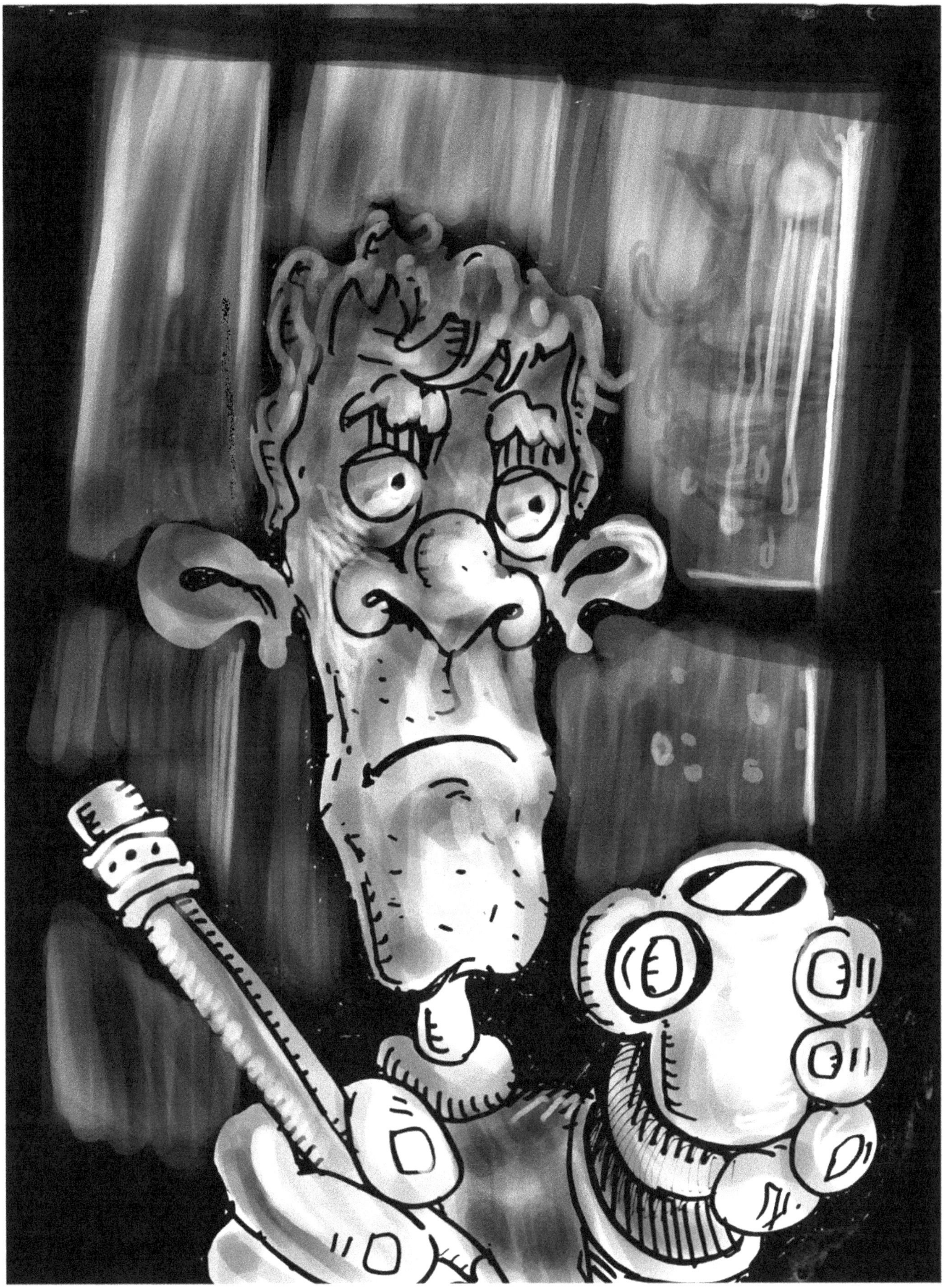

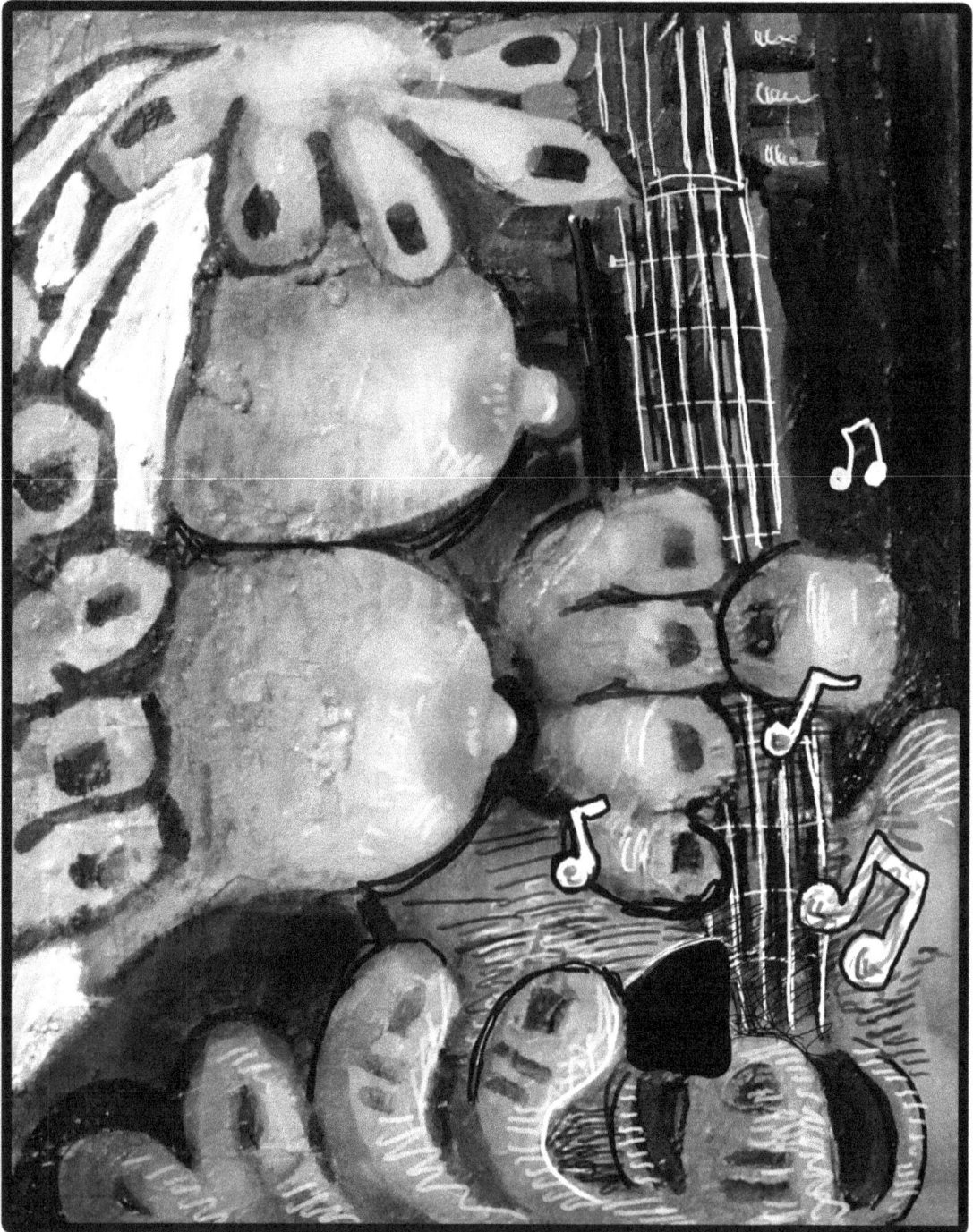

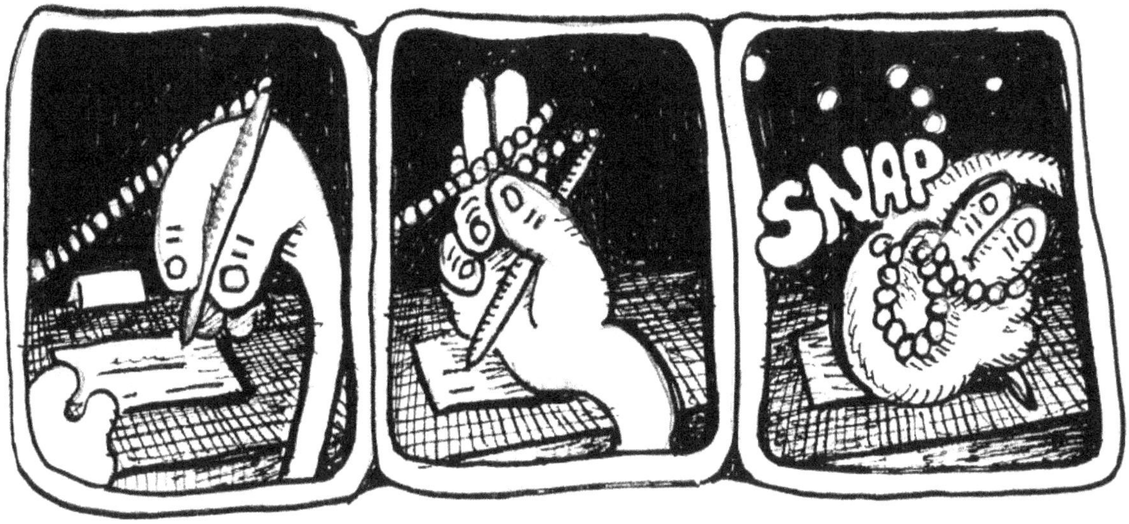
SNAP

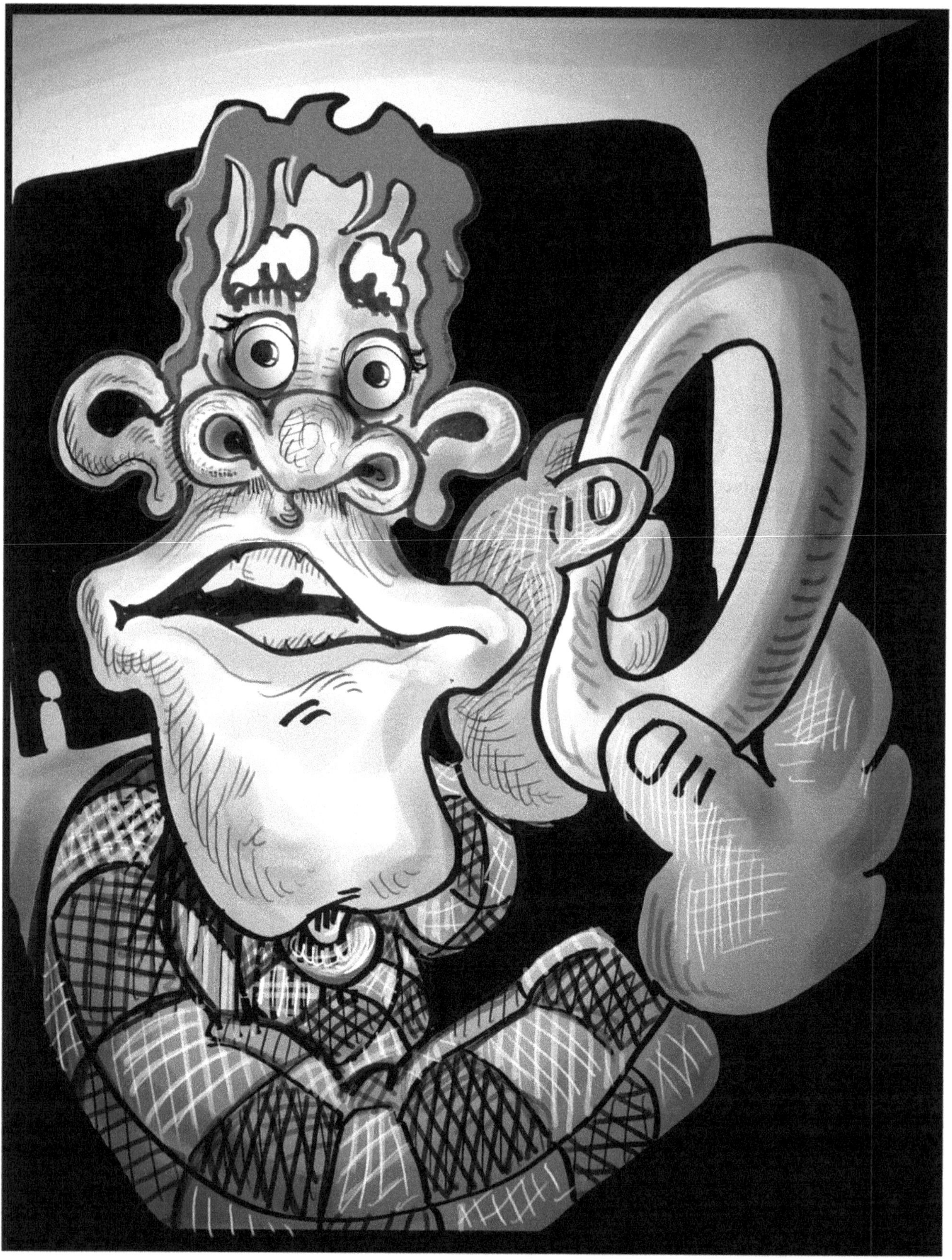

"TELL 'EM WILD BERNIE SENT YA!"

COFFEE CODEX

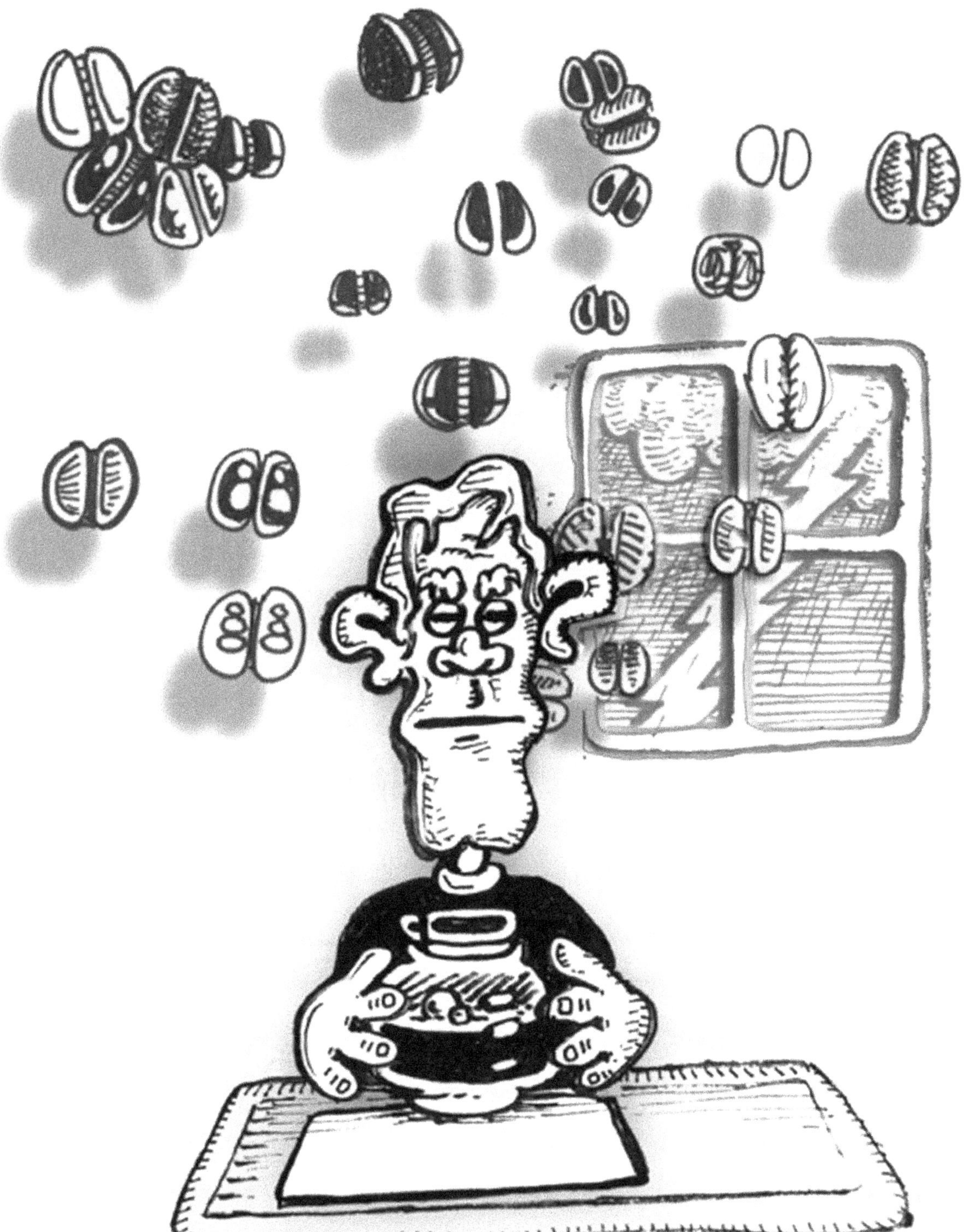

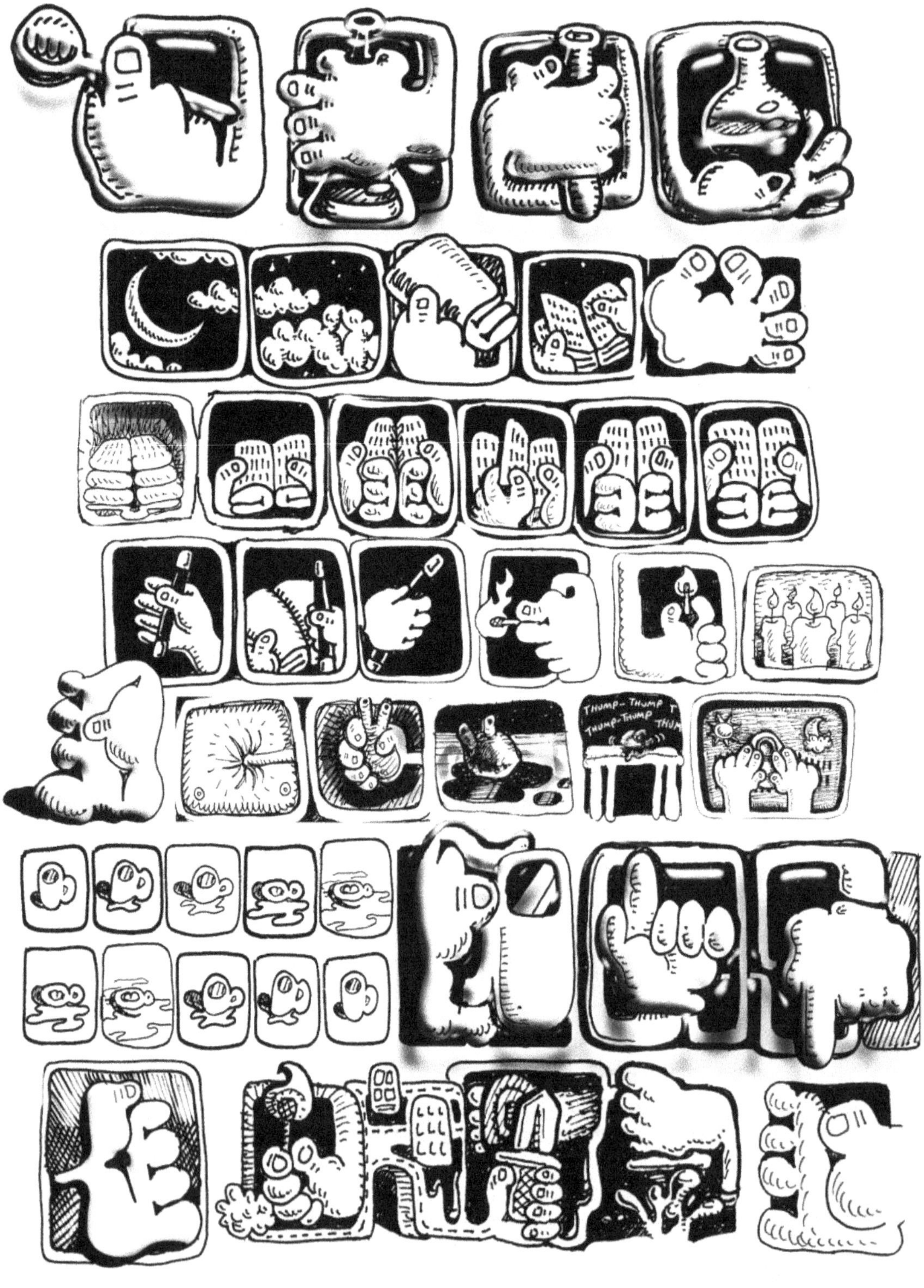
THUMP-THUMP
THUMP-THUMP

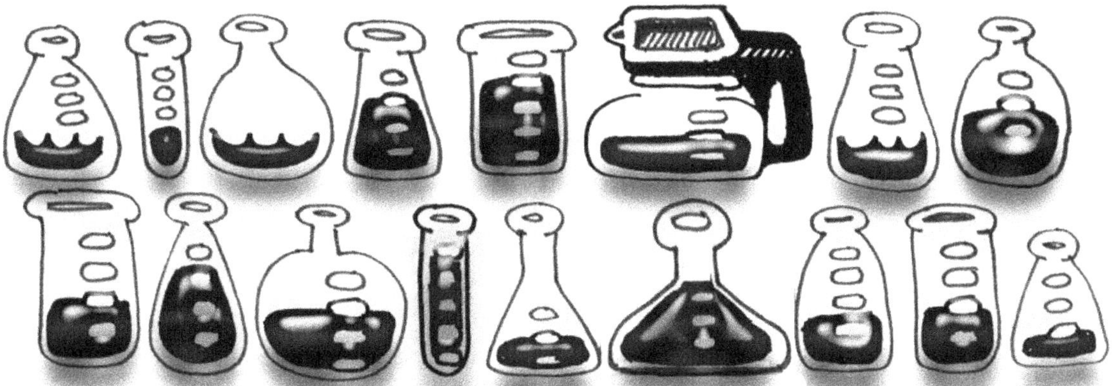

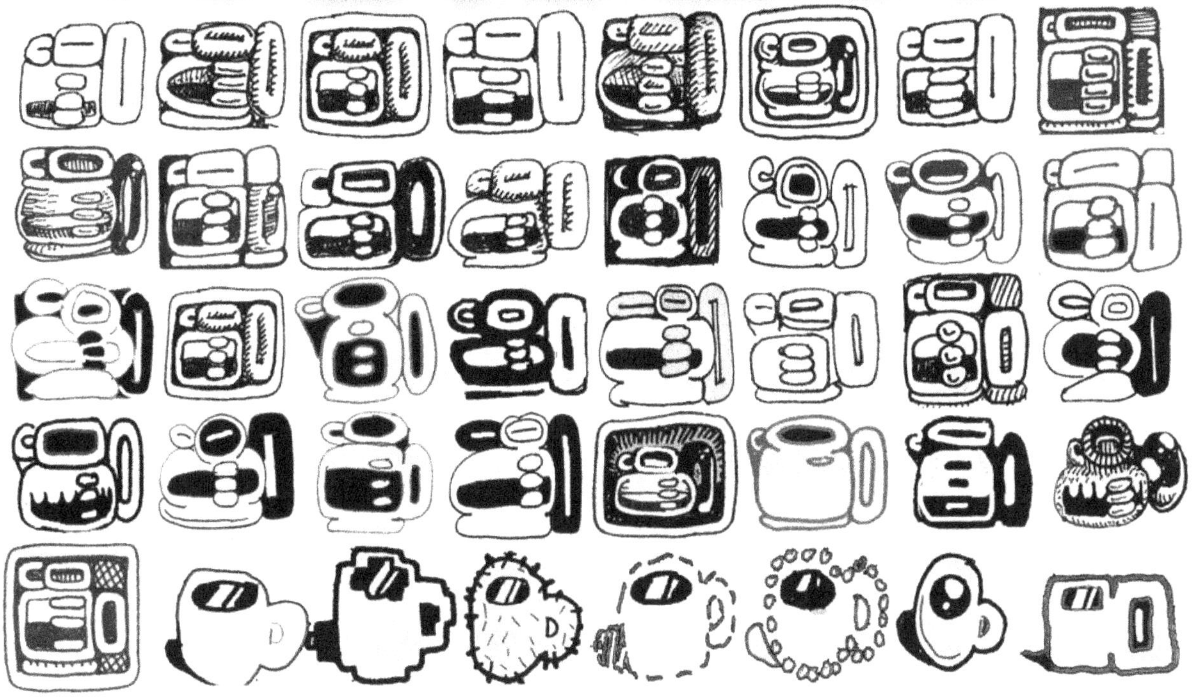

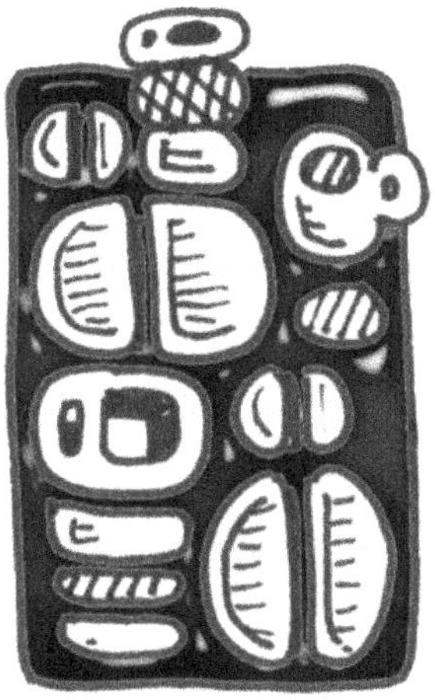

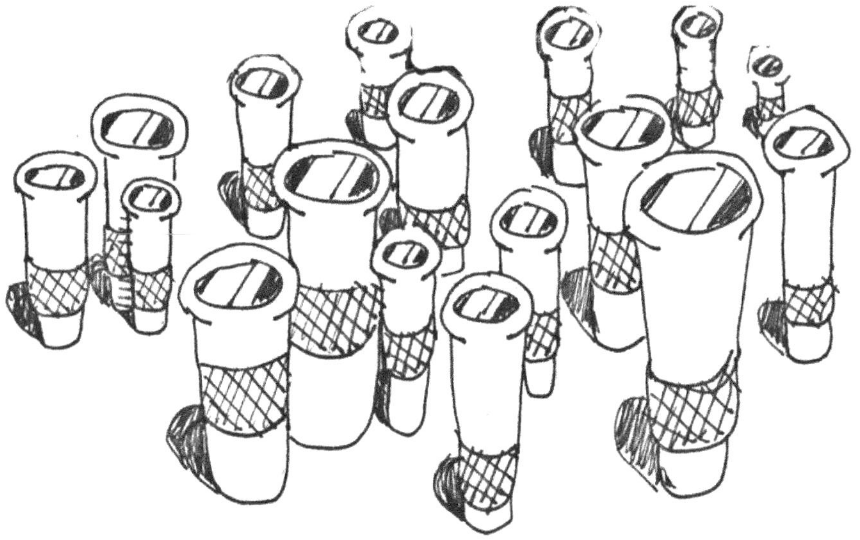

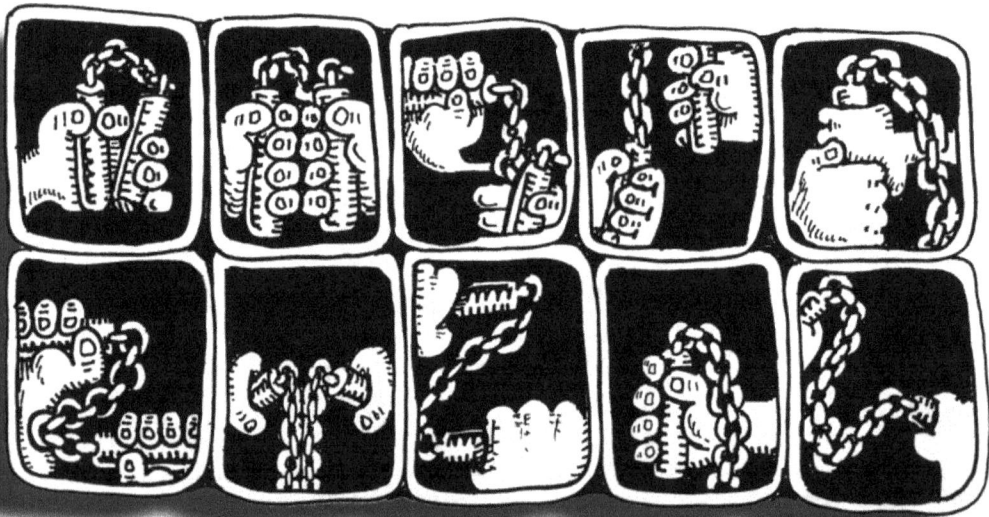

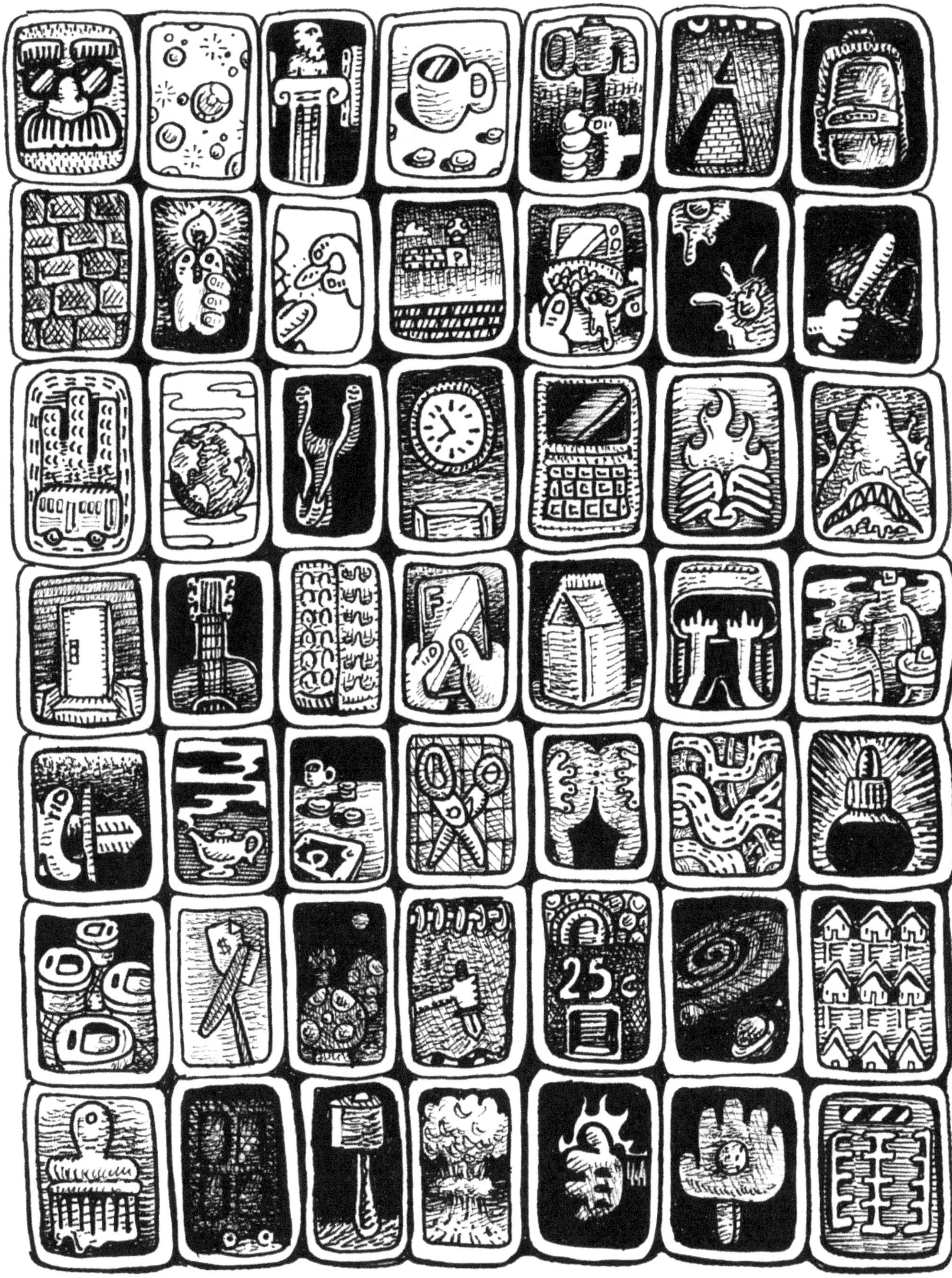
25¢

MAGIC KIT
OW!
INK
WTF
BAG OF WORMS
NICE BOOBS.
X-RAY
HOW TO MEET BABES
FAKE
MIND CONTROL
RABBIT'S FOOT
TRAP
POP

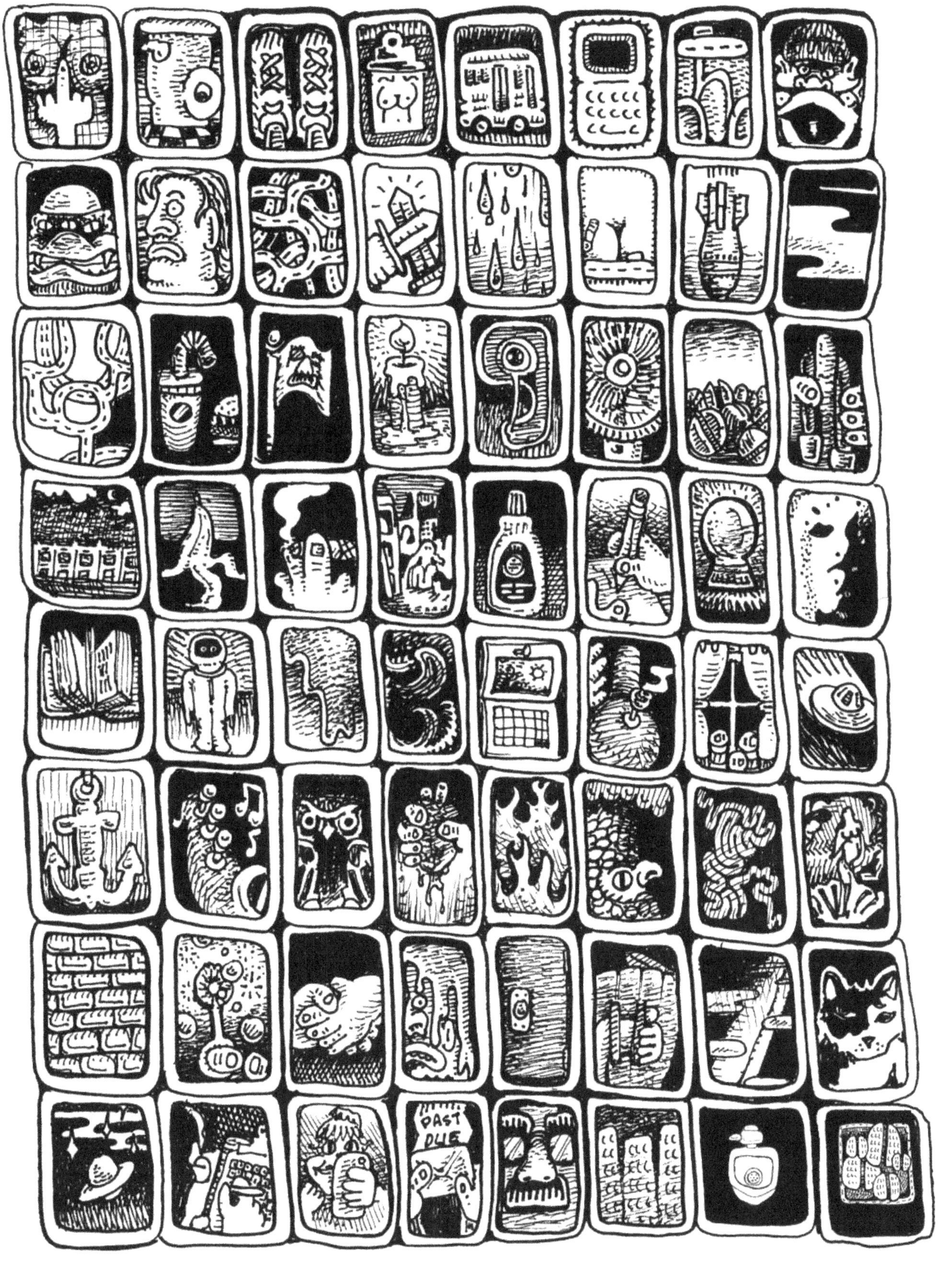
PAST DUE

PRESS
START

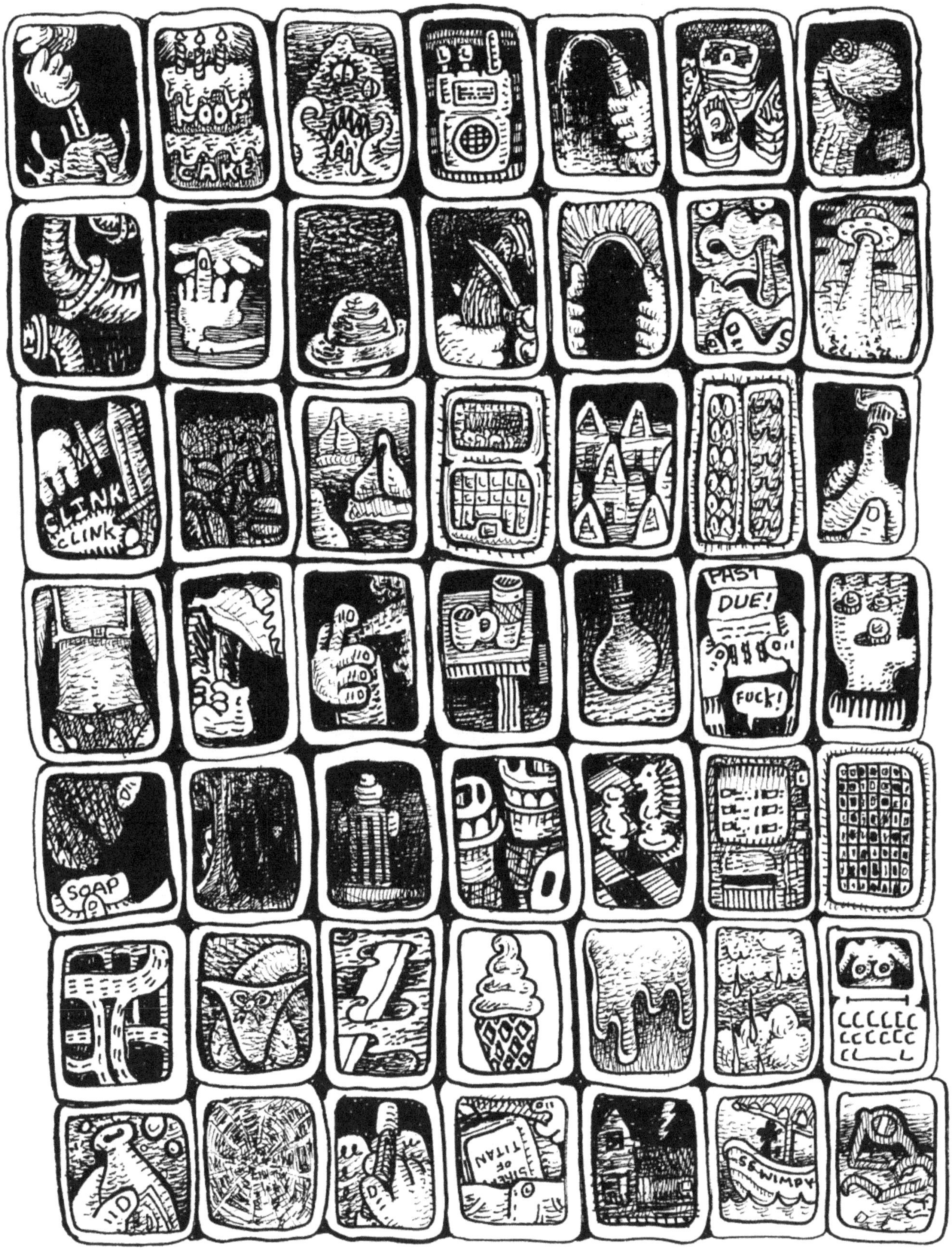
CAKE
CLINK
CLINK
PAST DUE!
FUCK!
SOAP
SS WIMPY

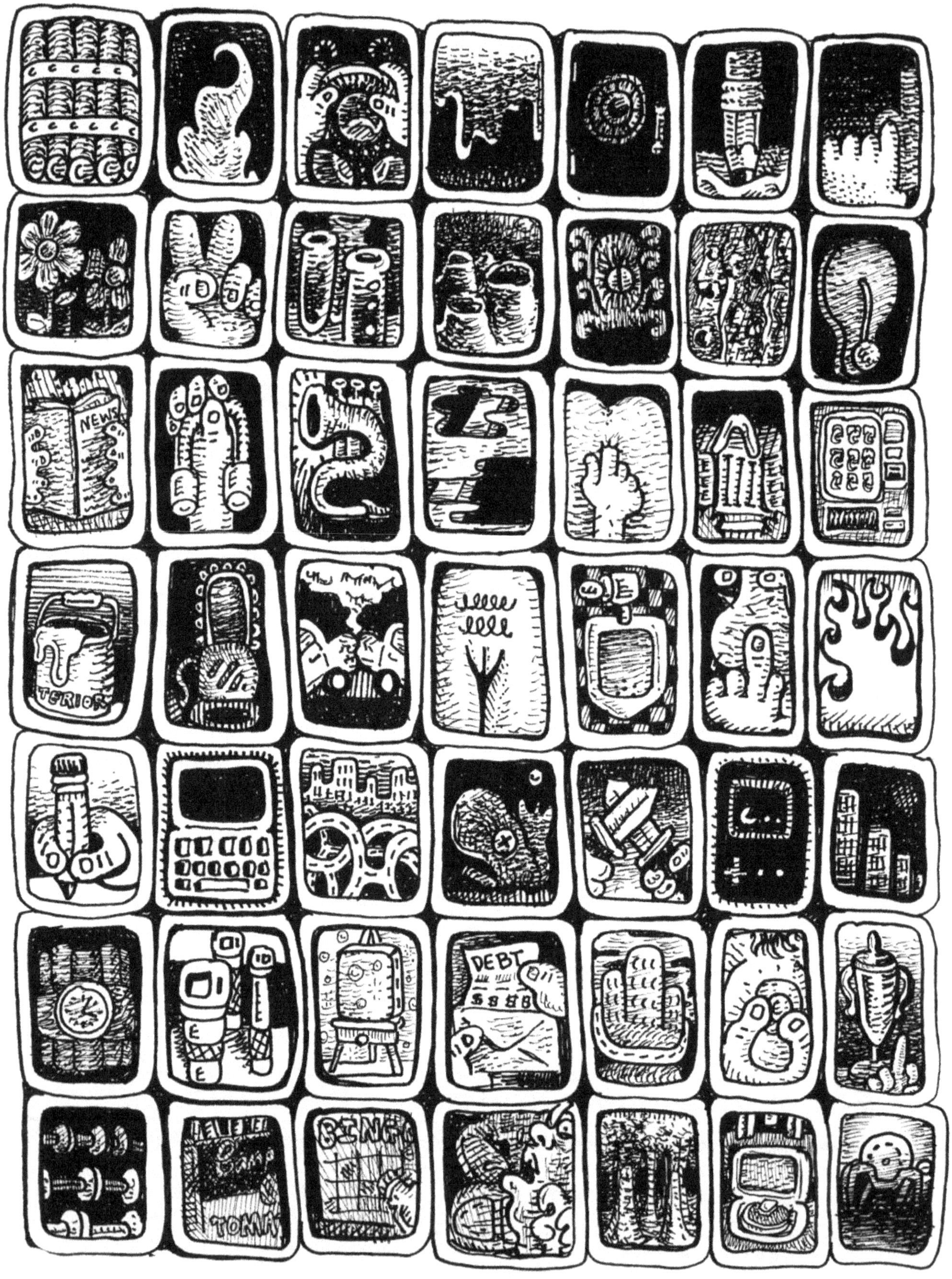
NEWS
TERIOR
DEBT

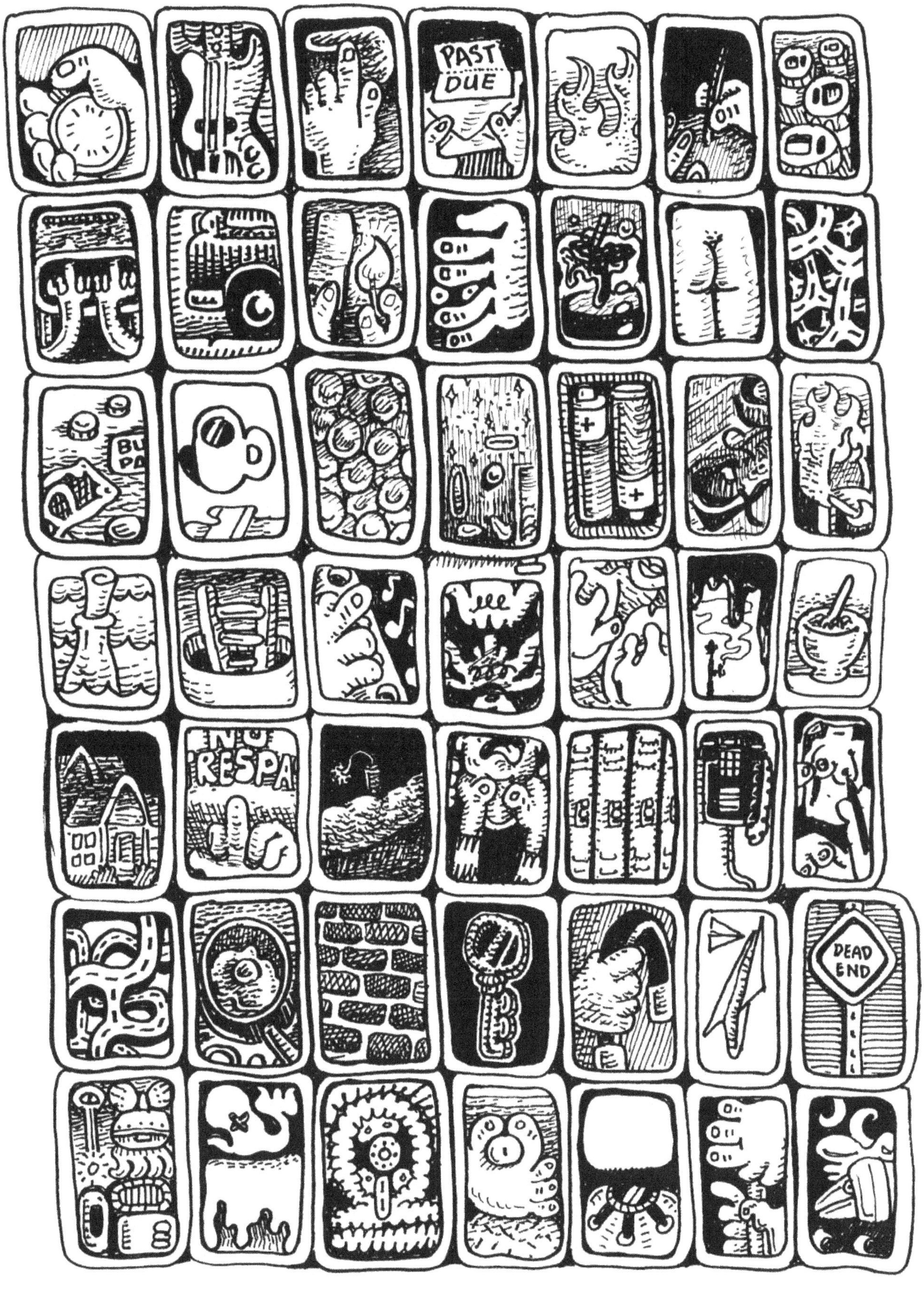
PAST DUE
RESPA
DEAD END

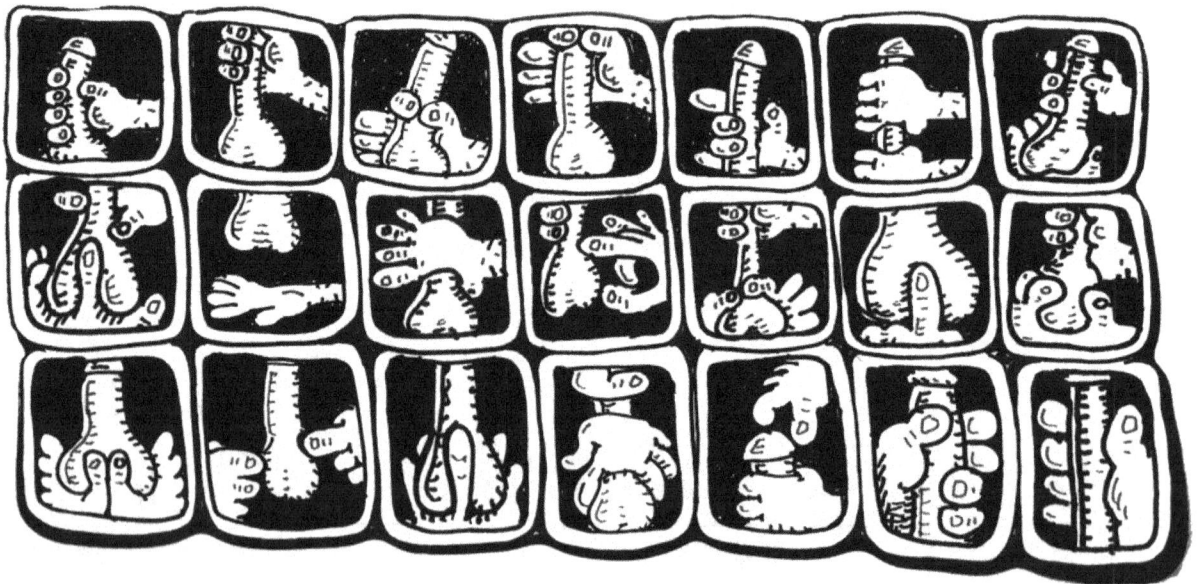

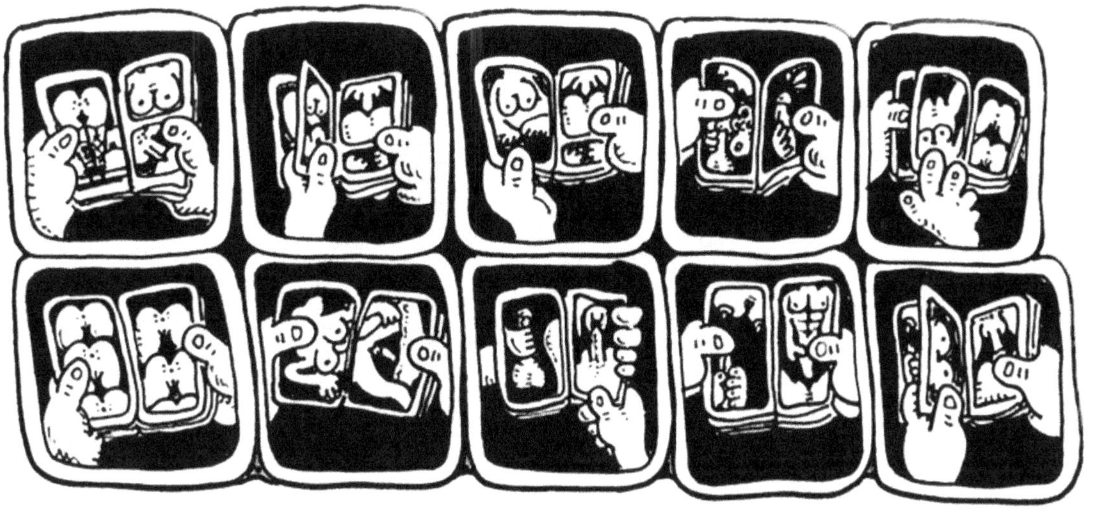

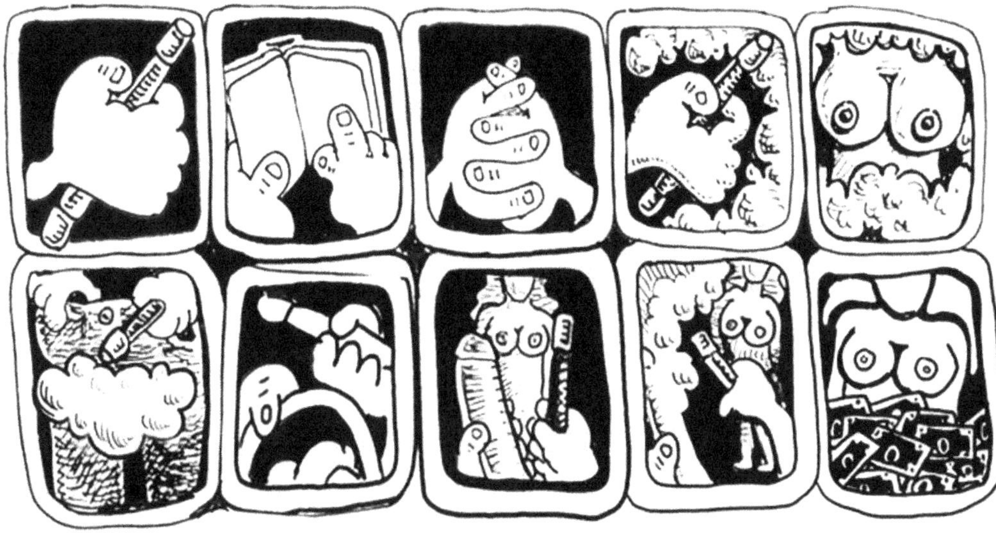

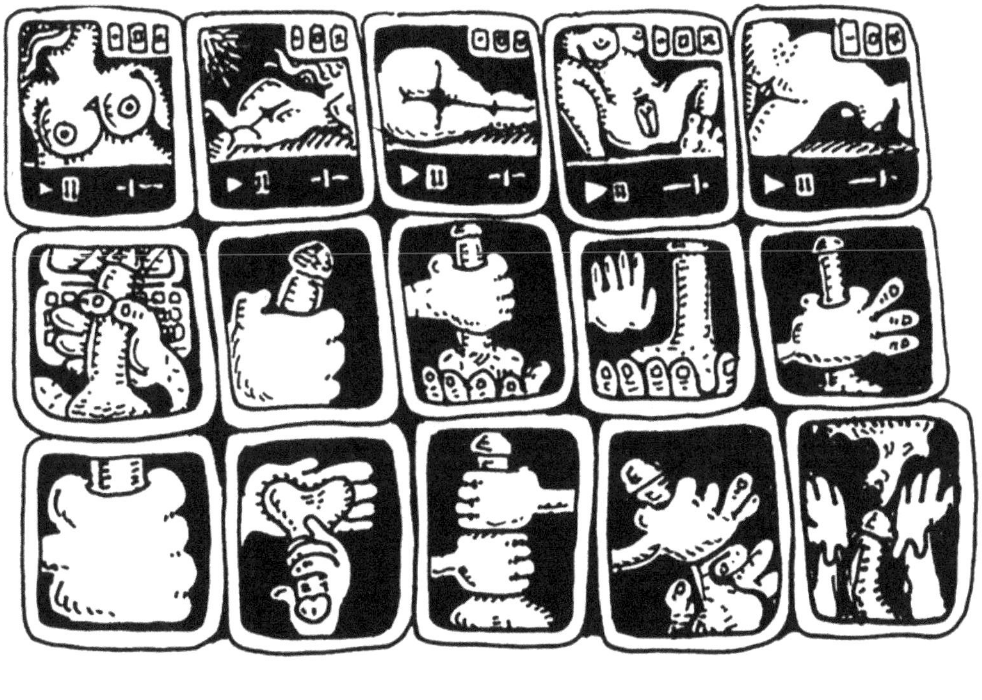

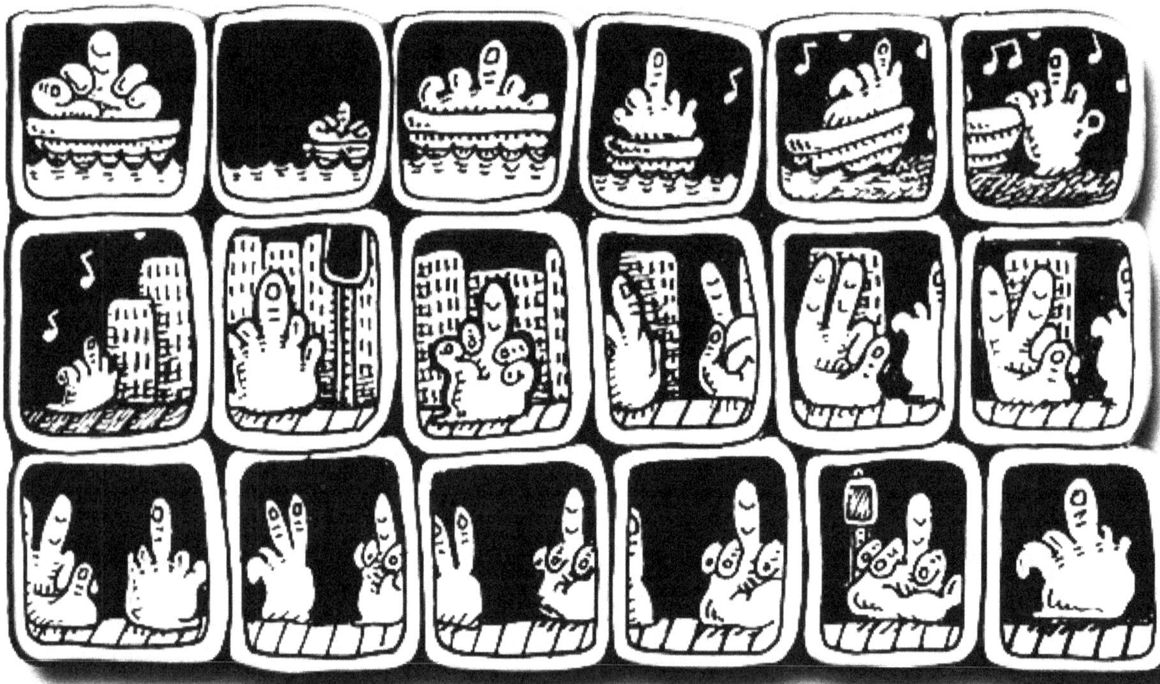

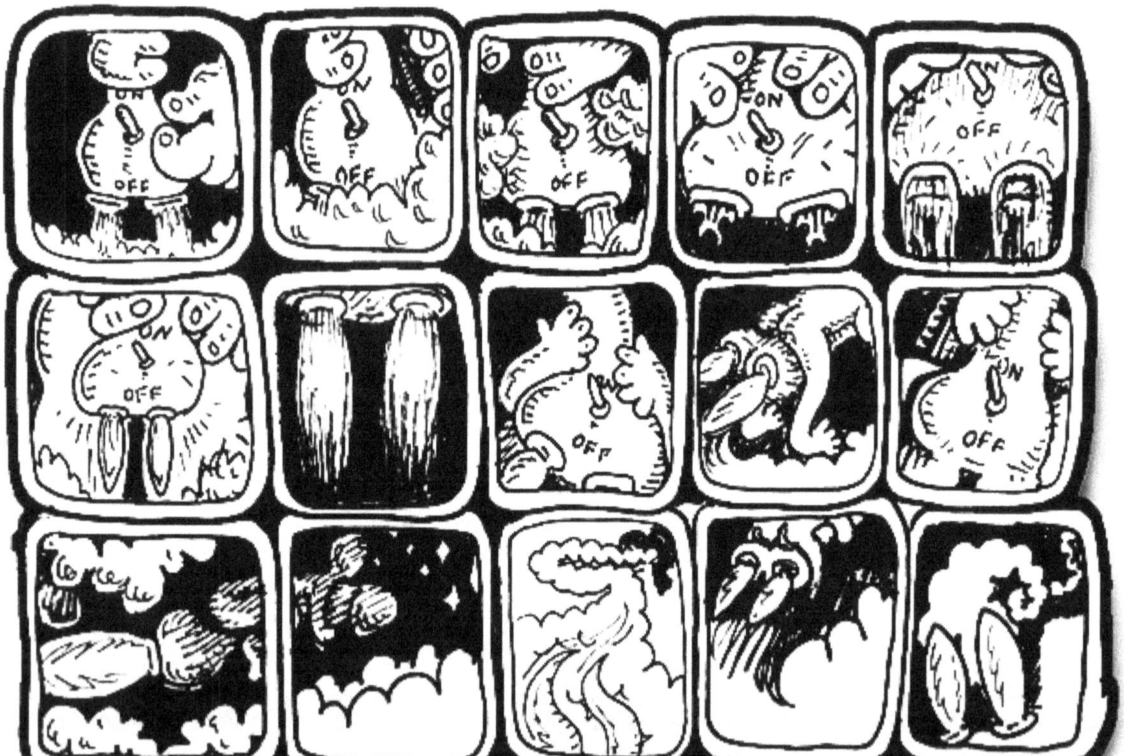
ON
OFF
ON
OFF
OFF
ON
OFF
OFF
ON
OFF
OFF
ON
OFF

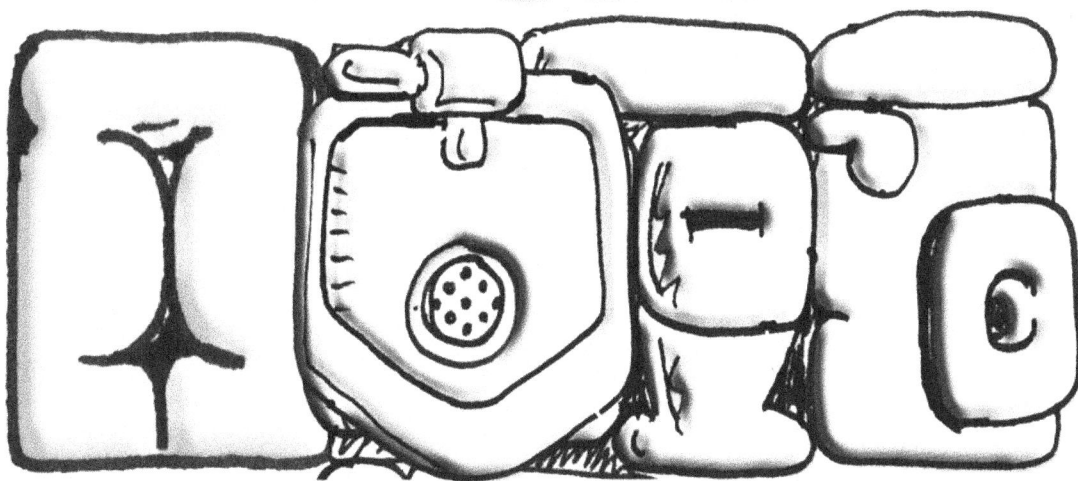

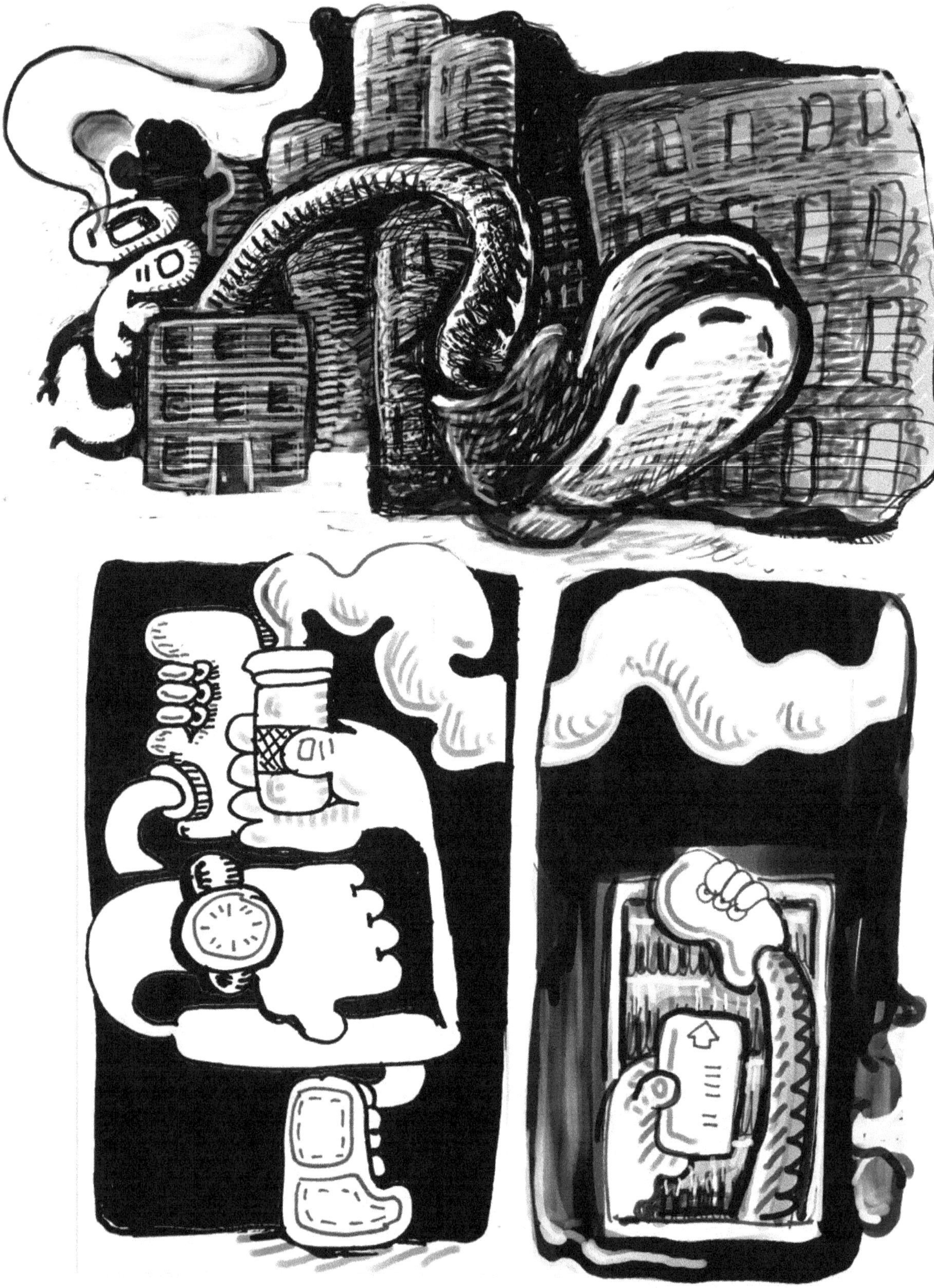

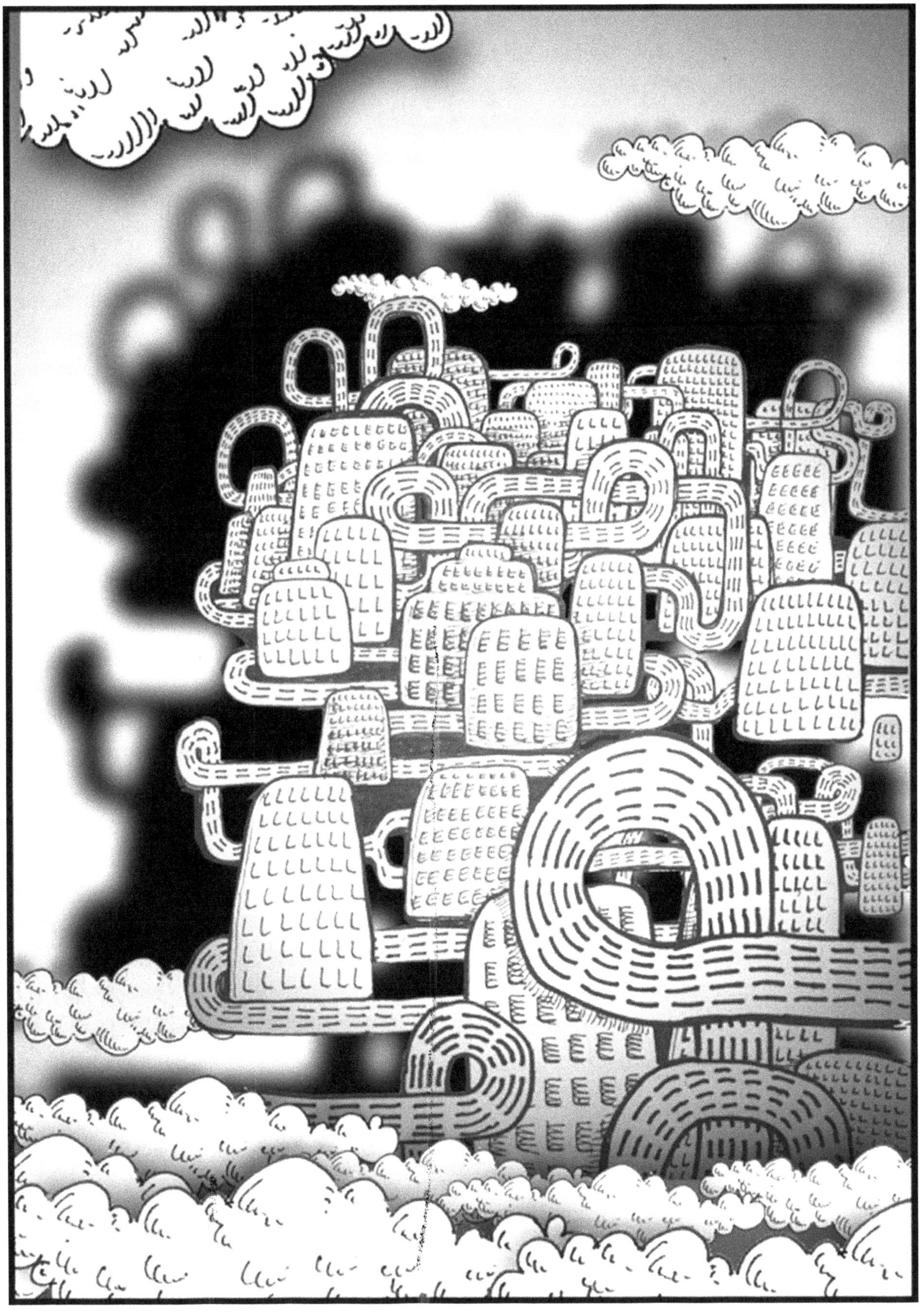

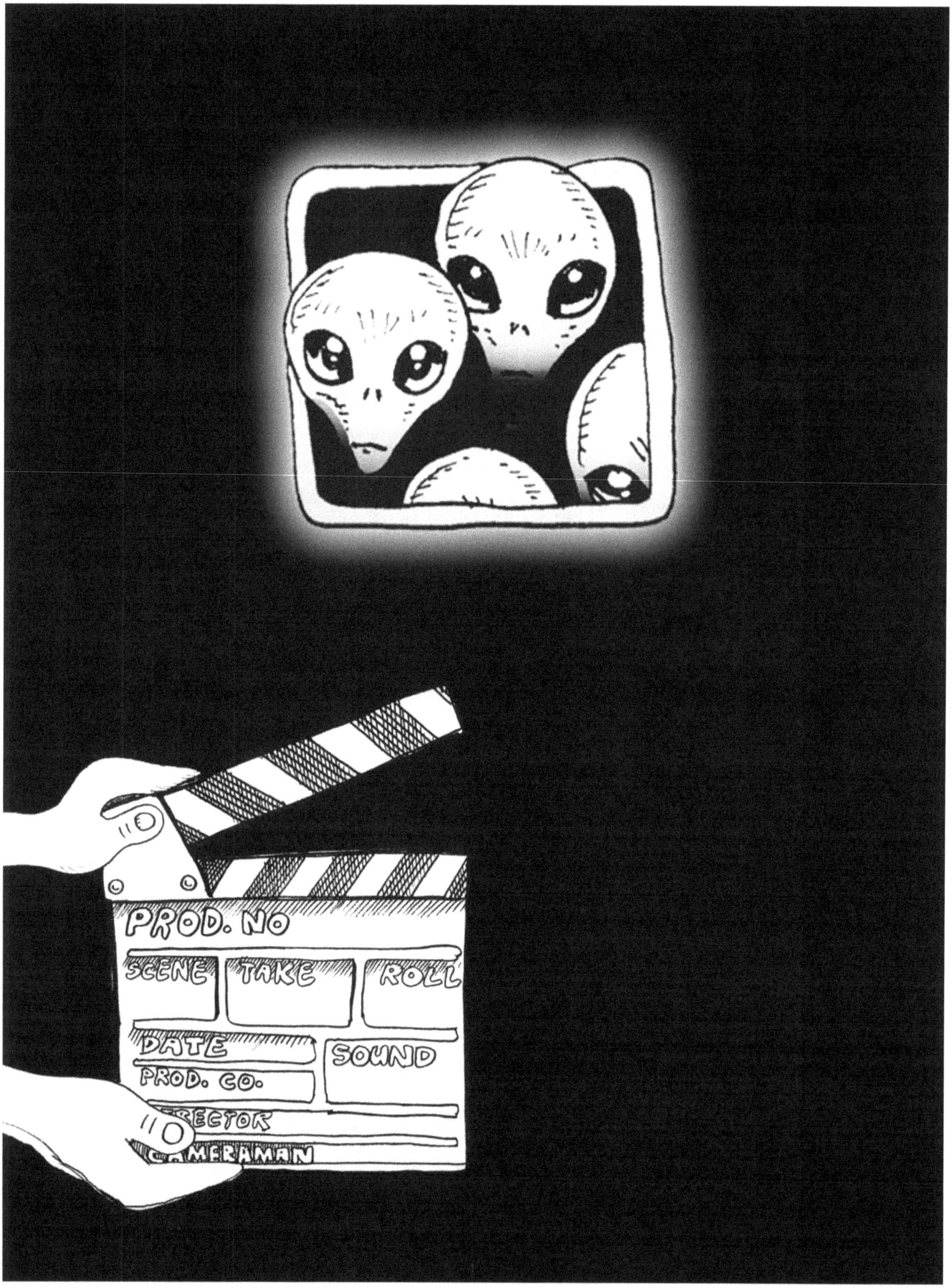
PROD. NO
SCENE
TAKE
ROLL
DATE
SOUND
PROD. CO.
CAMERAMAN

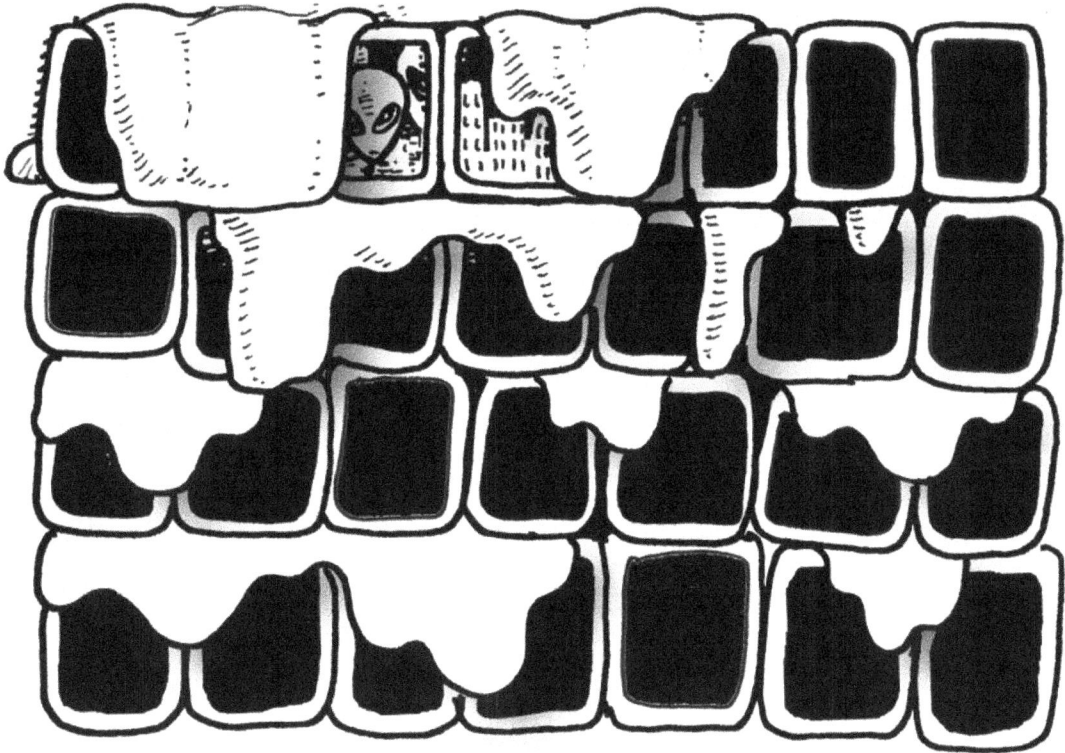

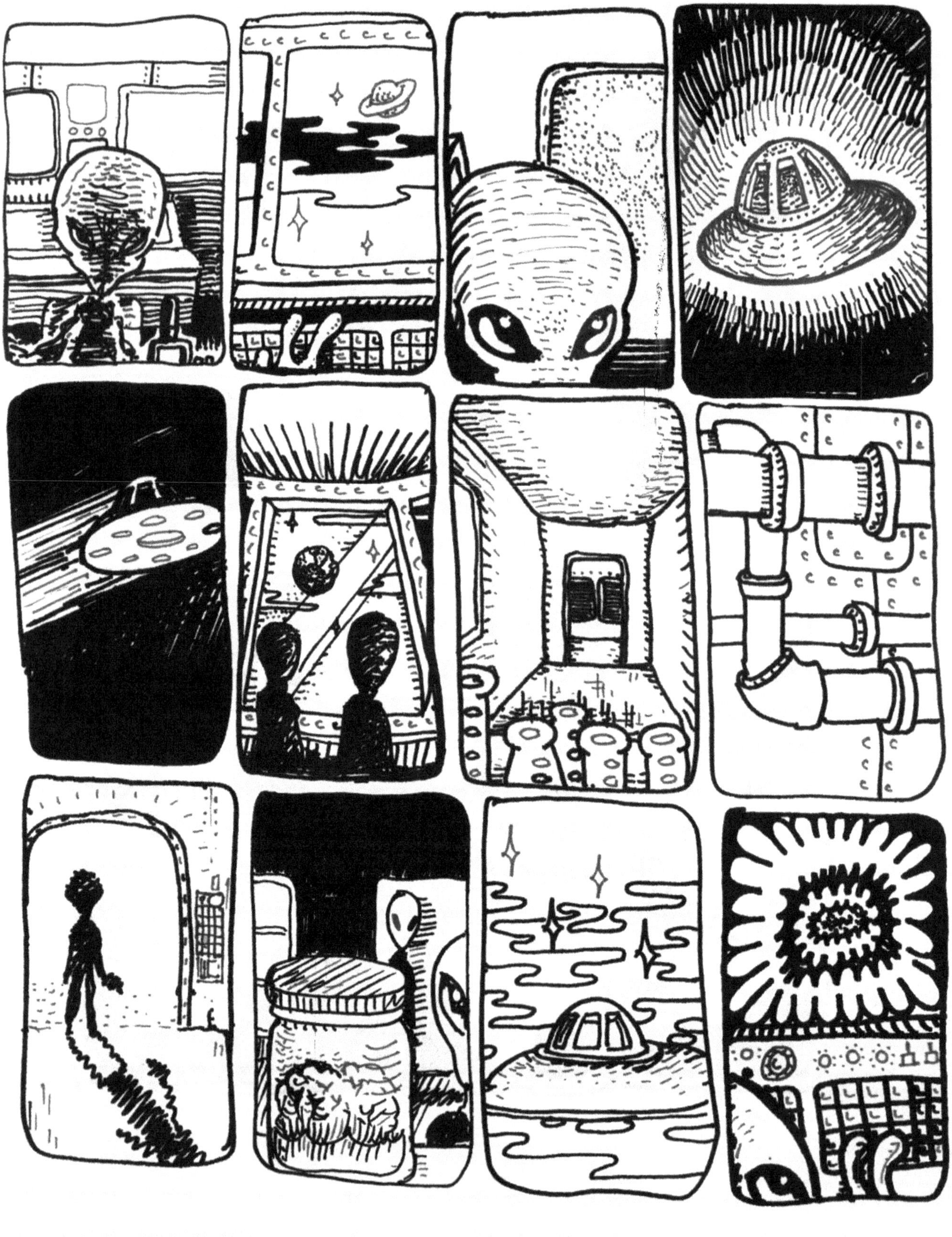

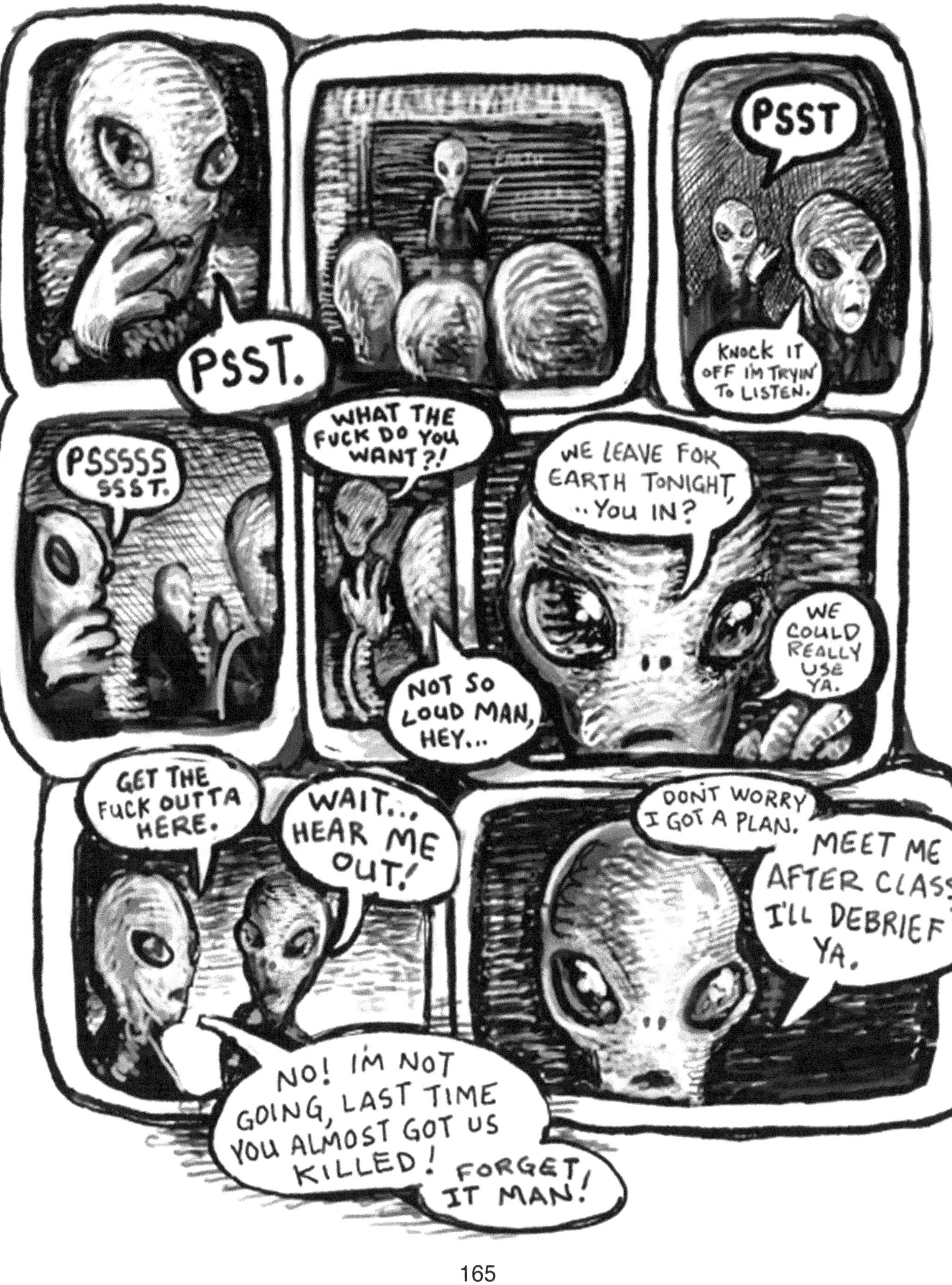

PSST.
PSST
KNOCK IT OFF I'M TRYIN' TO LISTEN.
PSSSSS SSST.
WHAT THE FUCK DO YOU WANT?!
NOT SO LOUD MAN, HEY...
WE LEAVE FOR EARTH TONIGHT, ..YOU IN?
WE COULD REALLY USE YA.
GET THE FUCK OUTTA HERE.
WAIT..., HEAR ME OUT!
NO! I'M NOT GOING, LAST TIME YOU ALMOST GOT US KILLED! FORGET IT MAN!
DON'T WORRY I GOT A PLAN.
MEET ME AFTER CLASS, I'LL DEBRIEF YA.

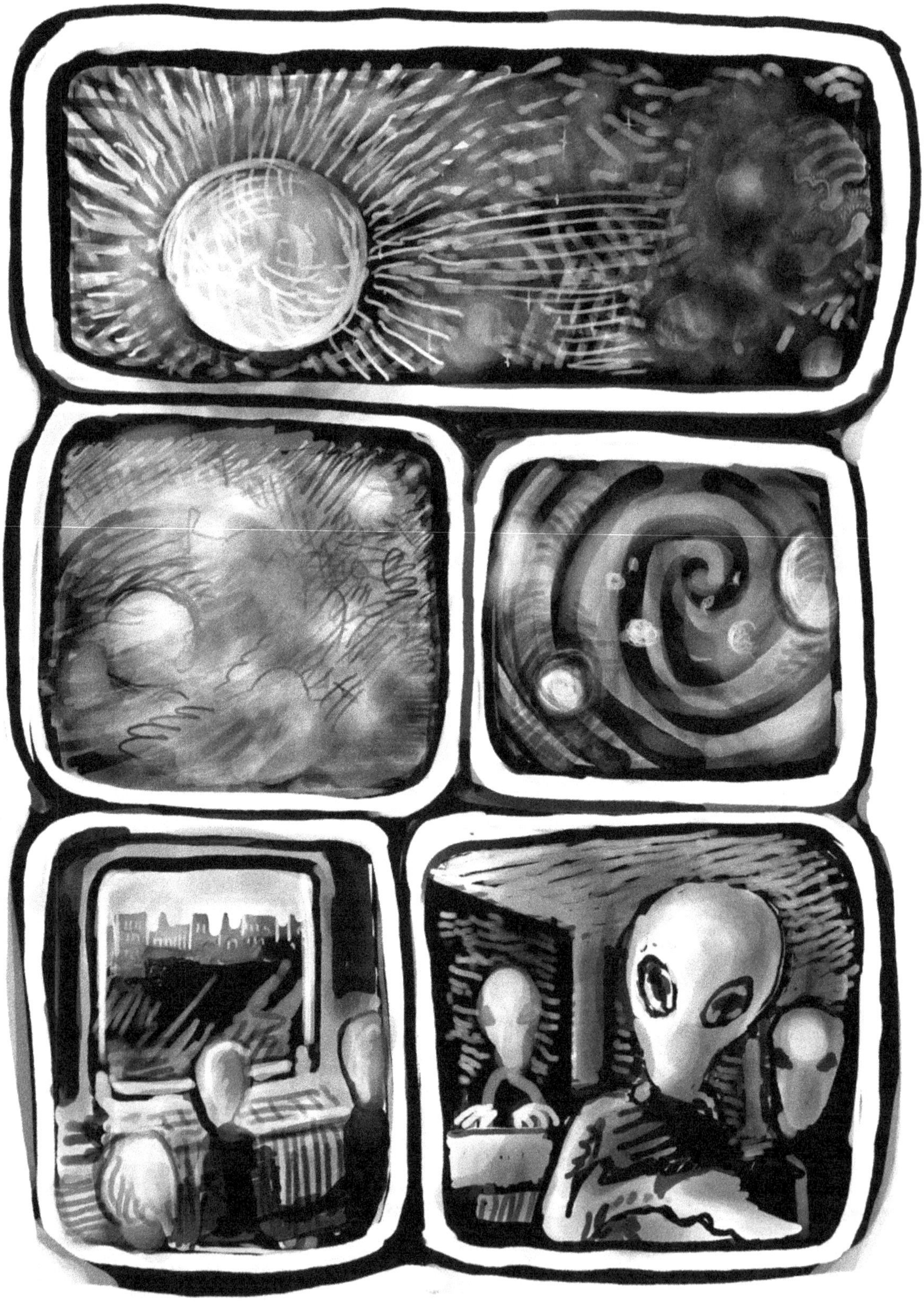

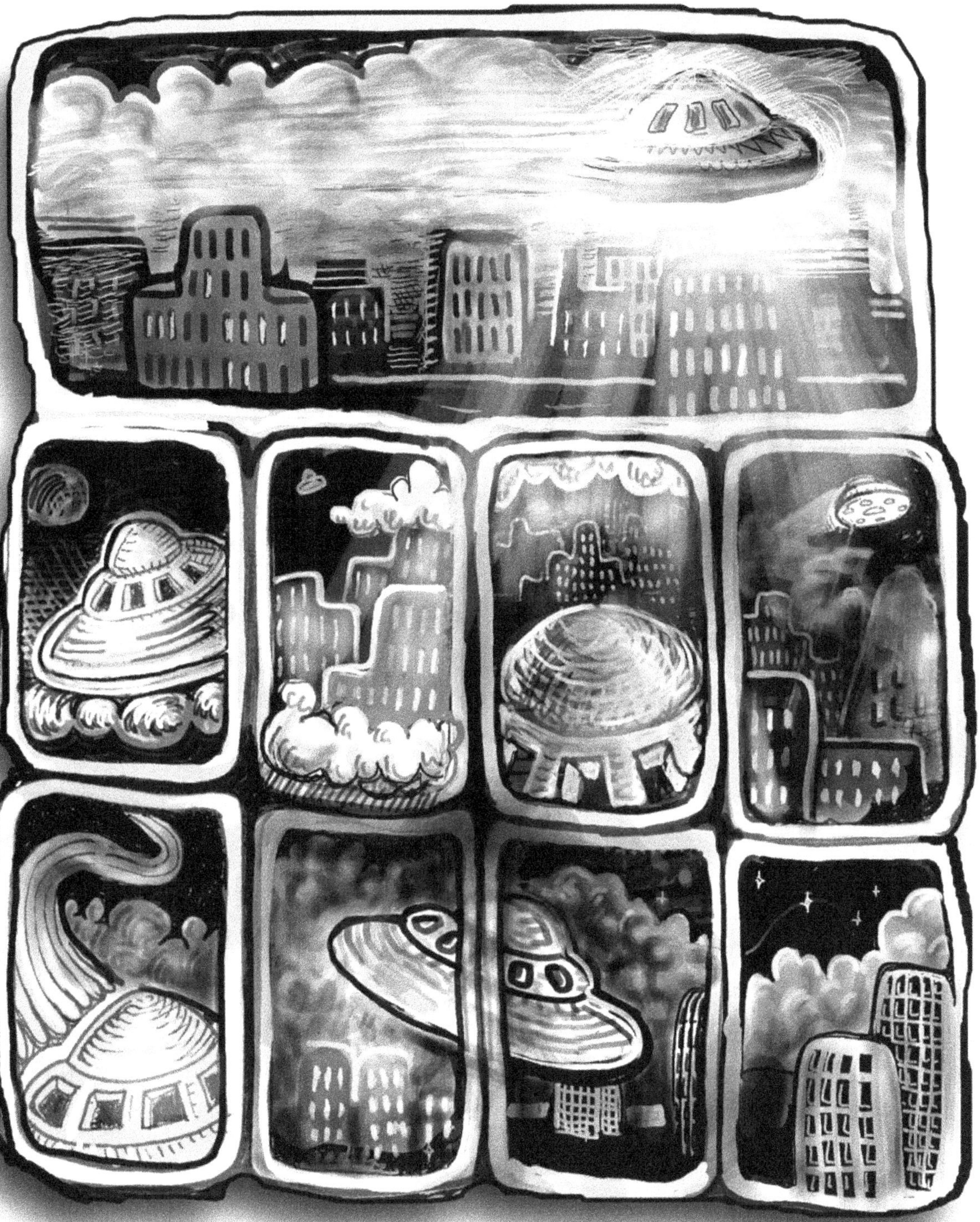

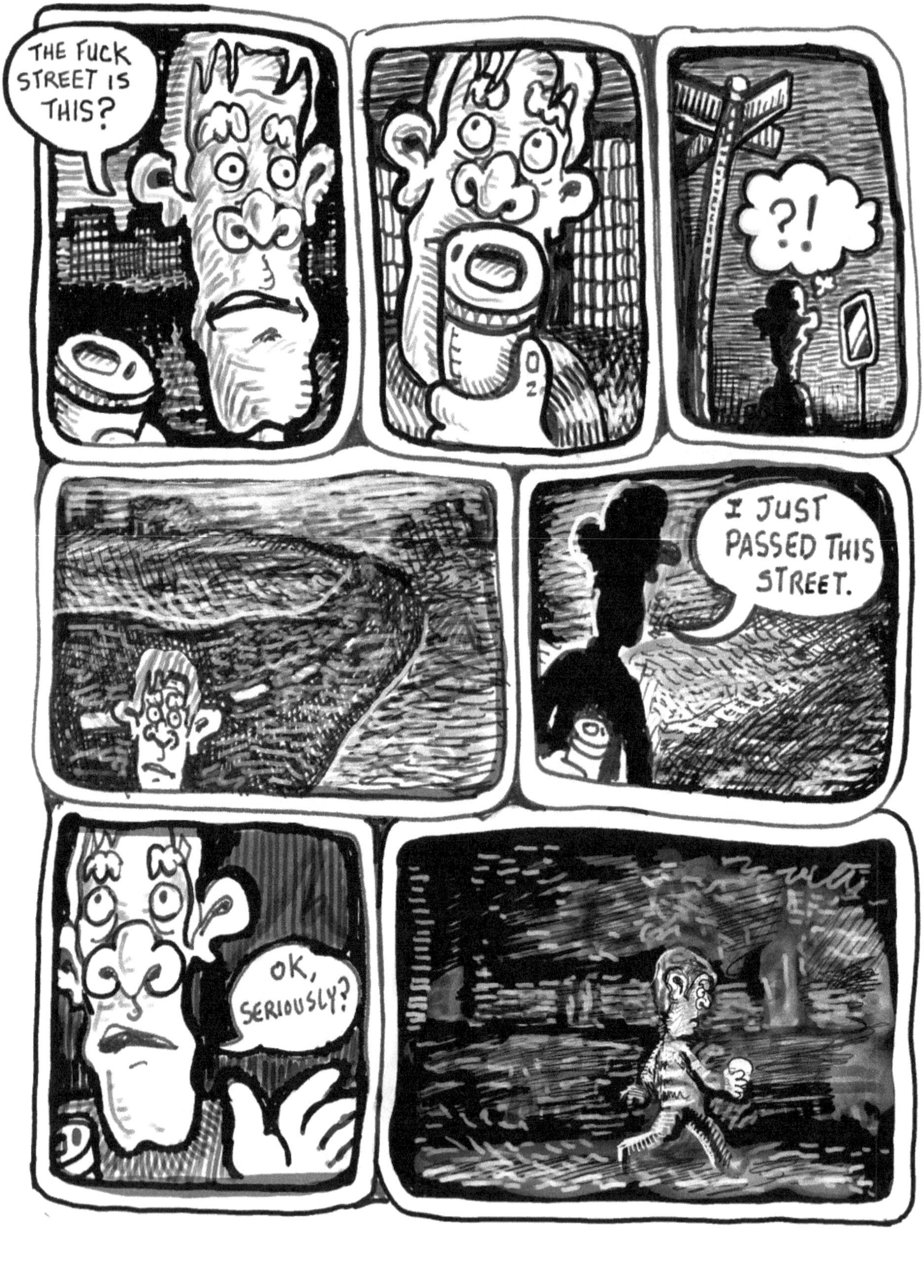
THE FUCK STREET IS THIS?
?!
I JUST PASSED THIS STREET.
OK, SERIOUSLY?

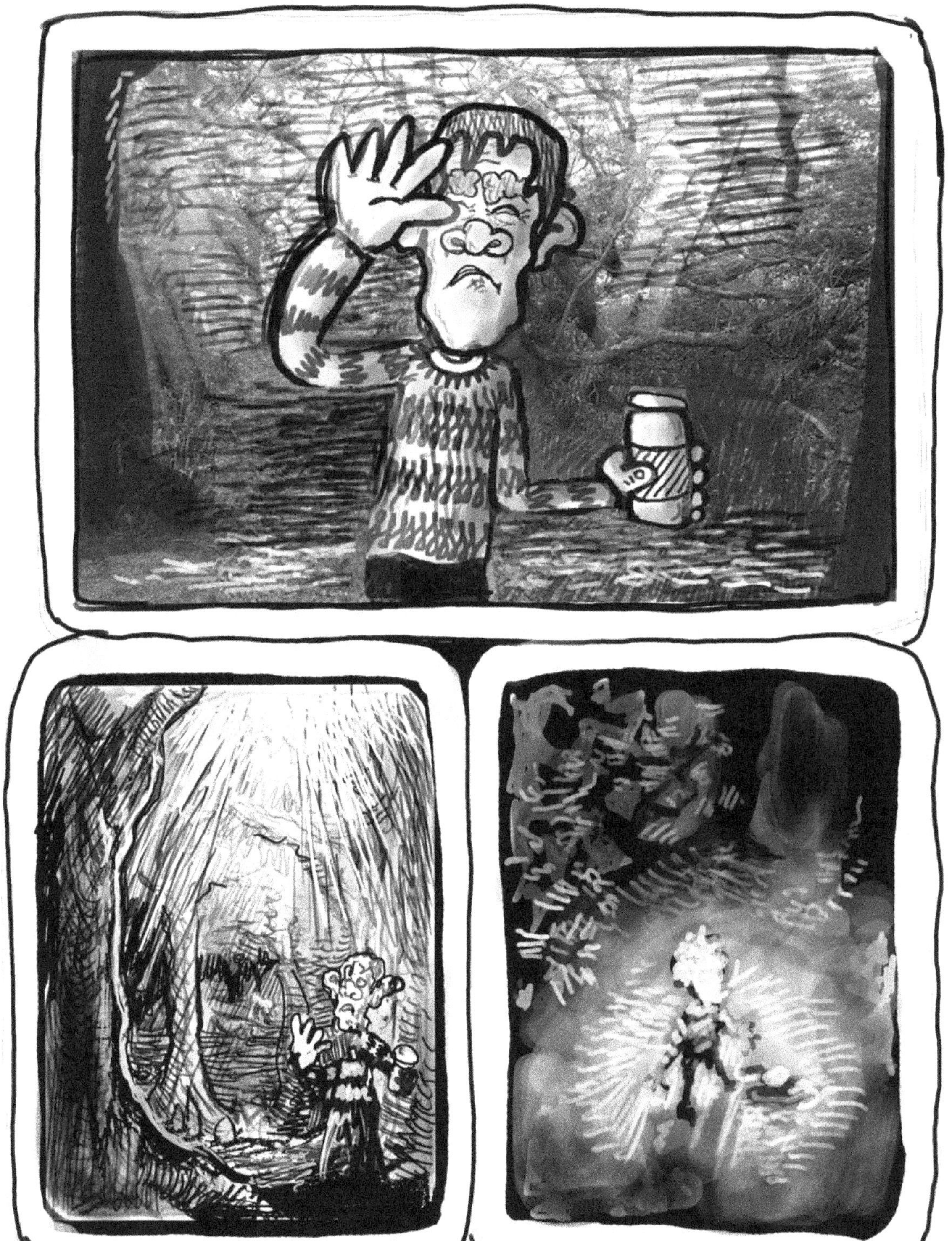

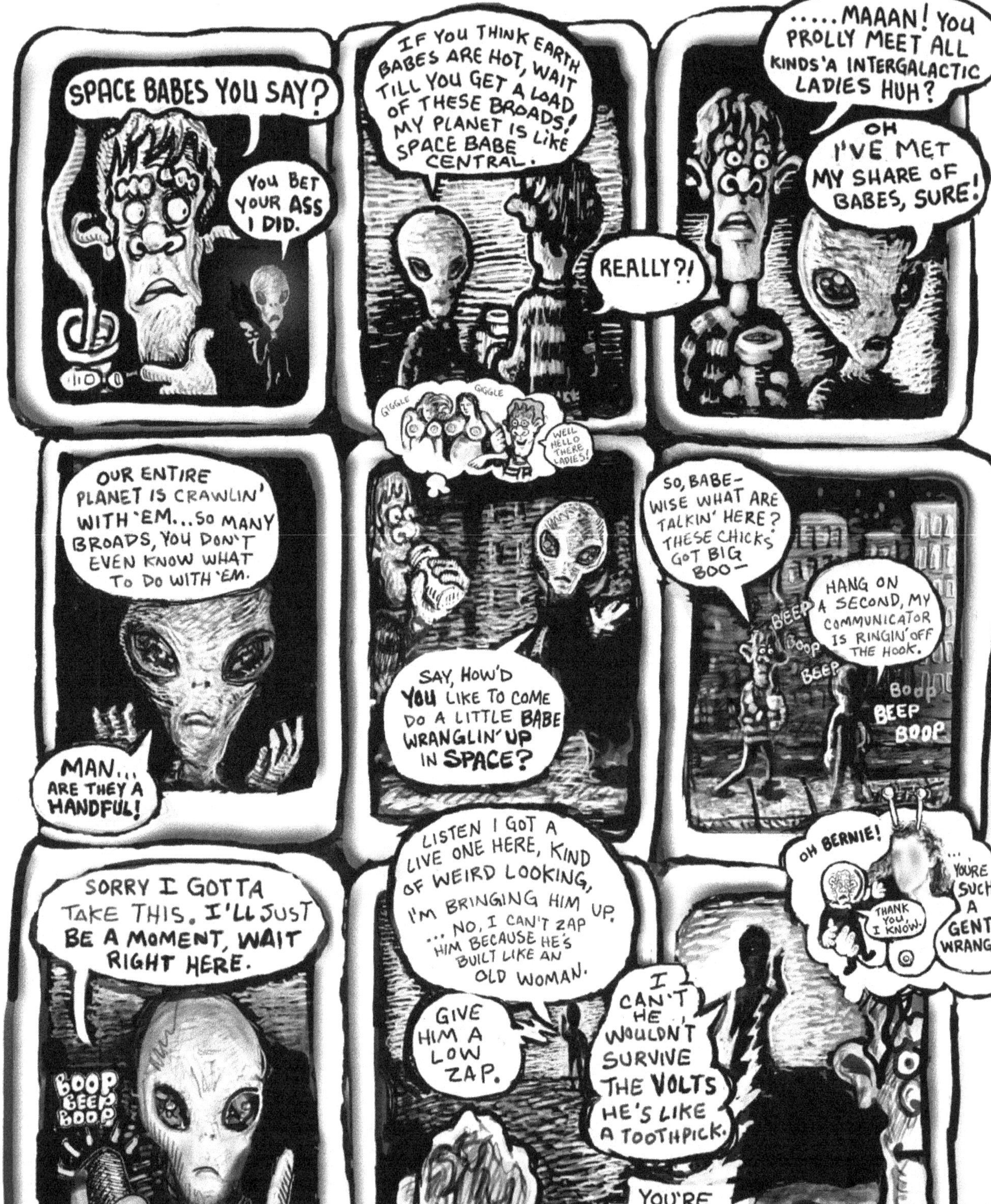
SPACE BABES YOU SAY?
YOU BET YOUR ASS I DID.
IF YOU THINK EARTH BABES ARE HOT, WAIT TILL YOU GET A LOAD OF THESE BROADS! MY PLANET IS LIKE SPACE BABE CENTRAL.
REALLY?!
GIGGLE GIGGLE
WELL HELLO THERE LADIES!
.....MAAAN! YOU PROLLY MEET ALL KINDS'A INTERGALACTIC LADIES HUH?
OH I'VE MET MY SHARE OF BABES, SURE!
OUR ENTIRE PLANET IS CRAWLIN' WITH 'EM...SO MANY BROADS, YOU DON'T EVEN KNOW WHAT TO DO WITH 'EM.
MAN... ARE THEY A HANDFUL!
SAY, HOW'D YOU LIKE TO COME DO A LITTLE BABE WRANGLIN' UP IN SPACE?
SO, BABE-WISE WHAT ARE TALKIN' HERE? THESE CHICKS GOT BIG BOO—
BEEP BOOP BEEP
HANG ON A SECOND, MY COMMUNICATOR IS RINGIN' OFF THE HOOK.
BOOP BEEP BOOP
SORRY I GOTTA TAKE THIS. I'LL JUST BE A MOMENT, WAIT RIGHT HERE.
BOOP BEEP BOOP
LISTEN I GOT A LIVE ONE HERE, KIND OF WEIRD LOOKING, I'M BRINGING HIM UP. ... NO, I CAN'T ZAP HIM BECAUSE HE'S BUILT LIKE AN OLD WOMAN.
GIVE HIM A LOW ZAP.
I CAN'T HE WOULDN'T SURVIVE THE VOLTS HE'S LIKE A TOOTHPICK.
OH BERNIE!
THANK YOU, I KNOW.
... YOU'RE SUCH A GENTLE WRANGLER.
YOU'RE NOT BRINGING A LIVE REDNECK ON THE SHIP, PUT HIM DOWN!

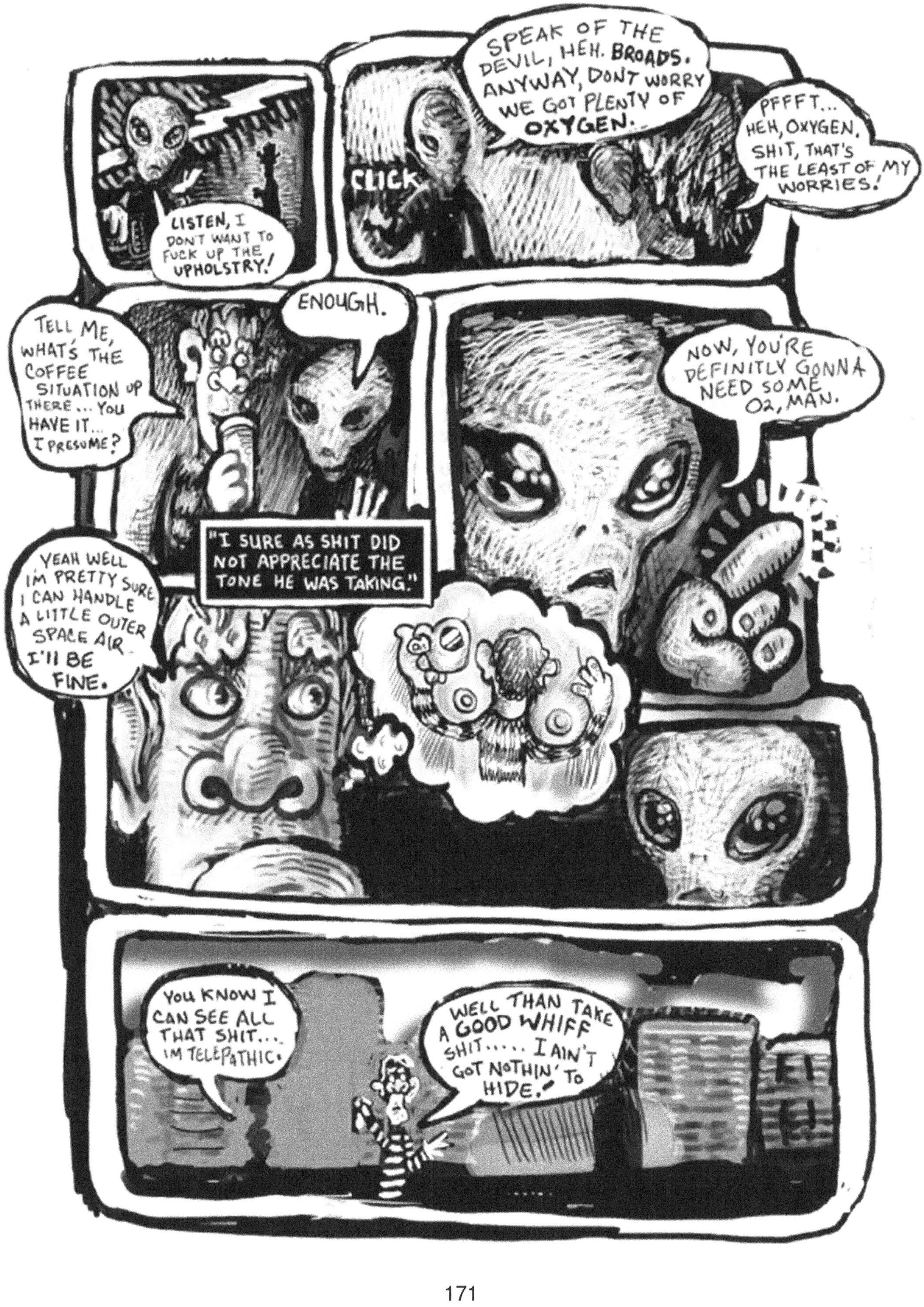
LISTEN, I DON'T WANT TO FUCK UP THE UPHOLSTRY!
CLICK
SPEAK OF THE DEVIL, HEH. BROADS. ANYWAY, DONT WORRY WE GOT PLENTY OF OXYGEN.
PFFFT... HEH, OXYGEN. SHIT, THAT'S THE LEAST OF MY WORRIES!
TELL ME, WHAT'S THE COFFEE SITUATION UP THERE... YOU HAVE IT... I PRESUME?
ENOUGH.
NOW, YOU'RE DEFINITLY GONNA NEED SOME O2, MAN.
"I SURE AS SHIT DID NOT APPRECIATE THE TONE HE WAS TAKING."
YEAH WELL IM PRETTY SURE I CAN HANDLE A LITTLE OUTER SPACE AIR. I'LL BE FINE.
YOU KNOW I CAN SEE ALL THAT SHIT... IM TELEPATHIC.
WELL THAN TAKE A GOOD WHIFF SHIT..... I AIN'T GOT NOTHIN' TO HIDE.

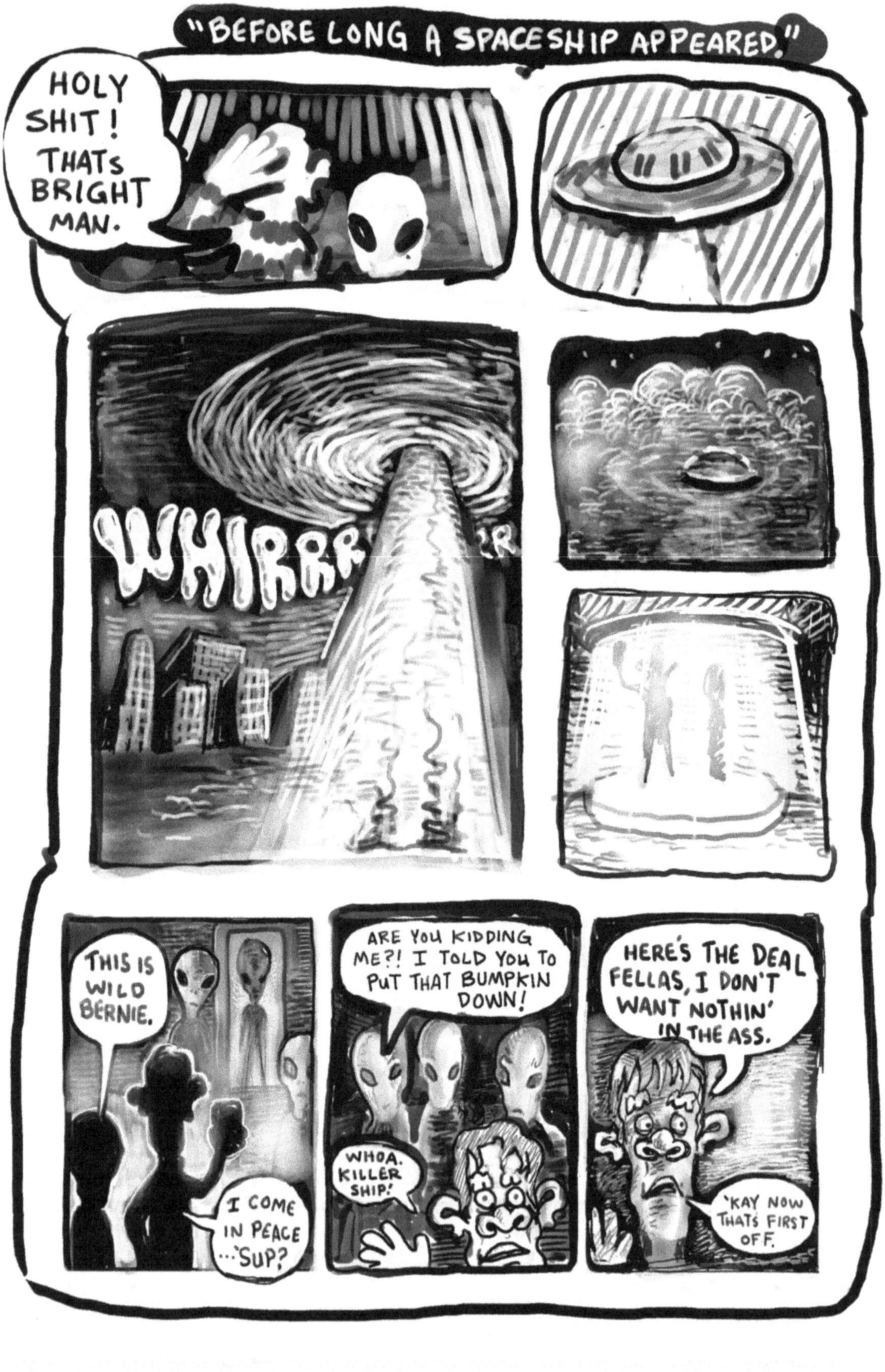
"BEFORE LONG A SPACESHIP APPEARED."
HOLY SHIT! THATS BRIGHT MAN.
WHIRRR
THIS IS WILD BERNIE.
I COME IN PEACE ...'SUP?
ARE YOU KIDDING ME?! I TOLD YOU TO PUT THAT BUMPKIN DOWN!
WHOA. KILLER SHIP!
HERE'S THE DEAL FELLAS, I DON'T WANT NOTHIN' IN THE ASS.
'KAY NOW THATS FIRST OFF.

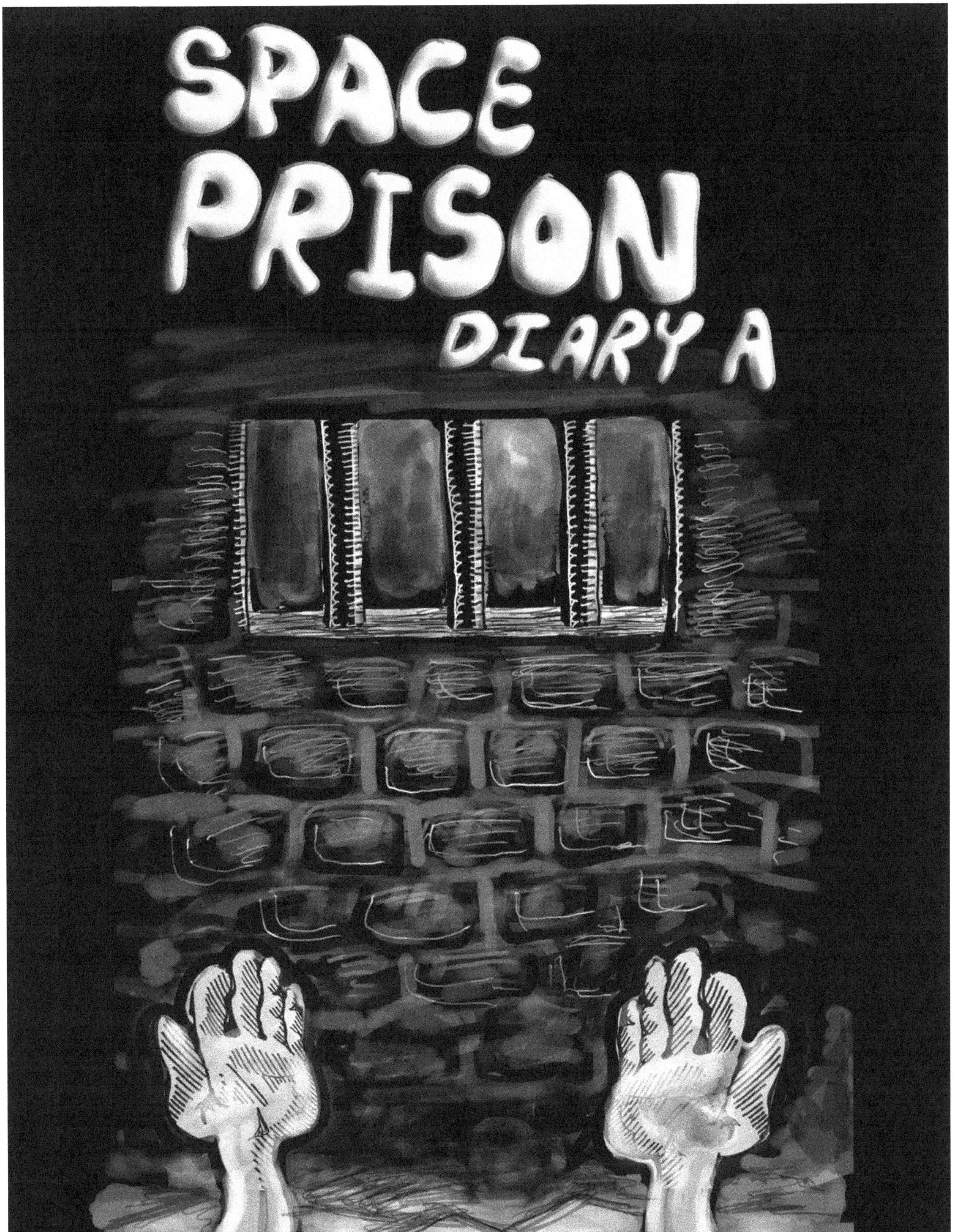
SPACE
PRISON
DIARY A

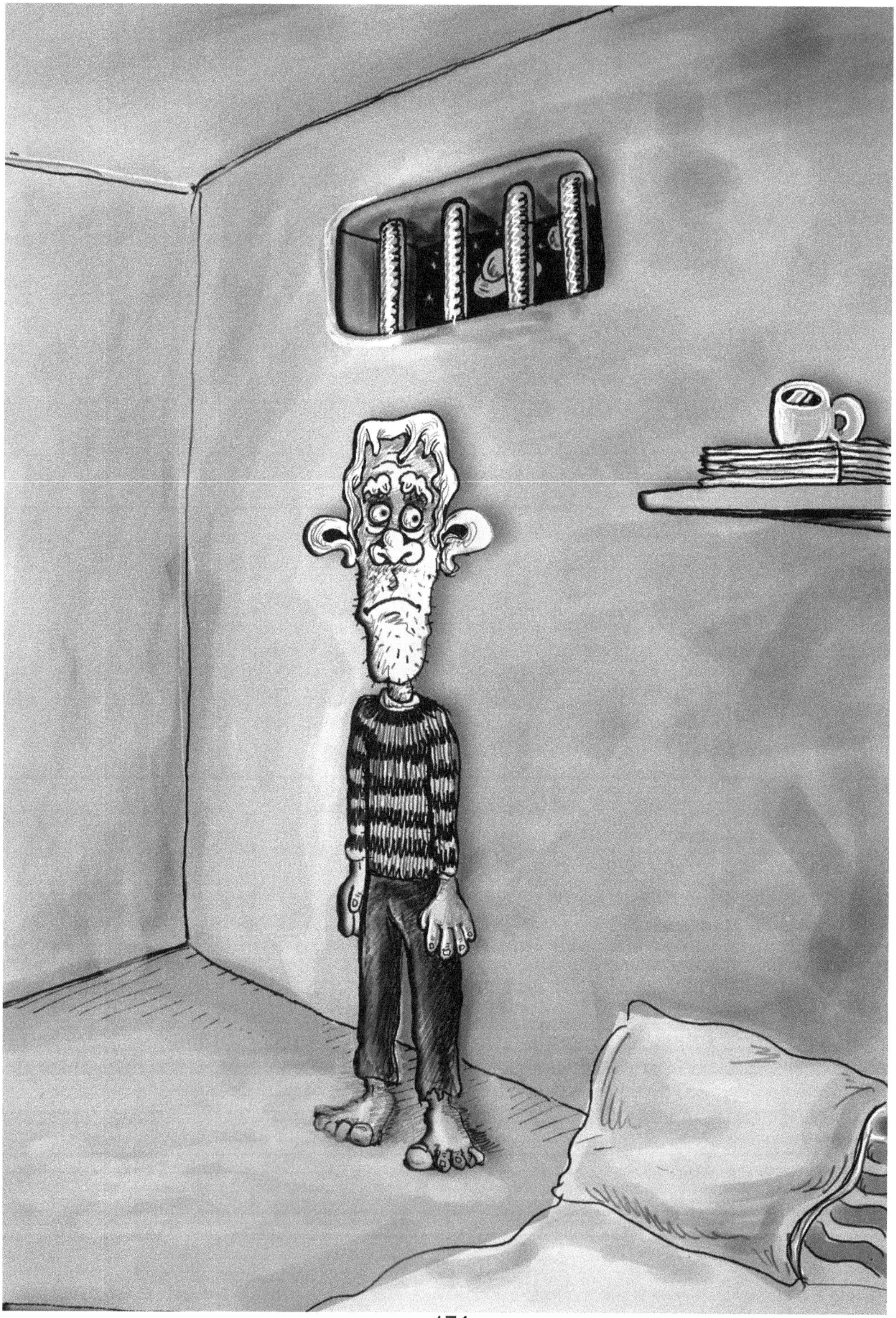

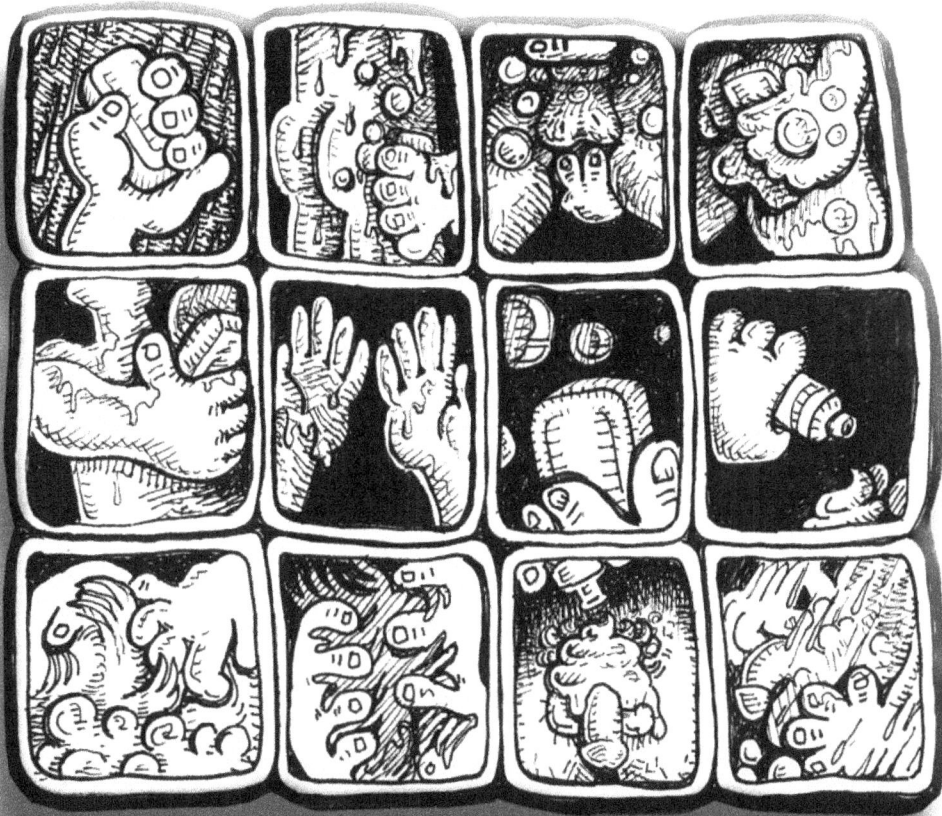

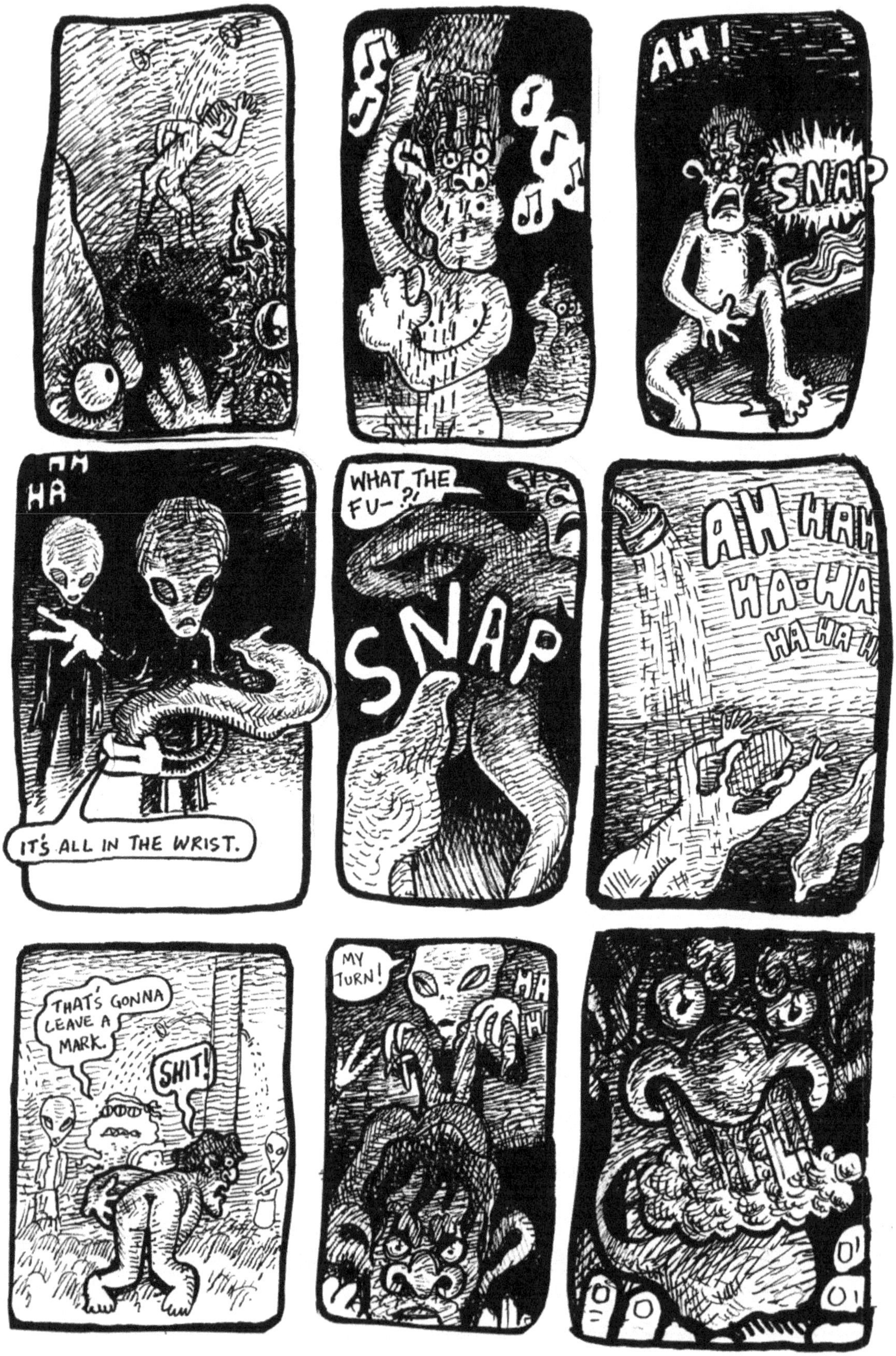
AH!
SNAP
HA HA
IT'S ALL IN THE WRIST.
WHAT THE FU-?!
SNAP
AH HAH
HA-HA
HA HA H
THAT'S GONNA LEAVE A MARK.
SHIT!
MY TURN!
HA H

YOU BOYS OKAY ?!
YEAH NO SWEAT.
LOOKIN' REAL PINK.
HA HA HA HA HA
KISS MY PINK FUCKIN' ASS ALL OF YA!
YOU SPANKED THE WRONG GUY!

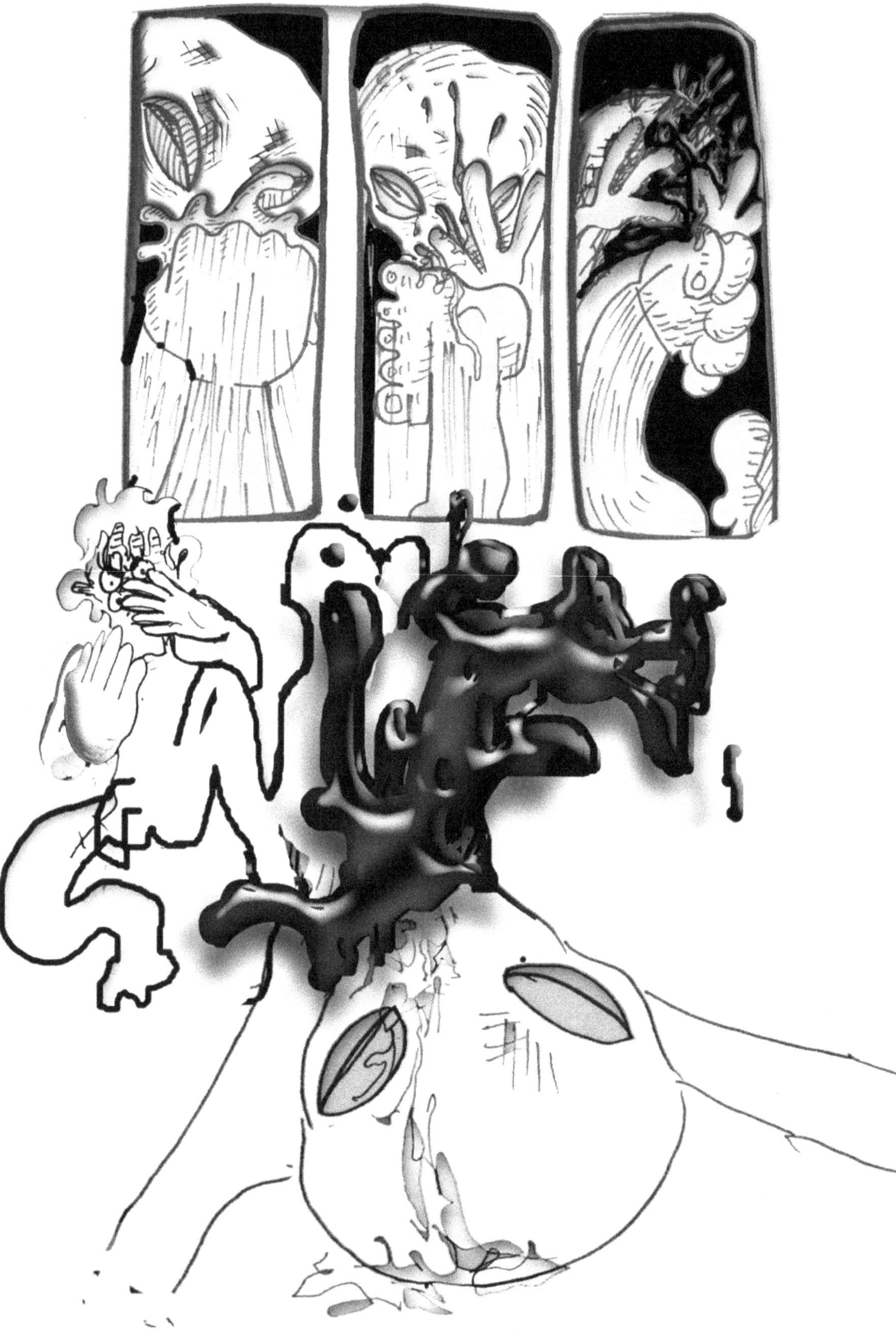

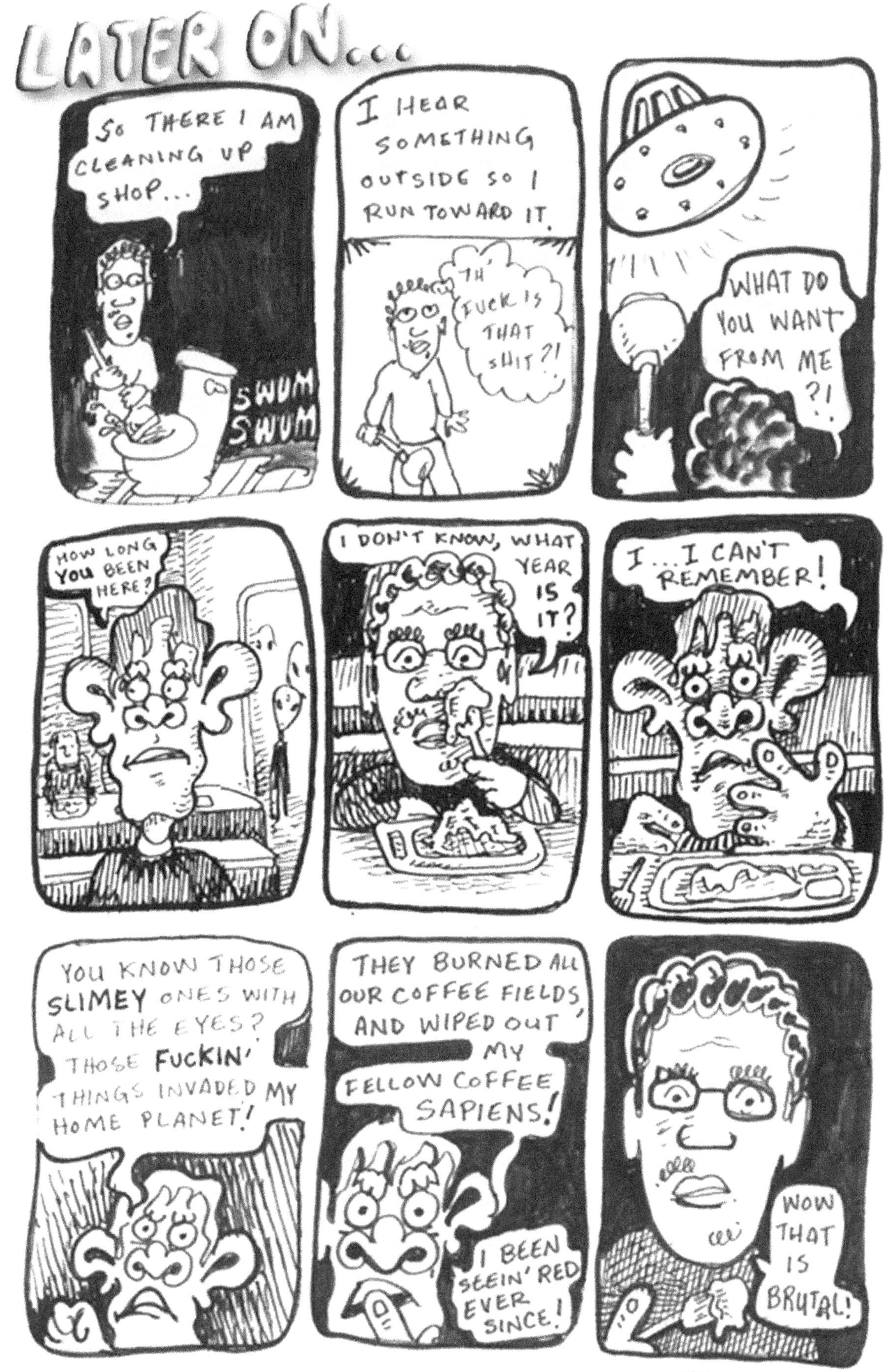
LATER ON...
SO THERE I AM CLEANING UP SHOP...
SWUM SWUM
I HEAR SOMETHING OUTSIDE SO I RUN TOWARD IT.
TH' FUCK IS THAT SHIT?!
WHAT DO YOU WANT FROM ME?!
HOW LONG YOU BEEN HERE?
I DON'T KNOW, WHAT YEAR IS IT?
I... I CAN'T REMEMBER!
YOU KNOW THOSE SLIMEY ONES WITH ALL THE EYES? THOSE FUCKIN' THINGS INVADED MY HOME PLANET!
THEY BURNED ALL OUR COFFEE FIELDS, AND WIPED OUT MY FELLOW COFFEE SAPIENS!
I BEEN SEEIN' RED EVER SINCE!
WOW THAT IS BRUTAL!

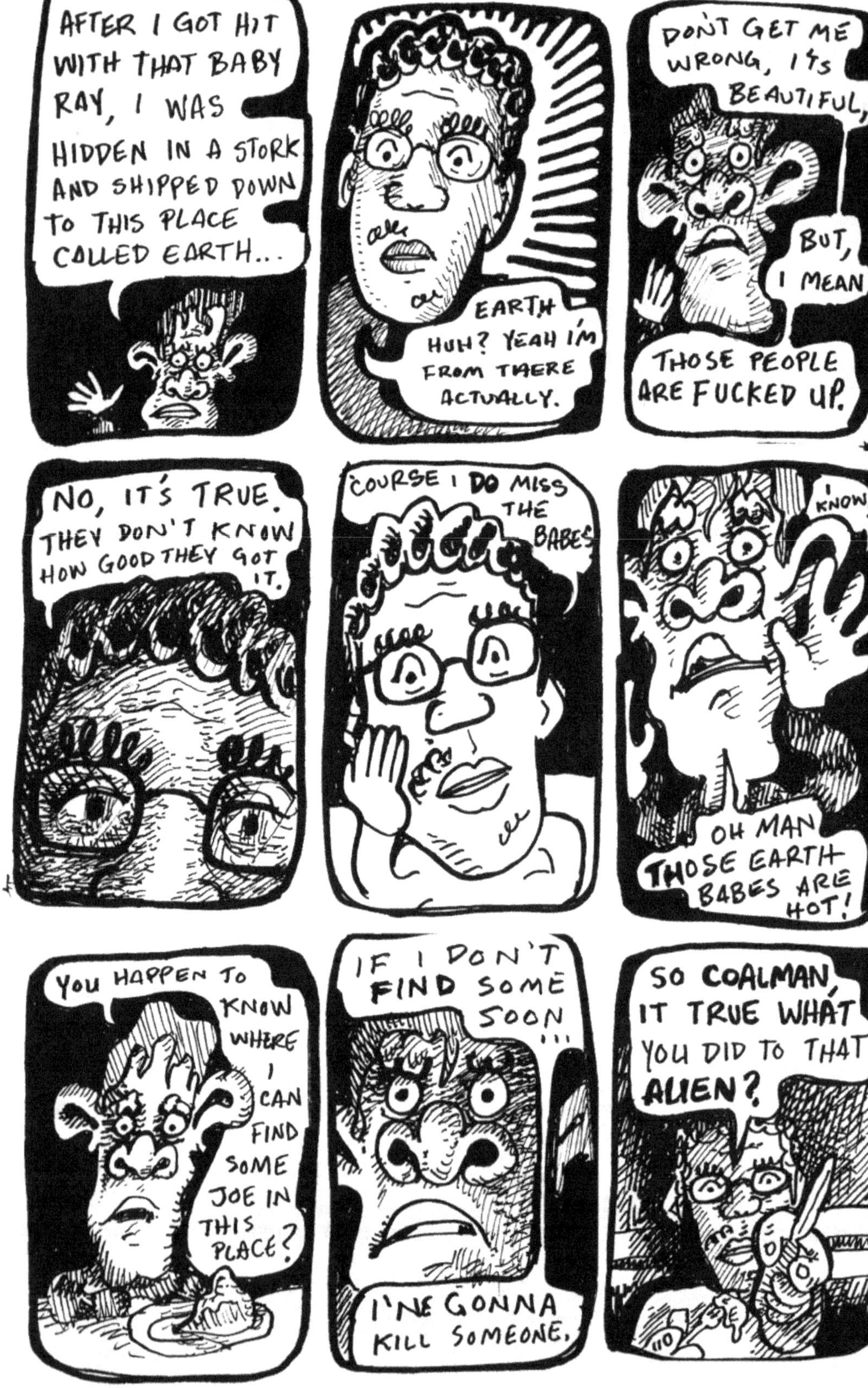
AFTER I GOT HIT WITH THAT BABY RAY, I WAS HIDDEN IN A STORK AND SHIPPED DOWN TO THIS PLACE CALLED EARTH...
EARTH HUH? YEAH I'M FROM THERE ACTUALLY.
DON'T GET ME WRONG, IT'S BEAUTIFUL,
BUT, I MEAN
THOSE PEOPLE ARE FUCKED UP.
NO, IT'S TRUE. THEY DON'T KNOW HOW GOOD THEY GOT IT.
COURSE I DO MISS THE BABES
I KNOW!
OH MAN THOSE EARTH BABES ARE HOT!
YOU HAPPEN TO KNOW WHERE I CAN FIND SOME JOE IN THIS PLACE?
IF I DON'T FIND SOME SOON...
I'M GONNA KILL SOMEONE.
SO COALMAN, IT TRUE WHAT YOU DID TO THAT ALIEN?

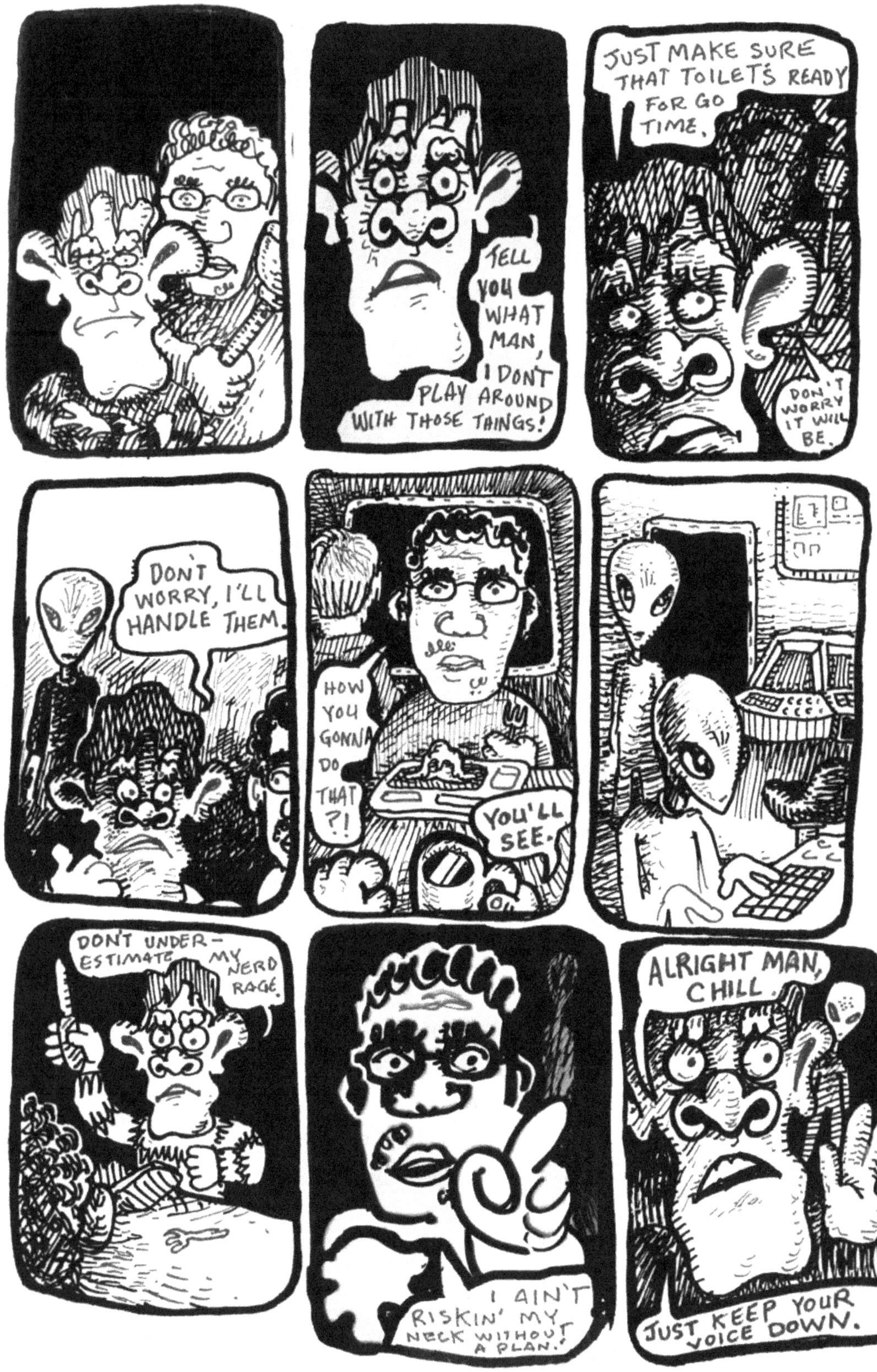
TELL YOU WHAT MAN, I DON'T PLAY AROUND WITH THOSE THINGS!
JUST MAKE SURE THAT TOILET'S READY FOR GO TIME.
DON'T WORRY IT WILL BE.
DON'T WORRY, I'LL HANDLE THEM.
HOW YOU GONNA DO THAT?!
YOU'LL SEE.
DON'T UNDER-ESTIMATE MY NERD RAGE.
I AIN'T RISKIN' MY NECK WITHOUT A PLAN.
ALRIGHT MAN, CHILL.
JUST KEEP YOUR VOICE DOWN.

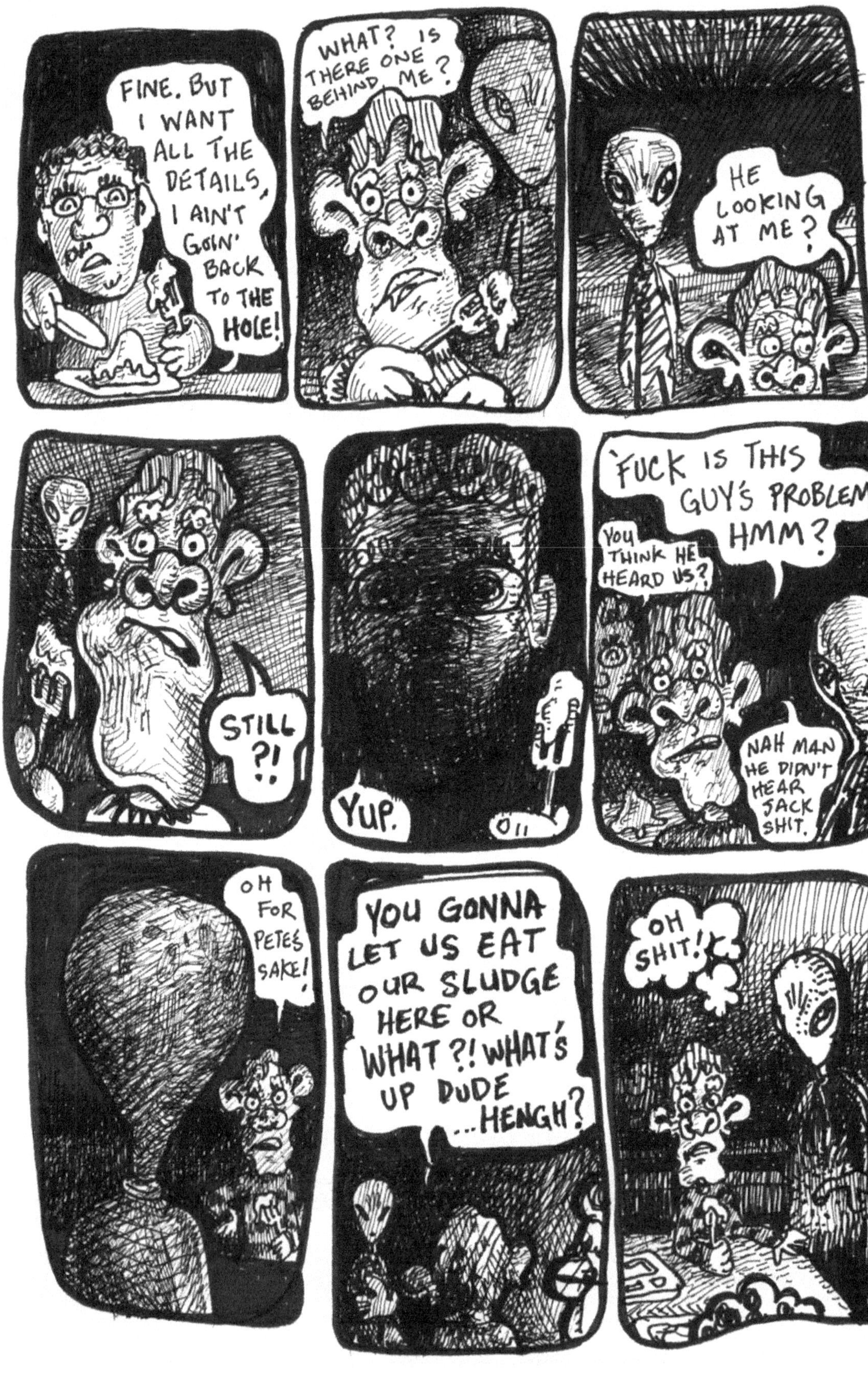

FINE. BUT I WANT ALL THE DETAILS, I AIN'T GOIN' BACK TO THE HOLE!
WHAT? IS THERE ONE BEHIND ME?
HE LOOKING AT ME?
STILL ?!
YUP.
`FUCK IS THIS GUY'S PROBLEM HMM?
YOU THINK HE HEARD US?
NAH MAN HE DIDN'T HEAR JACK SHIT.
OH FOR PETE'S SAKE!
YOU GONNA LET US EAT OUR SLUDGE HERE OR WHAT?! WHAT'S UP DUDE ...HENGH?
OH SHIT!

QUIT DIGGIN' IT IN, THAT SHIT HURTS... YOU 'BOUT DONE YET OR WHAT
HENGH ?
BZZZT BZZZT BZZZZ
BZZZT BZZZ ZZT
TOILET OOCH
YOU GOT SOME NERVE TALKIN' TO ME LIKE THAT PAL!
JUST HURRY UP ALREADY!
BZZZT BZZ
STUPID FUCKIN' ALIEN!
AND QUIT DRAGGIN IT!
TOILET OOCH

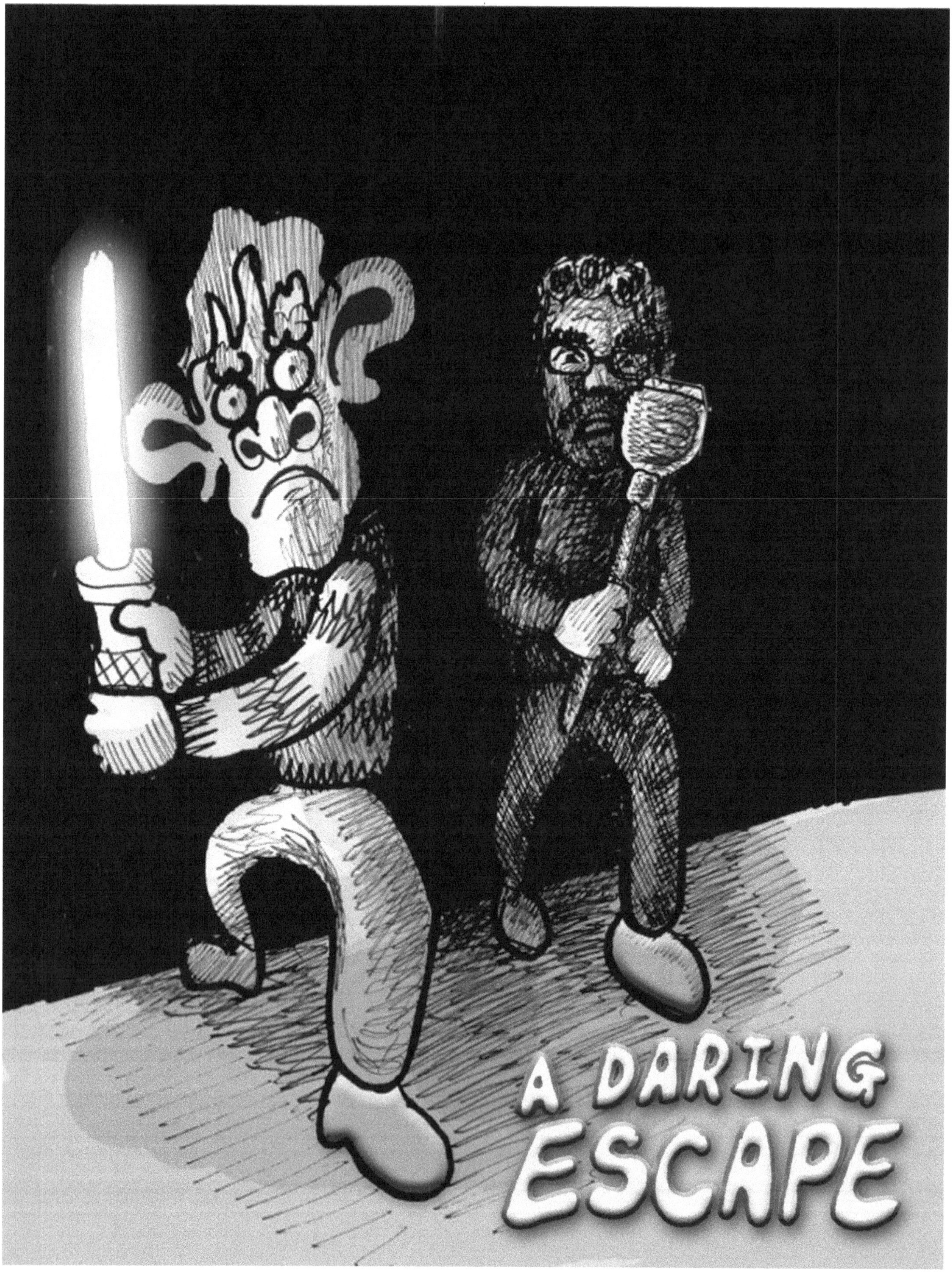
A DARING
ESCAPE

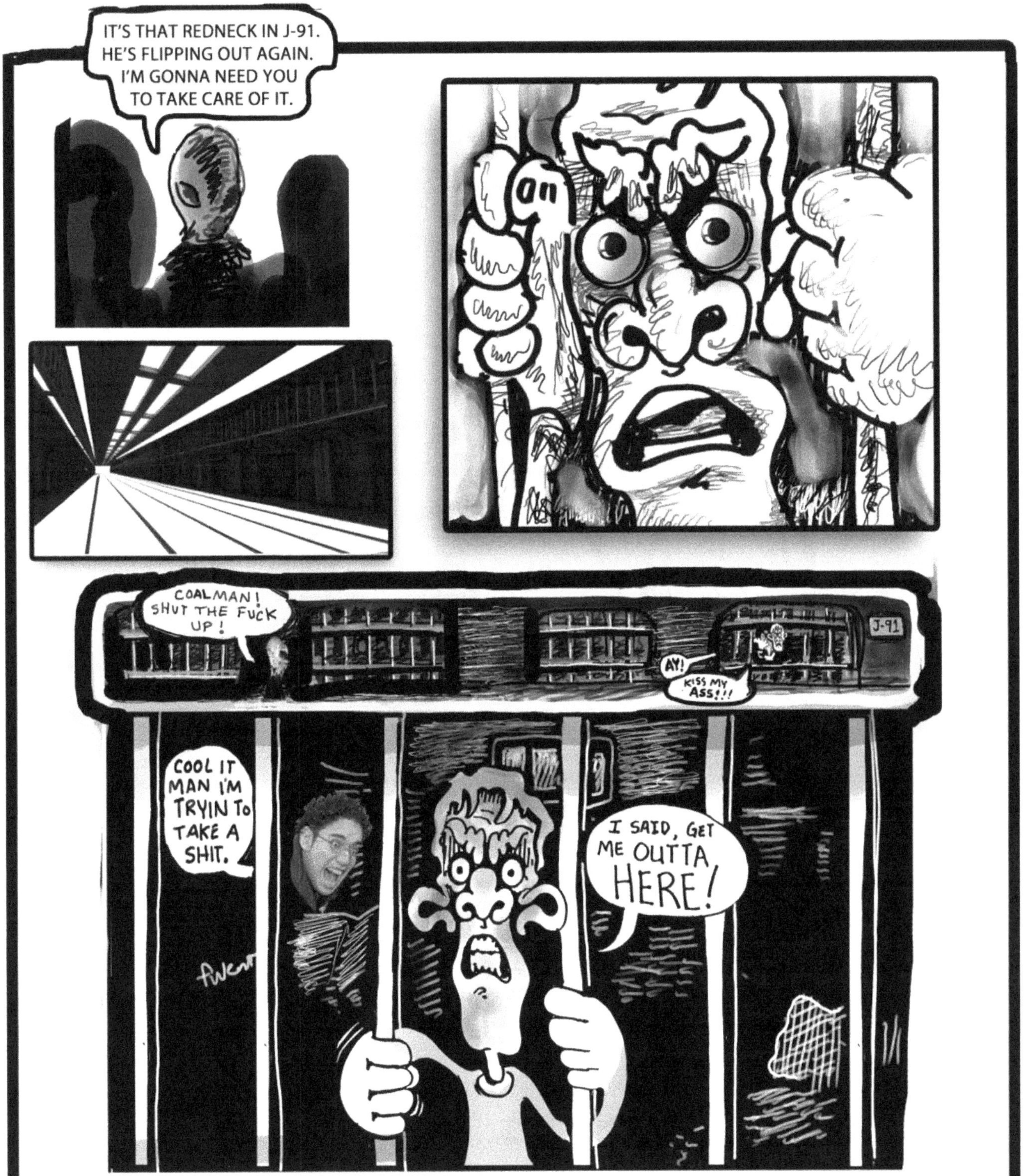
IT'S THAT REDNECK IN J-91.
HE'S FLIPPING OUT AGAIN.
I'M GONNA NEED YOU
TO TAKE CARE OF IT.
COALMAN! SHUT THE FUCK UP!
J-91
AY!
KISS MY ASS!!!
COOL IT MAN I'M TRYIN TO TAKE A SHIT.
I SAID, GET ME OUTTA HERE!

FILL IT UP WITH SOME OF THAT TOILET HOOCH AND WE'LL SEE WHAT THIS BABY CAN DO!
KAY NOW STAND BACK AND LET A PRO DO IT.
I'M SERIOUS I USED TO GO HUNTING WITH THE FELLAS ALL THE TIME ON MY HOME PLANET.
HOW HARD COULD IT BE?
HOLY SHIT!
OKAY. TURN IT OFF QUICK!
ZOOCH
ZZOOCH
YOU TRYIN' TO GET US ZAPPED ?!

NO WAY!
SCRATCH SCRATCH
HEY MELT SOME OF THESE BARS FOR ME MAN!
WELL,
OK.
HE'S COOL LET HIM OUT
THANK YOU SIR!
OH, THANK YOU!
THANK YOU!
NO PROB.

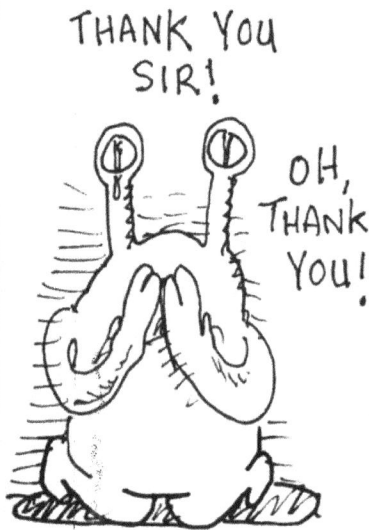

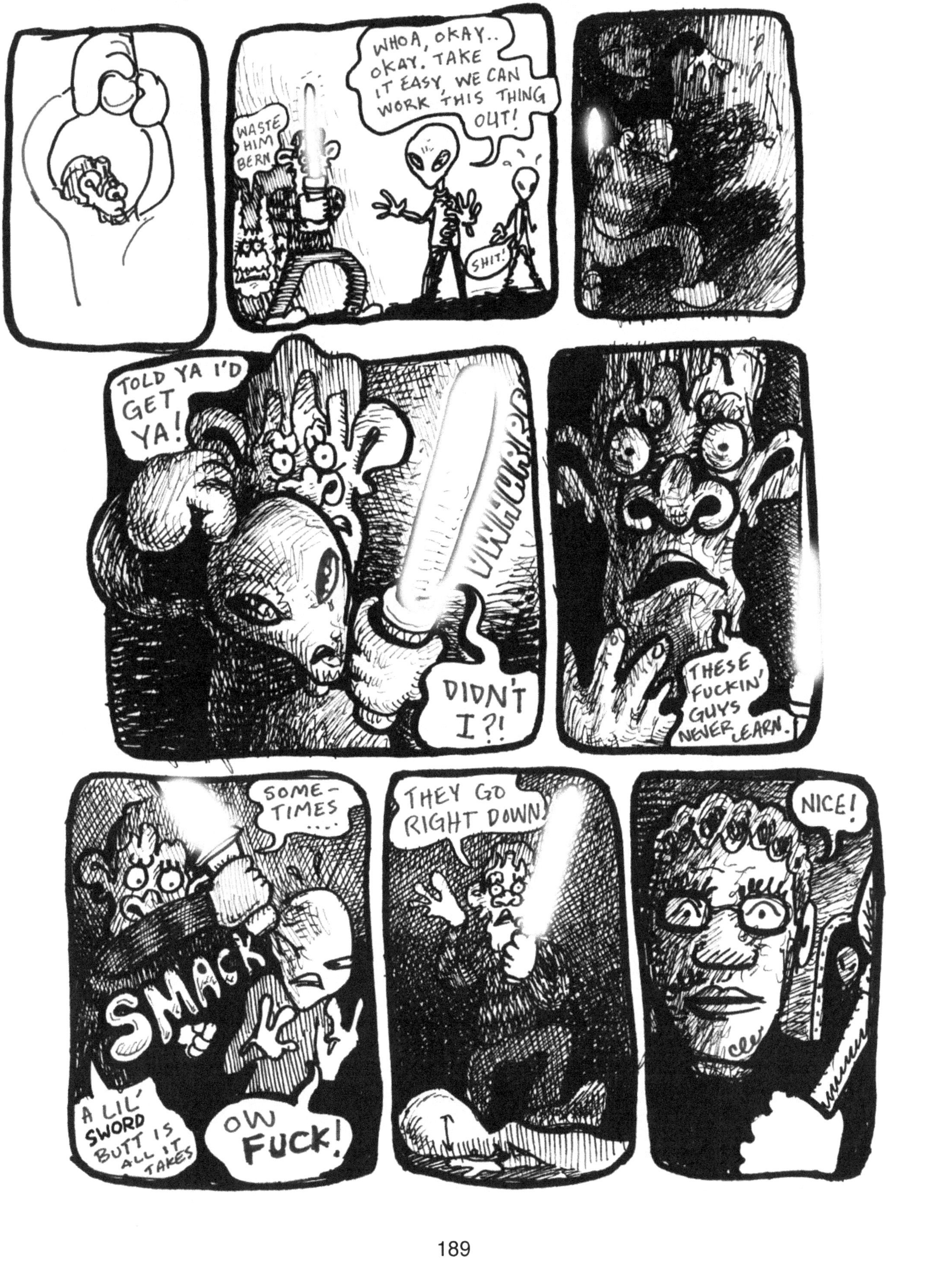
WASTE HIM BERN
WHOA, OKAY.. OKAY. TAKE IT EASY, WE CAN WORK THIS THING OUT!
SHIT!
TOLD YA I'D GET YA!
DIDN'T I?!
THESE FUCKIN' GUYS NEVER LEARN.
SOME-TIMES ...
SMACK
A LIL' SWORD BUTT IS ALL IT TAKES
OW FUCK!
THEY GO RIGHT DOWN
NICE!

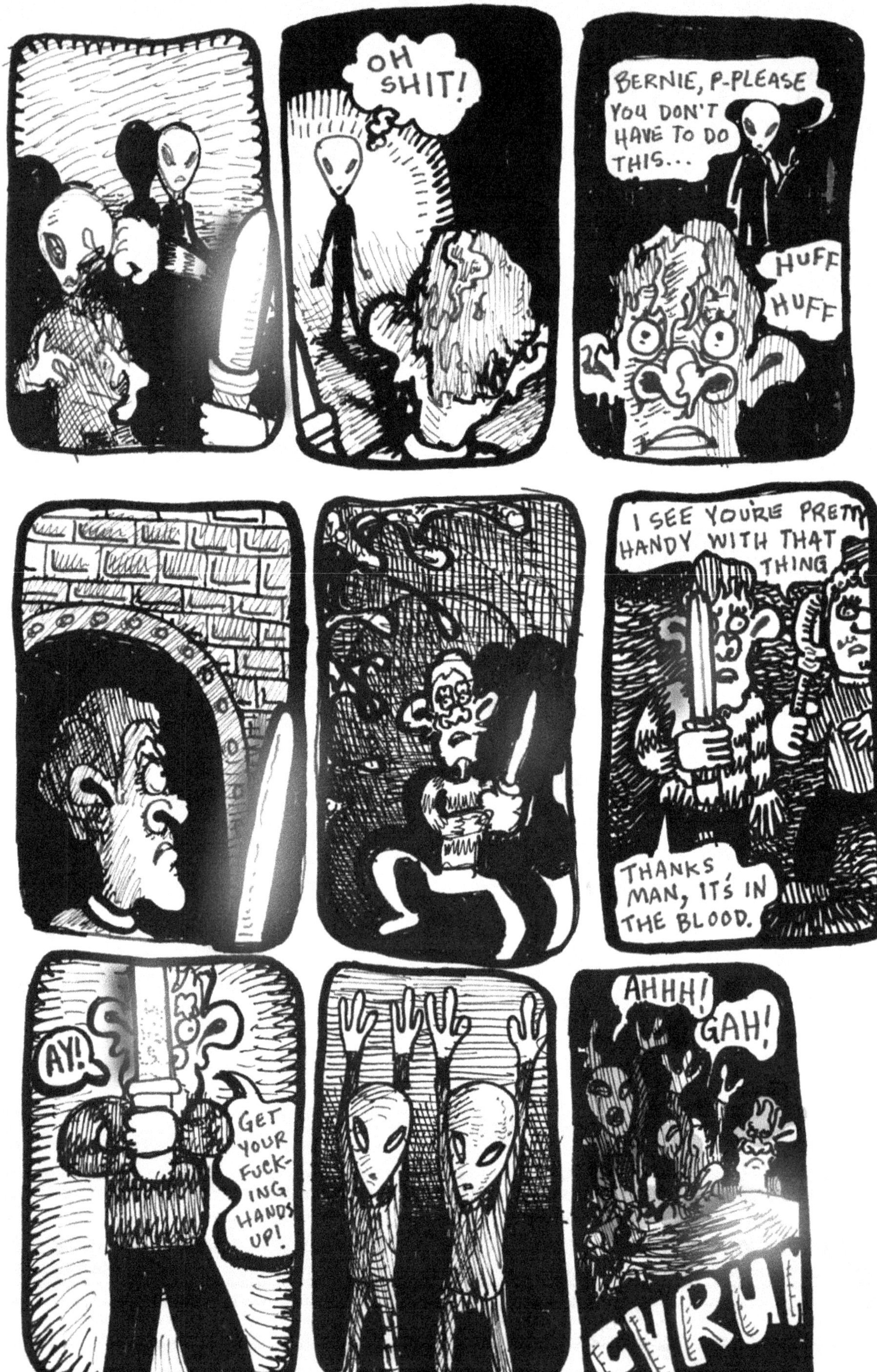
OH SHIT!
BERNIE, P-PLEASE YOU DON'T HAVE TO DO THIS...
HUFF HUFF
I SEE YOU'RE PRETTY HANDY WITH THAT THING
THANKS MAN, IT'S IN THE BLOOD.
AY!
GET YOUR FUCK-ING HANDS UP!
AHHH!
GAH!
FVRHH

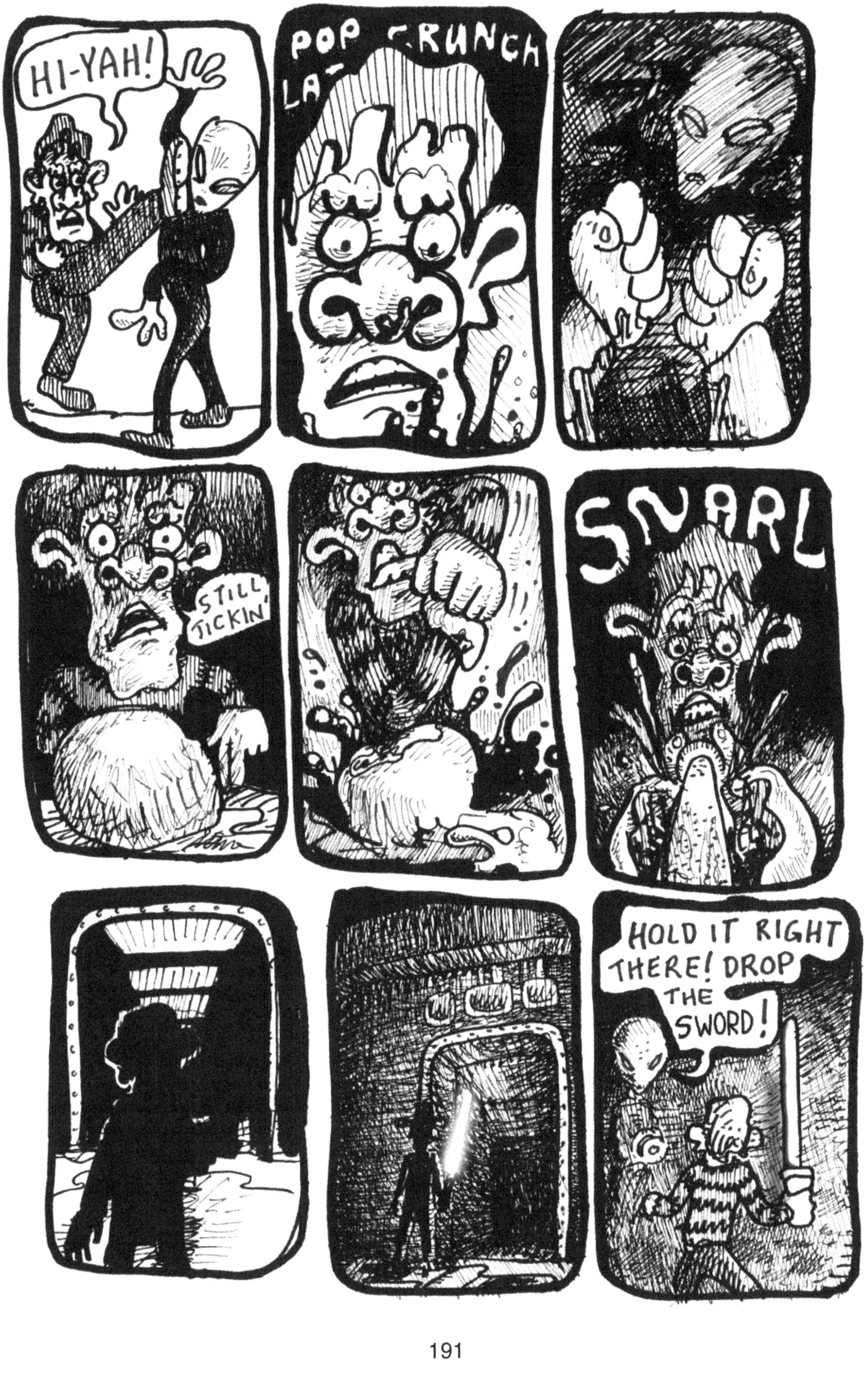
HI-YAH!
POP CRUNCH
STILL TICKIN'
SNARL
HOLD IT RIGHT THERE! DROP THE SWORD!

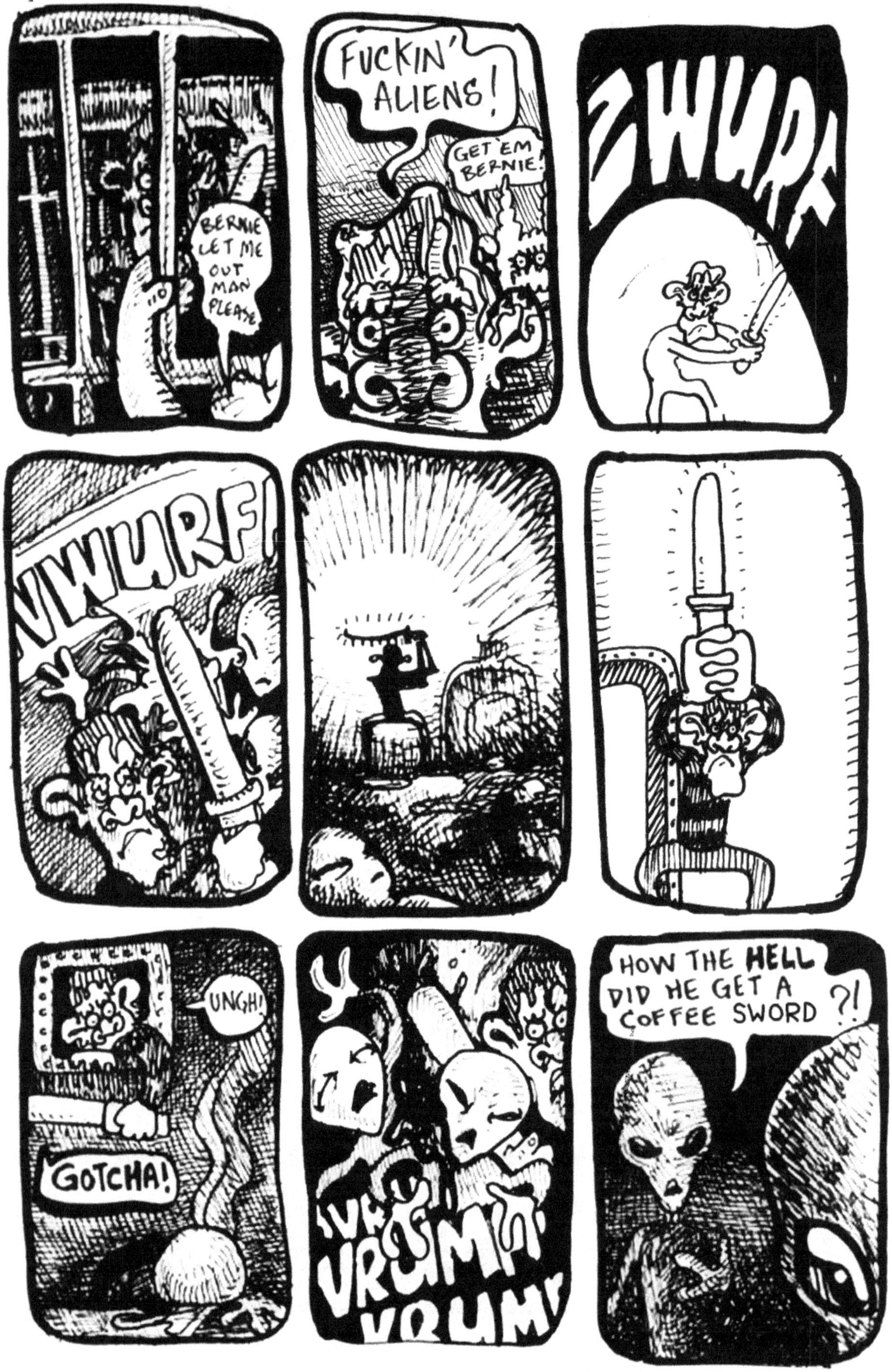
BERNIE LET ME OUT MAN PLEASE
FUCKIN' ALIENS!
GET 'EM BERNIE!
ZWURF
VWURF!
UNGH!
GOTCHA!
VRUMP
VRUMP
HOW THE HELL DID HE GET A COFFEE SWORD ?!

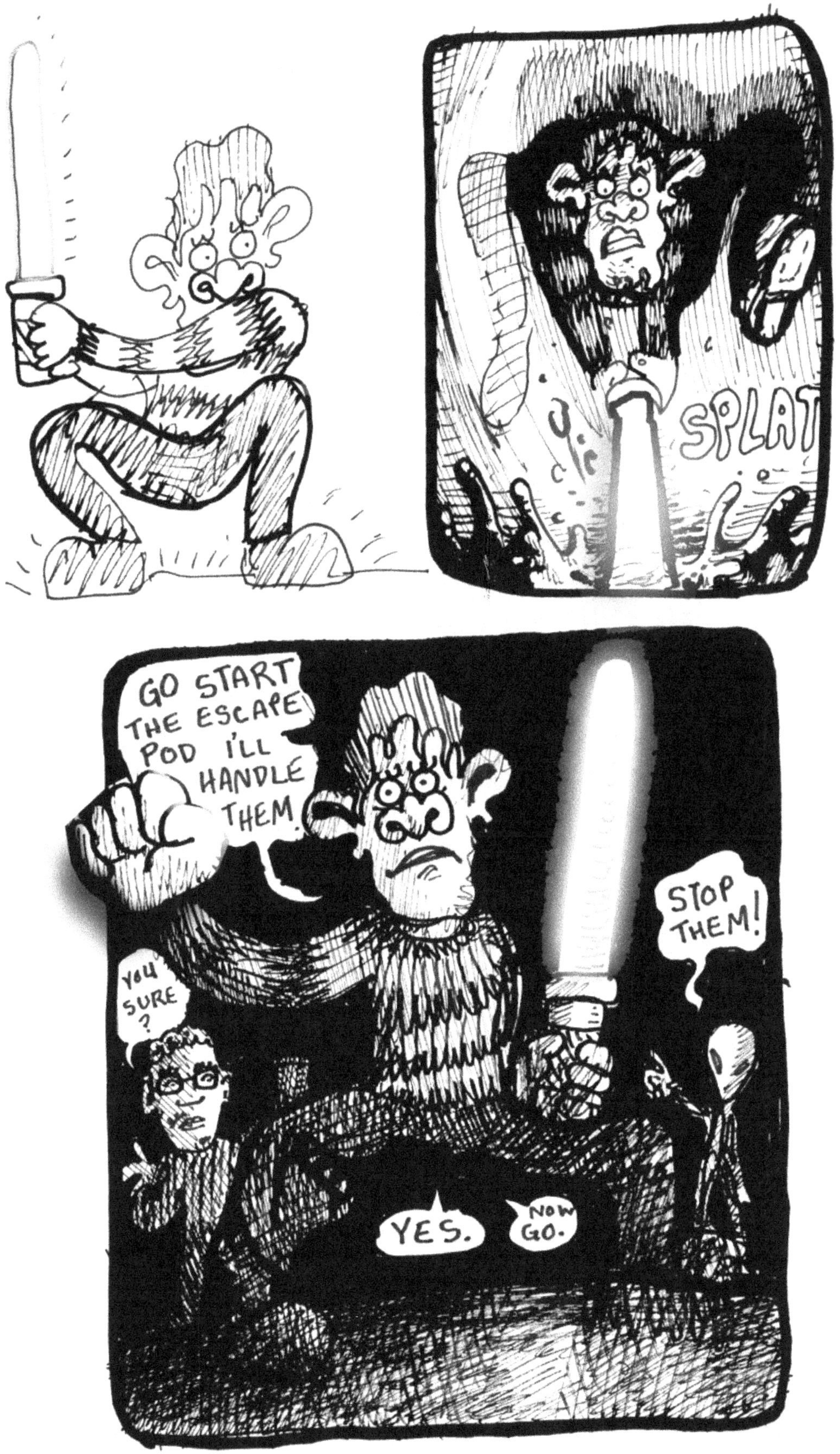
SPLAT
GO START THE ESCAPE POD I'LL HANDLE THEM.
YOU SURE ?
YES.
NOW GO.
STOP THEM!

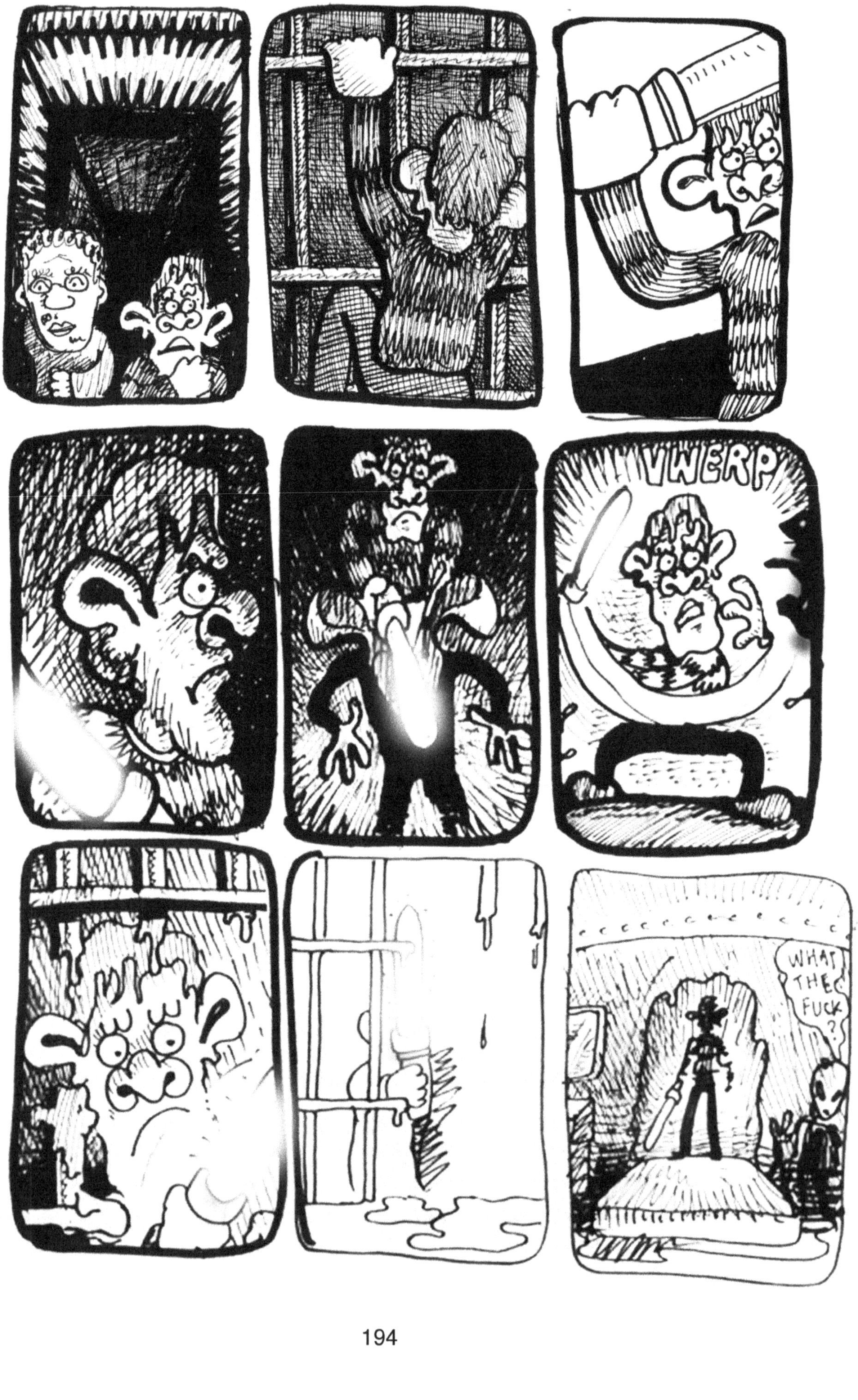
VWERP
WHAT THE FUCK?

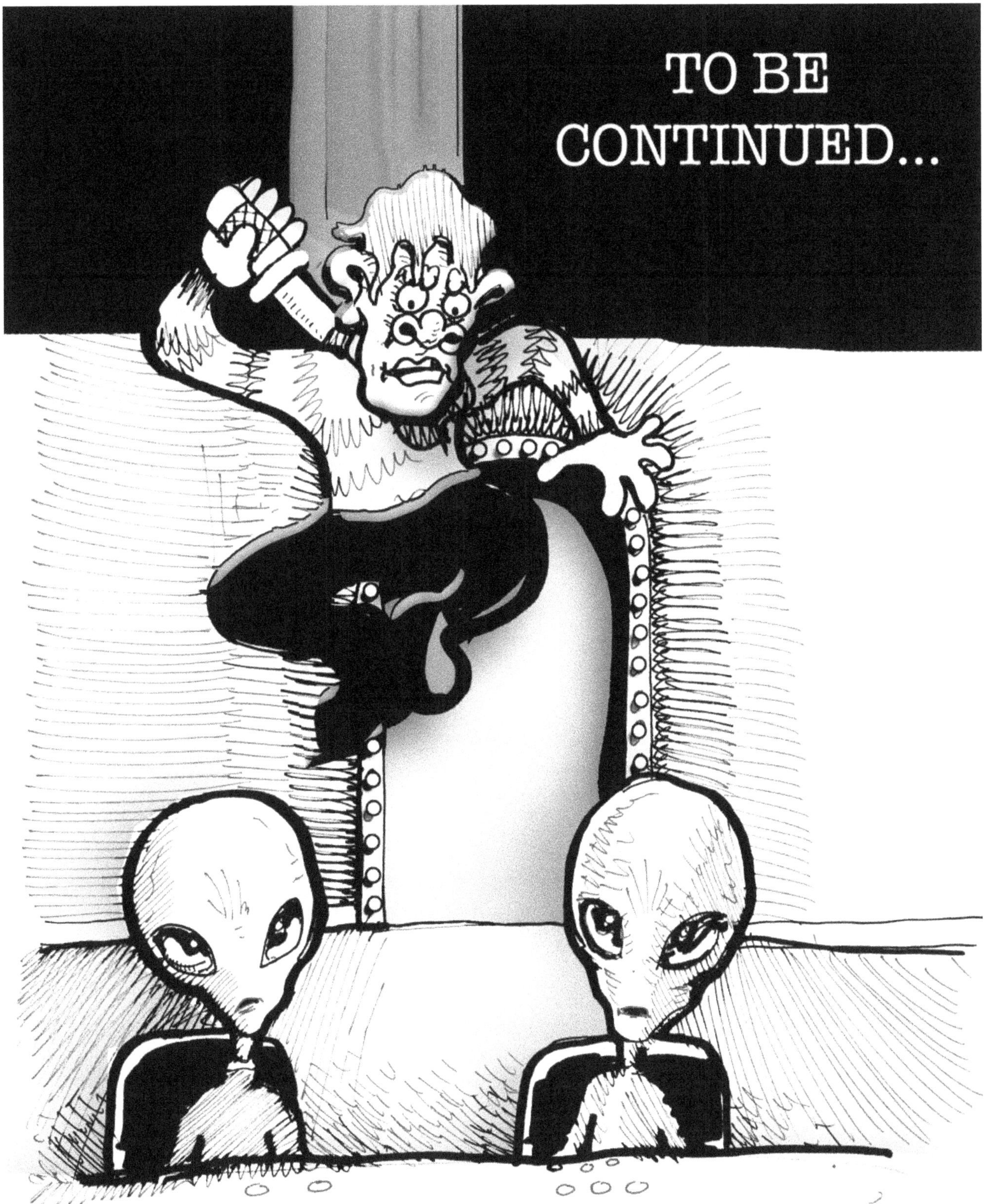
TO BE
CONTINUED...

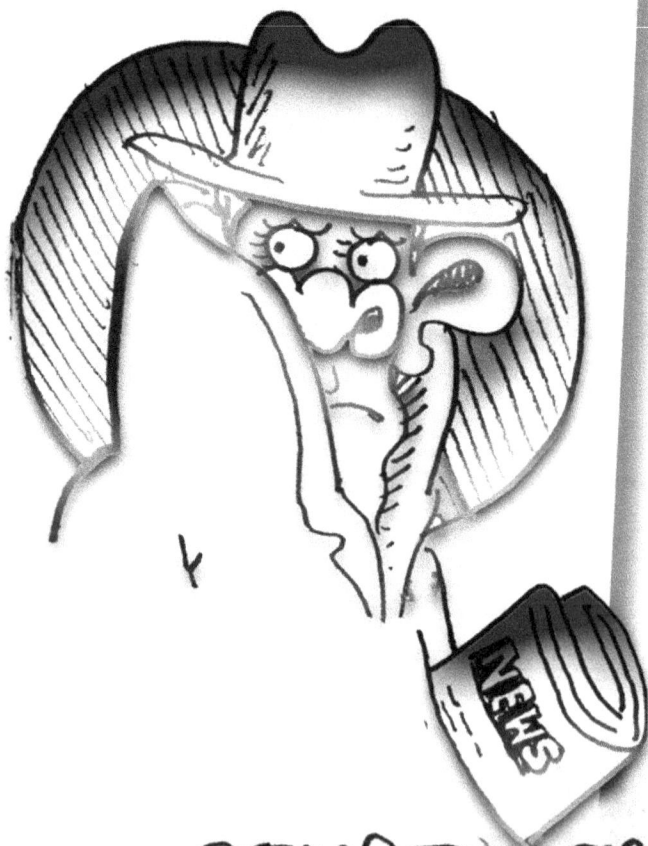

WILD BERNIE

WOMENS

PRIVATE EYE

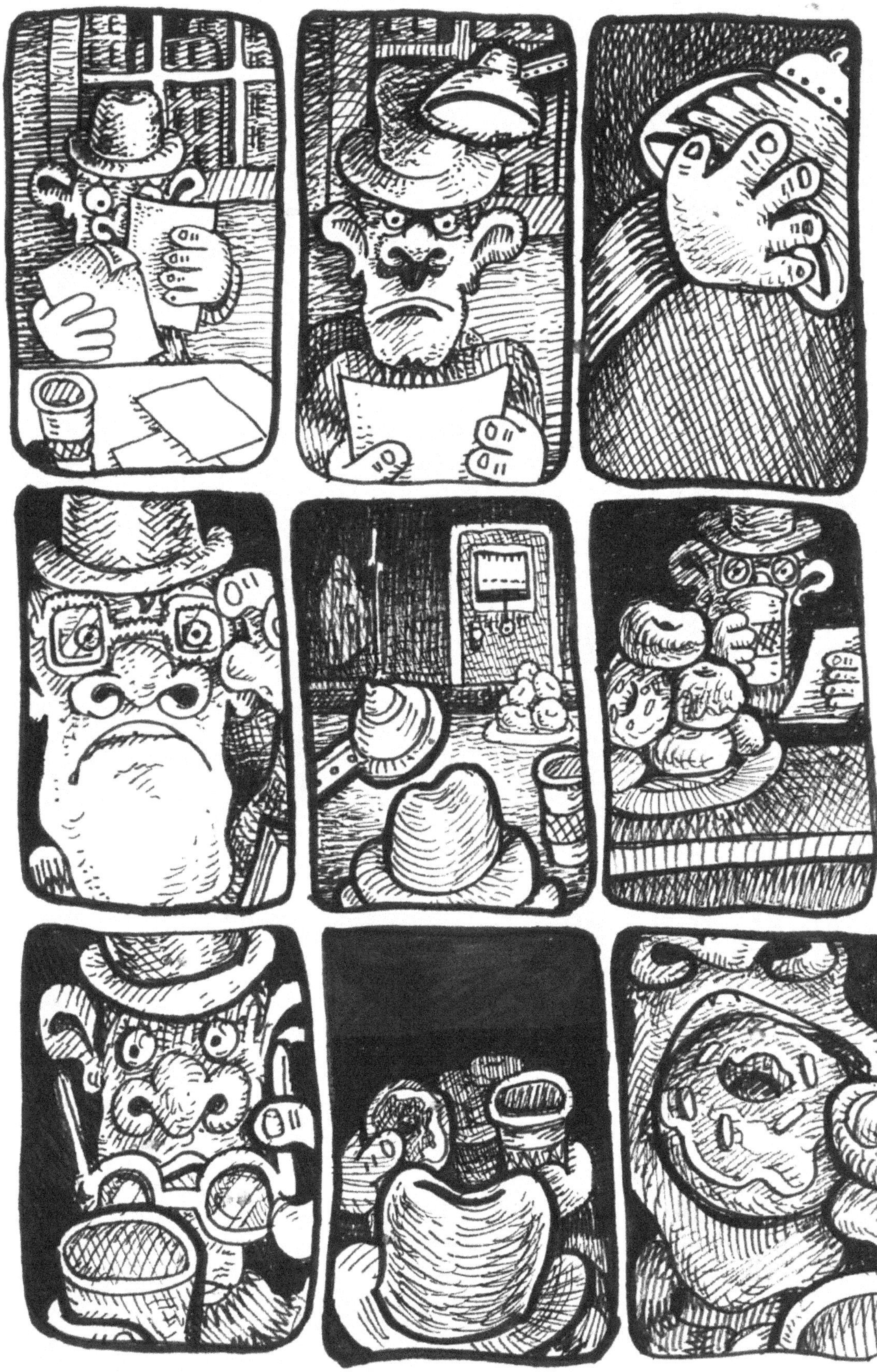

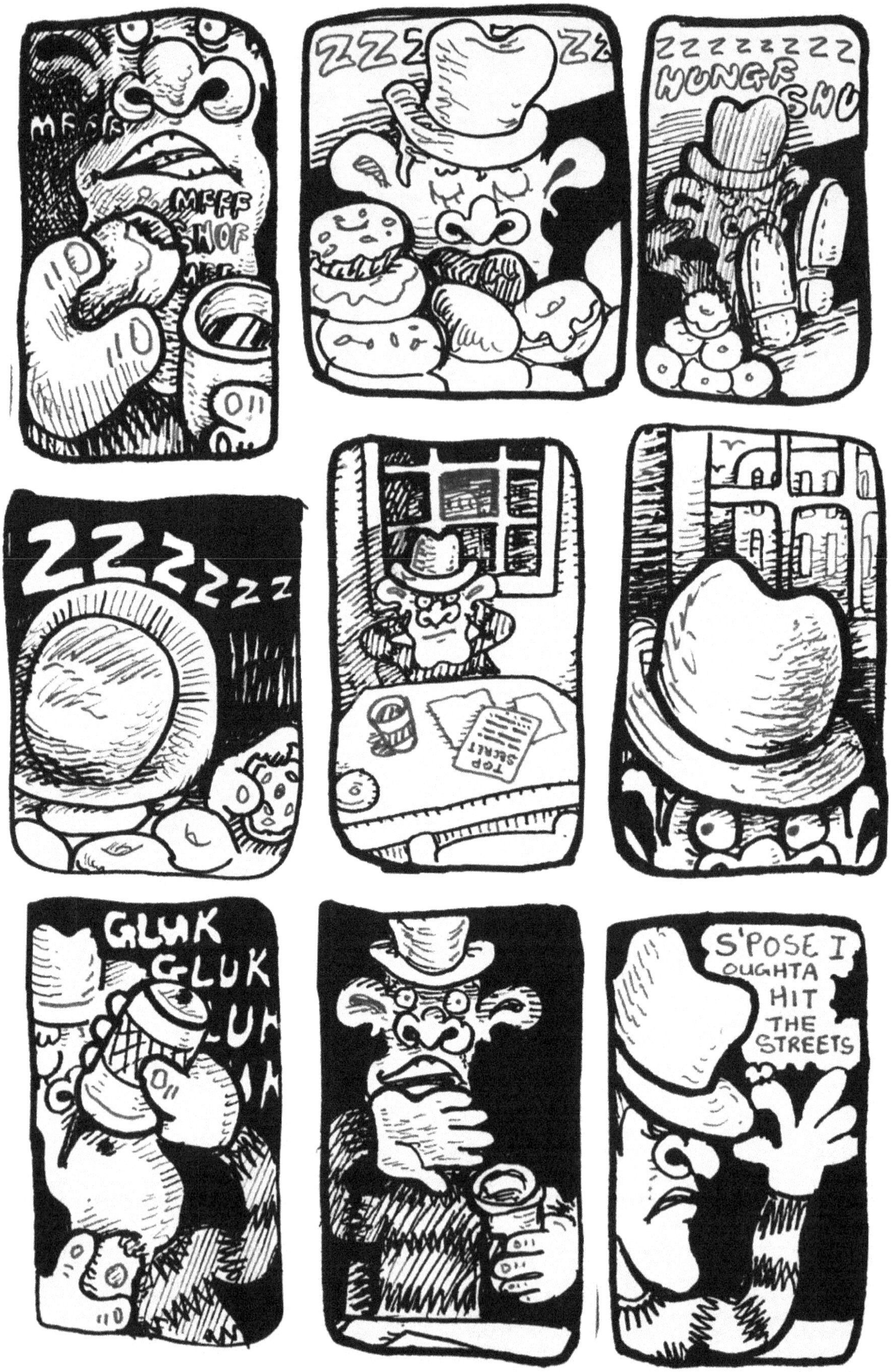
MFFF
SHOF
ZZZZZZZZZ
HONGF SHU
ZZZZzzz
TOP SECRET
GLUK
GLUK
S'POSE I OUGHTA HIT THE STREETS

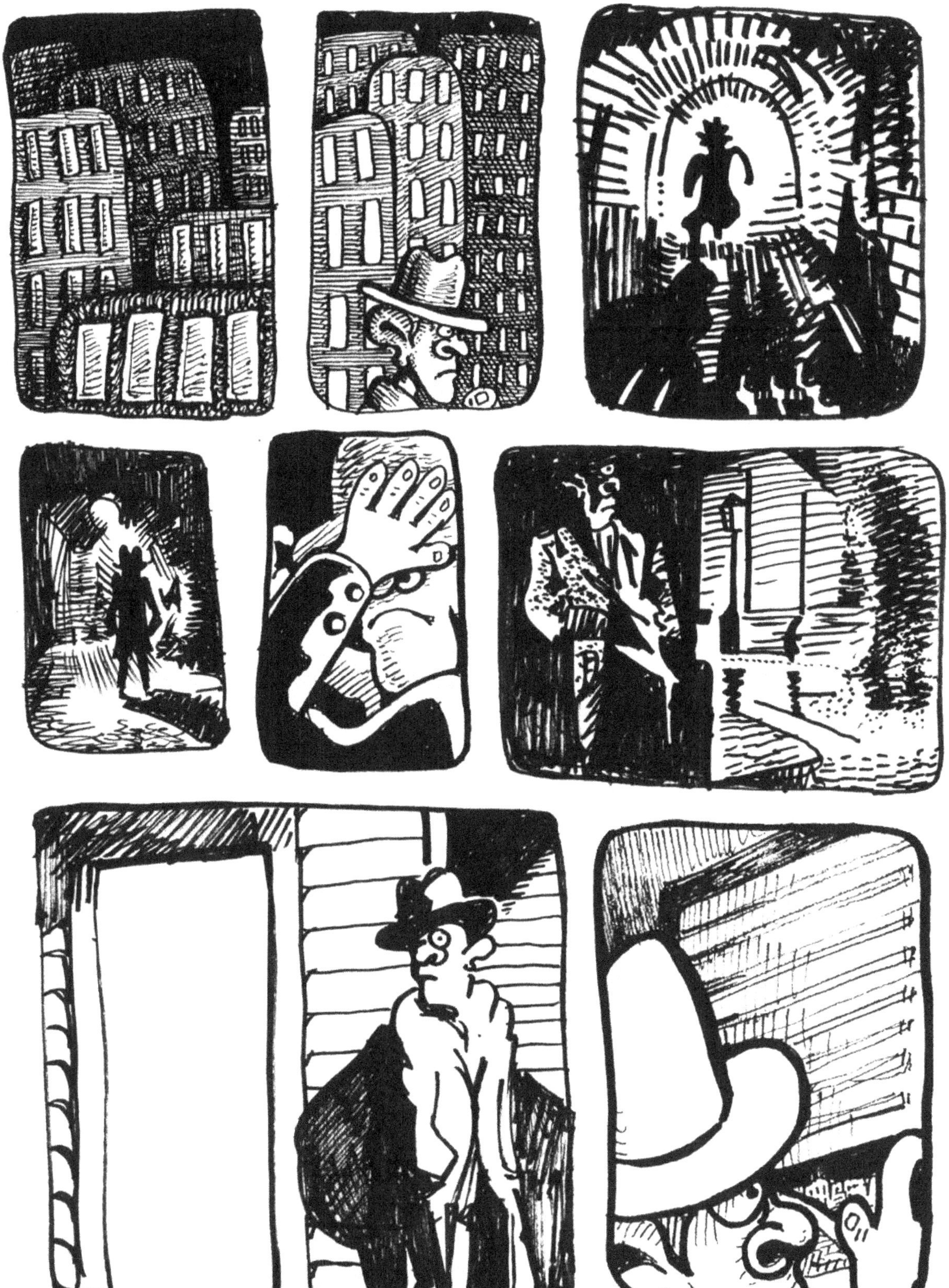

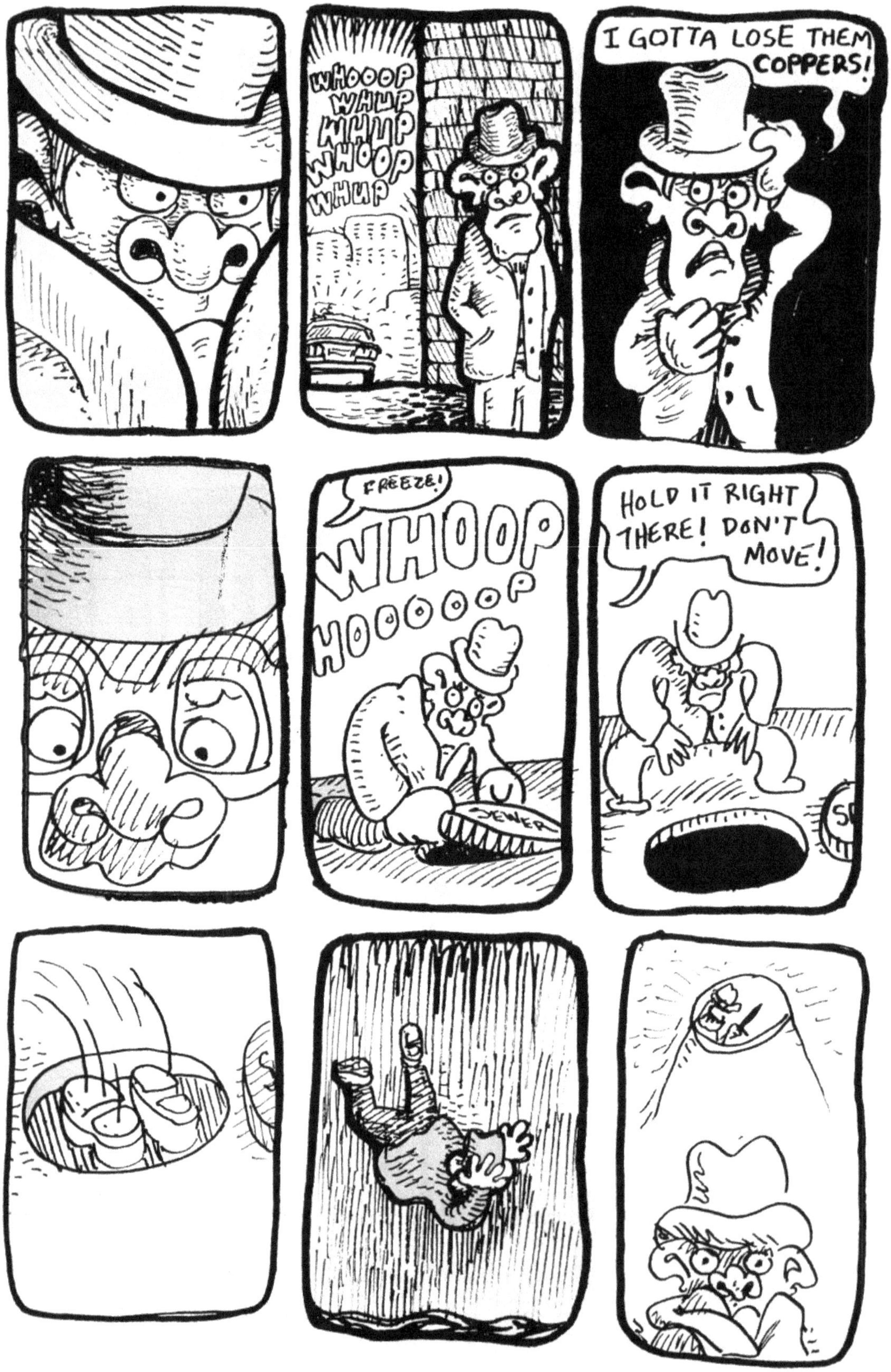
WHOOOP
WHUP
WHUP
WHOOP
WHUP
I GOTTA LOSE THEM COPPERS!
FREEZE!
WHOOP
HOOOOOOP
SEWER
HOLD IT RIGHT THERE! DON'T MOVE!

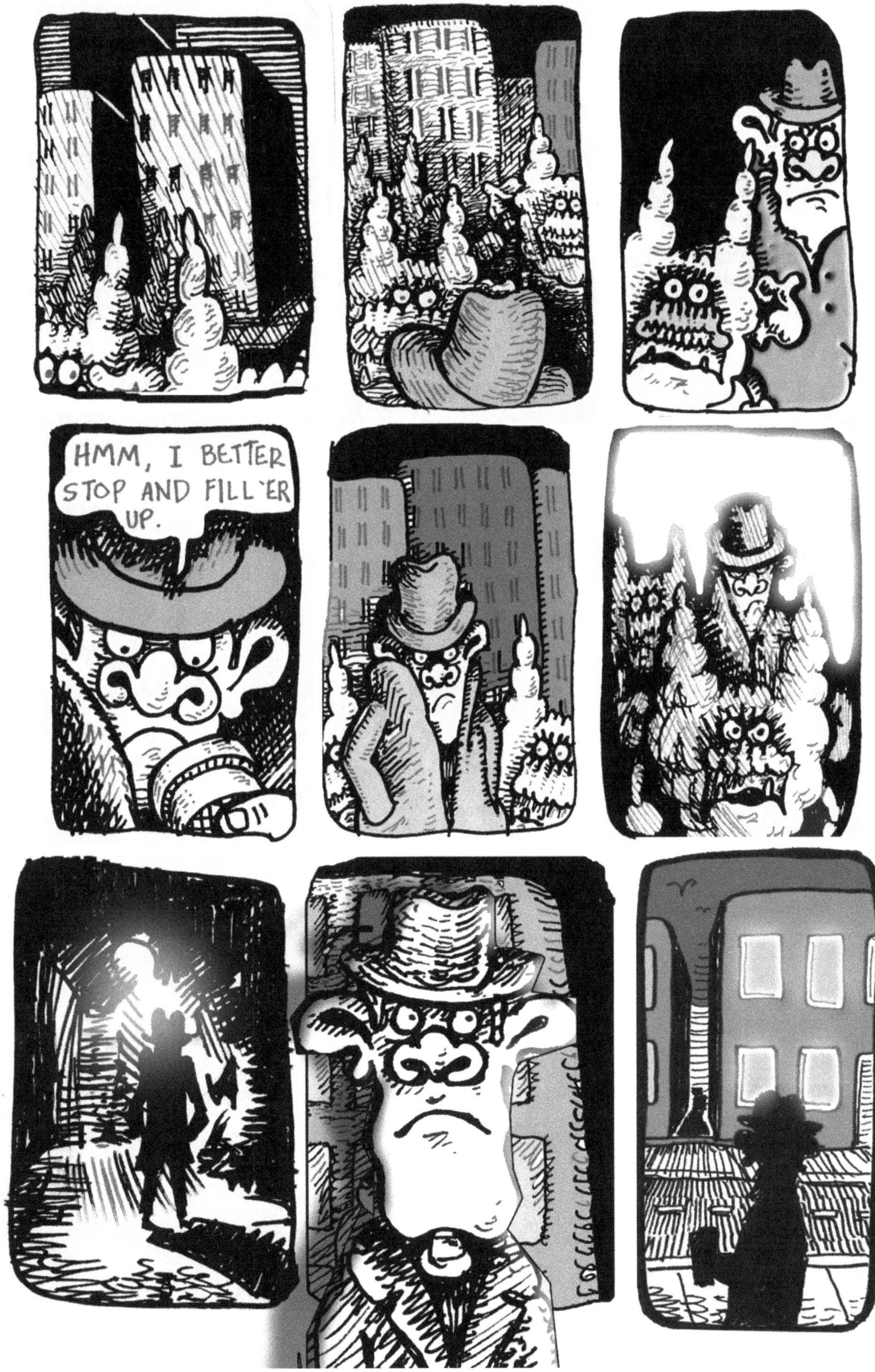
HMM, I BETTER STOP AND FILL`ER UP.

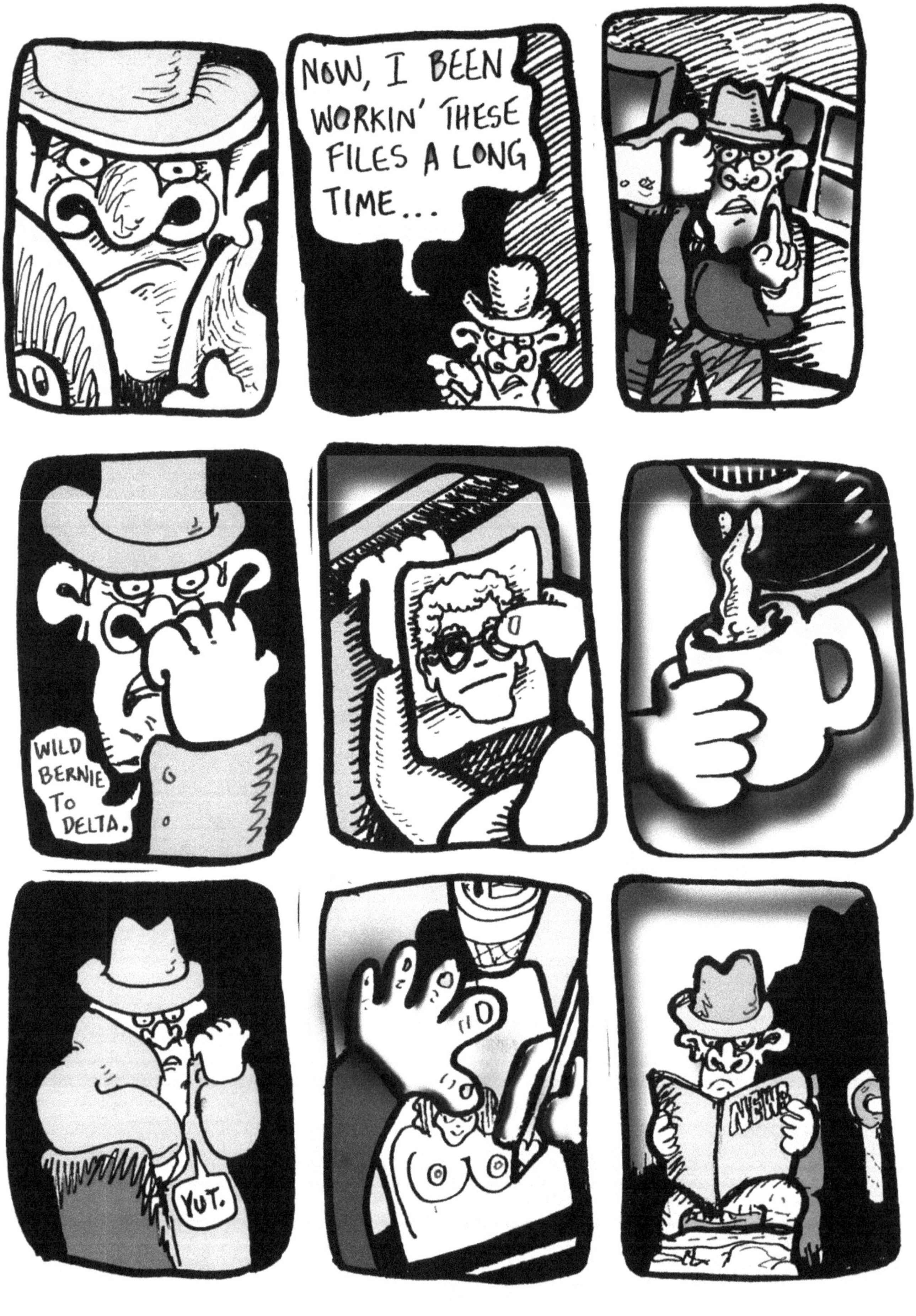
NOW, I BEEN WORKIN' THESE FILES A LONG TIME...
WILD BERNIE TO DELTA.
YUT.

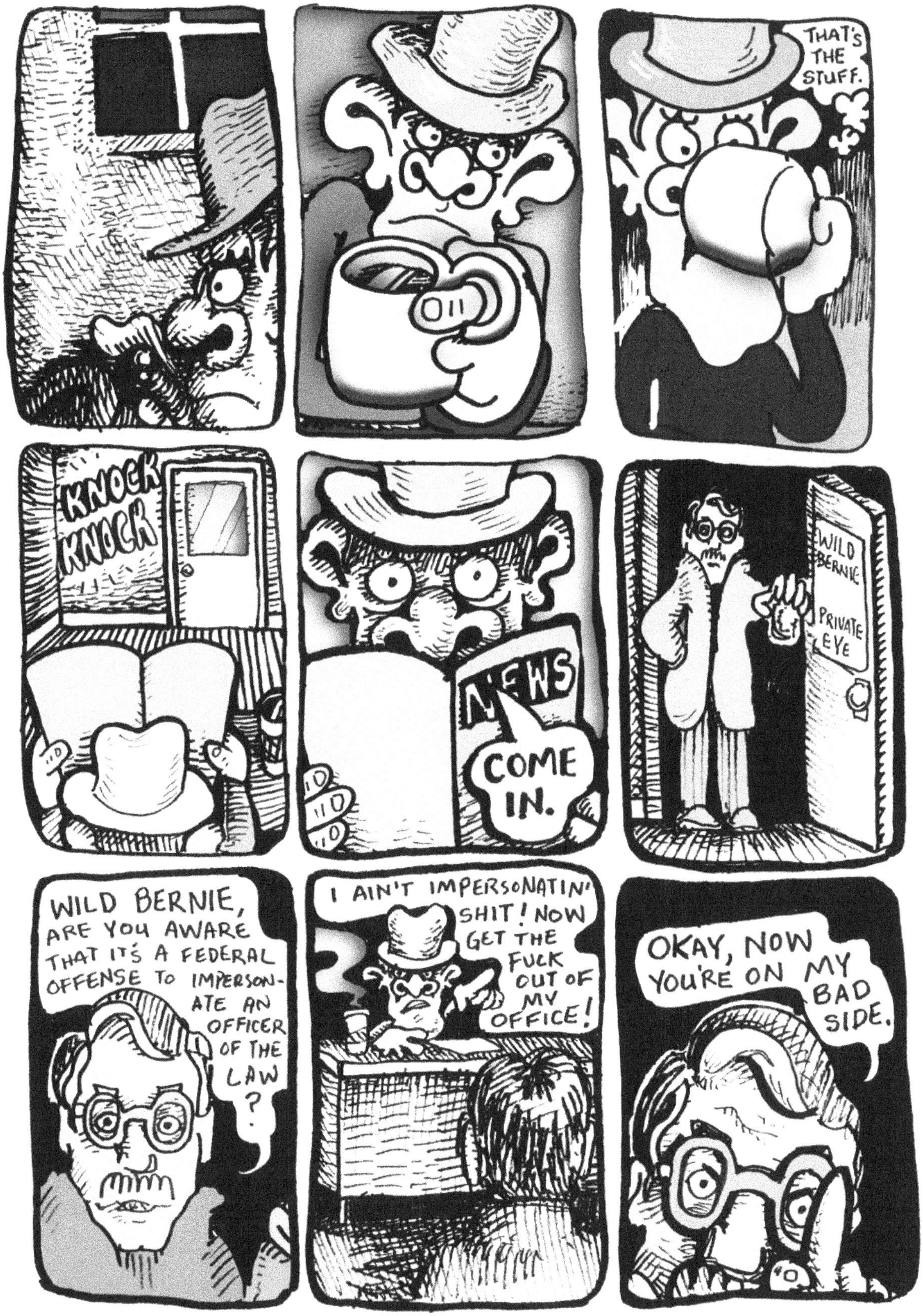
THAT'S THE STUFF.
KNOCK KNOCK
NEWS
COME IN.
WILD BERNIE PRIVATE EYE
WILD BERNIE, ARE YOU AWARE THAT IT'S A FEDERAL OFFENSE TO IMPERSON-ATE AN OFFICER OF THE LAW ?
I AIN'T IMPERSONATIN' SHIT! NOW GET THE FUCK OUT OF MY OFFICE!
OKAY, NOW YOU'RE ON MY BAD SIDE.

CASE FILES
TOP SECRET
EVIDENCE
CASE FILES

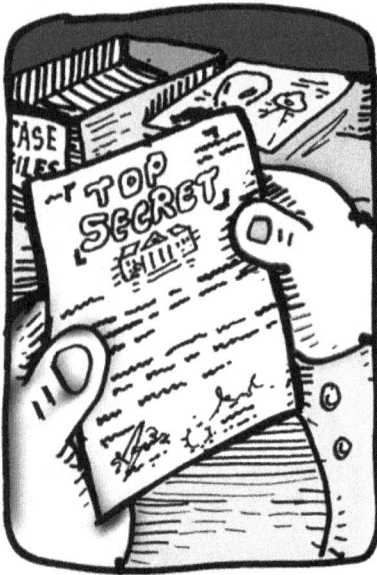

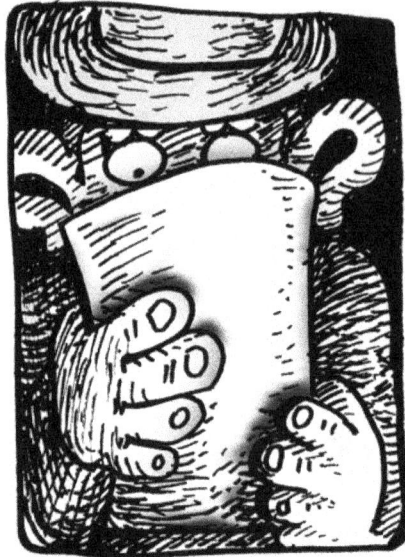

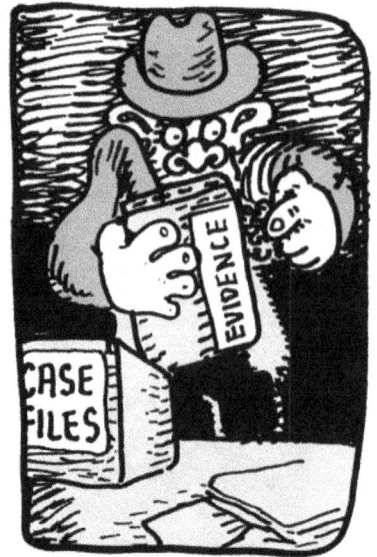

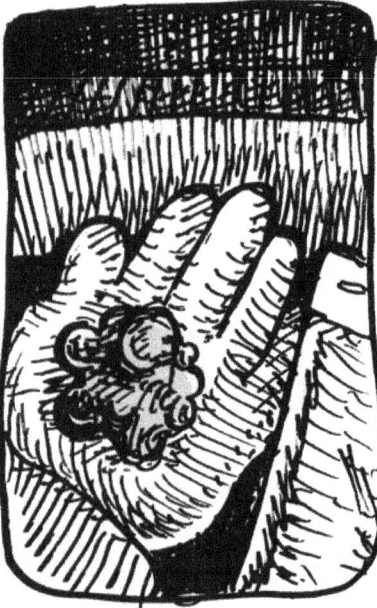

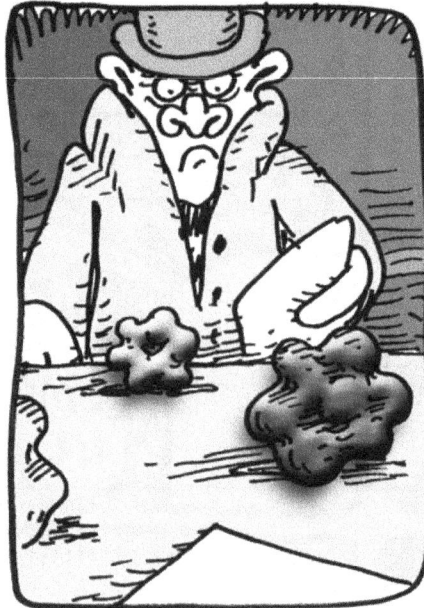

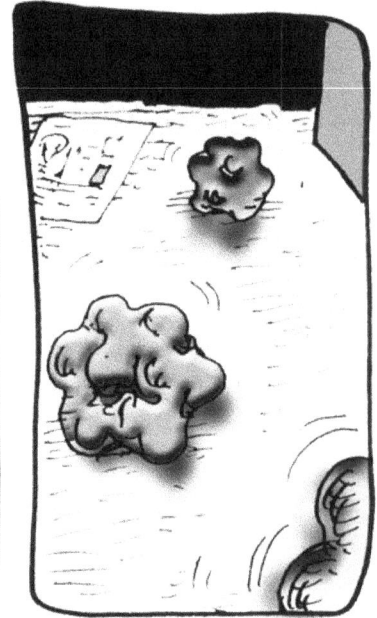

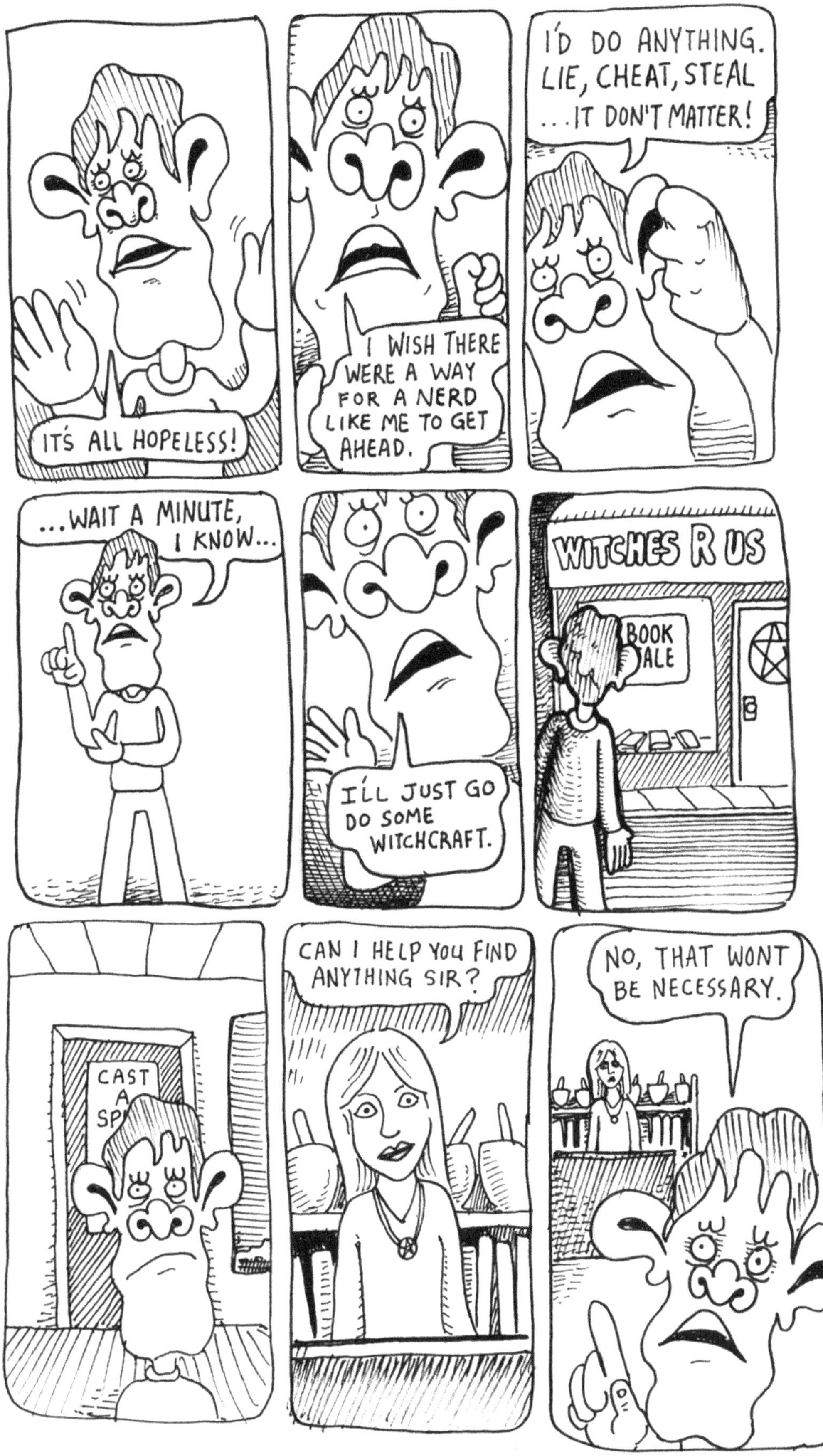
IT'S ALL HOPELESS!
I WISH THERE WERE A WAY FOR A NERD LIKE ME TO GET AHEAD.
I'D DO ANYTHING. LIE, CHEAT, STEAL ...IT DON'T MATTER!
...WAIT A MINUTE, I KNOW...
I'LL JUST GO DO SOME WITCHCRAFT.
WITCHES R US
BOOK
ALE
CAST
A
SP
CAN I HELP YOU FIND ANYTHING SIR?
NO, THAT WONT BE NECESSARY.

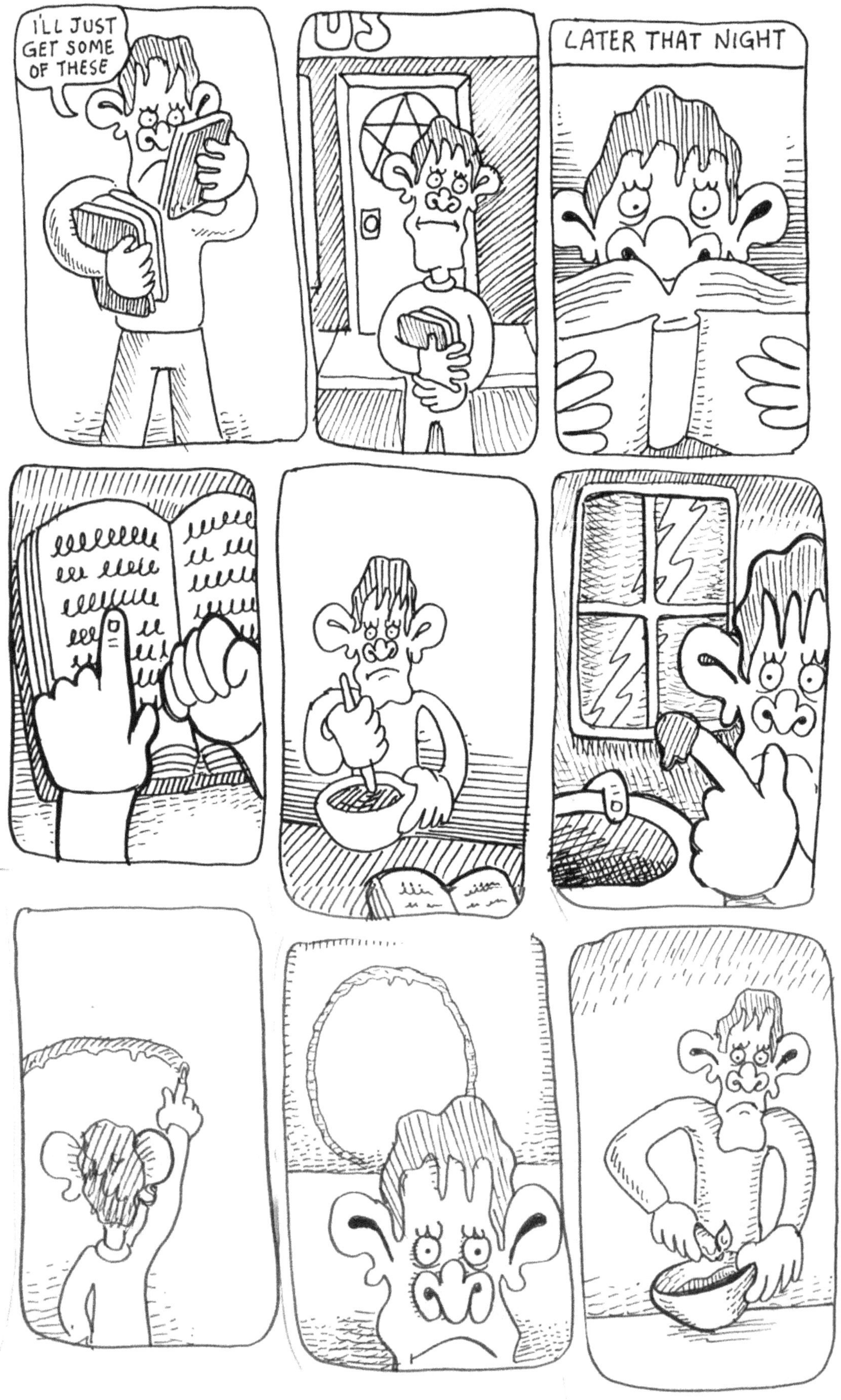
I'LL JUST GET SOME OF THESE
US
LATER THAT NIGHT

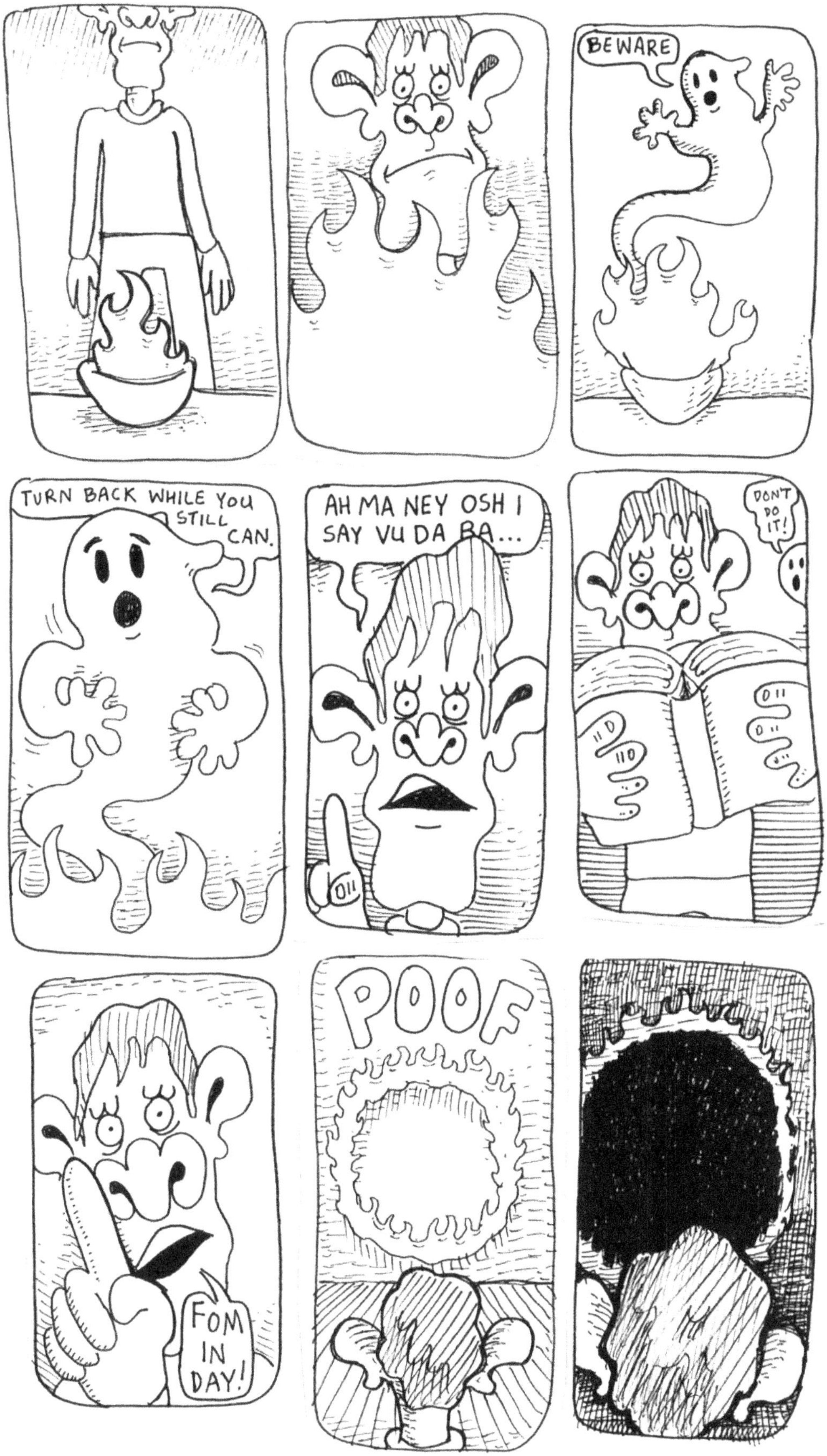
BEWARE
TURN BACK WHILE YOU STILL CAN.
AH MA NEY OSH I SAY VU DA BA...
DON'T DO IT!
FOM IN DAY!
POOF

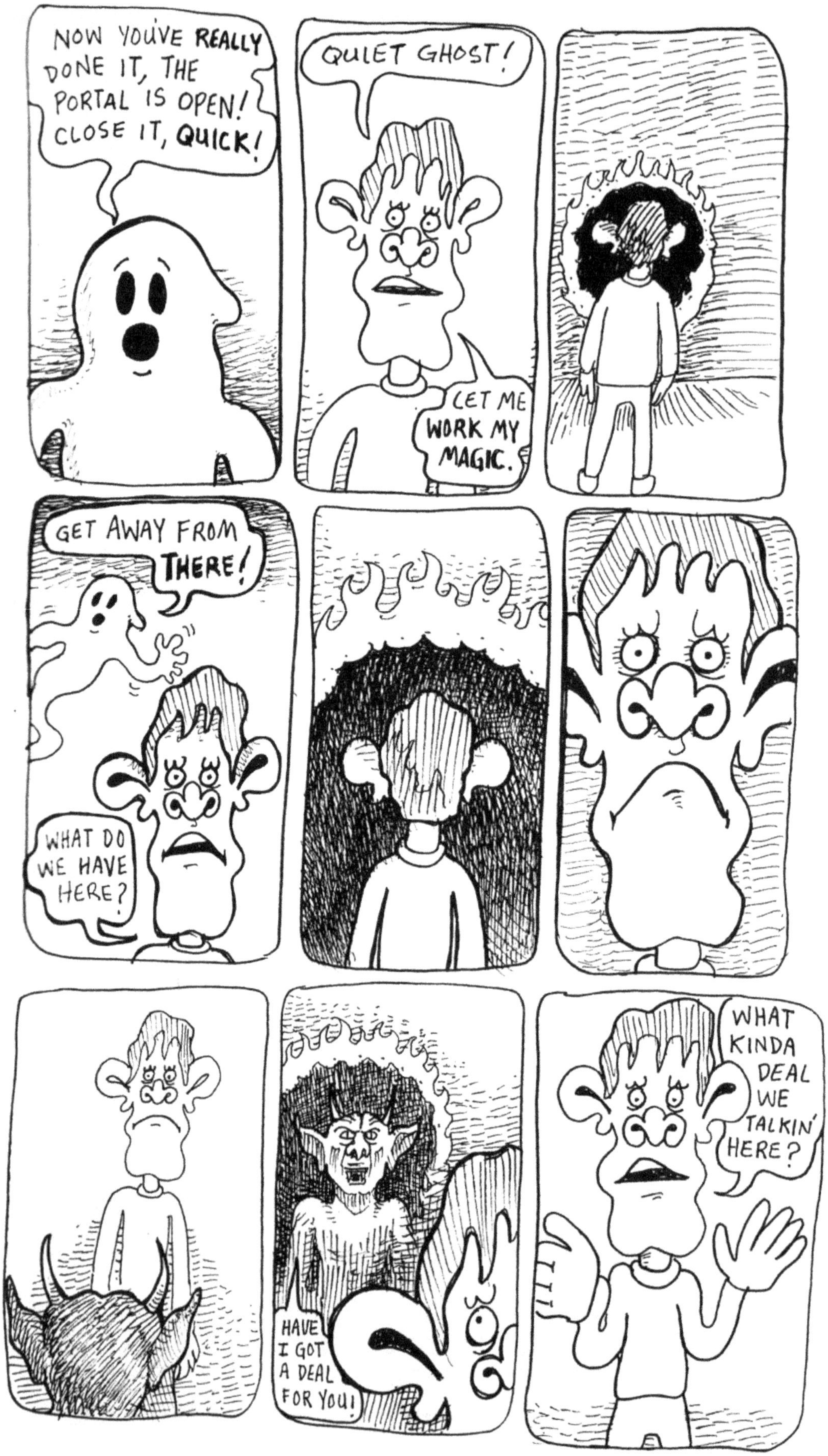
NOW YOU'VE REALLY DONE IT, THE PORTAL IS OPEN! CLOSE IT, QUICK!
QUIET GHOST!
LET ME WORK MY MAGIC.
GET AWAY FROM THERE!
WHAT DO WE HAVE HERE?
HAVE I GOT A DEAL FOR YOU!
WHAT KINDA DEAL WE TALKIN' HERE?

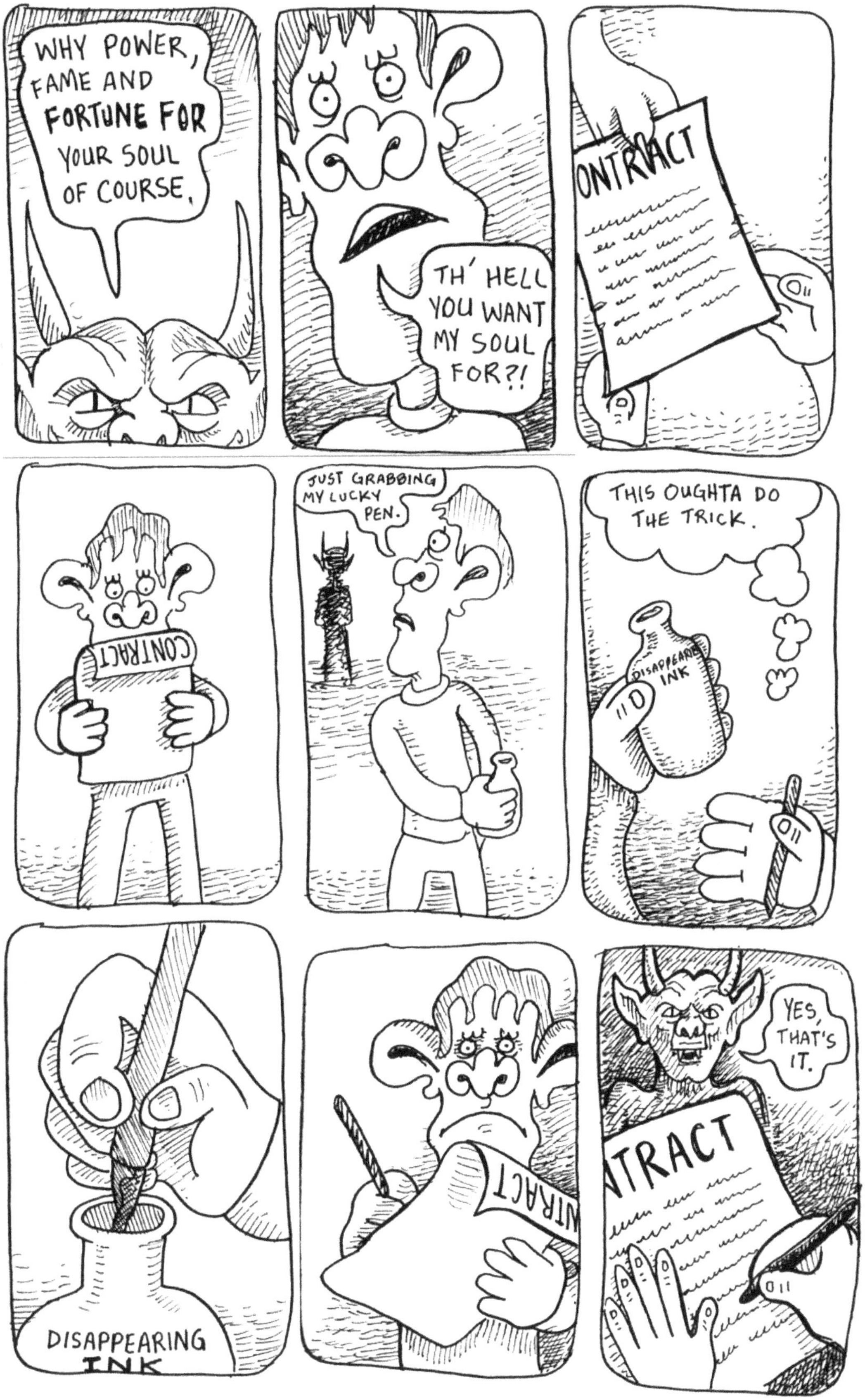
WHY POWER, FAME AND FORTUNE FOR YOUR SOUL OF COURSE.
TH' HELL YOU WANT MY SOUL FOR?!
JUST GRABBING MY LUCKY PEN.
THIS OUGHTA DO THE TRICK.
DISAPPEARING INK
YES, THAT'S IT.

CONTRACT
I'LL BE SEEING YOU SOON.
HA-HA HA-HA-HA!
WHAT HAVE YOU DONE!?
RELAX GHOST!

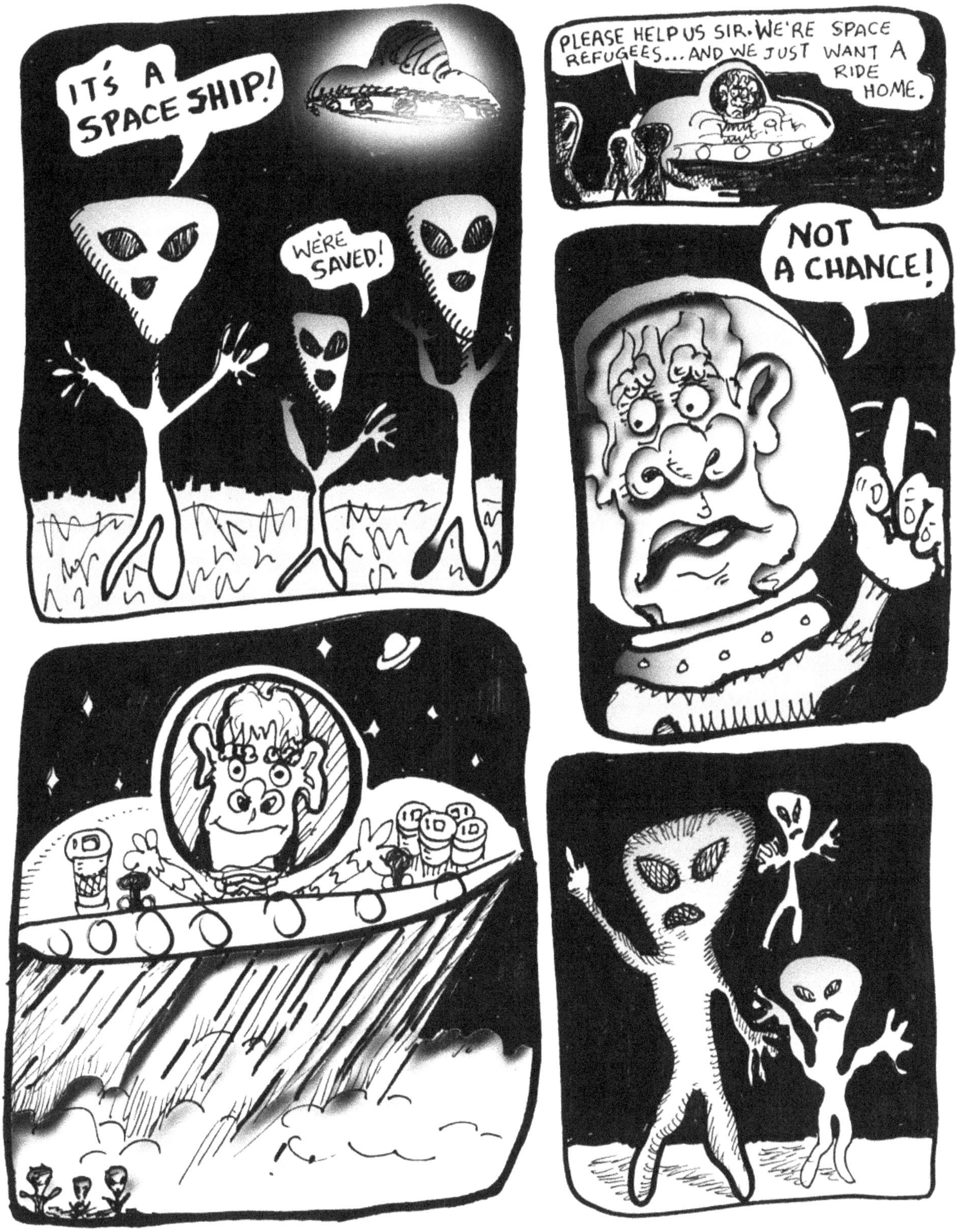
IT'S A SPACE SHIP!
WE'RE SAVED!
PLEASE HELP US SIR. WE'RE SPACE REFUGEES... AND WE JUST WANT A RIDE HOME.
NOT A CHANCE!

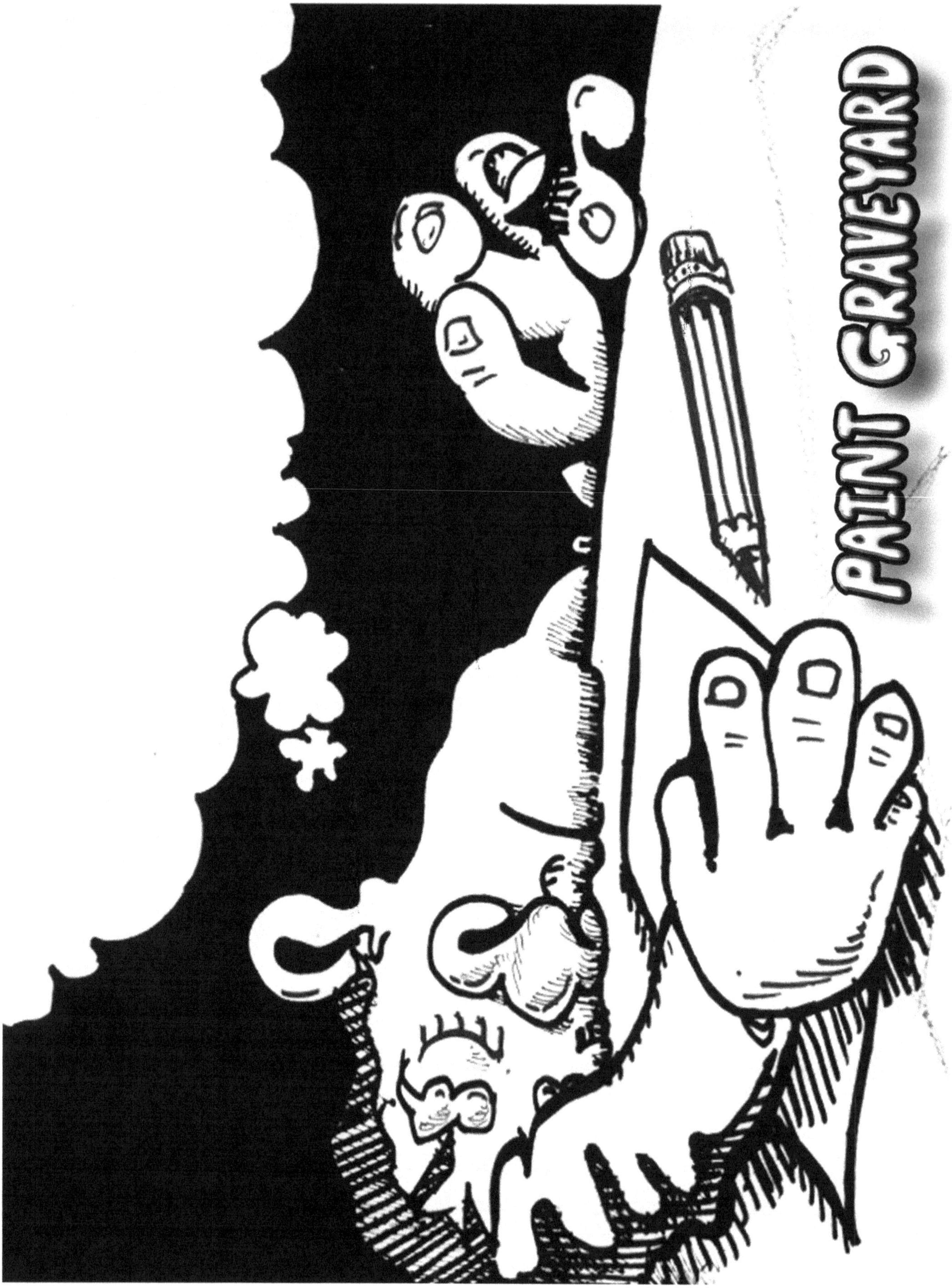
PAINT GRAVEYARD

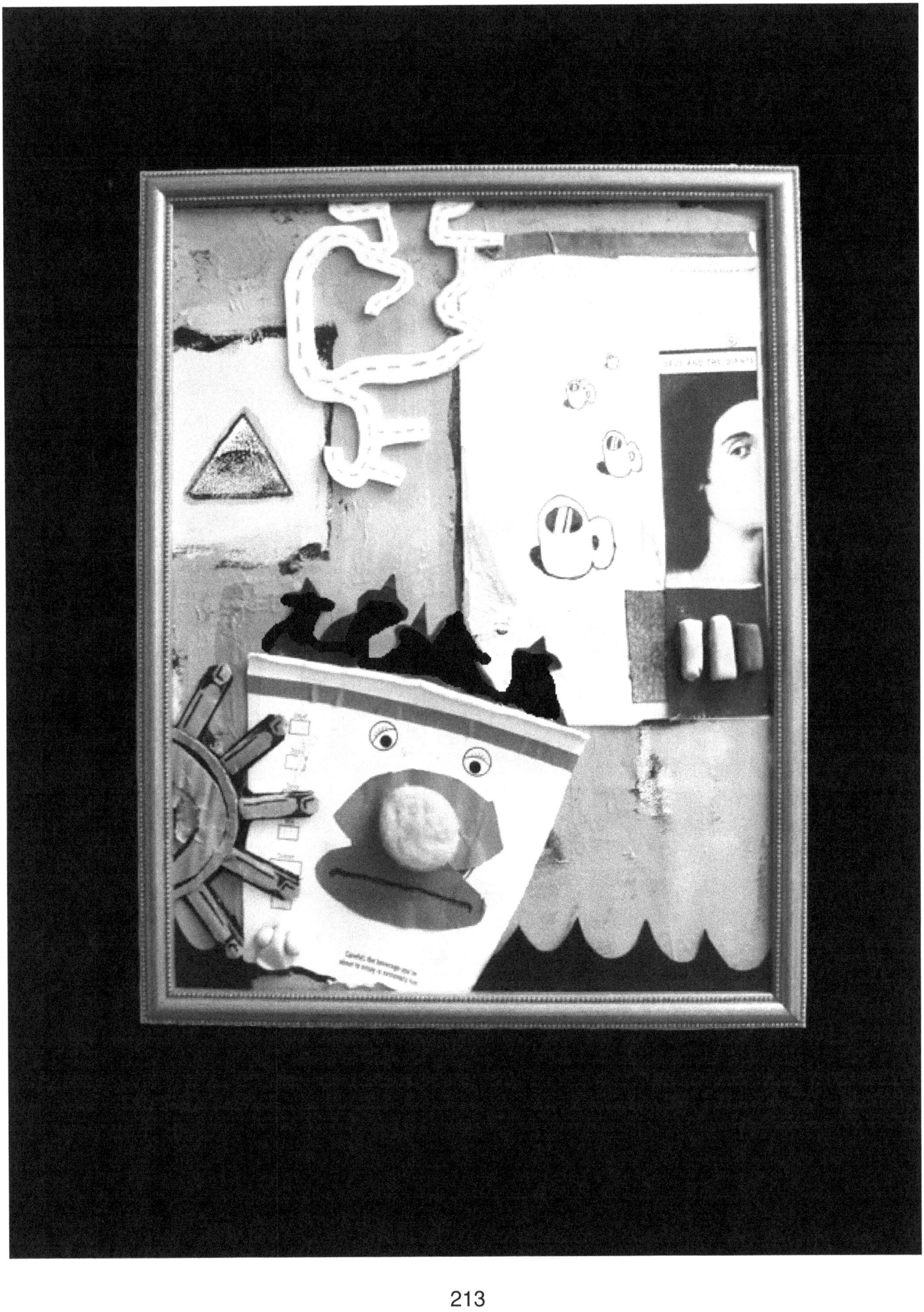

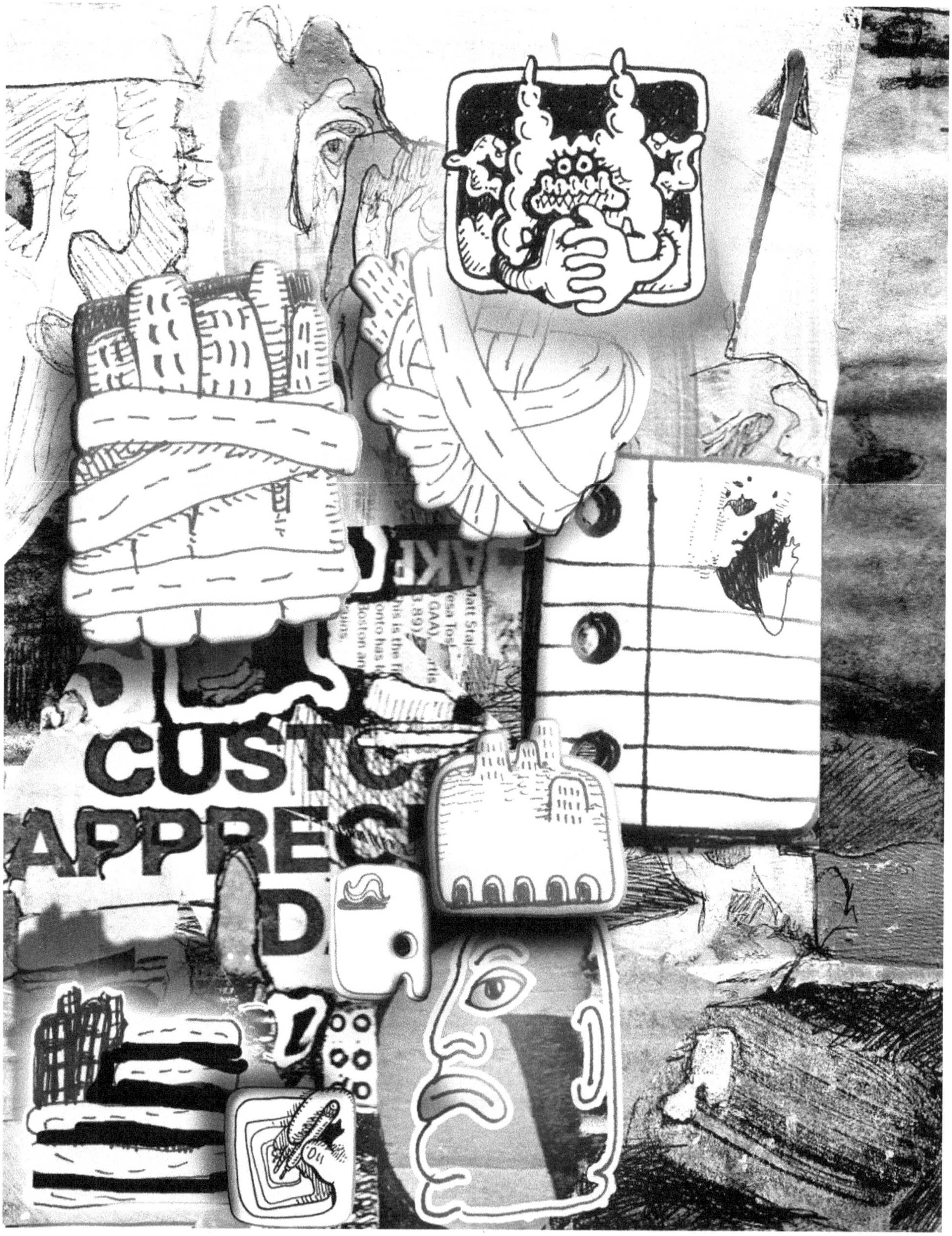
CUST
APPRE
D

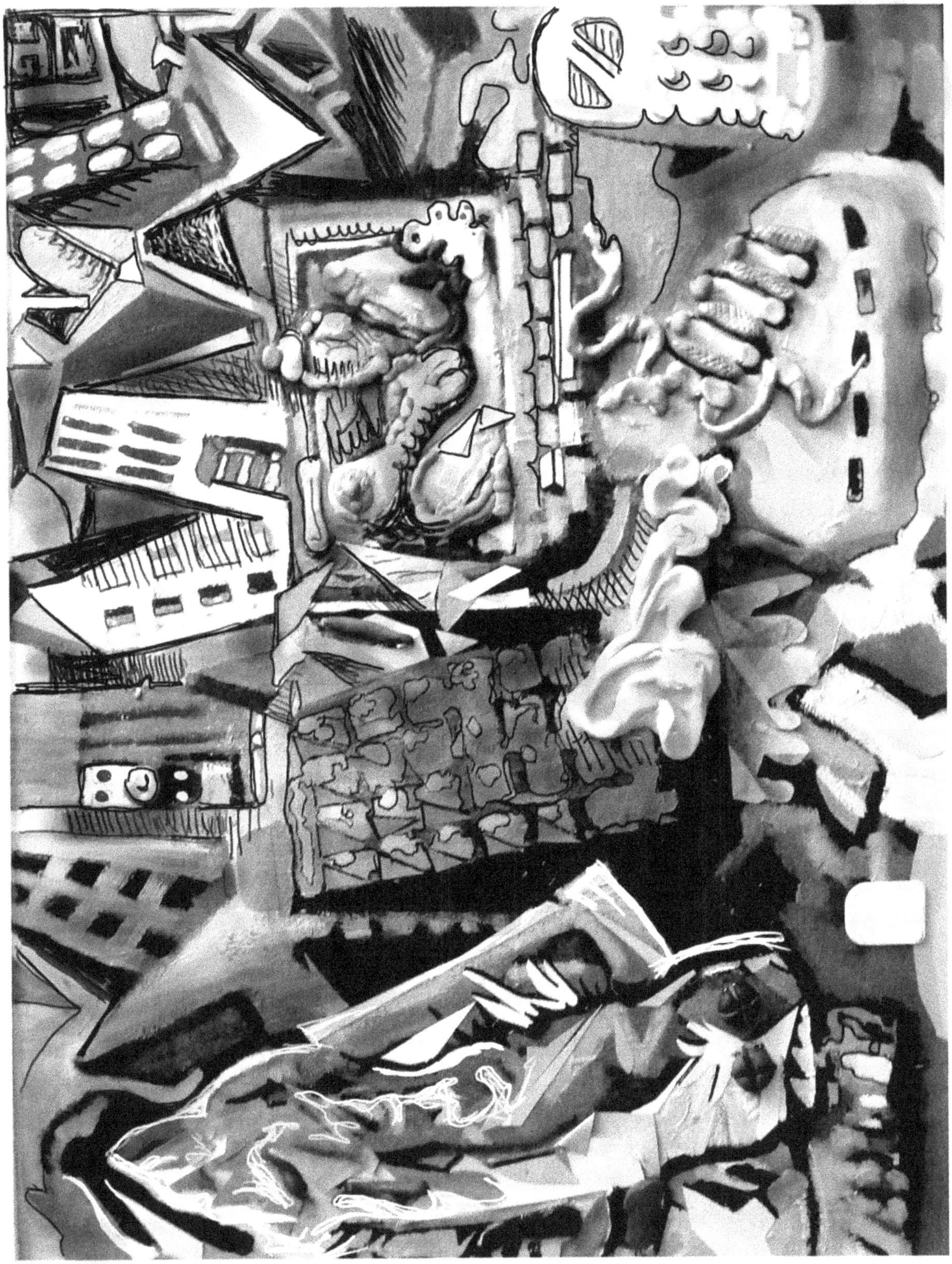

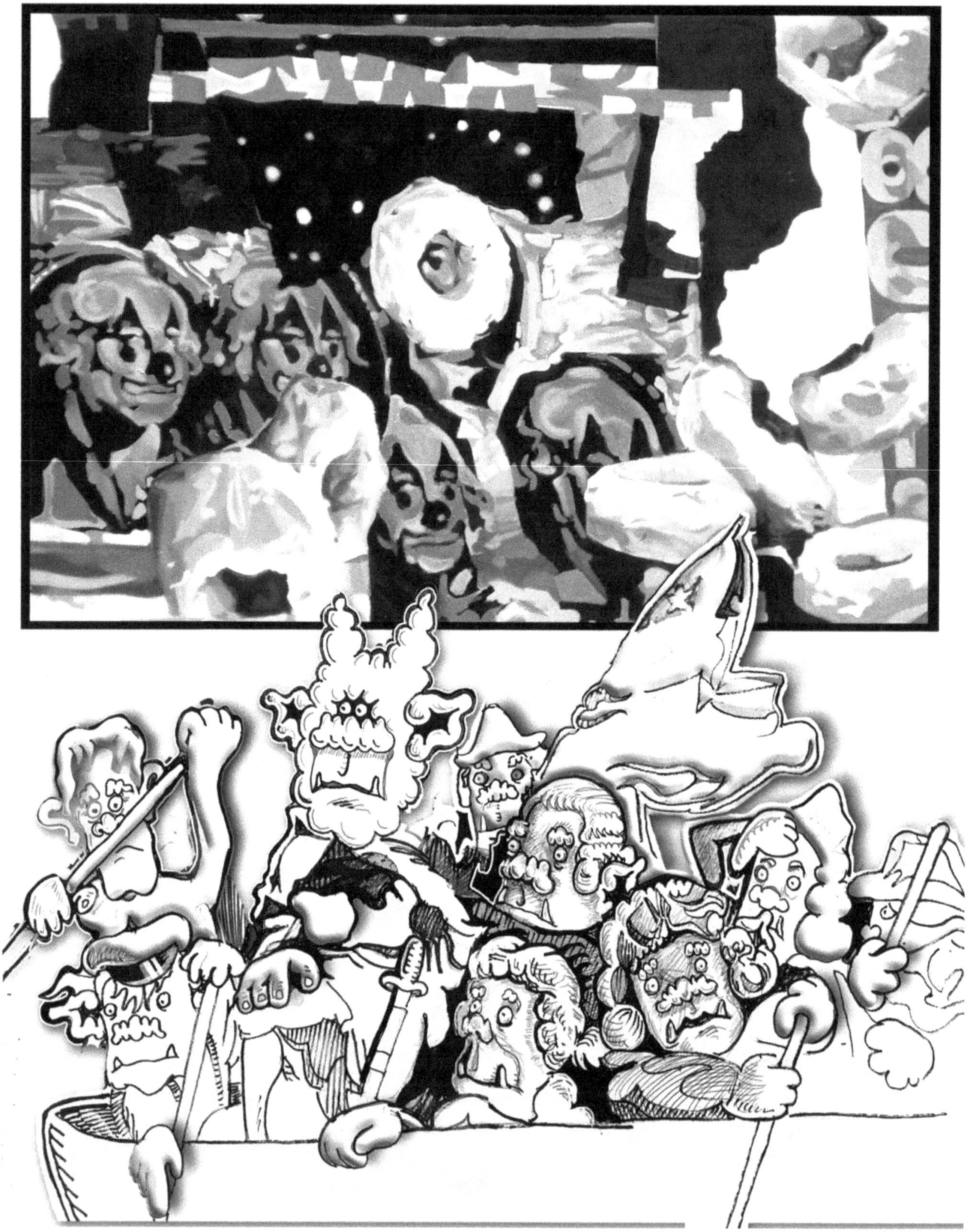

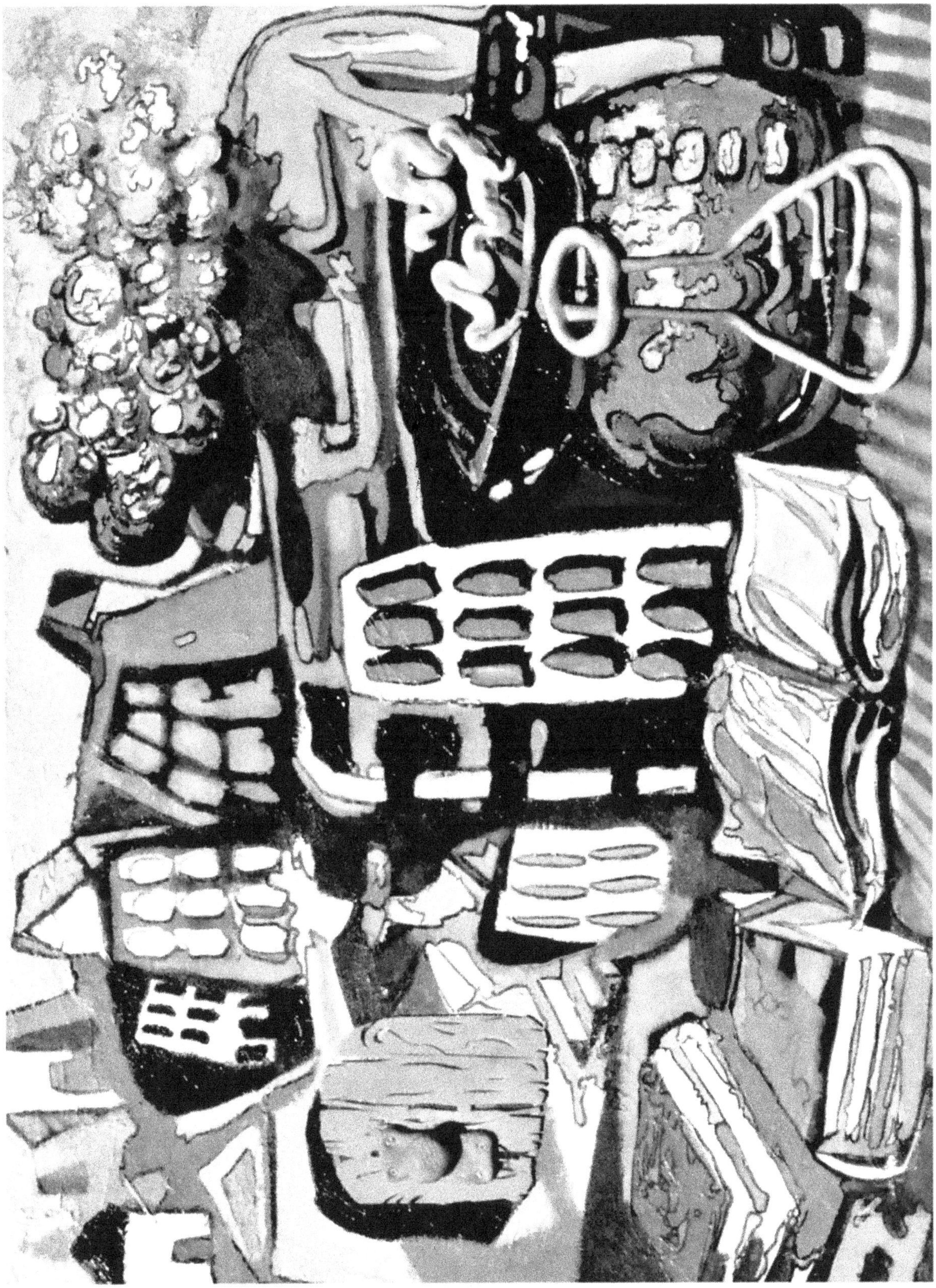

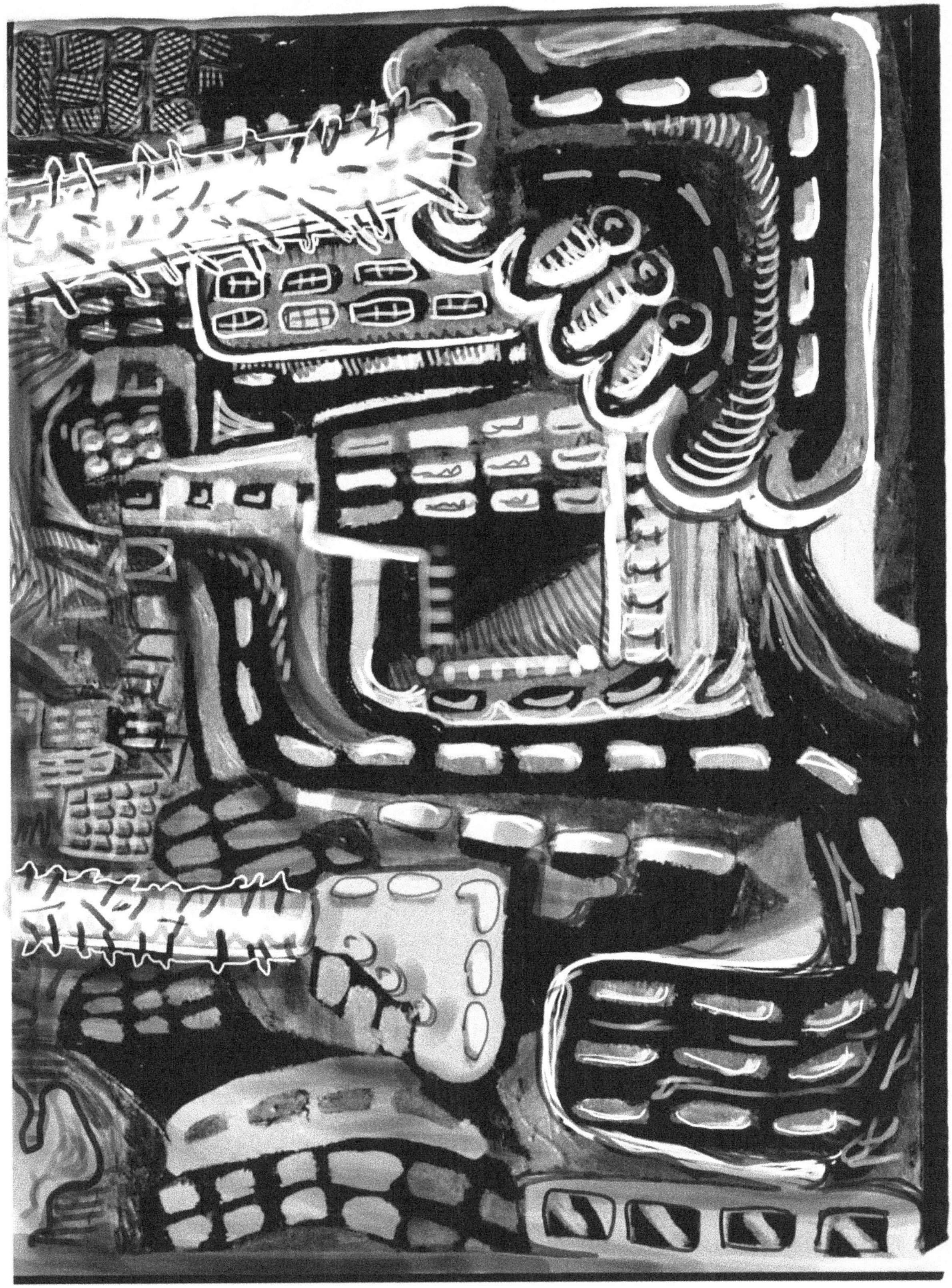

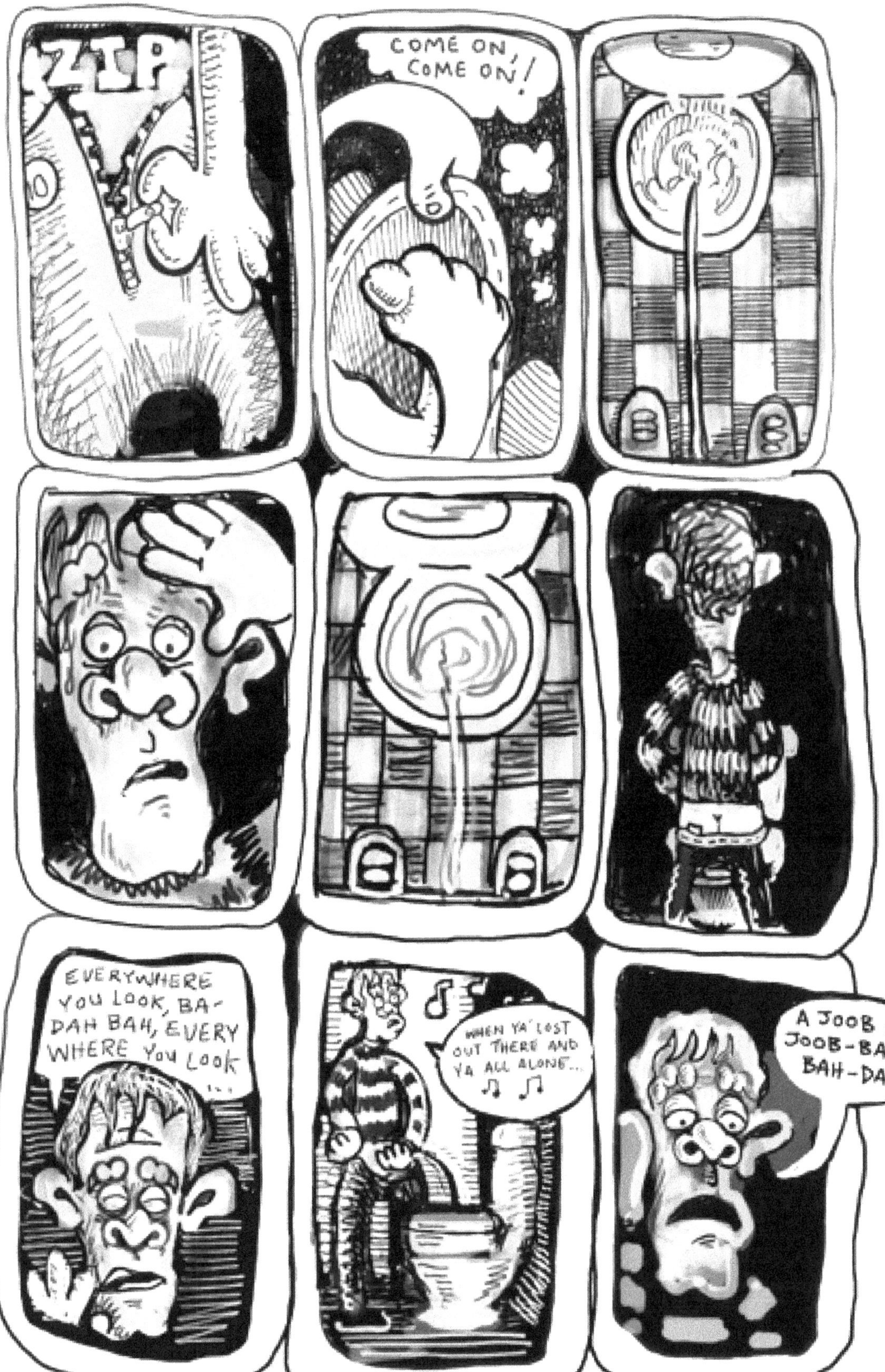
ZIP
COME ON, COME ON!
EVERYWHERE YOU LOOK, BA-DAH BAH, EVERY WHERE YOU LOOK ...
WHEN YA' LOST OUT THERE AND YA ALL ALONE... ♫ ♫
A JOOB A JOOB-BAH BAH-DAH!

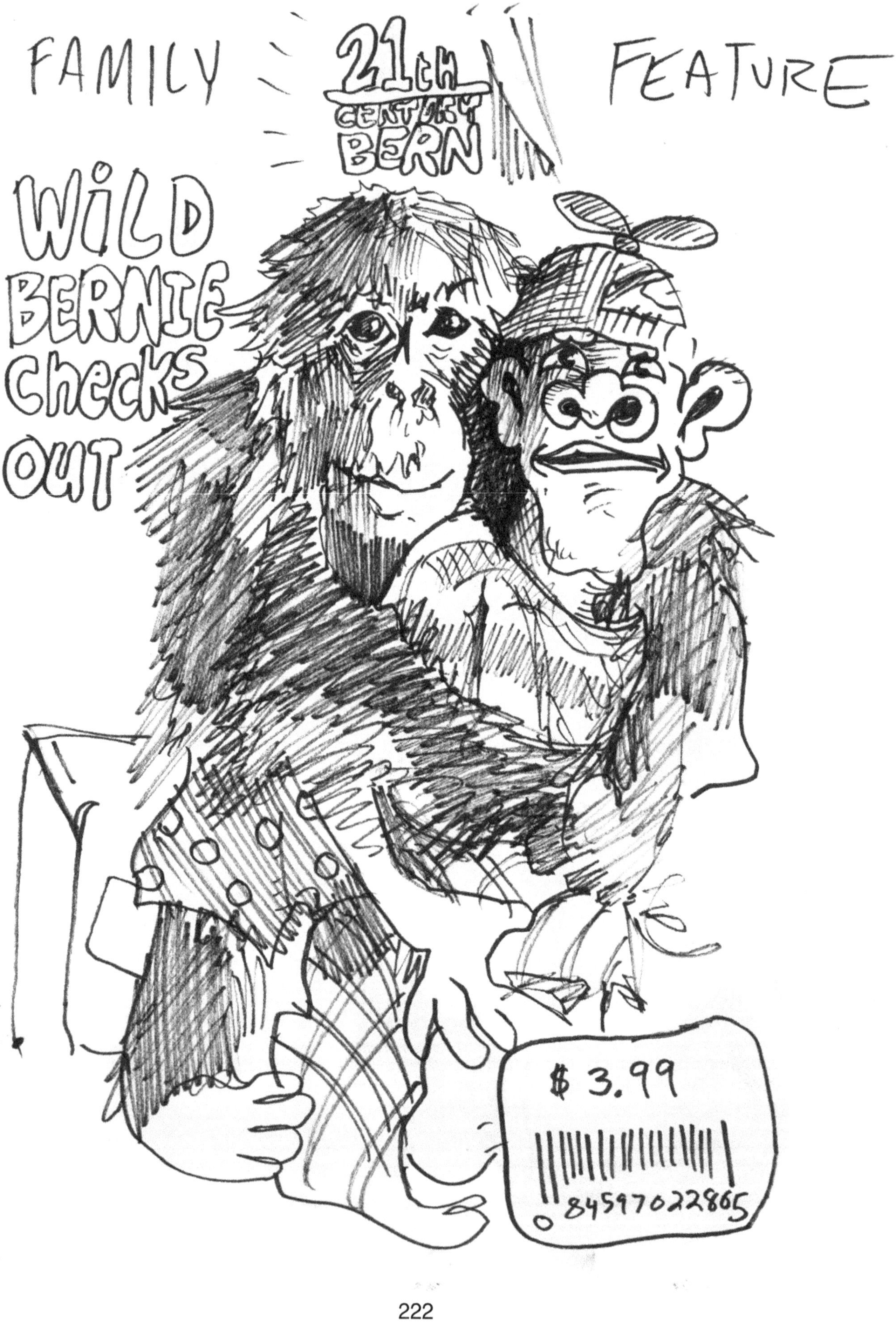
FAMILY
21th CENTURY BERN
FEATURE
WILD BERNIE checks OUT
$ 3.99
84597022865

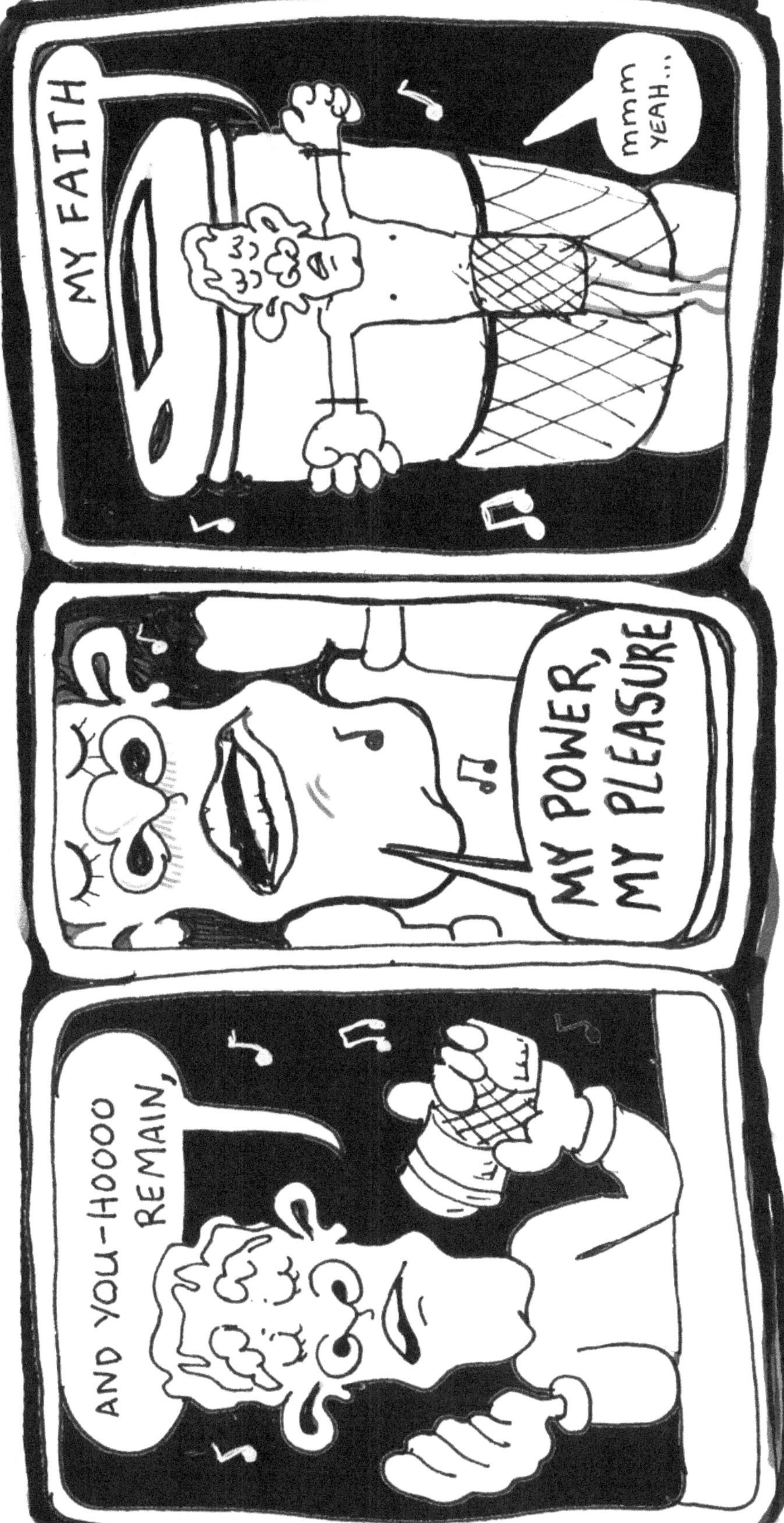
AND YOU-HOOOO REMAIN,
MY POWER, MY PLEASURE
MY FAITH
mmm YEAH...

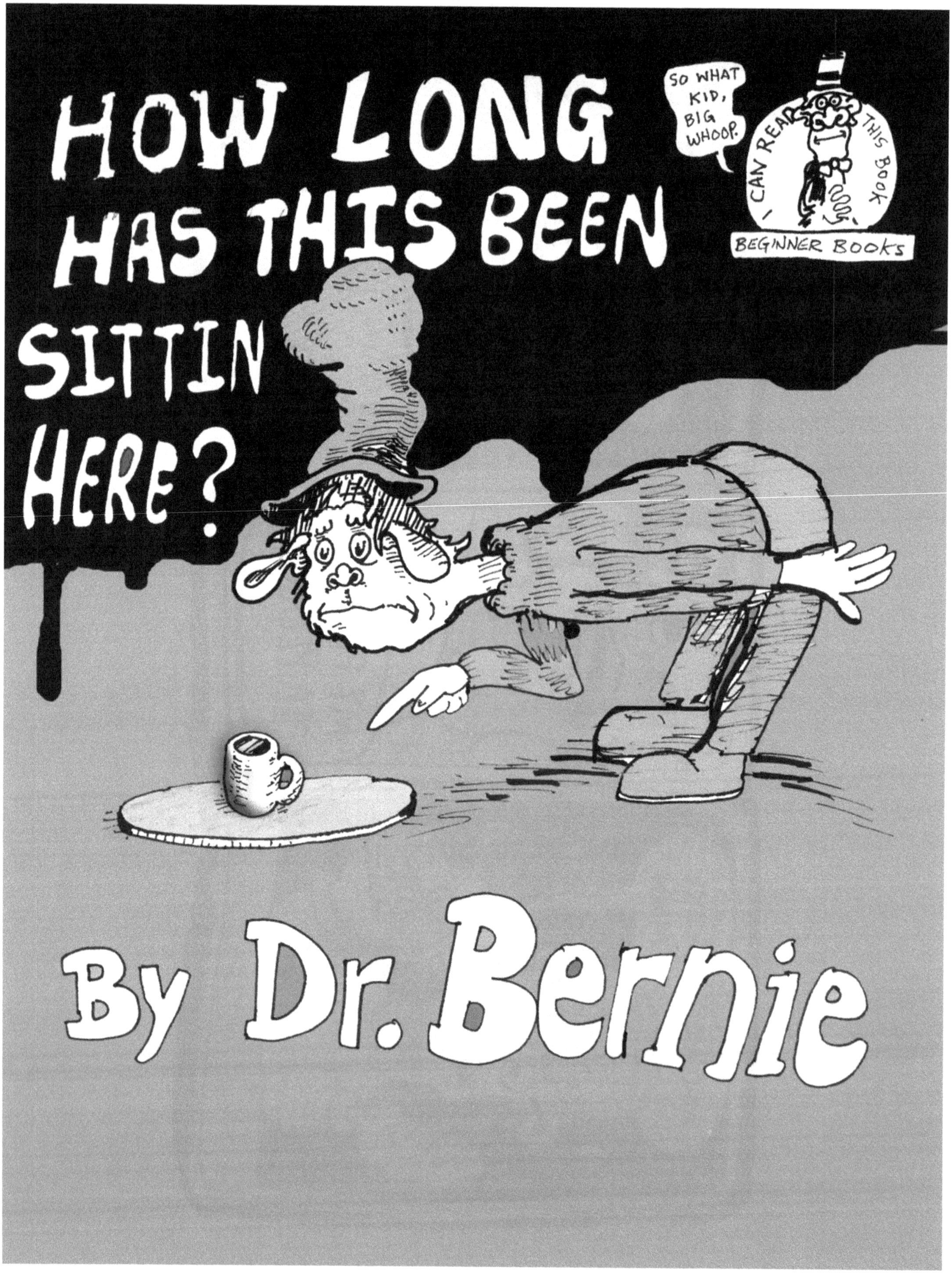
HOW LONG HAS THIS BEEN SITTIN HERE?
SO WHAT KID, BIG WHOOP.
I CAN READ THIS BOOK
BEGINNER BOOKS
By Dr. Bernie

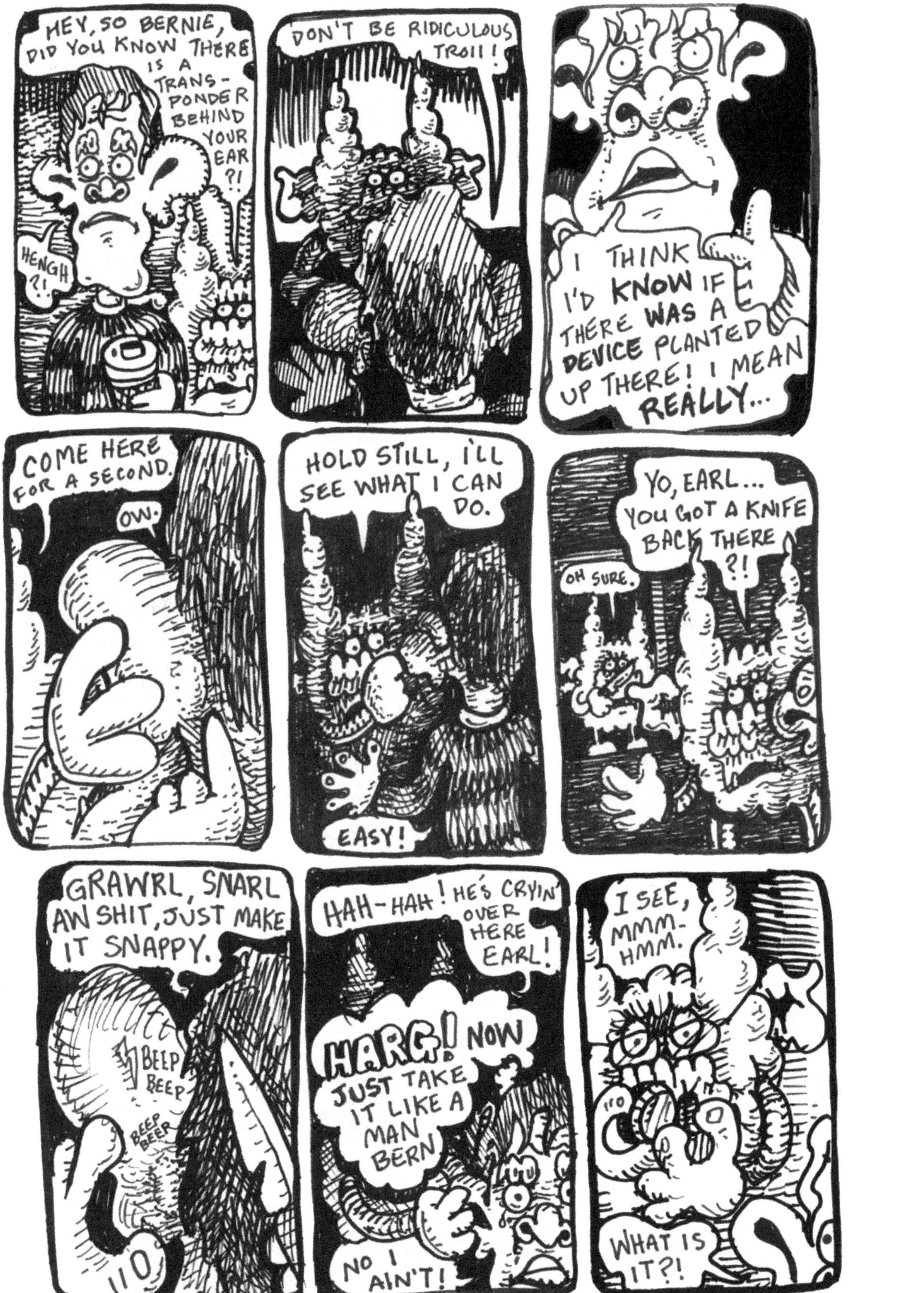
HEY, SO BERNIE, DID YOU KNOW THERE IS A TRANS-PONDER BEHIND YOUR EAR ?!
HENGH ?!
DON'T BE RIDICULOUS TROLL!
I THINK I'D KNOW IF THERE WAS A DEVICE PLANTED UP THERE! I MEAN REALLY...
COME HERE FOR A SECOND.
OW.
HOLD STILL, I'LL SEE WHAT I CAN DO.
EASY!
YO, EARL... YOU GOT A KNIFE BACK THERE ?!
OH SURE.
GRAWRL, SNARL AW SHIT, JUST MAKE IT SNAPPY.
BEEP BEEP
BEEP BEEP
HAH-HAH! HE'S CRYIN' OVER HERE EARL!
HARG! NOW JUST TAKE IT LIKE A MAN BERN.
NO I AIN'T!
I SEE, MMM-HMM.
WHAT IS IT?!

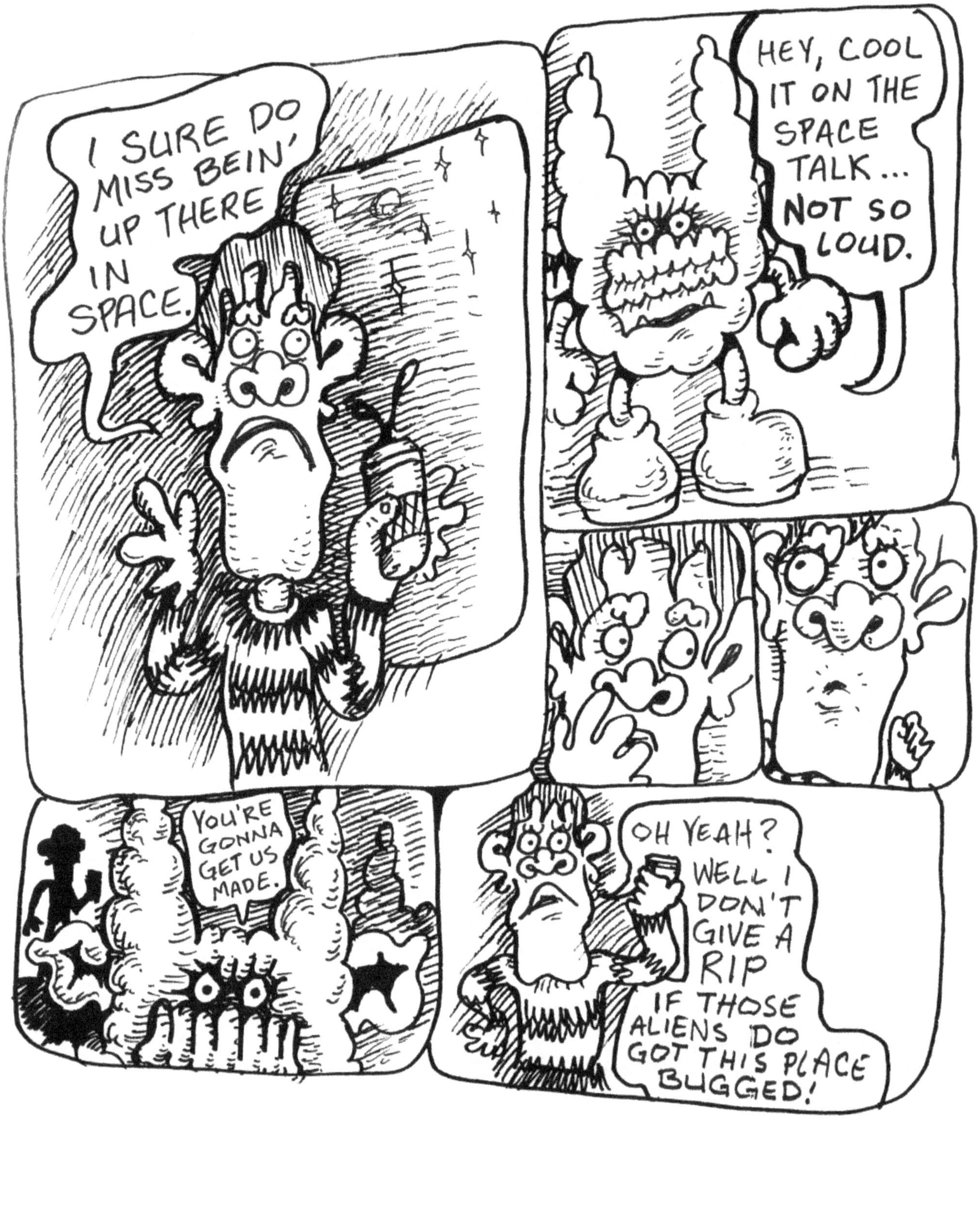
I SURE DO MISS BEIN' UP THERE IN SPACE.
HEY, COOL IT ON THE SPACE TALK... NOT SO LOUD.
YOU'RE GONNA GET US MADE.
OH YEAH? WELL I DON'T GIVE A RIP IF THOSE ALIENS DO GOT THIS PLACE BUGGED!

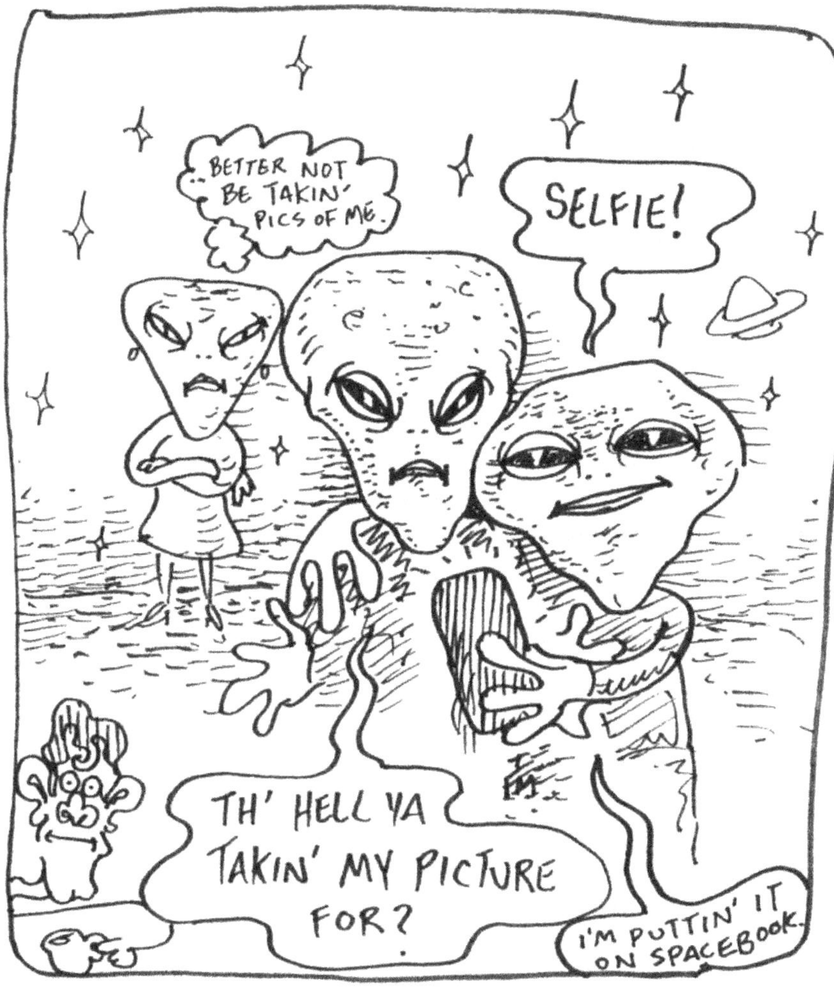
BETTER NOT BE TAKIN' PICS OF ME.
SELFIE!
TH' HELL YA TAKIN' MY PICTURE FOR?
I'M PUTTIN' IT ON SPACEBOOK.

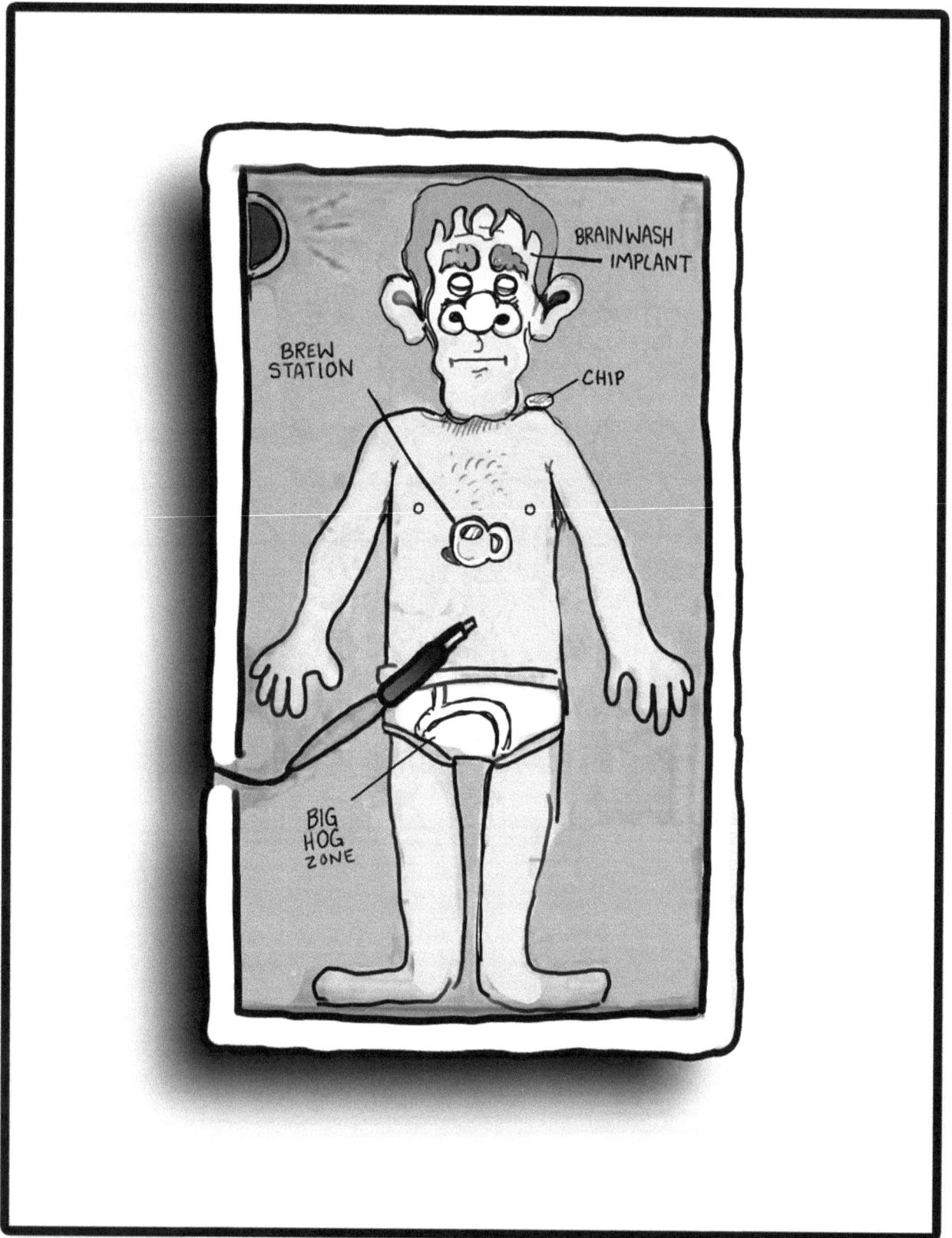

BRAIN WASH
IMPLANT

CHIP

BREW
STATION

BIG
HOG
ZONE

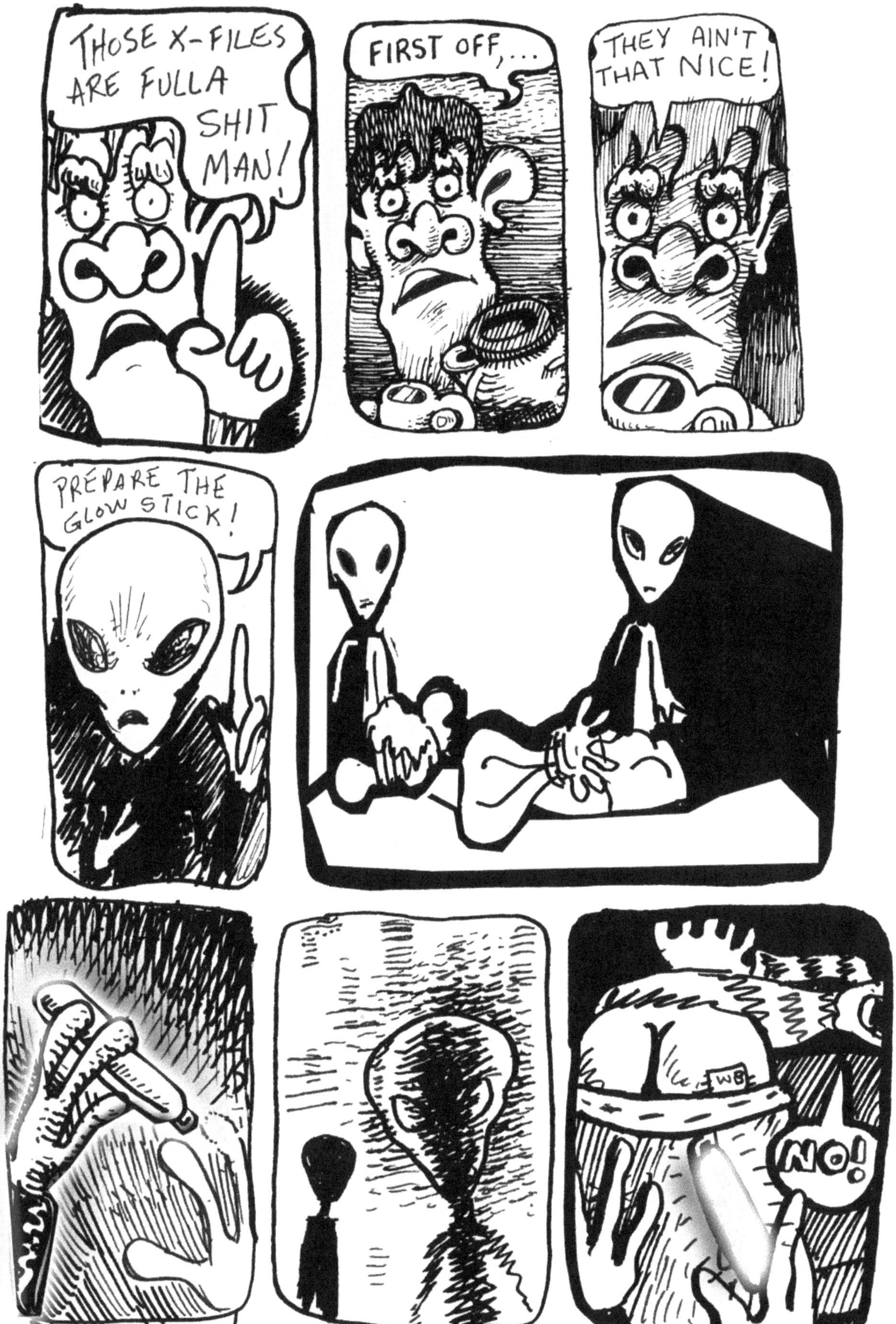
THOSE X-FILES ARE FULLA SHIT MAN!
FIRST OFF,...
THEY AIN'T THAT NICE!
PRÉPARE THE GLOW STICK!
WB
NO!

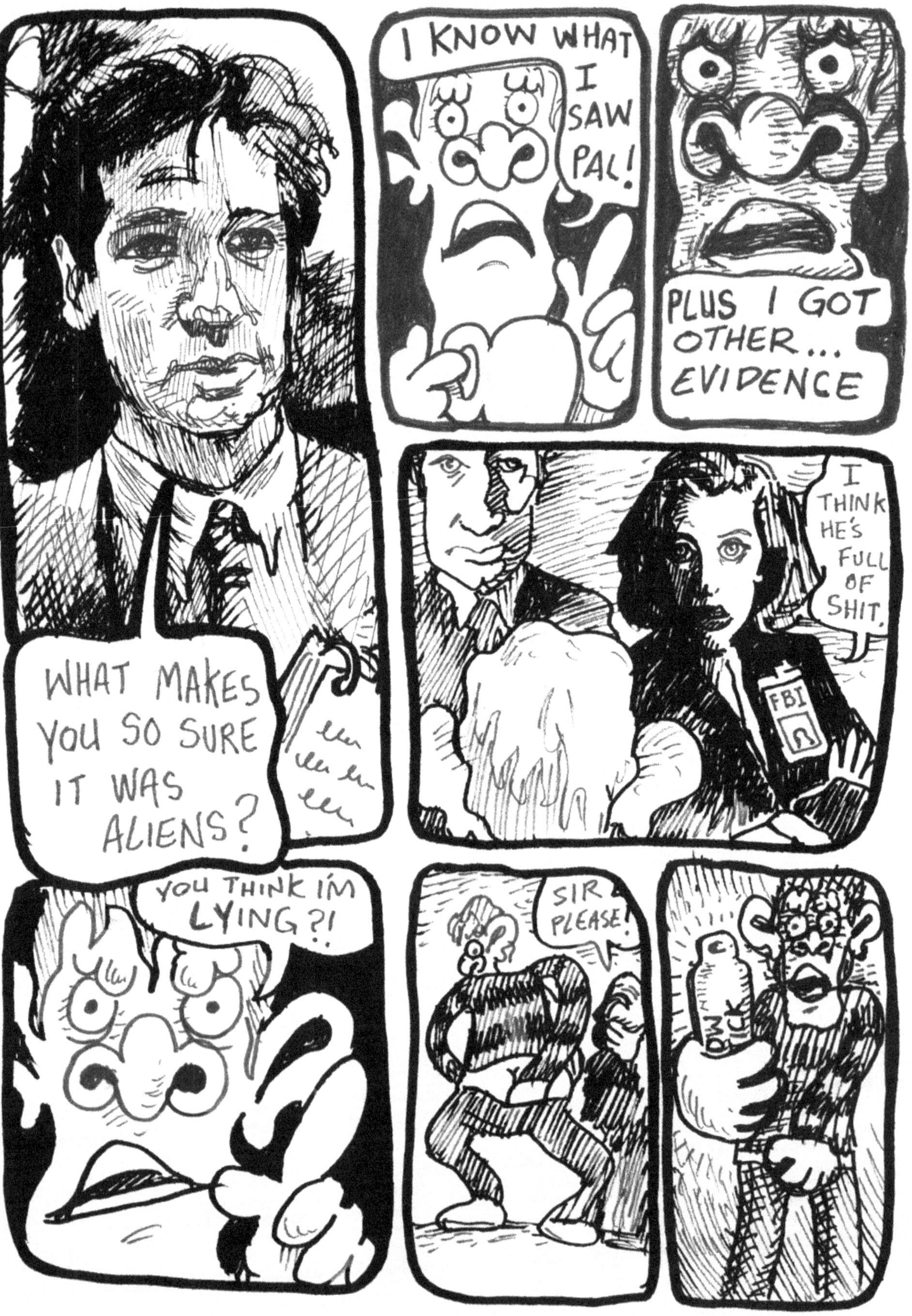
WHAT MAKES YOU SO SURE IT WAS ALIENS?
I KNOW WHAT I SAW PAL!
PLUS I GOT OTHER... EVIDENCE
I THINK HE'S FULL OF SHIT.
YOU THINK I'M LYING?!
SIR PLEASE!

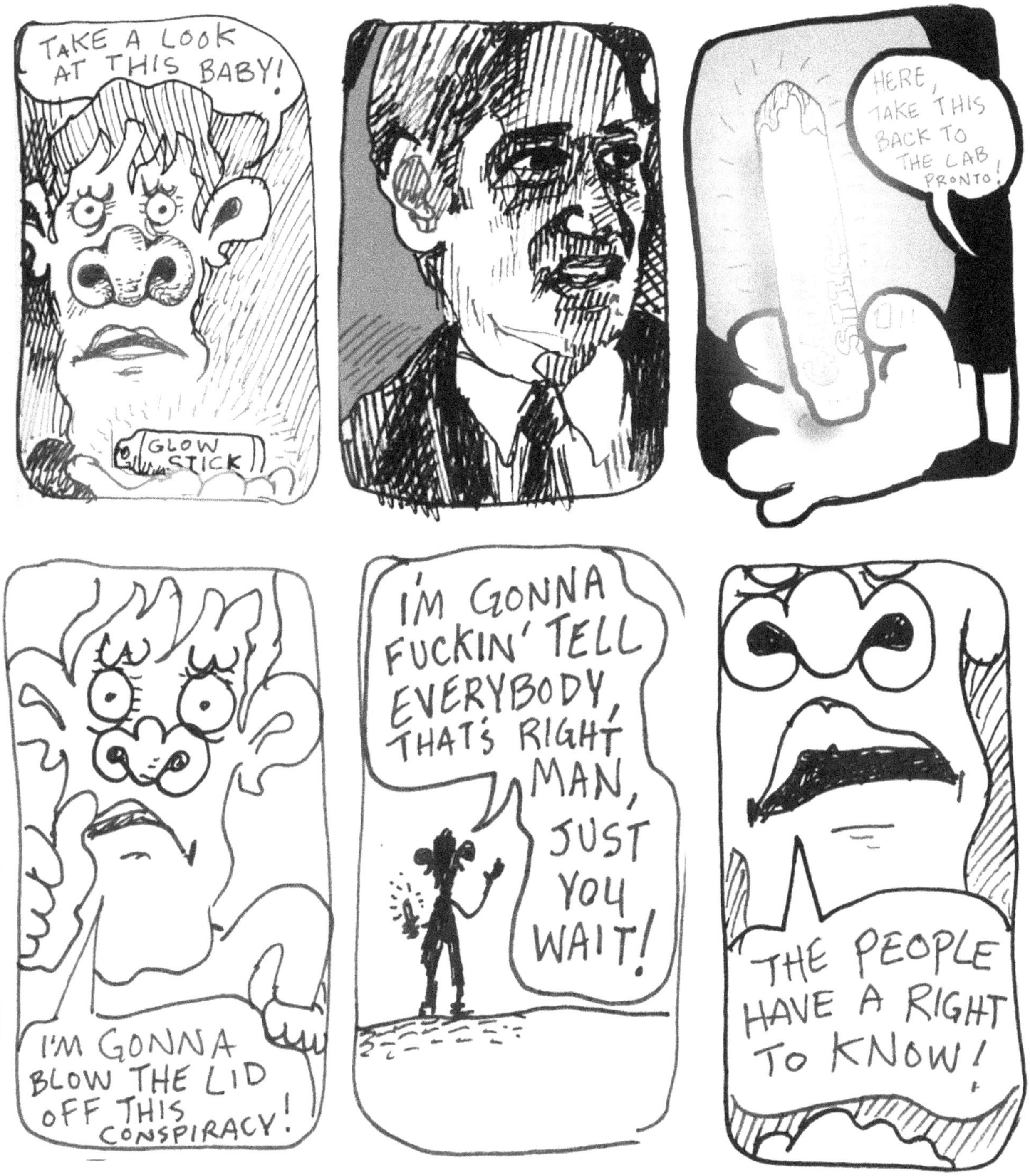

TAKE A LOOK AT THIS BABY!
GLOW STICK
HERE, TAKE THIS BACK TO THE LAB PRONTO!
I'M GONNA BLOW THE LID OFF THIS CONSPIRACY!
I'M GONNA FUCKIN' TELL EVERYBODY, THAT'S RIGHT MAN, JUST YOU WAIT!
THE PEOPLE HAVE A RIGHT TO KNOW!

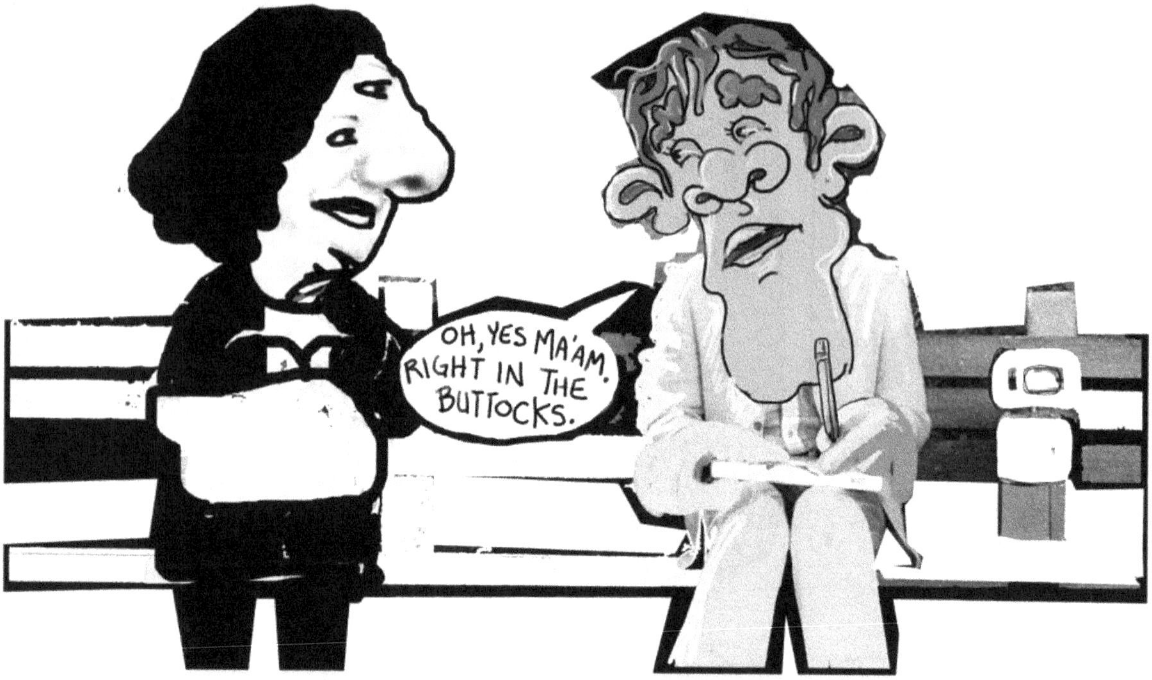
OH, YES MA'AM. RIGHT IN THE BUTTOCKS.

Too cold? I'll say.
Mother nature sure does like to test our patience huh?
Well, not this time Mother Nature, m'kay?
Not when its this damn cold!

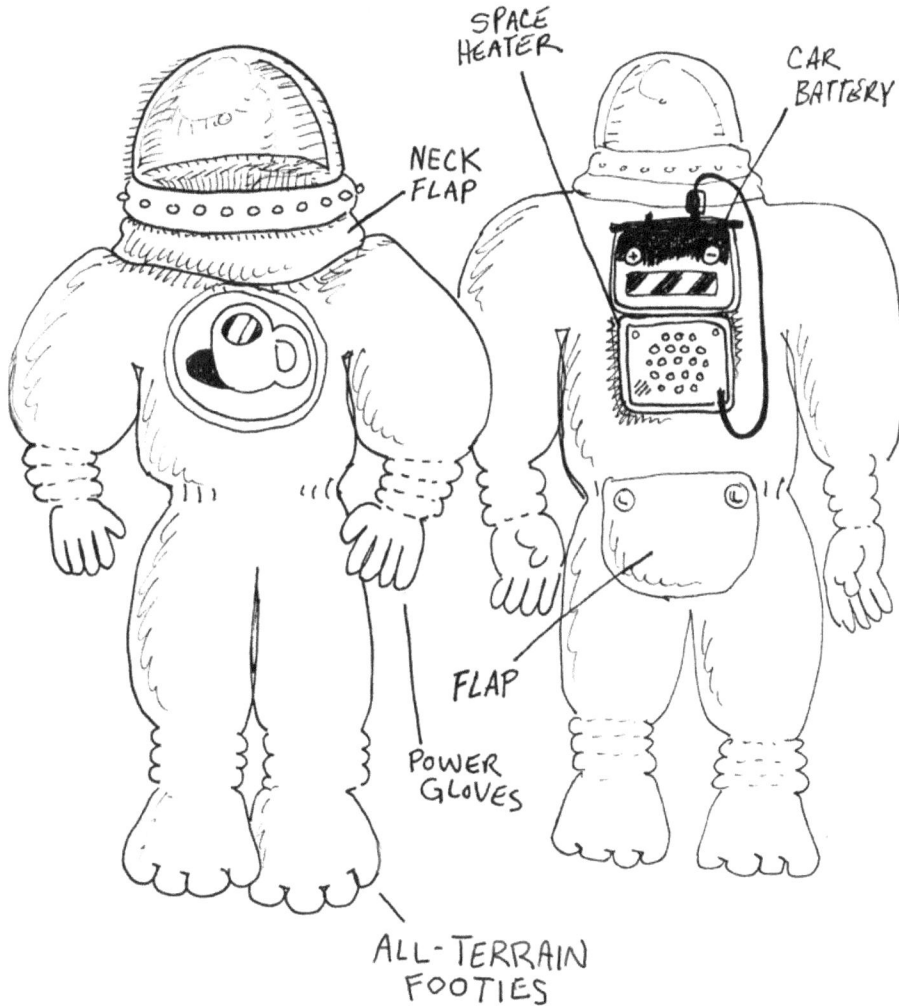

SPACE HEATER

CAR BATTERY

NECK FLAP

FLAP

POWER GLOVES

ALL-TERRAIN FOOTIES

Wild Bernie Brand Luxury Earthsuits.

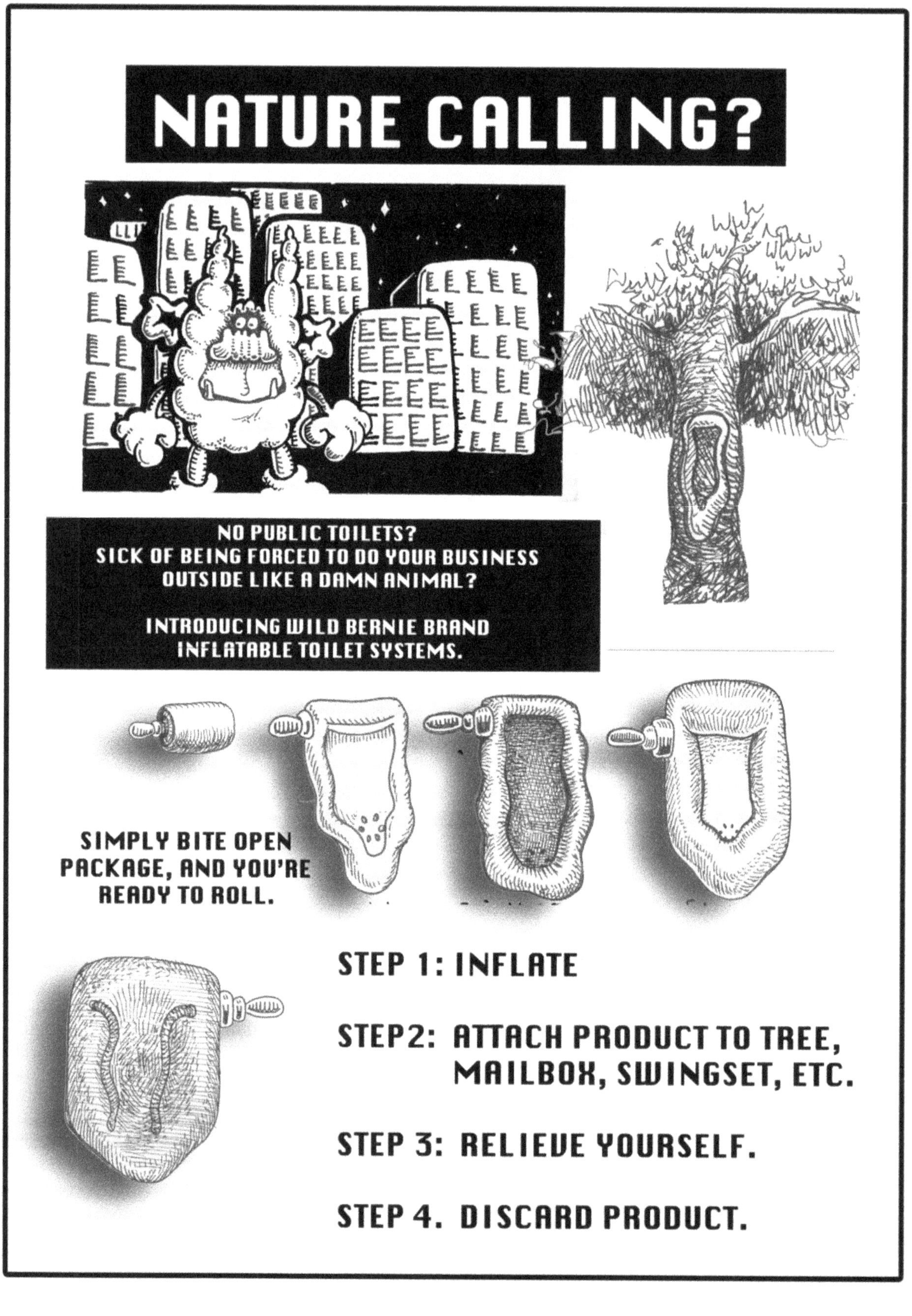
NATURE CALLING?
NO PUBLIC TOILETS?
SICK OF BEING FORCED TO DO YOUR BUSINESS OUTSIDE LIKE A DAMN ANIMAL?
INTRODUCING WILD BERNIE BRAND INFLATABLE TOILET SYSTEMS.
SIMPLY BITE OPEN PACKAGE, AND YOU'RE READY TO ROLL.
STEP 1: INFLATE
STEP2: ATTACH PRODUCT TO TREE, MAILBOX, SWINGSET, ETC.
STEP 3: RELIEVE YOURSELF.
STEP 4. DISCARD PRODUCT.

BEFORE

AFTER

PLUMBERS GROOMING

FRONT   SIDE

RIGHT ON MAN!

GEOMETRIC BEARD

WOMEN TOO!

BEFORE   AFTER

FRONT AND REAR BANG RE-ALIGNMENT

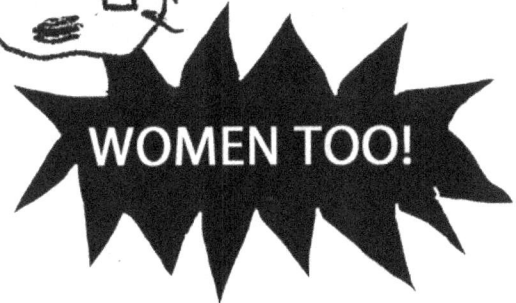

PLUMBER'S GROOMING SAVED MY MARRIAGE!

BEFORE   AFTER

I LOVE IT!

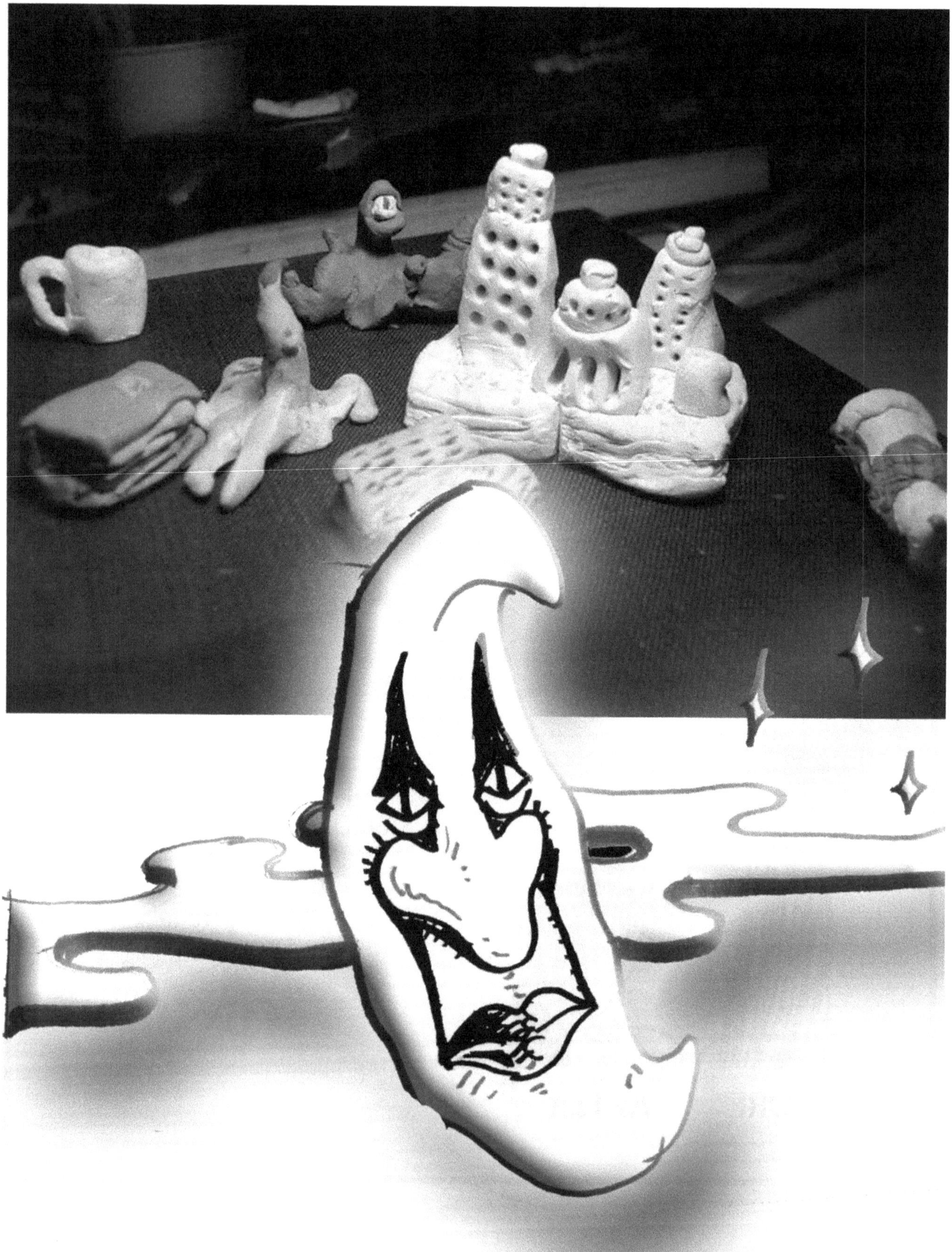

DANCE
COMPETITION
CASH PRIZE
NO WAY...
I'M A HAPPENING GUY, I GOT MOVES ...
HELL, I COULD REALLY WIN THIS THING!

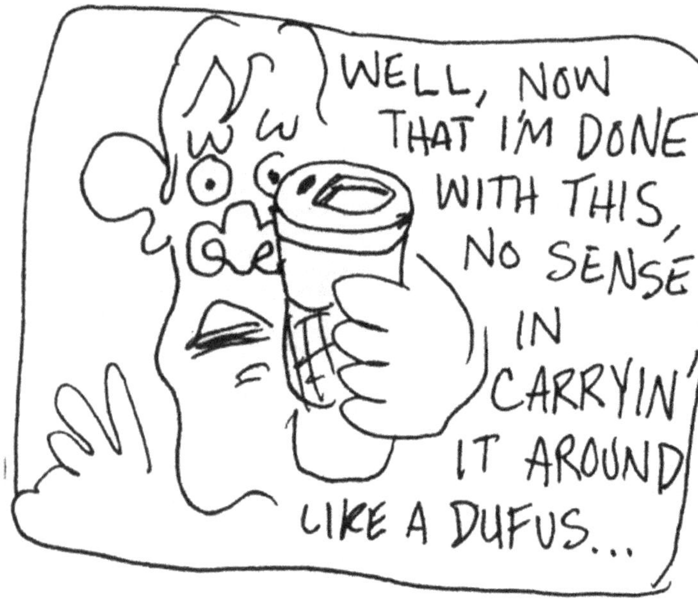
WELL, NOW THAT I'M DONE WITH THIS, NO SENSE IN CARRYIN' IT AROUND LIKE A DUFUS...

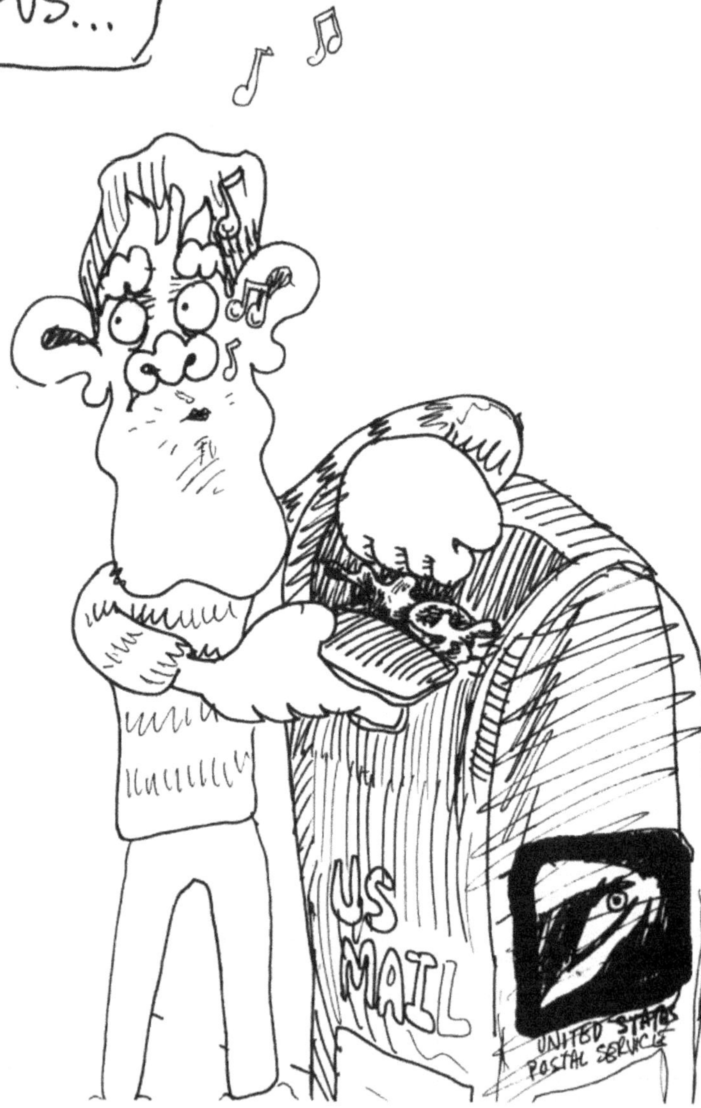
US MAIL
UNITED STATES POSTAL SERVICE

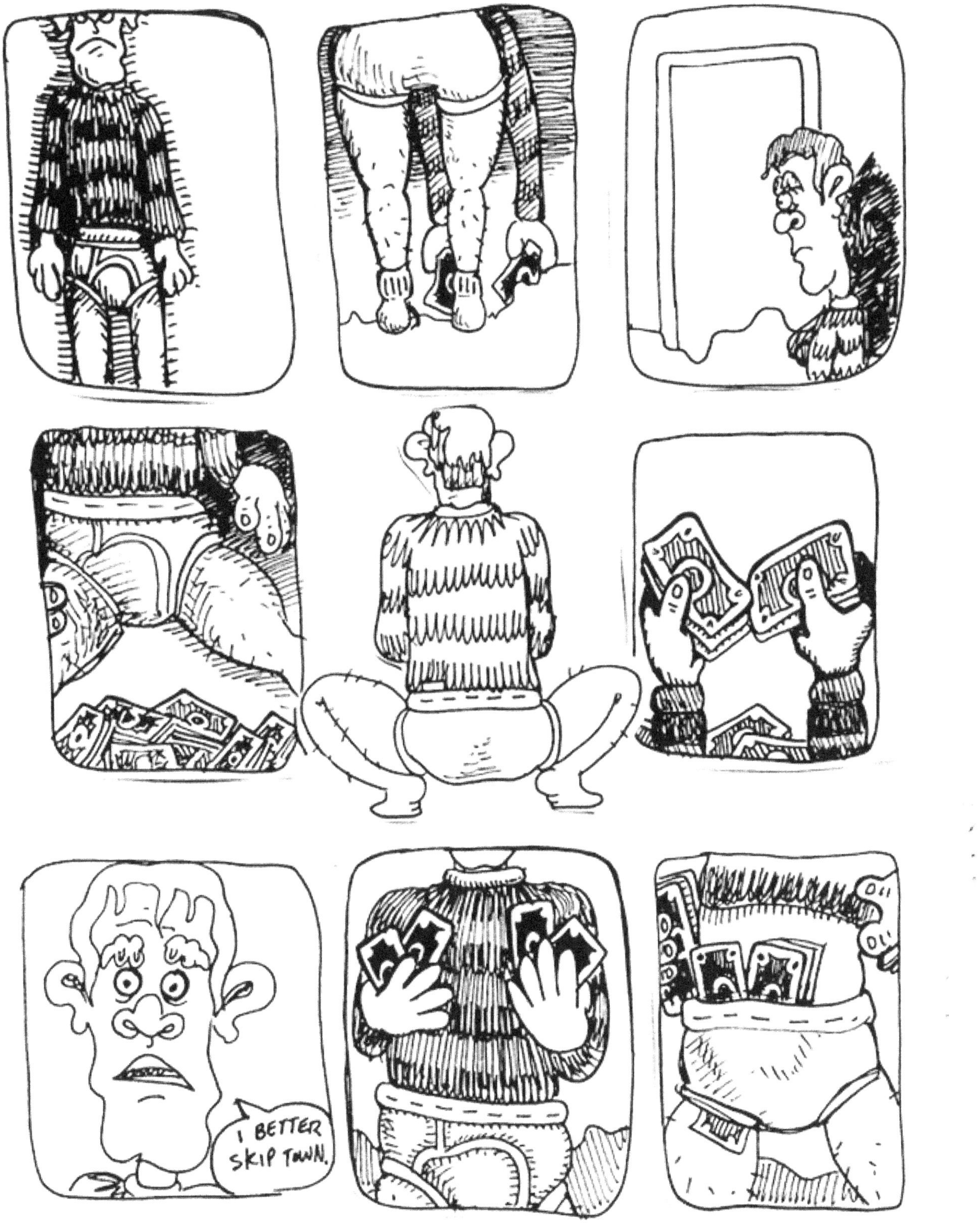
I BETTER SKIP TOWN.

IT SO HOT OUT! I CAN'T STAND IT!
I'M MELTING LIKE A DARN ICE CREAM CONE!
I BETTER GET OUT OF THE SUN!
OH DANG!
I DON'T WANT TO BE A PUDDLE! NOOOOOOO!

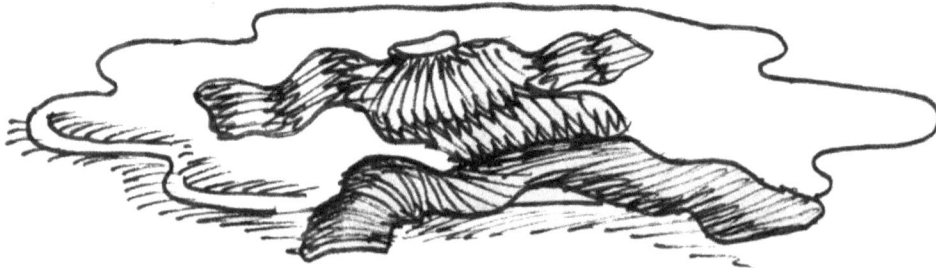

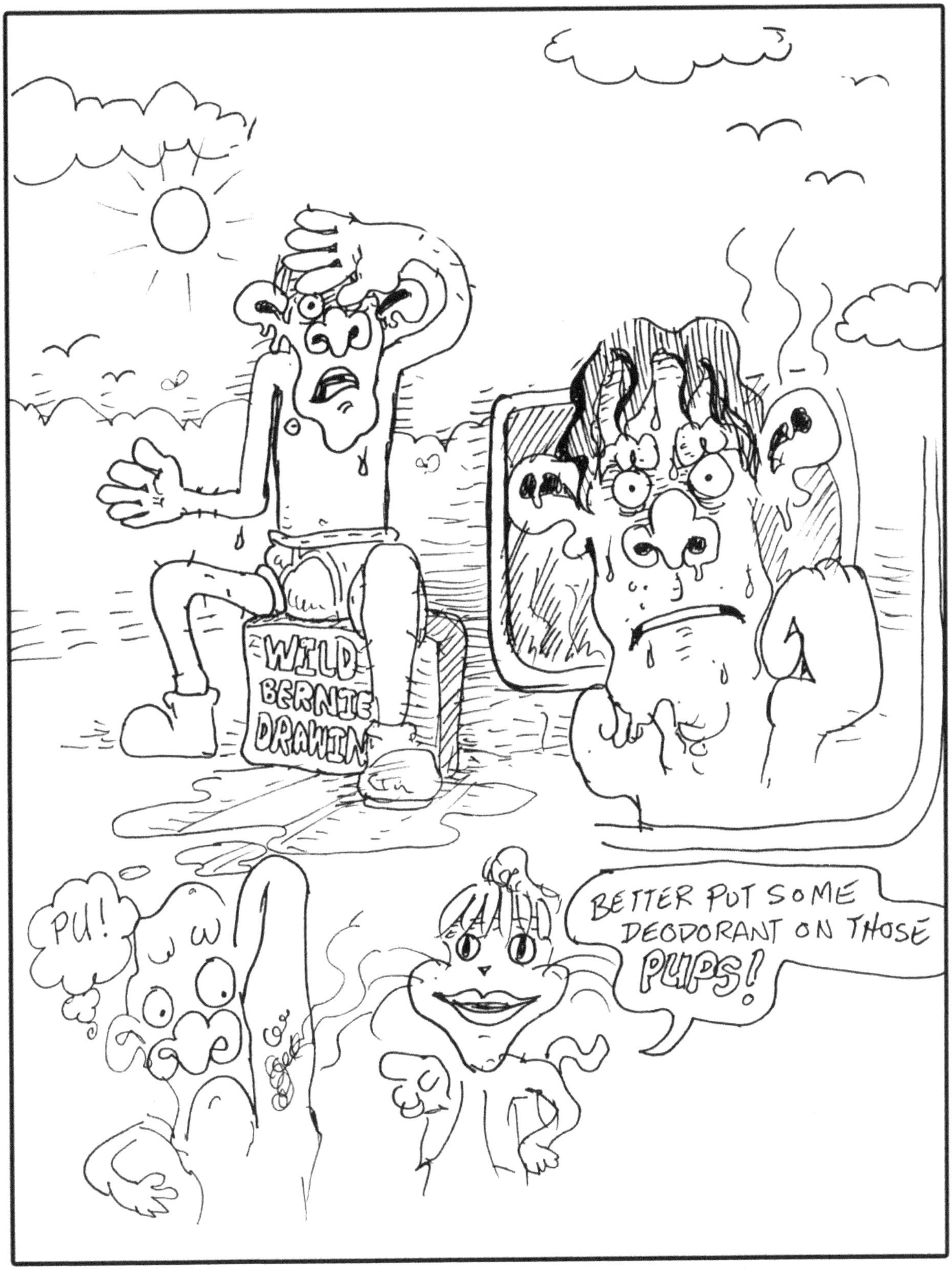
WILD BERNIE DRAWIN
PU!
BETTER PUT SOME DEODORANT ON THOSE PUPS!

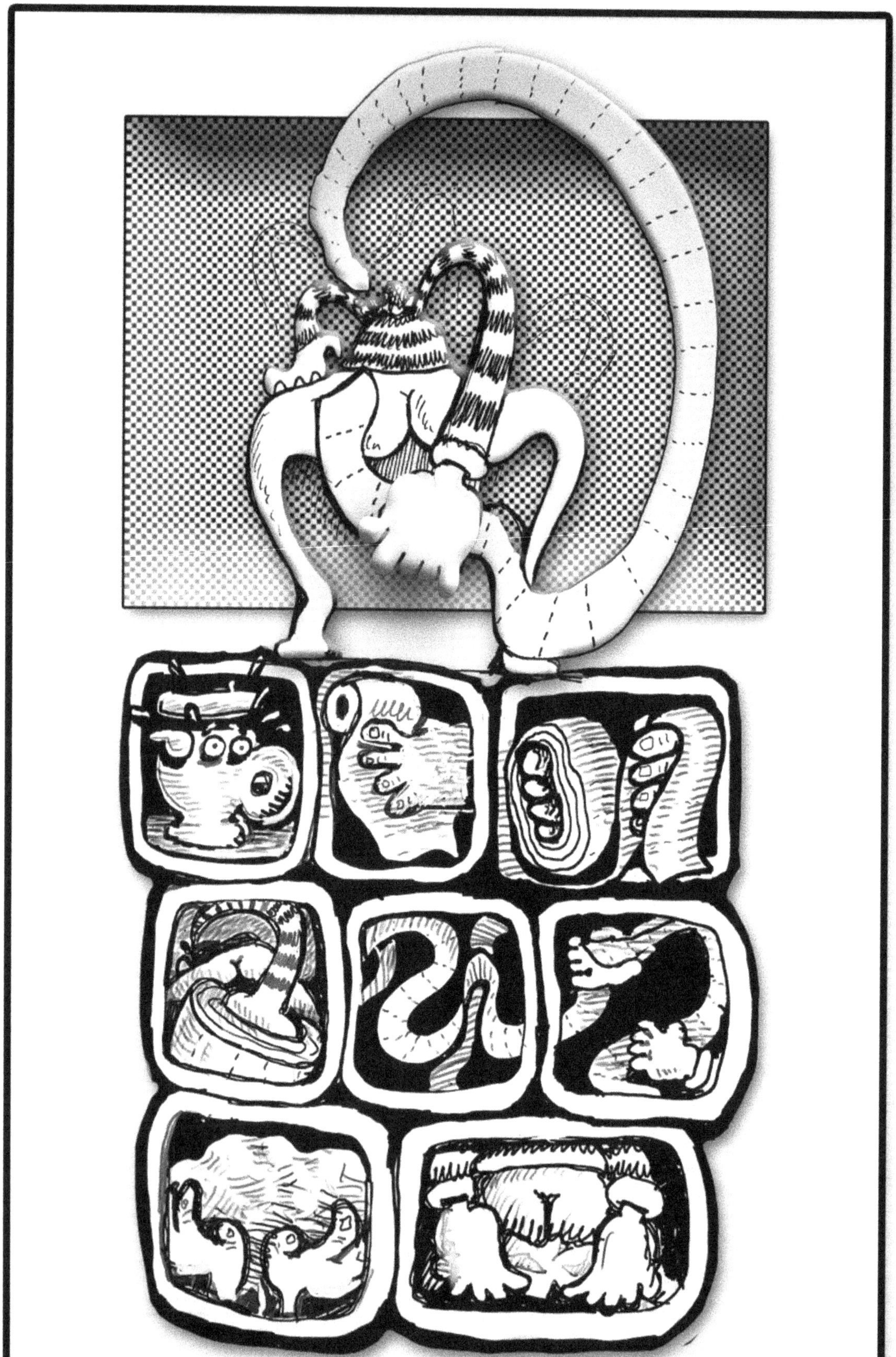

PLEASE:
FLUSH THE TOILET
AFTER USING
THANK YOU
THE MANAGEMENT

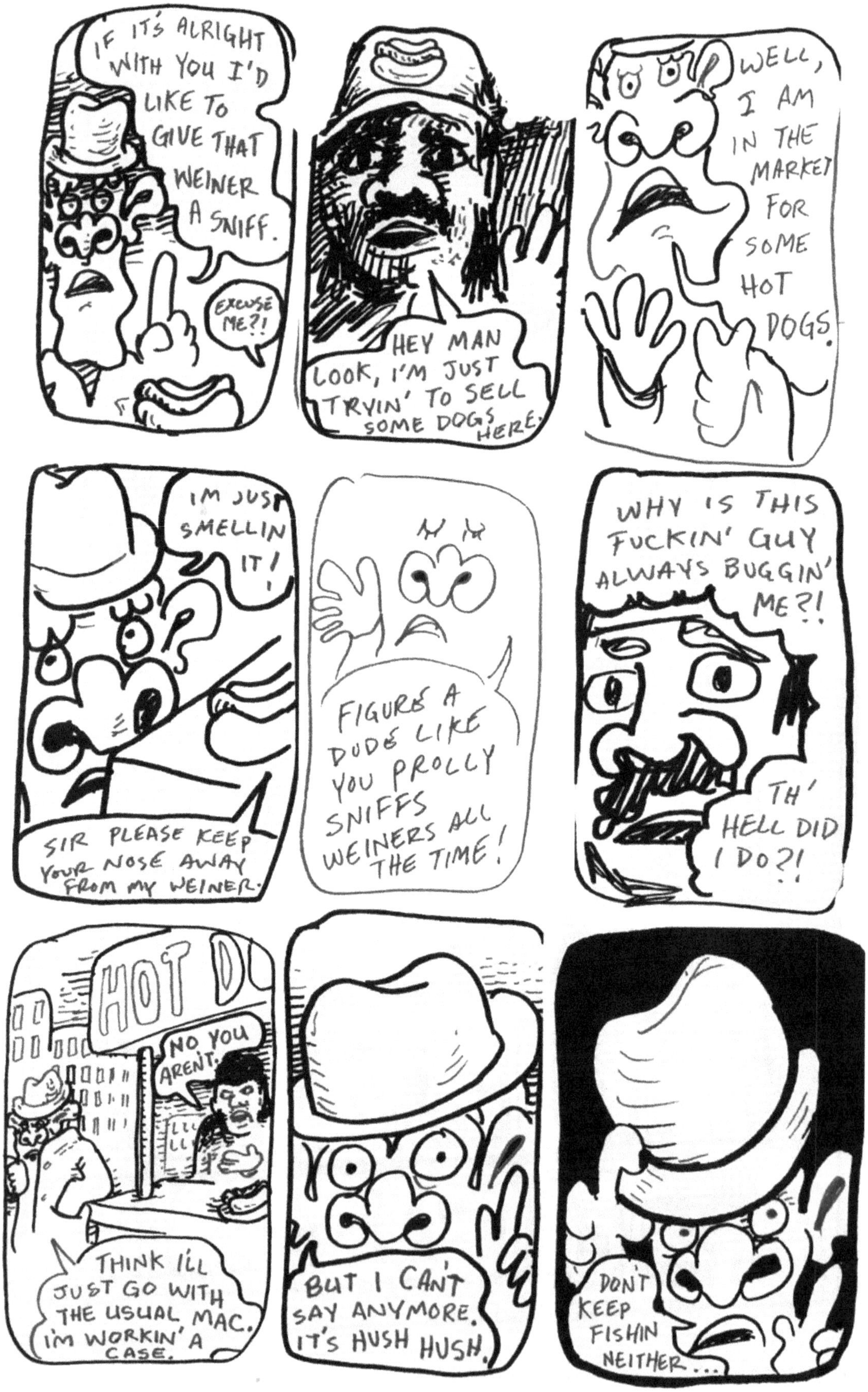
IF IT'S ALRIGHT WITH YOU I'D LIKE TO GIVE THAT WEINER A SNIFF.
EXCUSE ME?!
HEY MAN LOOK, I'M JUST TRYIN' TO SELL SOME DOGS HERE.
WELL, I AM IN THE MARKET FOR SOME HOT DOGS.
IM JUST SMELLIN IT!
SIR PLEASE KEEP YOUR NOSE AWAY FROM MY WEINER.
FIGURE A DUDE LIKE YOU PROLLY SNIFFS WEINERS ALL THE TIME!
WHY IS THIS FUCKIN' GUY ALWAYS BUGGIN' ME?!
TH' HELL DID I DO?!
HOT D
NO YOU ARENT.
THINK I'LL JUST GO WITH THE USUAL MAC. I'M WORKIN' A CASE.
BUT I CAN'T SAY ANYMORE. IT'S HUSH HUSH.
DON'T KEEP FISHIN NEITHER...

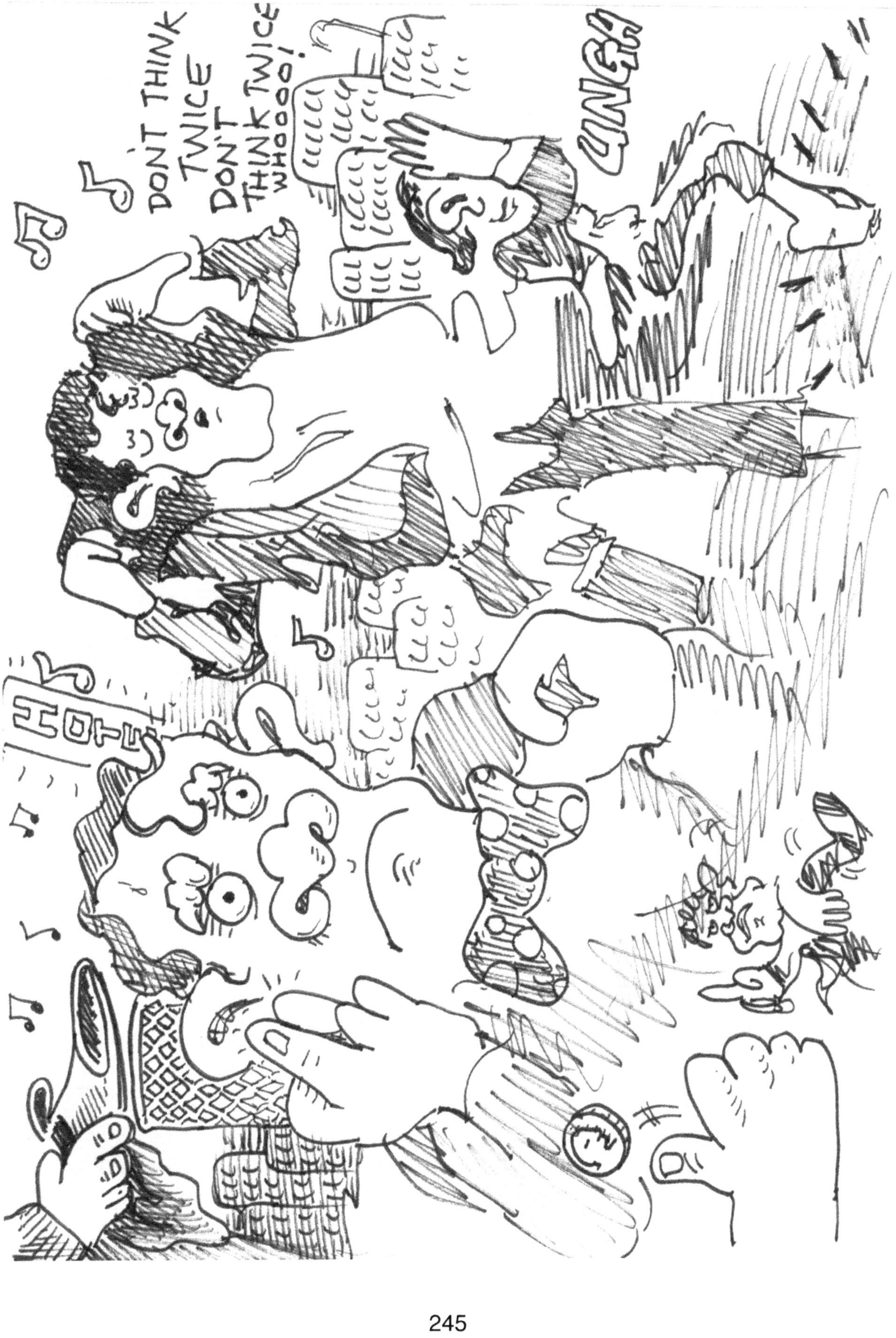
DON'T THINK TWICE
DON'T THINK TWICE WHOOOOO!
UNGH
HOT

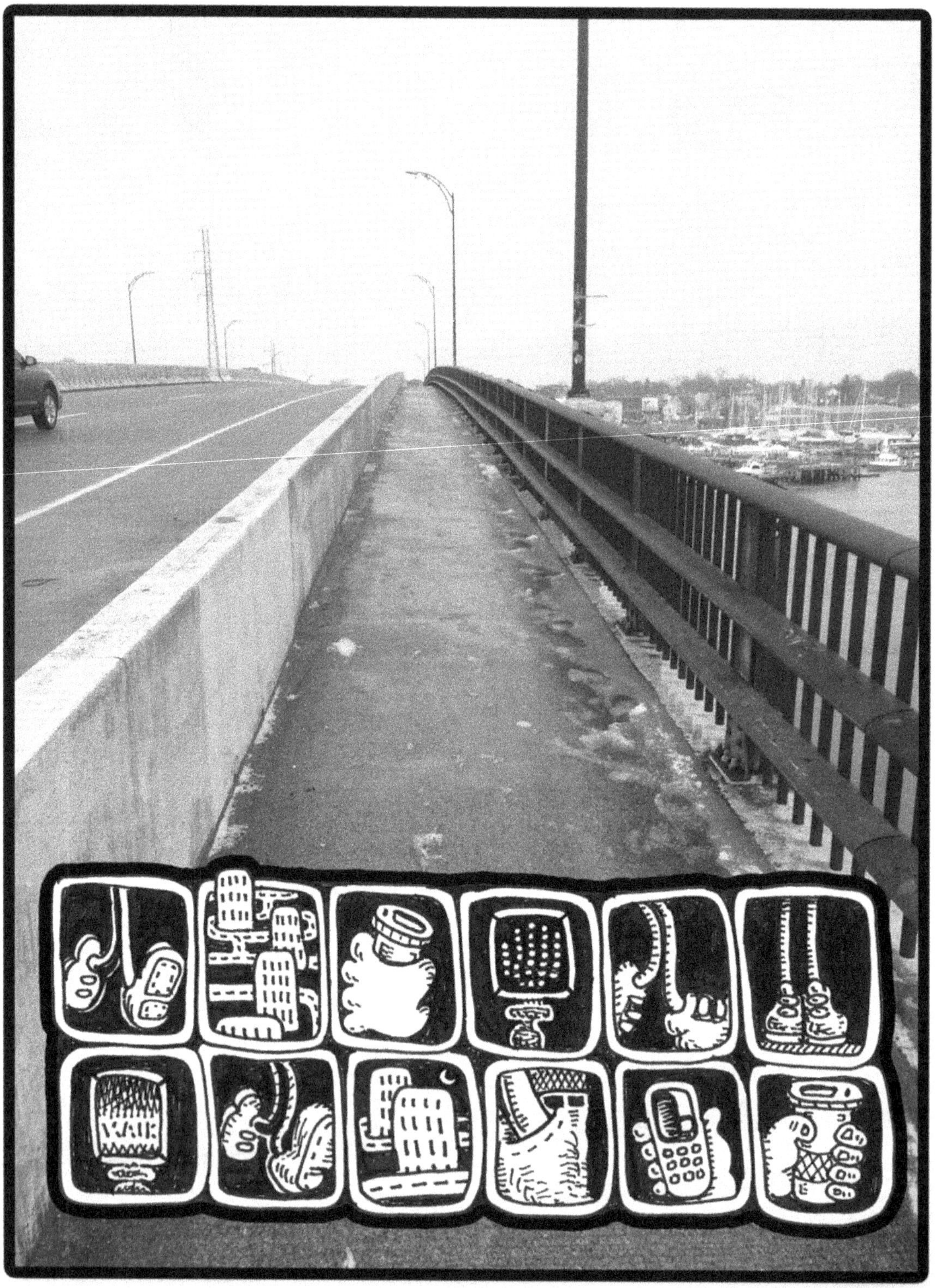

www.ingramcontent.com/pod-product-compliance
Lightning Source LLC
Chambersburg PA
CBHW081148090426
42736CB00017B/3228
9780692703892